ORDEAL OF THE PRESIDENCY

By David Cushman Coyle 1887-1969.

WITH ILLUSTRATIONS COLLECTED
BY M. B. SCHNAPPER

D1520642

GREENWOOD PRESS, PUBLISHERS
WESTPORT, CONNECTICUT

The Library of Congress has catalogued this publication as follows:

Library of Congress Cataloging in Publication Data

Coyle, David Cushman, 1887-1969.
  Ordeal of the Presidency.

    1. Presidents--United States--Biography.
I. Title.
E176.1.C8 1973   973'.099 [B]   72-10691
ISBN 0-8371-6612-8

PUBLISHER'S NOTE

For cooperation and permission in connection with the illustrations—most of which were assembled and captioned by the undersigned during Mr. Coyle's absence from the country—Public Affairs Press is deeply indebted to the following persons and institutions:

Bruce L. Felknor, Executive Director of the Fair Campaign Practices Commission; Julie d'Estournelles, Executive Director of the Woodrow Wilson Foundation; Herman Kahn, Director of the Franklin D. Roosevelt Library; Floyd McCaffree, Research Director of the Republican Party; Robert Oshins, Research Director of the Democratic Party; Clifford K. Shipton, Librarian of the American Antiquarian Society; James R. Wiggins, Executive Editor of the Washington Post; Mrs. Eleanor Roosevelt; Senator Clinton Anderson; the Library of Congress; the National Archives; and the New York Public Library.

For various courtesies in connection with *Ordeal of the Presidency*, Public Affairs Press is also indebted to Robert Cousins, Reed Harris, Robert L. Thompson, and Samuel T. Williamson.

M. B. SCHNAPPER
Editor, Public Affairs Press

Originally published in 1960
by Public Affairs Press, Washington, D. C.

Reprinted with the permission
of Public Affairs Press

First Greenwood Reprinting 1973

Library of Congress Catalogue Card Number 72-10691

ISBN 0-8371-6612-8

Printed in the United States of America

44,314

FOREWORD

". . . and as to you, sir, treacherous in private friendship and a hypocrite in public life, the world will be puzzled to decide, whether you are an apostate or an imposter; whether you have abandoned good principles, or whether you ever had any?"

This is what Tom Paine wrote to George Washington in July, 1796, when Washington was wearily finishing his second term in the Presidency. It is a fair sample of the kind of language that has poured over the head of many a President since Washington's time.

Today we can read Tom Paine's heated language with a cool mind; we do not feel it necessary to prove that Washington was no scoundrel. In 1796, neither his enemies nor his friends could consider such a question absurd. Similarly, in our own times we have seen the President of the United States called names that his enemies felt to be richly deserved but his friends took as indecent outrages. It may be useful under such conditions, or at least a comfort for the friends of a President, to recall the outrages of former generations. To aid in such a cooling exercise is the main purpose of this book.

In the following chapters are given samples of the treatment meted out to ten of our most-maligned Presidents, from Washington to Franklin Roosevelt.

The reader will observe that through all the changes of spelling and style, the insults offered to Presidents show traces of a pattern. Lying is perhaps the most common accusation, largely because a successful President has to deal with facts as they are, no matter what he may have expected, and promised as a candidate. He will also be solemnly charged with plotting to subvert the Constitution and make himself King, for the fear of royalty still lurks deep in the American breast—at least in the breast that specializes in hating Presidents. And in times of foreign tension or war, the President is commonly charged with treason.

A story written for this purpose cannot of course be the same thing as a history of the times or even a condensed biography of the vari-

iii

ous Presidents. Much of the story is necessarily made up of quotations, interlarded with commentary designed to explain what the President was doing to excite such fervid objurgations.

Not all those who criticize a President in heated language are necessarily paranoiacs, and not all are necessarily mistaken in their criticisms. The best of Presidents may make mistakes and the more active a President is the more conspicuous they are likely to be. Sometimes, of course, the critics have been more or less right; some of their criticisms are included in these pages as examples not of malignancy but of what Presidents have to bear.

As anyone familiar with history will immediately recognize the quotations used herein do not cover the field. A comprehensive cross-section of political calumny would be intolerably dull. The kinds of people who customarily hate Presidents are, it must be admitted, not usually bright; and if the reader of such material is to stay awake and appreciate what the haters are trying to say, it is necessary to pick out mainly the howls of rage that down through the years can still raise an echo of how they sounded when blood was hot and the victim was living in the White House. Some of the most fascinating material comes from critics who were never dull, such as Washington Irving in pursuit of Jefferson, Mark Twain on the trail of Theodore Roosevelt, or H. L. Mencken appraising the achievements of F.D.R. Unfortunately, however, a number of famous masters of invective will be found missing from these pages either because they did not devote their talents to attacking Presidents or because in their enthusiasm they do not come to a point in the time that a modern reader will wait.

The ultimate of criticism, of course, is assassination, which has succeeded with three Presidents, and numerous attempts have been foiled by the Secret Service. The assassins are a special group, not treated here. Many of the most paranoiac haters who call the President traitor, dictator, or communist often say among their fellows that someone ought to shoot him; but not many—unless perhaps in the case of F.D.R.—have really meant it. Moreover, the widespread gratitude that seems to have been anticipated by those who have shot Presidents has been conspicuously lacking. Surely Lincoln was hated by many Southerners who talked as if they wanted him removed, but when it was done, where were they? John Wilkes Booth was bitterly disappointed by the lack of appreciation he found for his success. His diary says: "After being hunted like a dog through swamps, woods, and last night being chased by gun boats till I was forced to return wet, cold, starving with every man's hand against me, I am here in despair, looked upon as a common cut-throat."

It is an unavoidable characteristic of the American form of political freedom that those who do not approve of the President will say what they think; and some of his opponents will use violent language even if they do not go so far as shooting. To examine an assortment of the verbal missiles that have been thrown at some of our Chief Magistrates may be a valuable exercise not only for the purpose of understanding what an active President may have to endure, but also to gain perspective on what comes in the daily newspaper or over the air. This is a free country in many important respects, one of which is freedom to curse the Head of State.

In the preparation of this book, I am happy to acknowledge, I have leaned heavily on the research contributed by my wife, Doris Porter Coyle, who put into the enterprise not only a vast amount of patience in the searching of ancient newspapers and other sources, but also a discriminating judgment which served as an invaluable help in the choice of materials to be included in the manuscript.

DAVID CUSHMAN COYLE

Washington, D. C.

ABOUT THE AUTHOR

David Cushman Coyle graduated from Princeton in 1908 with the degree of A.B., having studied Constitutional Government under Woodrow Wilson. In 1910 he received the degree of Civil Engineer from Rensselaer Polytechnic Institute. He entered the field of political economics in 1931 with a series of articles on government policies for meeting the depression.

In 1933 Mr. Coyle came to Washington and became a consultant to various government agencies during most of the next twenty years. In the course of intervals of government work he wrote a number of books and magazine articles on the New Deal. In 1938 he was winner of the Harper's $1,000 prize for the best essay on *The American Way*.

In 1942 Mr. Coyle was invited to London by the British Ministry of Information to lecture on America and he remained there several years as consultant to the U. S. Office of War Information on the interpretation of the United States to the British public.

Mr. Coyle's most recent book is *Conservation* (1957), a history of the movement that Theodore Roosevelt regarded as his chief claim to fame. His books *The U.S. Political System* (1954) and *The United Nations* (1955) have been widely translated and circulated, particularly by the U.S. Information Agency and the United Nations.

CONTENTS

CHAPTER I

KING GEORGE OF MOUNT VERNON

George Washington, being first in war, was naturally first in the hatred of his Tory countrymen during the Revolution. That much he could expect. What he did not expect was the sniping and obstruction that came from his own side, and the animosity that developed against him among some of his countrymen while he was President.

Later Presidents knew all too well that they would not be protected by the divinity that was supposed to hedge a king. Washington was the first to experience the unpleasant fact that the chief servant of the American people often finds he has a cruel master. He also was the first to illustrate the principle that the Presidents whom future generations will consider great are usually given the roughest treatment while they are in office.

The least of Washington's troubles was the venomous language aimed at him by the Tories during the Revolutionary War. The Tory attacks were especially bitter for the very reason that this was no revolt of the masses in which a united upper class was fighting for its life. This was a civil war that split the ruling class itself. Washington and the other Revolutionary leaders were men of substance, revolting against British laws that limited their industry and trade. Those who took the Loyalist side therefore looked on Washington as a traitor not only to his King but also to his class. They tried to shore up their own self-confidence by telling themselves that Washington could not possibly be a gentleman. In their eyes he was "the Great Captain of the western Goths and Huns." Indeed, according to the Tory New York *Gazette*, all the Revolutionary leaders were at best an assortment of "obscure, pettifogging attorneys, bankrupt shopkeepers, outlawed smugglers, wretched banditti, . . . the refuse of mankind."

In those days many people believed strongly in the virtue of political verse to disconcert and weaken their enemies. For example, one earnest loyalist, Jonathan Odell, minced no words in the following lines addressed to General Washington:

1

"Thou has supported an atrocious cause
Against thy king, thy country, and the laws;
Committed perjury, encouraged lies,
Forced conscience, broken the most sacred ties;
Myriads of wives and fathers at thy hand
Their slaughtered husbands, slaughtered sons, demand;
That pastures hear no more the lowing kine,
That towns are desolate, all—all is thine."

It may be doubted that Washington spent much time poring over such Tory denunciations or that he took them much to heart. What he did take to heart was the sniping and obstruction from his own side.

During the bitter winter of 1777-78, while Washington's army was suffering at Valley Forge, General Horatio Gates in the North was enjoying the prestige of his victory over Burgoyne. Encouraged by signs of discontent in the Army, a few of Washington's generals seized the occasion to organize a plot with the object of forcing him out and making Gates Commander-in-Chief. The conspiracy was soon named "Conway's Cabal," after its most conspicuous leader, General Thomas Conway, a French volunteer of Irish birth, who was distinguished by a vast and vocal appreciation of his own military genius. Another conspirator was Quartermaster-General Thomas Mifflin, whose mismanagement had been largely responsible for the hardships of Valley Forge. Gates himself gave at least tacit encouragement to the Cabal. Congress also created an awkward situation by appointing Conway Inspector-General of the Army, implying dissatisfaction with Washington's administration of his command.

Washington fought back, accusing Conway of being an "incendiary," and challenging Gates to show his hand. In the showdown the Army stood with Washington and the Cabal collapsed. Conway resigned his commission early in 1778 and returned to France.

As for Congressional sniping, Washington pointed out impatiently that it was easier "to draw remonstrances in a comfortable room by a good fireside than to occupy a cold, bleak hill and sleep under frost and snow, without clothes or blankets." In the end he kept his command and came through with general applause, but he had had a taste of the ingratitude of republics. He would have more and worse after the end of the war.

Even before he came under fire as President of the United States, he was subjected to barbs of disrespect for his role as President of the Constitutional Convention. One dissatisfied citizen, signing himself "Centinel," wrote in the *Independent Gazeteer* of October 5, 1787, that to talk of the Great Commander and the Great Philosopher was to talk nonsense, "for Washington was a fool from nature, and Franklin was a fool from age."

From the beginning of the war, many Americans were fearful lest there arise a native growth of monarchy in this country, and Washington was a victim of suspicions on this account, both during the Revolution and afterward as President. Many members of Congress were haunted by thoughts of Cromwell and Julius Caesar, and of the danger that the American people, after successfully escaping the tyranny of George of England, might wake up to find themselves the subjects of an all-powerful George of their own.

Thomas Jefferson was particularly concerned over the threat of monarchy, but he did not share in the common suspicions as to the sentiments of Washington. At the time of the adoption of the Constitution Jefferson was American Minister in Paris, and from there he corresponded at length with Washington in friendly vein. Like the latter, he was opposed to unlimited reelection of a President, a point that the new Constitution did not cover. As he put it, "This, I fear, will make that an office for life, first, then hereditary. I was much an enemy of monarchies before I came to Europe, and am ten thousand times more so since I have seen what they are. There is scarcely an evil known in these countries which may not be traced to their king as its source, nor a good which is not derived from the small fibres of republicanism existing among them. I can further say, with safety, there is not a crowned head in Europe whose talents or merits would entitle him to be elected vestryman by the people of any parish in America."

Washington had no desire to be King; what he wanted was to retire to a quiet life at Mount Vernon, from which he could conduct his highly profitable business as a real estate operator. He was already one of the richest men in the country, and the emoluments and duties of a monarch did not attract him. But when he became President in 1789 most of the men around him were "Federalists," the business men and landowners who had promoted the new Constitution in order to strengthen the Federal Government. On general principles, as he knew, the leading Federalists were by no means hostile to the idea of having an American King in whose court they could expect to obtain influential places. These feelings in the upper levels of the administration were bound to make trouble for the President.

When Jefferson returned to America and was appointed Secretary of State in 1790, he was shocked at the monarchical sentiments he heard in New York, where the Government was sitting. "Being fresh from the French Revolution, while in its first and pure stage, and, consequently, somewhat whetted up in my own republican principles," he observed in a letter, "I found a state of things in the general society of the place, which I could not have supposed possible. The revolution I had left, and that we had just gone through in the recent change of our own government, being the common topics of conversation, I was astonished to find the general prevalence of monarchical sentiments, insomuch, that in maintaining those of republicanism, I had always the whole company on my hands, . . . The furthest that anyone would go in support of the republican features of our new government would be to say, 'the present constitution is well as a beginning, and may be allowed a fair trial, but it is, in fact, only a stepping stone to something better.' "

These fears of Jefferson were echoed by irresponsible critics in intemperate language, including accusations that Washington himself was acting like a king. By 1790 there was already growing resentment at the Presidential ceremonials. One of Washington's friends wrote to him from Virginia that a certain Colonel had told him that "there was more pomp used there than at St. James's where he had been, and that Washington's bows were more distant and stiff." To which Washington replied, with a tinge of bitterness, that his bows were "the best I was master of. Would it not have been better to throw the veil of charity over them, ascribing their stiffness to the effects of age . . . rather than to the pride and the dignity of office, which, God knows, has no charms for me."

Washington explained to Jefferson that when he entered the Presidency, he had observed that he was ignorant of the forms used in other governments and, being "perfectly indifferent to all forms," had assigned such matters to General Henry Knox, "a man of parade," and to Colonel Humphreys, who had lived at a foreign court. Some of what they proposed Washington absolutely rejected, and at the end of his first term he called the Cabinet together and asked for advice

The unfortunate phrasing accompanying contemporary prints such as the above encouraged criticism of Washington by those who found it advantageous to accuse him of harboring monarchial ambitions.

Martha Washington's receptions strongly suggested royal levees to some.

Such adulation of Washington made his enemies feel justified in charging him with a secret desire to be treated like royalty despite his disavowals.

about changes in the ceremonies. Both Jefferson and Hamilton were agreed that there was too much pomp, but they were outtalked by Knox and Attorney-General Edmund Randolph.

Washington was so far from being friendly toward aristocratic privileges and ambitions that he was seriously worried by his entanglement with the Society of the Cincinnati shortly after its establishment in 1783. This fraternal order was founded at the suggestion of General Knox, with the active support of Baron von Steuben and other leading Generals. Membership was open to American and foreign officers of the Continental forces and their eldest male descendents. The stated purpose of the order was "to preserve the exalted rights and liberties of human nature for which they had fought and bled," as John Marshall described it with approval in his life of Washington. As soon as news of the Society's organization became public, it was violently attacked as an effort to found a hereditary aristocracy. Washington's deep attachment to his loyal comrades in arms did not prevent his having sympathy for the public doubts as to possible future developments of the Society. Years later Jefferson recounted in a letter to Martin Van Buren how Washington had talked with him on the subject, which they both had agreed was a matter of serious concern. According to this account:

"On his way to the first meeting [of the Cincinnati] in Philadelphia, which I think was in the spring of 1784, he called on me at Annapolis [where Congress was then sitting]. It was a little after candle-light, and he sat with me till after midnight, conversing, almost exclusively, on that subject. While he was feeling indulgent to the motives which might induce the officers to promote it, he concurred with me entirely in condemning it; and when I expressed an idea that if the hereditary quality were suppressed, the institution might perhaps be indulged during the lives of the officers now living, and who had actually served; 'no,' he said, 'not a fibre of it ought to be left, to be an eyesore to the public, a ground of dissatisfaction, and a line of separation between them and their country.'"

On his return from the meeting Washington reported that at first he had prevailed on most of the officers to reject the idea of the Cincinnati when Major L'Enfant arrived from France with applications for membership in the order from the French officers who had served in America, together with a solemn act of the King of France permitting them to wear its insignia. This turned the tide so strongly that all Washington could do was to obtain "a suppression of the hereditary quality." In the end he could not secure even that much; for the action of the May, 1784, national meeting abolishing hereditary membership failed of ratification by the state societies, and so the order did not die out with the original members.

Americans are today so used to hereditary societies having no political importance that it may be somewhat hard to imagine two men such as Washington and Jefferson talking from candle-light till midnight about the danger of developing an American House of Lords. But for these eighteenth-century men to believe that any great nation could long endure without monarchical institutions was still only an act of faith. Whether in fact the democratic growth of the American system in the next century was an inevitable effect of western pioneering or whether it was mainly due to Jefferson himself and his victory over the Federalists in 1800 may be arguable. But it is certain that these two men discussing their country's future in 1784 would have been astonished if they could have been told of the entire absence of political activity for or against the present Society of the Cincinnati, with its headquarters in the Capital City which the government under either party often rents as a convenient palace for the entertainment of visiting royalty.

When Washington was President, he continued to be criticized for his connection with this seemingly dangerous institution. A distressed Philadelphian, for instance, after discussing the constitution of the Cincinnati, commented: "Never perhaps was a foundation more deep and less equivocal laid for a new order in the state, than in the instrument we have been describing. . . . It is wonderful that many officers, and particularly the illustrious Washington, whose integrity was unquestionable, and whose characteristic quality had ever been wariness and caution could have been deceived in a business of so extreme magnitude. His conduct in this affair is perhaps the only blot, that can be fixed on the character of this venerable hero. It is impossible however wholly to exculpate him."

During the first two years of Washington's administration he was relatively free from personal attack. For a while he was actually treated much like a king, and held by most people to be above all political disputes—an attitude he himself regarded as most proper for a President. It was Alexander Hamilton, Secretary of the Treasury and the President's closest friend and adviser, who bore the weight of the opposition to the government's policies. But by 1792 those who opposed Hamilton's economic measures were beginning to blame Washington for "shielding himself behind the Secretary of the Treasury," and letting Hamilton "usurp the legislative powers of Congress" by proposing acts for Congress to pass. Since many of these acts were regarded by important sections of the public as injurious, their effect was to arouse partisanship and focus criticism on the administration, including Washington as its chief.

The Federalist policies advanced by Hamilton—particularly the protective tariff, excise taxes, and assumption of responsibility for the war debts of the states—were designed to establish a strong public and private financial structure as a basis for growing American manufacture and trade. Opposed to Hamilton from the start were the back-country agrarians and the city mechanics and small tradesmen, who in time came to look upon Jefferson as their leader. Naturally partial to states' rights, they at first called themselves anti-Federalists. They soon recognized, however, that the increasing prosperity of the country had rendered it futile to oppose the new Constitution itself; accordingly they began using the name "Republicans," which to them meant simply that they were against kings. It was later that they became "Democratic Republicans" and finally "Democrats." Most of them continued for some time to join fervently in singing "God Save Great Washington," to the tune of "God Save the King;" for Washington's name still bore some of the sacred quality that today is attached to the Stars and Stripes. Even those who opposed some of his policies had not all forgotten that fifteen years earlier his stubborn courage had been the very banner of freedom.

But the fact that the President was not really above the political battle, and that he inevitably had to be held responsible for the actions of his administration, began to take effect. Whatever he might think his position ought to be, he was not only human, but also a Federalist and therefore fair game. As the party struggles increased in bitterness the game was going to be harried without mercy. Washington had hoped a division of the country into rival parties or "factions," might be avoided, but that turned out to be impossible, and the home-grown conflicts were aggravated by the stirring news from

France. Events abroad forced Washington to make decisions that involved raising bitter controversies between political parties at home.

The French Revolution, which began in 1789, was at first greeted in the United States with general satisfaction, much as the Kerensky revolution in Russia was received in 1917 before it was overrun by the Bolsheviks. The French Revolution was regarded as a flattering imitation of our own, as indeed it was in part. Washington himself congratulated Lafayette and gratefully accepted the key of the Bastille which Lafayette sent him after the fall of the prison-fortress on July 14, 1789. That key is preserved at Mount Vernon to this day.

But the Revolution soon turned violently radical and took the form of a mass revolt against the upper classes. Feeling about it in this country divided along class lines, and disputes about what was going on overseas soon began to sharpen American party differences. The Federalists tended to sympathize with the French aristocracy while the Republicans became more vigorous in their opposition to Washington through their support of the Revolutionary movement in France.

As early as November, 1791, the Republican press was complaining of the Federalist attitude. A writer signing himself "Aratus" began a series of letters in the *American Daily Advertiser*, viewing with disgust those in America who feared the example of the events in France. As the Revolution had frightened the kings of Europe, so "a kindred panic has reached America. Great mischief appears to be apprehended from its widely spreading influence among the people; and champions of no common size have arose to combat it, by warning their countrymen of its fatal tendency." Aratus did not point the finger, but his readers understood that he referred to the Federalists surrounding Washington.

In the summer of 1791 there came to the seat of government a Frenchman who boded ill for the President's peace of mind. Philip Freneau was a young man of Huguenot ancestry who had been a friend of Madison's at Princeton College, and later a captain in the Revolutionary War. Madison evidently introduced him to Jefferson, who gave him a job in the State Department as a French translator. In the autumn Freneau began publishing a newspaper called the *National Gazette*. This paper and the Philadelphia *Aurora*, published by Franklin's grandson, Benjamin Franklin Bache, became the leading organs of the Republican Party, and were widely quoted by Republican papers throughout the country.

In February, 1792, the *Gazette* criticized the fact that Washington's birthday had been made the occasion for a parade by some of the Philadelphia militia. This was beginning to be a sore point with the Republicans, for no one had ever heard of celebrating the birthday of any public figure except the King. Signs of increasing disrespect for the Washington administration began to appear in the press before the middle of 1792. In May a letter signed "Anti-Puff" remarked: "Notwithstanding all the pains taken by those, who *call themselves the friends and admirers of the government,* to *thrust* their honeyed bolusses of adulatory PUFF *down the gaping throat of credulity,* the people cannot swallow such *choaking morsels* by which their faith would *certainly be strangled.*"

Hamilton himself wrote much for the Federalist press, defending the Administration and attacking Jefferson. Deeply disturbed by the growing enmity between these two members of his Cabinet, Washington addressed notes to both of them but got scant comfort from their replies. Hamilton, who was quite capable of showing impatience with his chief, refused to "recede at the present" and charged Jefferson with trying to "render me and all the objects connected with my administration odious," and to "subvert the government." In his reply Jefferson told the President: "No government ought to be without censors; and where the press is free no one ever will. If virtuous it need not fear the free operation of attack and defense." After Jefferson himself became President he was no longer so carefree about the operation of attack, but he never ceased to believe in the value of a free press.

By the end of 1792 there were open attacks on Washington's administration as pro-British. The courts were enforcing the collection of debts owed to British subjects, one critic complained, despite the failure of Britain to live up to her side of the peace treaty. He accused the government of "blind adherence to certain fashionable and courtly maxims of the day, by which it is endeavored to be inculcated that peace, and a good understanding with Great-Britain, must be preserved at any price . . . maxims which, in the opinion of the great body of the yeomanry of America, flow from the partial system of things, wherein the advantage of the many is made subservient to the emolument and aggrandizement of the few."

As Washington entered his second term he found himself faced with increasingly serious foreign problems. In the spring of 1793 came news that the revolutionists in France had guillotined King Louis XVI, and, a few weeks later, that they had declared war on England. Whatever Washington might do about this war was bound to offend one party or the other in the United States.

The Federalists were strongly opposed to any action that would offend the British, for American trade was mainly with England and British colonies. The Republicans, on the other hand, were more and more pro-French; chopping off the head of the French King did not offend them. Now was the time, in their opinion, to repay America's debt to France by helping her against England. Jefferson himself, as the responsible head of the State Department, favored keeping out of the war for the same reason that Washington did— the United States was too young and frail to take part in such a battle of the giants. But the less responsible Republicans were hot and wild.

There were also plenty of complications that Washington had to think about which were not so plain to private citizens with strong partisan views. He had no illusions about the pure unselfishness of French attachment to the United States, either under the King or under the Republic. He knew that when the American commissioners, Franklin, Jay, and John Adams, were negotiating peace with England after the Revolution, they discovered that the French were secretly manoeuvering to limit the Americans to the eastern coast, reserving the Mississippi Valley and the West for France and her ally Spain. The British, on the other hand, preferred to strengthen the Americans rather than the French and Spanish, and secretly agreed to recognize not only independence but American sovereignty as far west as the Mississippi. So the seeds were sown not only for American growth beyond the mountains, but also for distrust of France.

There were also seeds of controversy with England. In the peace treaty the British obtained assurances that Congress would advise the states to restore the properties confiscated from the Tories, and would put no obstacles in the way of collection of debts. The British in return promised to send back the slaves that they had carried off from the Southern states, and to evacuate their forts in the West. These promises were not fulfilled to anyone's satisfaction. The net effect was that the Jeffersonians, who were emotionally attached to

France, accused Jay and Adams, and the whole conservative party of which Washington was the head, of selling out to the British.

In April, 1793, Washington consulted, quite properly, with his Cabinet, and on April 22 he proclaimed American neutrality. From this point on, Republican attacks on Federalist monarchism took second place, and the spotlight was thrown on the accusation that the Federalists were pro-British and tainted with treason. Washington, as the man responsible for foreign policy, was directly in the line of fire.

Three years later Washington's memorandum to his Cabinet on the problem of neutrality came into the hands of the *Aurora*, which printed it in full as evidence of "treachery" to the nation's interests. In the memorandum, dated April 18, 1793, Washington asked the Cabinet members to consider and advise him on thirteen questions, covering such matters as whether the United States, under its treaties with France, had any right to remain neutral; and if so, whether neutrality would be expedient; and further, if the French Republic should send a Minister to the United States, whether he should be received. These entirely legitimate questions, which had in fact brought replies, even from Jefferson, favoring neutrality, were viewed as plain evidences of Washington's guilt:

"The foregoing queries were transmitted for consideration to the heads of the departments, previously to a meeting to be held at the President's house. The text needs no commentary. It has stamped upon its front in characters brazen enough for idolatry itself to comprehend, perfidy, and ingratitude. To doubt in such a case was dishonorable, to proclaim those doubts treachery. For the honor of the American character & of human nature, it is to be lamented, that the records of the United States exhibit such a stupendous monument of degeneracy. It will almost require the authenticity of holy writ to persuade posterity, that it is not a libel ingeniously contrived to injure the reputation of 'the saviour of his country'."

Since Jefferson was one of those to whom the secret document had been addressed, there was suspicion that he had leaked it, but he denied this vigorously. "In Bache's Aurora, of the 9th instant, which came here by the last post," he wrote to Washington, "a paper appears, which, having been confided, as I presume, to but few hands, makes it truly wonderful how it should have got there. I cannot be satisfied as to my own part, till I relieve my mind by declaring, and I attest everything sacred and honorable to the declaration, that it has got there neither through me nor the paper confided to me. This has never been from under my own lock and key, or out of my own hands."

While the problem of neutrality was plaguing Washington's mind a new source of disturbance appeared. On April 8, 1793, the frigate *L'Ambuscade* sailed into Charleston harbor, bringing Edmond Charles Genet, Minister Plenipotentiary from the French Republic to the United States Government. Citizen Genet took his title "plenipotentiary" at face value; upon arriving in Charleston he immediately set about buying American ships and commissioning them as French privateers to prey on British shipping. The news of his activities reached Philadelphia on April 22, the day the President issued his neutrality proclamation. Genet traveled slowly overland toward the capital, being feted as a popular hero all the way; the cheering crowds made him feel that he, rather than Washington, was the idol of the people.

While Genet was enjoying his triumphal progress by land, his frigate sailed from Charleston to Philadelphia, taking British prizes along the way and sending them into American ports to be sold. She even took the British vessel *The Grange* inside Delaware Bay. Since this vessel was captured in American waters, Washington directed Jefferson, as Secretary of State, to order her restored to her owners. The situation was already strained by the time Genet arrived in the capital on May 16; Washington received him with cold formality.

Genet, feeling confident that the people were with him, was offended but not discouraged. He requested that the government pay him the remaining $2,300,000 of its war debt owing to France, in advance of the due date, so that he could spend it for supplies; and he proposed to negotiate a new treaty, "a true family compact." When these were refused, he became even more offended.

At one point Genet had the local Republicans so aroused that mobs of them paraded the streets and threatened to attack Washington and other members of the government. Jefferson had a house in the suburbs, but John Adams, many years later, described in a letter to him how it felt at the time to be in the middle of the turmoil:

"You certainly never felt the terrorism excited by Genet in 1793, when ten thousand people in the streets of Philadelphia, day after

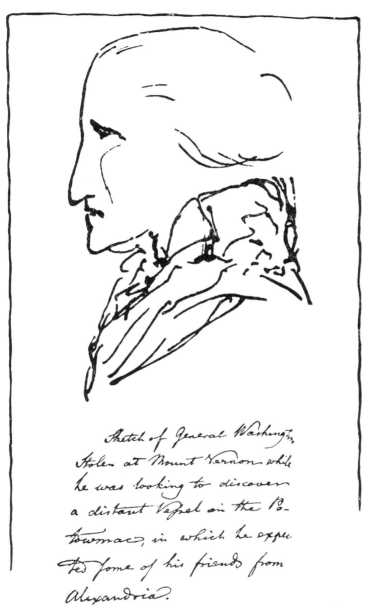

Sketch of General Washington, Stolen at Mount Vernon while he was looking to discover a distant Vessel on the Po- towmac, in which he expec- ted some of his friends from Alexandria.

Washington's haggard look, caught in this little known sketch by architect Benjamin H. Latrobe, reflected something of his bitterness because of vilification he was frequently subjected to in the course of his final years as nation's chief executive.

Entitled "Mrs. General Washington Bestowing Thirteen Stripes on Britania" this engraving in London's Rambler Magazine of 1783 shows Washington wearing a skirt as he brandishes a "cat" over weeping Britannia. Adjoining the caricature was a purported extract from the Pennsylvania Gazette of November 11, 1782, to the effect that Martha Washington confessed to a clergyman that the General was a woman.

day, threatened to drag Washington out of his house, and effect a revolution in the government, or compel it to declare war in favor of the French revolution, and against England . . . when Market Street was as full as men could stand by one another, and even before my door; when some of my domestics, in phrenzy, determined to sacrifice their lives in my defence; when all were ready to make a desperate sally among the multitude, and others were with difficulty and danger dragged back by the others; when I myself judged it prudent and necessary to order chests of arms from the war office, to be brought through by lanes and back doors; determined to defend my house at the expense of my life, and the lives of the few, very few, domestics and friends within it."

Genet is credited with having introduced into the American language the word "democrat" for the good people, and "capitalist" for the bad ones. At about the same time the Federalists began calling the Republicans "Jacobins," after certain radical societies in France, and also "levelers." In England a leveler was a radical who wanted to "soak the rich."

Genet's arrival stimulated Freneau to step up his criticisms of Washington which began to get under the President's skin. Jefferson says in his diary for May 23, 1793, that Washington "adverted to a piece in Freneau's paper of yesterday, he said he despised all their attacks on him personally, but that there had never been an act of the government, not meaning in the Executive line only, but in any line which that paper had not abused. . . . He was evidently sore and warm, and I took his intention to be that I should interpose in some way with Freneau, perhaps withdraw his appointment of translating clerk in my office. But I will not do it. His paper has saved our constitution which was galloping fast into monarchy, & has been checked by no means so powerfully as by that paper. . . . The President, not sensible of the designs of the party, has not with his usual good sense, and sang froid, looked on the efforts and effects of this free press, & seen that tho' some bad things had passed thro' it to the public, yet the good preponderated immensely."

The offending issue contained a long letter from "A Democrat," reprinted from a Boston paper, denouncing neutrality as an act of perfidy to the French nation, and suggesting that the states nullify it by taking unneutral measures such as levying stiff harbor charges on British ships and not on French. "An American" wrote to suggest that the paper reprint, as a public reproach to the President, the relevant articles of the French treaty of February 6, 1778, which it did.

In the same issue "An Old Soldier" said: "Let the mercenary band, who bask in the sun-shine of court-favour, and who, in the accumulation of wealth, forget the dignity of man, . . . let *these* declare themselves neutral . . . Thanks-be to our God, the *sovereignty* still resides with THE PEOPLE, and that neither proclamations nor *royal demeanor and state* can prevent them from exercising it . . . it is a disgrace to America to place France upon the same footing with the powers with whom she is at war . . . rather let America join in the combat with France than forfeit her honor and her virtue."

Indignantly Washington wrote to Henry Lee on June 21: "The publications in Freneau's and Bàche's papers are outrages on common decency." But "I have a consolation within that no earthly effort can deprive me of, and that is, that neither ambition nor interested motives have influenced my conduct. The arrows of malevolence, therefore, however barbed and well pointed, never can reach the most vulnerable part of me, though, while I am up as a mark, they will be continually aimed."

A particularly awkward incident came early in July. The *Little Sarah*, an English merchantman, was captured by a French frigate and brought into Philadelphia, where she was refitted as a privateer and rechristened the *Petite Democrate*. Washington had issued orders forbidding the outfitting of privateers in American ports, but he was at Mount Vernon, and Jefferson was left in charge. When Genet was told that the ship must not sail he flew into a rage against the President and threatened that the crew would resist any attempt to prevent her departure. He stormed that if Washington refused to behave properly he would appeal over the President's head to the people. Then he calmed down a little and told Jefferson that after all the ship would not be fit for sea before the President's return.

The Republicans were excited and defiant. On July 10th someone signing himself "Juba" protested in the *Gazette* that Washington had allowed the *Little Sarah* to be armed and to sail under the command of a notorious British privateersman, but when she became a French ship he had tried to forbid her sailing:

"The Minister of France. I hope," declared Juba, "will act with firmness and with spirit; the people are his friends, or the friends of France, and he will have nothing to apprehend; for, as yet, the people are the sovereign of the United States. If one of the leading features of our Government is pusillanimity, when the British Lion shows his teeth let France and her Minister act as becomes the dignity and justice of her cause, and the honor and faith of nations." This was plain talk, assuring the French Minister that he could defy the President with impunity.

When Washington returned the next day he sent Jefferson a note asking: "Is the minister of the French Republic to set the acts of this government at defiance *with impunity*,—and then threaten the executive with an appeal to the people? What must the world think of such conduct? and of the government of the United States in submitting to it?" Jefferson assured the President that the *Petite Democrate* was not ready for sea. But Genet had fooled him; she slipped away.

The President was vilified in a French poem which the public attributed to Genet and which he did not deny. Another attack, in prose, the Minister admitted to be the work of his private secretary. Genet was quoted as saying of Washington that the old man was in his dotage, but that the people would put him in his place. But as word spread that the French Minister had threatened to appeal to the people, his popularity faded. Millions of Americans were still partial to France as against England, but for a foreigner to ask them to discipline George Washington was too much.

On the other hand, as the effects of pro-French partisanship piled on top of the resistance to Federalist domestic policies, the President became more and more sensitive to the increasing attacks against him. Jefferson records that early in August, when Secretary Knox spoke of a recent libel on the President, in a moment the face of Washington grew red with anger: "He got into one of those passions when he cannot command himself, ran on much on the personal abuse which had been bestowed on him, and defied any man on earth to produce one single act of his, since he had been in the Government, which had not been done on the purest motives. He had never repented but once having slipped the moment of resigning his office, and that was every moment since; and, by God! he had rather be in his grave than in his present situation. He had rather be on his farm than be emperor of the world; and yet they were charging him with wanting to be a king."

The Secretary of State had become increasingly embarassed by Genet's activities. He was particularly worried by news that the Frenchman's agents were organizing American armed forces for an attack on Louisiana, which at that time belonged to Spain. Information came from the American legation in London that France proposed to take the territory around New Orleans and the coast westward to Mexico, and would not object to an American conquest of Florida. But Jefferson was already thinking of the need for American control of New Orleans, and Genet's projects threatened to bring that territory into stronger hands than those of the feeble Spanish Crown.

At last Washington decided that Genet would have to go, and in August Jefferson wrote to Gouverneur Morris, the American Minister in Paris, asking for his recall. His letter suggests that he was thoroughly tired of the French envoy. He told Morris: "Genet, not content with using our force, whether we will or not, in a military line, against nations with whom we are at peace, *undertakes also to direct the civil government;* thus in his letter of June 8th, he promised to respect the political opinions of the President, *till the representatives should have confirmed, or rejected them,* as if the President had undertaken to decide what belonged to the decision of Congress: In his letter of June 14th, he says more openly, that the President *ought not* to have *taken on himself* to *decide* on the subject of the letter, but that it was of importance enough to have consulted congress thereon; and in that of 22nd June, he tells the President, in *direct terms,* that congress *ought* already to have been consulted on certain questions which *he had been too hasty* in deciding, thus making *himself,* and not the President, the *judge* of the *powers* assigned by the constitution, and *dictating* to him the occasion when he shall exercise the power of convening congress."

Genet was not sent back to France, for his friends had fallen from power and the government had ordered his arrest. He moved to Jamaica, New York, where he settled down and married the daughter of Governor Clinton. He outlived both Washington and Jefferson, and died a respected gentleman farmer and civic leader. In 1827 an Edmond Charles Genet and Mr. Eugene Robertson advertised for subscriptions to a project of air navigation "to secure to these Republics, the additional scientific honour, after having first improved the navigation of the waters by the power of steam to be also the first to improve the navigation of the air by aerostatic machine."

After Washington was rid of the irrepressible French Minister he still found no peace, for the British were encroaching so seriously on American shipping that by 1794 there was growing danger of war with England. Washington therefore sent John Jay, then Chief Justice, to London to see if he could negotiate a settlement. Jay signed a treaty on November 19, 1794, but the ships were so slow during the winter that no copy reached Philadelphia until the following March. Congress by that time had adjourned and gone home. Washington did not make public the terms of the treaty, but on June 8 he laid it before the Senate in special session.

The Republicans began to make trouble long before seeing the text of the treaty. News had arrived that Jay had been courteously received, which on the face of it led them to suspect that he had sold himself to the British. It was also reported that he had kissed the Queen's hand, and they cried out that he had prostrated the sovereignty of the people at the feet of majesty and richly deserved to have his lips blistered to the bone.

During May and June Washington came under violent criticism for holding the treaty secret. The Senate, while it ratified the treaty, made an attempt to keep it classified, but it leaked out and was published by Bache of the *Aurora*. Copies of the treaty were rushed by the Republicans to all parts of the country, and they created vast excitement. The British had driven a hard bargain. They did not promise this time to return or pay for the slaves they had carried off during the Revolution, but the United States promised help in collecting private debts owed to British creditors, mainly by Southern planters. There was no relief from British seizure of seamen out of American ships, and in many other details the treaty was favorable to England and hostile to France. One permanent result of the treaty was that many of the Southern planters, who had been shy of Jefferson's leveling tendencies, now came over to the Republican party.

Mass meetings of protest were held all over the country. In Philadelphia the Republicans called a meeting by distributing handbills that expressed their feelings toward the administration: "Citizens! assemble at the State-House on Thursday afternoon, the 23rd instant, at 5 o'clock, then and there to discuss the Momentous Question, viz.: Are the People the Legitimate Fountain of Government? There is creeping into your Constitution an insidious Serpent, whose venom, once infused, will exterminate every remaining Spark of Gratitude and National Faith! Attend! Your rights are invaded! France is our avowed Friend, and in the hour of Adversity was our vigorous and undaunted Advocate. Great Britain is the universal Foe of *Liberty;* and you, from your Regeneration to the present moment, have been the guiltless victims of her Infernal malice."

During the summer the heat built up. The Republicans stoked the fires by burning Jay in effigy, and Washington came under direct attack. "Valerius" for instance, belabored him with some fairly heavy sarcasm: "To the President: . . . Suffer me to observe, once for all, that in the analisis of your political character, I shall be constrained to shew myself more the enemy of your heart than of your head. I promise not to wound your self love, by the ambiguous apology for your conduct, which has so often flowed from the lips of those who call themselves your friends. *They* could vouch for your *political honesty*, on the score of *wisdom* they have generally been silent . . . whatever deviations from the constitutional orbit may have marked your political course, have arisen from the deficiency of your knowledge, or from the misdirection of your mind by the erroneous information of others!"

In a later communication "Valerius" added: "For, Sir, we are free, and are with one mind, determined to remain free. Your voice may have been heard when it called to virtue and glory, but it will be lost in the tempest of popular fury, whenever it shall speak the language of lawless ambition. The American People, Sir, will look to death, the man who assumes the character of an usurper."

The Republican press decried the notion that the fate of the nation could hang on Washington or that he should be held above criticism. We are no longer free, it warned, if the magic of the despot's name is allowed to shield a violation of principle and Constitution, "and if the mantle of infallibility constantly invelops him."

A writer in the *New York Journal* criticized the President because he had politely thanked the New York Chamber of Commerce for approving his conduct and had refused to apologize to many other bodies that had disapproved the Jay treaty. Did the common people mean to put themselves on a par with the merchants and traders? "Were five thousand of the mass to weigh against four hundred stockholders? . . . Let the swinish creatures not approach the presidential sanctuary with their gruntings. Was he to be pestered with their opinions and have his nerves unstrung by their advice? Was he not soverign, infallible, immaculate, omniscient? Hardened and presumptuous wretches, they did not deserve so good a monarch."

In September a letter signed "Atticus" went so far as to suggest that the country could hardly survive if Washington remained President.

"A solemn, an awful silence pervades the world of American politics portentous of some great event. The signature, the unexpected signature of the President to the Treaty, has momentarily paralyzed the American mind . . . He has thwarted the affections of the people, and in contempt to their attachment to the Republic of France, and aversion from Great Britain, he has deceived the one and crouched to the other. . . . Shall he greet the tyrant George as his *great, good and dear friend,* and shall we be obliged to recognize such sacrilege of liberty?

"In signing the treaty the president has thrown the gauntlet, and shame on the coward heart that refuses to take it up. . . .

"Fellow citizens, we are on the eve of some great event; our liberties are in jeopardy, and we must either rescue them from the precipice, or they will be lost to us forever. One hope offers itself to us, and a consolatory one too, the house of Representatives of the United States. . . . As our application to the President has been treated with scorn, let us make our appeal to that body which has the power of impeachment, and we shall not find them the stepfathers of their country . . . let us then, my fellow citizens, rally round our representatives, and we may still be free!"

The Republicans charged that Washington had violated the Constitution, observing irrelevantly that he had made a treaty with a nation that is the abhorrence of our people, and had treated our remonstrances with pointed contempt. "Louis XVI, in the meridian of his splendor and his power, never dared to heap such insults upon his subjects. The answers to the respectful remonstrances of Boston and Philadelphia and New York sounded like the words of an omnipotent director to a seraglio. He had thundered contempt upon the people with as much confidence as if he sat upon the throne of Indostan. As he had been disrespectful to his people, he should no longer expect them view him as a saint." Then, as now, many critics bandied the word "unconstitutional" who had never read the Constitution. That document nowhere requires the President to be guided solely, or at all, by "the weight of the mail."

A letter to the editor of the *Aurora* sadly informed the President that "The name of Washington like the inscription on the ring of Solomon, was a protection to all who were happy enough to be leagued against the people. Like an ignis fatuus it has led us astray thro' bogs and quagmires till it has brought us to the brink of destruction. Times are now changed, the people begin to see that you are not infallible, to perceive that you have erred, and to distrust the high sounding encomiums so often reechoed by the pretended Federalists."

In the *New York Journal* "A Calm Observer," believed to have been John Beckley, Clerk of the House, accused Washington of drawing several thousand dollars more from the Treasury than the salary of $25,000 a year that he was entitled to. "Is there any other man," the Calm Observer inquired, "Who would have dared to ask such a favor? How can the people feel respect for the rulers who trample on the laws and the Constitution of the land? What will posterity say of the man who has done this thing? Will it not say that the mask of political hypocrisy has been worn by Caesar, by Cromwell, and by Washington alike?"

Harking back to the charge of monarchism, one correspondent deplored Washington's loss of his old folksy ways and his assumption of regal manners: "Time was when he, more than any other, indulged the manly walk and rode the generous steed. Now to behold him on horseback or afoot is the subject of remark. The concealing carriage, drawn by supernumerary horses, expresses the will of the President, and defies the loyal duty of the people. He receives visits. He returns none. Are these republican virtues? Do they command our esteem?" "Happily," said another commentator, "the public mind is rapidly changing. Hitherto the name of Washington has been fatal to the popularity of every man against whom it was directed. Now it is as harmless as John O'Nookes or Tam O'Stiles. To be an opposer of the President will soon be the passport to popular favor."

Even the legislature of Virginia voted down a resolution expressing undiminished confidence in Washington, and another, disclaiming any doubt of his motives, barely passed.

The House that met on December 7, 1795, was controlled by the Republicans. On the second day, shortly after Washington read his address in person, the Congressmen began looking for ways to insult him. It had been customary to adopt courteous answering resolutions and then march in procession to the President's house and deliver them to him. To neglect this formality would be an insult, so it was moved that a committee visit the President and tell him that the House would consider his recommendations. After some bitter recriminations this motion was voted down, but 18 members voted for it. Then there were objections to the proposed answer, especially to a paragraph that referred to "that probably unequalled spectacle of national happiness, which our country exhibits," and to "the undiminished confidence of your fellow-citizens." After a nasty fight during which the words "probably unequalled" were dropped, the address was recommitted for changes to meet criticisms. When it came back there was nothing in it about "confidence."

Another opportunity for Congress to insult the President came on February 22, 1796. Despite Republican objections the custom of celebrating Washington's birthday had grown until, without any official sanction, it had become a general holiday, and Congress itself was accustomed to express its respect by adjourning for half an hour. This time it voted not to do so, and there was an outburst of denunciation in the Republican papers. The President was called "the American Caesar," and "the stepfather of his country."

People in those days were patient with long-winded political poetry, and the Republicans rejoiced in masterpieces such as the following, which came out on February 20, 1796:

"Excisemen, Senators, and army Hectors,
All hail the day in clear or squalid notes,
Place-hunters, too, with lordly Bank directors,
Loud in the general concert swell their throats.

❊   ❊   ❊

"The splendid Levee, too, in some degree,
Must Caesar's dignity and power display;
There Courtiers smooth approach with bended knee,
And hoary Senators their homage pay.

"Tho' 'faction most detestable,' most vain,
Hath on Jay's Treaty curses dire conferred—
What! self-created scum! dare you complain,
Or say infallibility hath erred?

"Dare you (ye swinish herd of infamy)
Against your country's father thus transgress—
Who for his Wisdom and Integrity
Doth 'undiminished confidence' possess?

"Against that rock—that adamantine wall—
Ye Sons of Whiskey, aim your blows—
Slanders against great Caesar's name must fall,
'Like pointless arrows shot from broken bows.' "

The language here indicates that the writer had not forgotten the Whiskey Rebellion of 1794, nor forgiven Washington for his report on it to the Congress, in which he reproached "certain self-created societies," meaning the Democratic societies of Philadelphia, New York, and Pittsburgh, which had been loud in their condemnation of the excise laws.

On March 2, 1796, Washington sent the Jay Treaty to the House for the appropriations necessary to carry it out, and there was a long argument over whether a treaty, passed by only the President and the Senate, could really be the supreme law of the land. The Republicans took a position somewhat like that of Senator Bricker 150 years later, but in the end the Federalists won, and the effort to nullify the

Constitutional treaty power failed for that time. Washington by then was used to being called unconstitutional.

After Congress adjourned in June, Washington returned to Mount Vernon to rest and to prepare his announcement that he would not run for a third term. We have a picture of him as he looked at that time, drawn by Benjamin Latrobe, who afterward was architect of the capitol. Visiting Mount Vernon in the summer of 1796, he described Washington in his journal as a courtly gentleman carrying with unbending fortitude the burden of his office and the curses of his political enemies, but often distrait and under evident strain. Latrobe's portrait shows a man still alert but worn and tired.

Meanwhile, an old Revolutionary warhorse and friend of Washington's, Thomas Paine, was composing a long and bitter attack on him. Paine was an Englishman whom Benjamin Franklin had induced to come to America in 1774. He published the famous pamphlet *Common Sense* in January, 1776, urging the American people to stand up against the King. Washington said of this pamphlet that it "worked a powerful change in the minds of men." In 1787 Paine returned to England and then visited France, where he got in trouble with the Jacobins and was jailed on the ground he was a British subject. While he was in jail James Monroe arrived in Paris as American Minister and wrote Paine a cordial letter assuring him that Washington and all the American people considered him to be a United States citizen. Monroe promised to work vigorously for his release, which in fact he effected some months later and then took him into his own house.

Though just out of a French jail, Paine was still violently pro-French and bitterly opposed to American neutrality, as well as to the aristocratic tone of Federalist policies in general. He determined to devote his talents to denouncing the President in an open letter. This famous letter covers 60 pages as published in pamphlet form by Bache in Philadelphia. Dated at Paris July 30, 1796, it starts without greeting:

"As censure is but awkwardly softened by apology, I shall offer you no apology for this letter. The eventful crisis to which your double politics have conducted the affairs of your country requires an investigation uncramped by ceremony. . . .

"The part I acted in the American Revolution is well known; I shall
not here repeat it. I know also that had it not been for the aid
received from France in men, money, and ships, that your cold and
unmilitary conduct (as I shall show in the course of this letter) would,
in all probability, have lost America; at least she would not have been
the independent nation she now is. You slept away your time in the
field till the finances of the country were completely exhausted, and
you have little share in the glory of the final event. It is time, sir,
to speak the undisguised language of historical truth.

"Elevated to the chair of the Presidency you assumed the merit
of every thing to yourself, and the natural ingratitude of your constitution began to appear. You commenced your Presidential career by
encouraging and swallowing the grossest adulation, and you travelled
America from one end—to the other, to put yourself in the way of
receiving it. . . . As to what were your views, for if you are not
great enough to have ambition you are little enough to have vanity,
they cannot be directly inferred from expressions of your own; but
the partizans of your politics have divulged the secret.

"John Adams has said (and John, it is known, was always a speller
after places and offices, and never thought his little services were
highly enough paid) John has said, that as Mr. Washington had no
child, that the Presidency should be made hereditary in the family
of Lund Washington. John might then have counted upon some
sine-cure for himself and a provision for his descendants. He did
not go so far as to say also, that the Vice Presidency should be hereditary in the family of John Adams. He prudently left that to stand
upon the ground, that one good turn deserves another." Paine threw
in this gibe without bothering to think what it would be like to have
both a hereditary President and a hereditary Vice President.

He went on to complain that Washington had neglected to put all
possible pressure on the French Government to get him out of prison:

"It was the duty of the executive department in America to have
made (at least) some enquiries about me . . . Mr. Washington owed
it to me on every score of private acquaintance, I will not now say,
friendship; for it has for some time been known, by those who know
him, that he has no friendships; that he is incapable of forming any;
he can serve or desert a man or a cause with constitutional indifference;
and it is this cold hermaphrodite faculty that imposed itself upon

the world, and was credited for a while by enemies as by friends, for prudence, moderation, and impartiality. . . .

"It is as well the ingratitude as the pusillanimity of Mr. Washington and the Washington faction, that has brought upon America the loss of character she now suffers in the world, and the numerous evils her commerce has undergone, and to which it is yet exposed. The British ministry soon found out what sort of men they had to deal with, and they dealt with him them accordingy; and if further explanation was wanting, it has been fully given since in the snivelling address of the New York Chamber of Commerce to the President, and in that of sundry merchants of Philadelphia, which was not much better. . . .

"If there is sense enough left in the heart to call a blush into the cheek, the Washington administration must be ashamed to appear. —And as to you, sir, treacherous in private friendship (for so you have been to me, and that in the day of danger) and a hypocrite in public life, the world will be puzzled to decide, whether you are an apostate or an imposter; whether you have abandoned good principles, or whether you ever had any?"

Paine's attack was impossible for Washington to comprehend, for he believed his conduct to have been correct. He was friendly to France, and had understood and sympathized with the idea of a revolt against the King, led by his friend Lafayette and Jefferson's friends in Paris. But when the masses began murdering the gentlemen, he was shocked, and he could not follow Paine's unswerving devotion to the bloodstained French Republic. The attack on Federalist domestic policies seemed equally baffling. What else could they have done? When the frontiersmen of Western Pennsylvania rose in the "whiskey rebellion" of 1794 against Hamilton's excise tax on whiskey, Washington sent the Army to suppress it without a qualm. He could not understand so complicated an idea as the "tyranny" of a tax imposed by the small minority of citizens who owned property and had votes, on the backwoods farmers who were used to putting their rye in liquid form so that they could carry it over rough trails to market. Washington saw nothing wrong in the property qualifications for voting, under which, according to an estimate given by Woodrow Wilson, out of about 4,000,000 people, only some 120,000 had votes.

Washington's education was meager, confined to the three Rs and surveying. Albert Jay Nock has pointed out that when Paine's letter reached him, he did not have the background of knowledge or ideas to comprehend what Paine was driving at. "Paine's bitter condemnation of him for having turned the country over to the tender mercies of monopolists and speculators merely wounded his sensibilities without ever reaching his understanding. Why, to whom else should the country be turned over?—to the ignorant rabble of workingmen and farmers?"

As for Washington's coldness, of which Paine so bitterly complained, John Bach McMaster, no friend to the Jeffersonians, in speaking of the resignations of Hamilton as Secretary of the Treasury and Knox as Secretary of War at the end of 1794, remarks that at this time "Washington was deprived of the services of the only two men his cold heart ever really loved."

Washington could probably have been easily reelected for a third term in 1796, but he had had enough. On September 17th he made public his Farewell Address, now considered one of the greatest of American state papers, but not so regarded by the Republicans at the time. If it had been a second proclamation of neutrality, or an open declaration of war against the French, as McMaster points out, it could not have provoked more anger among the Republicans. Here, they shouted, was proof aplenty that Washington was a man without character: "His temper is arbitrary. His disposition is avaricious. He has a great passion for being seen. Without any skill as a soldier he has crept into fame by the places he has held and by the success of the cause he espoused. . . . If it be merit to have laid a tax that raised an insurrection, then he shares it with the British ministers who provoked the Revolutionary War. If it be a merit to have burdened the many to enrich the few, then he shares it with that infatuated monarch who brought about the present state of France. . . . History will yet tear the page devoted to his praise. It was France and his country that, in defiance of England, gave him fame, and it is France and his country that will, in defiance of England, take that fame away."

According to one critic, his conduct no longer appeared to be guided by candor. In departing from that wise course, he had refused to the representatives of the people the papers they had a right to see. From that moment the brightness of his countenance faded. When he signed the Jay Treaty, the glory that once shone round him dissolved in mist. The enemies of liberty and his country claimed him as their own, and the name of Washington sank from the high level of Solon and Lycurgus to the mean rank of a Dutch stadholder, or the insignificance of a Venetian doge. Posterity would look in vain for any marks of wisdom in his Administration. They would, instead, behold a national debt, the worst of all diseases that ever inflict a state. They would see an excise arming freemen against their fellow-men, and they would say the great champion of American liberty retained the barbarous usages of the feudal system by keeping men in livery, and, twenty years after the founding of the Republic, still owned five hundred slaves.

The complaints about the national debt refer to Hamilton's policy of "assuming" or accepting responsibjlity for the war debts of both the Constinental Congress and the states, and paying them off, to the great advantage of the bondholders, many of them speculators, and many of them Federalist members of Congress. The Federal debt, which in our day horrifies so many conservatives, was much more realistically viewed by both Hamilton and his opponents, as the solid foundation under the portfolios of corporations and an instrument for the accumulation of capital—which the Federalists desired, and which the back-country people feared and hated. The complaint about withholding papers refers to a request by the House of Representatives in March, 1796, that the President hand over all the papers concerning the negotiations that had led up to the Jay Treaty with England. The Republicans wanted to fish for proofs of unconstitutionality or possibly undue British influence on Mr. Jay. The President, like many of his successors, refused to let hostile Congressmen fish in his files.

The part of Washington's Farewell Address that is now best remembered was the one most criticized at the time. " 'Tis our true policy," he said, "to steer clear of permanent alliance with any portion of the foreign world." The Republicans were enraged. What did this mean? Why were the United States suddenly cautioned not to extend their connections with European powers? The reason was plain. Washington had lately forced the United States into a treaty with Great Britain. The treaty gave great privileges to England, and now, lest similar concessions should be granted to France, he would have all political connections with Europe closed.

The Republican press accused Washington of magnanimously declining to run again because he knew he might be defeated by a clever manipulation of Republican votes in the Electoral College. This argument refers to the fact that under the original Constitution, each elector voted for two names without distinction, and if one candidate received the votes of a majority of the electors he was elected President, the runner-up becoming Vice President. While the electors had begun to follow party lines by 1796, they were by no means rubber stamps, and the parties at that stage of development had no definitely nominated candidates to whom the electors could be pledged as a party matter. In the election of 1796, as it turned out, thirteen men received electoral votes. Adams was elected with 71 votes and Jefferson was elected Vice President with 68. If Washington had been running it was conceivable that the Republicans might have concentrated enough of their own votes on Adams to humiliate Washington by reducing him to second place.

When Congress met in December, the Republicans again took the occasion of the President's Message to show their lack of respect. Although the customary courteous reply was passed, twelve members voted against it.

A correspondent in the *Aurora* complained that the Message was the same kind of bombast that characterized the speeches of George of England, and ridiculed the President's claim that the country was prosperous. He accused Washington of wanting Congress to build a national university "to tinsel the rattle of his age, the city of Washington," and raised the question whether he was so much concerned with the Capital city because it was named after him, or because of its neighborhood to his property. "Certain it is, however, that there has been a devotion to the spot more fervent than would have been inspired by patriotism alone." The writer went on to say that the country's prospects had been sacrificed to Washington's lust for power, and his previously good character had been brought into disgrace by the idolatrous worship of his followers.

Another correspondent took the trouble to lay down the proper line for future historians: "If ever a nation was debauched by a man, the American nation has been debauched by Washington. If ever a nation has suffered from the improper influence of a man, the American nation has been deceived by Washington. Let his conduct then be an example to future ages. Let it serve to be a warning that no man may be an idol, and that a people may confide in themselves rather than in an individual.—Let the history of the federal government instruct mankind, that the masque of patriotism may be worn to conceal the foulest designs against the liberties of a people."

One writer went to great pains to prove that President Washington had committed murder and Bache impugned his courage by digging up and printing a number of forged letters that had been published under Washington's name nineteen years earlier, during the war. The story was that when Fort Lee surrendered, a Negro servant of General Washington's fell into the hands of the British. In his possession, reportedly, was a portmanteau containing seven letters of a distinctly defeatist nature. Some were addressed to Lund Washington, some to Mrs. Washington's son John Parke Custis, and one to Mrs. Washington. Washington was made to talk to his own family in language indicating that the cause of the Revolution was hopeless. The fact was that he had never written any such letters and his servant had never been captured by the British.

The republication of these forgeries in the last months of Washington's term of office was a shrewdly aimed blow, warning him that his enemies would try to deprive him of the place he had earned in history by contributing to the Revolution what no other American was able to supply—a lofty example of undaunted courage and hope. Deeply hurt by what he sensed, he drew up a solemn declaration that none of the letters had been written by him. He handed his statement to the Secretary of State for placement in the archives. This statement, dated March 3, 1797, declared: "At the time when these letters first appeared, it was notorious to the army immediately under my command, and particularly to the gentlemen attached to my person, that my mulatto man Billy had never been one moment in the power of the enemy. It is also a fact that no part of my baggage or any of my attendants were captured during the course of the war. . . . The letters herein described are a base forgery, . . . I never saw or heard of them until they appeared in print." The unpleasant necessity of preparing such a denial for the record was what the President had on his mind the day before he turned over the office to his successor.

Finally came March 4 and Washington could go home to Mount Vernon, pursued, however, by the *Aurora*. That paper praised the Lord in its issue of March 6: " 'Lord now lettest thou thy servant depart in peace, for mine eyes have seen thy salvation,' was the pious ejaculation of a man who beheld a flood of happiness rushing in upon mankind—if ever there was a time that would license the reiteration of the exclamation, that time is now arrived; for the man who is the source of all the misfortunes of our country, is this day reduced to a level with his fellow citizens, and is no longer possessed of power to multiply evils upon the *United States* . . . the *name* of WASHINGTON from this day ceases to give a currency to political iniquity, and to legalize corruption." The writer went on to express astonishment that one man could have so far succeeded in breaking down the principles of republicanism, as to have threatened to destroy the Republic. "Such, however, are the facts, and with these staring us in the face, this day ought to be a JUBILEE in the *United States*."

Two months after Washington got back to Mount Vernon he was greeted by the publication of a seemingly outrageous letter by Thomas Jefferson. The Republican philosopher had known well that Washington was no royalist, but a deep concern about monarchism among leading Federalists continued to haunt him. This worry he had expressed in 1796 in a letter which, when it appeared in print in garbled form, created a furor and was taken by many people to be a direct attack on Washington. This was the famous Mazzei letter.

Philip Mazzei was an Italian who came to America in 1773 to settle and plant vines and olives. Jefferson met him and persuaded him to buy a place at Colle near Monticello. They became close friends, and corresponded after Mazzei returned to Europe in 1779. Jefferson wrote a long letter to Mazzei in April, 1796, in which there was one paragraph on the state of public affairs.

"The aspect of our politics has wonderfully changed since you left us. In place of that noble love of liberty and republican government which carried us triumphantly through the war, an anglican monarchical aristocratical party has sprung up, whose avowed object is to draw over us the substance, as they have already done the forms, of the British government. . . . It would give you a fever were I to name to you the apostates who have gone over to these heresies, men who were Samsons in the field and Solomons in the council, but who have had their heads shorn by the harlot England. In short, we are likely to preserve the liberty we have obtained only by unremitting labors and perils. But we shall preserve it; and our mass of weight and wealth on the good side is so great, as to leave no danger that force will ever be attempted against us. We have only to awake and snap the Lilliputian cords with which they have been entangling us during the first sleep which succeeded our labors."

A French translation of this paragraph got into the Paris press, from which in time it came to the United States, where it was retranslated into English and published in May, 1797. The French translator had added a paragraph of his own, to the effect that the conditions described by Mr. Jefferson explained the conduct of America toward France. It said that of all nations there was none from which France had a right to expect so much help and good will as from the United States. France was the Americans' true mother country. She had given the States their liberty and independence. Ungrateful children, they had deserted her when they should have armed in her defence. England and Mr. Pitt had dictated it all.

By the time Jefferson's remarks with the French additions were being published as a single quotation in New York, Jefferson had taken the oath as Vice President of the United States under President John Adams. The letter was seized upon as a gratuitous attack on Washington, and as proof that Jefferson's first loyalty was to France and that he was no fit person for high office in America.

Years later, in a letter to Martin Van Buren dated June 29, 1824, Jefferson stated emphatically that he had never had any disagreement with Washington over the Mazzei letter, nor in fact any personal disputes with him at any time, and continued: "My last parting with General Washington was at the inauguration of Mr. Adams, in March, 1797, and was warmly affectionate; and I never had any reason to believe any change on his part, as there certainly was none on mine.

"This letter to Mazzei has been a precious theme of crimination for federal malice. It was a long letter of business, in which was inserted a single paragraph only of political information as to the state of our country. . . . This paragraph, extracted and translated, got into a Paris paper at a time when the persons in power there were laboring under very general disfavor and their friends were eager to catch even at straws to buoy them up. To them, therefore, I have always imputed the interpolation of an entire paragraph additional to mine, which makes me charge my own country with ingratitude and injustice to France. . . .

"The original, speaking of an Anglican, monarchical and aristocratical party . . . states their object to be 'to draw over us the substance, as they had already done the *forms,* of the British Government.' Now the 'forms' here meant, were the levees, birthdays, and pompous cavalcade to the state house on the meeting of Congress, the formal speech from the throne, the procession of Congress in a body to re-echo the speech in an answer, &c., &c. But the translator here, by substituting *form* in the singular number, . . . made it mean the frame or organization of our government, or its form of legislative, executive and judiciary authorities, coordinate and independent; to which *form* it was to be inferred that I was an enemy. . . . Now General Washington perfectly understood what I meant by these forms, as they were frequent subjects of conversation between us."

Washington was not as much disturbed as Jefferson by the uproar over the Mazzei letter, for he knew that he and Jefferson felt the same way about monarchy, and that Jefferson was well aware of it; moreover, the Republican wolf-pack was off howling at the heels of President Adams. Most of the criticism fell on Jefferson, because of the anti-American sentiments that had been added in France. Mount Vernon at the last was a fairly quiet haven.

On December 13, 1799, Washington took a chill and came down with a septic sore throat, from which he died the following day. Once he was dead, the Republican papers entirely ceased reviling him. Even the *Aurora* spoke respectfully of him as "Commander in chief of the American armies during the revolution, caused by the tyranny of Great Britain: in this distinguished character, his name will live to the latest posterity among the greatest men who have ornmented history, by the support of liberty and their country against tyranny— As we can offer no higher Eulogium to the memory of a character elevated by fortune, talents, and the voice of his country to so high a station among the benefactors of mankind—we confine ourselves to that alone, recommending the principles for which he fought with so much honor to himself and his fellow citizens, and to the freedom of his country, to the careful and steadfast conservation of those who survive him."

On December 20th the same paper printed a letter from Alexandria describing Washington's last illness—"by some called the Crupe, by others an Inflammatory Quinsey"—and referring to his death not as the nation's happy release from "improper influence" but as a "mournful event." The item was even enclosed in heavy black lines. In later issues the *Aurora* printed President Adams's Message to Congress on the death, a notice of the funeral—also in heavy black lines—and an account of a memorial meeting of the Cincinnati in Philadelphia. On December 24 it announced the suspension of the paper for two days, "in honor of the memory of the immortal leader of the American armies to independence, GEORGE WASHINGTON, lately deceased." Finally on the 27th it printed a detailed and respectful story of the funeral.

So, even in the leading opposition newspaper, at last George Washington was allowed to rest in peace. Not all his successors have been so fortunate.

CHAPTER II

PERFIDIOUS PATRIOT

As the election of 1796 drew near it was clear that Washington's hope of a one-party country had not been realized. There were two parties well enough defined to recognize and attack their enemies. The Republicans sometimes praised John Adams as a left-handed way of belittling Washington, but in the main they aimed their fire at Adams as the front-running Federalist candidate.

Adams had long since learned the sensation of being hated by his fellow citizens and of stubbornly going his way amid catcalls and missiles; for it was he who in 1770 had acted as counsel for the British soldiers who were tried for murder after the "Boston massacre." This experience had been an educational one for a young lawyer with an interest in political affairs.

The "massacre" had culminated a winter of rising tension between the Bostonians and the soldiers of the 19th and 29th British Regiments who were stationed in the city to overawe the population. The local youths, in particular, had been stimulated by the tense atmosphere to attack the soldiers with stones and snowballs loaded with ice. Workmen from the waterfront also felt the urge to express their patriotic feelings by picking fights with the redcoats. Finally, on the moonlit evening of March 5, open rioting broke out in a square near the waterfront. The mob attacked a sentry, who called for help; a small squad of soldiers rushed to his defense; the mob closed in with sticks and showers of oyster shells, shouting "Lobsters! Bloody-backs! Let's burn the sentry box!" A soldier was knocked down, and the rest, with their backs to the wall, fired, killing five attackers or bystanders.

The Royal Governor, fearing widespread rebellion, promised that the soldiers would be duly tried for murder, but feeling ran so high that they could find no lawyer—even among the Tories—who would dare to take their case. Finally two said they would serve if John Adams, the well-known patriot and member of the Sons of Liberty, would join with them. Adams was sure that if he consented it would be political suicide; but for the honor of Massachusetts he could not refuse. Fortunately the trial was postponed until autumn, giving some time for passions to cool, and the political penalties of Adams's courageous stand did not seem to be as drastic as he had expected. His fellow members of the Sons of Liberty, after a short period of angry disbelief and then of reproach, turned around and elected him to the state legislature. The mob, on the other hand, did not forgive him. Stones came through the windows of his house. As he walked home after dark, voices from hidden corners would call out "Bloody-back!" and soon a mudball would fly past his head. Worse still, notorious Tories greeted him cordially, as if he had come over to their side.

When the trial came up in November the defense was able to obtain jurymen from outside Boston. The evidence plainly showed self-defense; Adams made an effective appeal to the New England conscience, and the soldiers were acquitted. In the city, however, feeling among the extremists ran higher than ever. Someone posted on the Town-House a "seditious paper" containing an adaptation of a passage from a current play, *Venice Preserved*:

"To See the Sufferings to my fellow Townsmen and own my self a man, to See the *Court* cheat the injured people with a *Shew* of *Justice* which yet we ne'er can taste of, drive us like wrecks down the rough tide of power while no hold is left to save us from destruction. All that Bear this are Slaves and we are such not to rise up at the great call of Nature and free the world from such Domestic TYRANTS.

No rebellion came, however, at that time, for the British Government adopted a more conciliatory attitude for the moment. Though there was much indignation over the acquittal of the "murderers" and over the solid legal arguments that Adams had used in court, he had gained stature as a man who had taken the case on behalf of the honor of Massachusetts law and justice when others were afraid of the mob. After the trial he devoted himself to his law practice, still thinking he was politically dead; but within a few years he found himself once more plunged into public life. In August, 1774, he was sent to Philadephia as one of the Massachusetts delegates to the Continental Congress.

There in the stress of later developments the man who, in the name of English law, had once saved his Majesty's soldiers from death, rose on May 15, 1776, and introduced the preliminary motion for independence with the words:

"Whereas his Brittanic Majesty, in conjunction with the lords and commons of Great Britain, has . . . excluded the Inhabitants of these United Colonies from the protection of his crown . . . it is necessary that the exercise of every kind of authority under the said crown should be totally suppressed, and all the powers of government exerted, under the authority of the people of the colonies . . ." Adams wrote to Abigail, his wife: "is it not a saying of Moses—*Who am I, that I should go in and out before this great people?*—When I consider the great Events which are passed, and those greater which are rapidly advancing, and that I may have been instrumental in touching Some Springs and turning Some Small Wheels, which have had and will have Such Effects, I feel an Awe upon my Mind which is not easily described."

Now it was twenty years later. It was 1796, and the country was independent but divided. Adams was up as a mark for the Republicans to shoot at. His treatment in this campaign however—the first to be contested in the young republic—was mild, compared with what came to him as President and what has happened to candidates in campaigns since 1796.

Boston's *Independent Chronicle,* for instance, mildly pointed out that Jefferson would be much less likely than Adams to found a Royal Family. Jefferson's writings marked him off as one of the most useful observers of the age, while those of Adams betrayed his aristocratical tastes. Adams had sons: these were no doubt the "well-born," who, according to their father's principles, ought one day to become lords and seigneurs of the land. Jefferson had only daughters who could hardly be dangerous as his political heirs. Adams hated the French Revolution; Jefferson, by his advice, had helped the people of France to find themselves. Elect Jefferson and the French would be conciliated at once, for they knew him to have a leaning in their favor; in America the mass of the people would be strongly drawn to the government, knowing his principles of Republican equality. Adams was said to be attached to the policies of Washington; but the people could not help remembering the time when, in a day of great gloom for the Republic, he had joined a faction that strove

Doughty arch-Federalist John Adams had personal characteristics that did not endear him among Republicans or members of his own party. Alexander Hamilton accused him of lacking "solidity of understanding" and being guilty of "great and intrinsic defects in his character." Moreover, Hamilton charged, Adams was afflicted by a "vanity without bounds and a jealousy capable of discoloring every object." The only Federalist elected President, Adams was outspoken about his uneasiness regarding democracy. Republicans never forgave him for once saying: "Democracy has never been so desirable as aristocracy or monarchy, but while it lasts, is more bloody than either. Remember, democracy never lasts long. It soon wastes, exhausts, and murders itself. There never was a democracy that did not commit suicide."

While the devil and Britain embolden his efforts, Federalist editor Peter Porcupine spews out lies about Jefferson and derision of democracy. Real name of Porcupine was William Cobbett, ex-British soldier.

A crude caricature of Federalists and Republicans fighting in Congress.

to pull down General Washington and raise up another to the supreme command.

This last accusation was wholly uncalled-for. As Adams's friends immediately pointed out, it was *Samuel* Adams who at first opposed Washington, and John Adams who sat up two whole nights to dissuade him. As for the fact that John Adams had sons to his name, the *Chronicle* would have been surprised at the road through which its prophecy would come to a sort of fulfilment. John Quincy Adams would indeed become President, but long before that he would have joined the Republican Party and would have come under the patronage of none other than Thomas Jefferson himself.

The *Aurora* was somewhat more severe in harping on Adams's political writings. It accused him of being a monarchist and a lover of titles, and noted that he used freely such terms as "well-born" and "canaille multitude," which could only apply under a monarchy. It raised the question whether the American people could risk electing a man who "believes the honors should fall to the well-born, and the hewing of wood and the drawing of water to the canaille multitude."

After Election Day the fact was plain that the electoral vote was going to be close between Jefferson and Adams. The electors had been chosen in various ways, for the Constitution provided then, as it does now, that each state would have the right to appoint its electors in any way the legislature might choose to adopt. Of the 138 electors, 70 had been appointed by state legislatures, 36 had been chosen in general state elections, and 32 had been elected by districts. Jefferson feared that neither he nor Adams would get a majority, and that the election might be thrown into the House; accordingly, he urged his friends not to work for him among the electors. He said Adams was an old friend and that he deserved the Presidency; Jefferson would not oppose him.

Alexander Hamilton was already hostile to Adams, and did his best to knife him among the Federalist electors, using his influence to shift votes to Thomas Pinckney of South Carolina, the secondary Federalist candidate, in the hope of making him President and throwing Adams once more into the Vice-Presidency. As the vote came out, however, Pinckney got only 59 electoral votes, and Aaron Burr 30, to 68 for Jefferson and 71 for Adams.

So John Adams became President and the leader of the opposing party became Vice President. The new President, in fact, felt more friendly to Jefferson than to Hamilton.

When Adams was inaugurated on March 4, 1797, his address was so conciliatory and non-partisan that for several months he had a honeymoon. Even the Republican papers praised him, saying that he was evidently going to be above parties and "was not chief of a faction." Then word came that the French Government, stung by the Jay Treaty, had refused to receive the new American Minister, Charles Cotesworth Pinckney, whom Washington had sent to replace Monroe. This action was accompanied by drastic decrees against American shipping and heavy depredations by French privateers. The French believed that if they put pressure on the Americans the opposition party would rise and overthrow the Adams Government. Pinckney had been forced out of France and was in Amsterdam. Faced with this news Adams called Congress in special session on May 15, and attacked the French actions in an Address that at once brought down on his head the wrath of the Republicans.

The speech was called a war-whoop and a war-song, and he was derided as "the President by three votes." According to the *Aurora*, whatever else might be said of him, he was, at least, a most admirable dissimulator. From the day of his inauguration he had completely deceived the people. Misled by his inauguration harangue, they supposed him to be of no party, and under the influence of no man. "But the mask is now put off. The cloven foot is in plain sight. . . . He is pleased to talk of foreign influence. What a pity he is not as free from British as he is of French influence! What a patriot he is, to be sure!" cried the editor with bitter sarcasm. "How truly American! With what indignation does he dwell on the treatment we get from belligerent powers! How the patriot blood mounted to his face as he spoke of the robberies of Great Britain, of the impressment of our seamen, of the savage conduct of England when she aroused the Indians to kill our settlers and burn our frontier towns, and urged on the Algerine pirates to filch us of our property on the sea! Hear him, too, speak of France, who aided us in the Revolutionary War! His notes are like those of the dying swan! What a friend to the rights of man, to the Republic of France, to the peace of the United States is not John Adams!"

The Republicans also took umbrage because the President had called for united support for the Government. "By the Government is to be understood John Adams," they sneered. "It is not for ME to hesitate. . . . Were the man in his second childhood, this egotism would be excusable. If he will own himself to be in his dotage, it will be pardonable even now. But for the President by three votes to talk in this wise is ridiculous." Rubbing in the fact of his narrow electoral majority, they pointed out that many of his electors had been chosen by state legislatures and not by the people, who no doubt would have voted for Jefferson if they had been given the chance. "Does he really think," they demanded, "that the people and himself are of one mind? That the people are partial to Great Britain? That they are for war measures against France?"

After some discussion in the Government it was decided in July to send three commissioners to France to see what terms could be made that would stop the unofficial war on American shipping and restore diplomatic relations. Pinckney, John Marshall, and Elbridge Gerry were chosen. The President, after starting the three off to France, went home to Braintree for a vacation. It would be spring of 1798 before he could hear what success the mission might have achieved.

In November, when Adams set out from Braintree to return to Philadelphia, his journey through Federalist New England was marked by parades and banquets, and the Federalists in Philadelphia suggested that the militia should turn out and escort the President into town. But most of the militia were Republicans, and Pennsylvania had voted for Jefferson in 1796. The Republicans seized the occasion to give the President a cold welcome.

When Washington was President, they pointed out, there was no turning out of the militia to escort him when he went to and from Mount Vernon. Even on his birthday when a tribute smacking of royalty was offered him, it was excused by alluding to his great services during the war. But what had John Adams done to deserve such honors? "Yet the merchant must quit his counter, the artisan put aside his tools, the tradesman close his shop, and all go forth and greet—the Duke of Braintree, the libeller of Republican government

in America. Let the British faction go if they wish, and bear a litter
with them, and put the godlike man in it and carry him home, lest a
spring break, or a wheel come off his carriage, and a life so dear
to our countrymen be placed in jeopardy."

The Republicans particularly resented the fact that in state after
state at the banquets in the President's honor, there was never a toast
to Jefferson, "the second officer of the nation." Why then should
Pennsylvania, which had not voted for Adams, do homage to him
now? "Are the militia a set of asses to bear every burden made
ready for their backs?"

Republican papers gleefully reported that only a few militiamen
paraded. One troop had twelve men, another had eighteen, and still
another as many as twenty-four. These set out in solemn array in the
forenoon. At three in the afternoon they came back, marching before,
behind, and around the carriage in which sat his Serene Highness
of Braintree. Naval officers and collectors of excise brought up the
rear. "The greatest possible order prevailed. Not a whisper was
heard. No gaping multitudes rent the air with shouts. No martial
music disturbed the quiet of the scene. A funeral could not have
been more decorous. Two or three constables, to be sure, attended
at his Highness's door, and sought to make some disturbance. 'Huzza!'
cried they as his Highness mounted the steps. But all was still as
death. 'Huzza!' again shouted the constables, 'won't you huzza for
the President?' Thereupon some boys cried 'Huzza!' and the President went in and shut the door." The Federalists denied the accuracy
of this story, but, true or imaginary, it stung.

The three commissioners who had been dispatched to France reached Paris in October, but were unable to make any direct contact with
the Government. Instead, various persons visited them, and made
it clear that they would have to apologize for parts of what President
Adams had said to Congress, give France a large loan, and also pacify
certain members of the Government with a "douceur" of 1,200,000
livres, equivalent to £50,000 sterling. The Americans said no; the
weeks went by; the French go-betweens talked of war. The commissioners reported in code to Washington, and on March 19, 1798,
Adams announced that the mission had failed and that the country
should prepare for defense.

The Republicans burst out in fury against what they called the

President's "War Message." Here, they declared, is food many will find hard to digest: gunpowder and red-hot cannon balls. They complained that the President "has not thought proper, yet, to *decypher* the later dispatches for *public* or *legislative* information!" Evidently he preferred to keep the facts to himself while he dragged the country into the European war. As the Republicans saw it, the Federalists themselves were terrified now that the crisis which they had so long been asking for had at last arrived. "Our hot-headed Federalists are now in the suds. They know not what to do, what to communicate."

But when the text of the reports was made public on April 3, it took the wind out of the Republicans' sails. The country was swept by a wave of patriotism. Theater crowds in the cities demanded that the orchestra play the *President's March* instead of the *Marseillaise*. A popular actor, looking for a way to ride the tide, persuaded Joseph Hopkinson to write a set of verses for the music of the *President's March*, and on April 25 in the New Theater in Philadelphia he taught a wildly enthusiastic audience to sing the new song, *Hail, Columbia*. Another product of this same period that has come down to us in our school histories, was the Federalist slogan, inspired by the French demands, "Millions for defense, but not one cent for tribute." But the Republicans were only momentarily disconcerted. By the middle of May they were burning the President in effigy here and there and writing bad verse about him. One verse of a long song to the tune of *Yankee Doodle* went:

> See Johnny at the helm of state,
>   Head itching for a crowny;
> He longs to be, like Georgy, great,
>   And pull Tom Jeffer downy.

The Federalist *Massachusetts Mercury* reported the colorful details of an effigy burning in Connecticut which had been inspired by the President's proclamation of a day of fasting:

From Danbury, (Conn.) June 11.
"The burning of the Effigy of the President of the United States at North-Stamford . . . on the morning of the 16th of May last, having occasioned much conversation, and contradictory reports, the

Editors after waiting some time in expectation of receiving from some gentlemen in the town a particular statement of the transaction, without success, are induced to give the following account from a Postrider, whose veracity [even though no gentleman] may be relied on—viz. That on the morning of the 16th of May he heard a report of a cannon, at North Stamford, and at about 8 o'clock he passed the Meeting-house, in front of which was placed a cannon, on the left the effigy of a man tarred and feathered appeared to have been hung on a low gallows, the rope burnt off, and the effigy yet unconsumed was lying in a fire kindled under it. In the centre stood a post about three feet high with a board pointing to the effigy, on which was painted the following words:

JOHN ADAMS
Those who venerate this intended Despot, may here
pay their last homage to his remaining ashes

"There was also written on a paper and fastened to the board, the following lines:

Adams the great,
In envy'd state,
Issu'd a proclamation,
That each free state
Abstain from meat
With deep humiliation.
Let 'Ristocrats,
Those scurvy brats,
Keep fast with fear and mourning;
But we'll conspire
To build a fire,
And put his image burning.

"This proves the spirit of jacobinism, as it will appear, whenever it dare to show itself. Let those who whine at a French cockade's being taken from an obscure fellow's hat [also no gentleman], read the above account and be silent."

In view of the large number of Irishmen among the Republicans, the trace of brogue is not surprising.

Despite some Republican outbursts, for the moment the tide favored Adams. On July 6, 1798, for instance, Stephen Decatur in the sloop-of-war *Delaware* captured a French privateer that had been marauding near the coast and brought her in, much to the improvement of American morale.

Then the French Government, disappointed by the failure of the Republicans to stage a revolution, approached Vans Murray, the American Minister at the Hague, with flattering assurances that if the United States would send another minister he would be received "with the respect due to the representative of a free and independent nation." President Adams, meanwhile, in his Message of December, 1798, had taken a pacific line, saying that he would be willing to send another minister on assurance that he would be properly received. This line he had adopted against the strong opposition of Timothy Pickering, the Secretary of State, and others in the Cabinet.

Adams had made the mistake of retaining Washington's Cabinet, which had become accustomed to looking for leadership to Hamilton in his New York law office, and continued to do so. James Truslow Adams points out that Hamilton expected to guide the Administration's policies, and looked to the President to be contented with the appearance of power while actually it would be secretly exercised by others. Adams, however, was a strong character, and the result was a bitter and devastating struggle. Here we see the first clear violation of the conservative principle of the weak Presidency, which was violated again in the choice of Lincoln, with equally discordant results.

When encouraging letters from the Hague at last arrived in February, 1799, Adams, without consulting his Cabinet, sent the name of Vans Murray to the Senate for confirmation as Minister to France. The members of the Federalist inner circle, caught off guard, were outraged at this boldness, and the Senate was cold to the nomination. In order to avoid a bitter fight, Adams decided to nominate Murray and two others as negotiators and ministers, and the Senate confirmed them. Hamilton was bitter, however.

News came in March, 1799, that the U.S.S. *Constellation* had captured one of the crack frigates of the French Navy, *L'Insurgente,* off St. Kitts in the West Indies. The news was welcomed with celebrations by the Federalists, but the Republicans were critical, and there were widespread riots in Pennsylvania against the collection of a war tax on real estate.

During the summer of 1799 Adams' envoys to France were delayed while the President waited for French assurance that they would be well received. The assurance came in August, but meanwhile France was in confusion; French armies had been routed in Italy and on the Rhine. The Cabinet urged Adams to put off the sailing of the American mission until the dust settled. Then on October 8 the Pennsylvania election was held and the Republicans carried the Governorship. Congress was still Federalist, but Adams could feel the tide turning against his party, and he decided to send the mission off to France, in the hope of pacifying public opinion. So the mission was dispatched, but it was nearly a year later, on September 30, 1800, that a peace treaty was signed.

Secretary Pickering was enraged at the President's decision, and others in the Cabinet were also alienated. Hamilton was pulling strings, and Adams knew it. The Federalist Party was in trouble.

Hamilton's enmity was not all that was wrong with the propects of President Adams. For in the middle of 1798, the Federalists, thinking that they had the Republicans on the run, had passed the Alien and Sedition Laws, which in the end played a large part in the defeat of Adams for reelection in 1800, and in the death of the Federalist Party.

The Alien Law allowed the President to deport any foreigner whom he might consider dangerous. This law was aimed at the wild Scotch-Irish, English, and French immigrants who were hostile to England and liked to stir up the native Republicans. The Sedition Law provided penalties for criticizing the Government or the President, and it was vigorously enforced against Republican pamphleteers and newspaper editors. The effect on public opinion was disastrous to the Administration, especially along the frontier.

When the news of the Sedition Law reached the West, the hardy pioneers immediately struck a blow for liberty by violating it. The *Mirror*, a Kentucky paper, for instance, protested on July 21:

"At a period when the overbearing hand of an infatuated administration is stretched over the freemen of America; when those who dare to doubt the infallibility of our rulers are marked as victims, to be offered at the shrine of aristocracy; when the liberty of the press, the most important of the privileges of freemen, is groaning under oppression on the Atlantic shore; it becomes the citizens of the west to assume the most decided aspect. . . . When that government, to which we are attached, so far degenerates from its native purity as to receive the aid of penal statutes and a suppression of the voice of its citizens . . . it is a desertion of the cause of freedom to be silent or tamely submissive. . . . The day appears to be at hand, when the gaping minions of administration, with appetites keen as vultures, will surround our peaceful habitations and encircle us in the net of treason and sedition now preparing for us. . . . But it is to be presumed, that the citizens of the West, far removed from the contaminating influence of European politics, are too firmly devoted to their sacred rights to be deterred by the infliction of unmerited pains and penalties."

One of the victims of the Sedition Law was Thomas Cooper. He was an Englishman who had fled England for political reasons and in 1797 had applied to President Adams for a government job but without success. In 1799 he was editor of the Sunbury and Northumberland *Gazette* in Pennsylvania, and issued copies of a violent address in favor of the Republican candidate for Governor, Thomas McKean. When a reader asked if he was the same Cooper who had wanted to serve under Mr. Adams two years before he replied that indeed he was, and that it was not he that had changed but the President who had shown himself in his true character. In 1797, he declared, the President "was hardly in the infancy of political mistake." At that time he had not yet sanctioned the Alien and Sedition Laws and the abolition of trial by jury; had not saddled the country with the expense of a standing army; had not inflicted it with a permanent navy; had not brought its credit so low as to borrow money at eight per cent; had not planned embassies to Russia, Prussia, and the Sublime Porte, nor interfered with the course of justice, nor delivered poor Robbins to the mock trial of a British court-martial. Robins's case, unhappily, was little known, he remarked, but it ought to be well known, and before the next election, should be.

"Robbins" was a sailor with a strong Irish brogue, who was arrested in Charleston in February, 1799, at the request of the British Consul, charged with being a mutineer named Thomas Nash from the British frigate *Hermione,* which had been seized in 1797 by her crew and sold in a Spanish port. The sailor swore that he was Jonathan Robbins of Danbury, Connecticut. But the Court decided that he was Irish. He was turned over to the British, court-martialed, and hanged. He was reported to have admitted on the way to the gallows that he was Thomas Nash, but to the Republican press he was an innocent victim of Federalist truckling to England.

Cooper was convicted under the Sedition Law and punished with a fine of $400 and six months in jail. Others who were penalized under the law included Charles Holt of the New London *Bee,* Anthony Haswell of the *Vermont Gazette,* Abijah Adams of the *Independent Chronicle,* and James Thompson Callender.

Callender was a free-lance pamphleteer who worked in the 1790s for various Republican leaders, chiefly Benjamin Franklin Bache, George Mason, and Thomas Jefferson. He became notorious as the most violent of the writers who took aim at Washington and Adams; in later life he turned his venomous pen against President Jefferson. As late as 1894, Richard W. Thompson, an ex-Congressman writing his recollections of Presidents he had seen from Jefferson on down, recalled that as a boy he had been shown a pamphlet against Washington, "by an Irishman named Calender who was hired for the purpose, and supplied with whiskey, in order to stimulate his faculties. . . . It was the foulest and most mendacious publication I ever read— exceeding by far, anything to which the readers of the present day are accustomed. I personally knew the survivor of a bloody duel it produced." (Callender is more credibly reported to have been a Scot.)

Callender was working on the *Aurora* when the Sedition Act was passed. He fled to Virginia where he found refuge at Gunston Hall under the protection of George Mason. While passing his time there he wandered out to a nearby distillery and was picked up covered with mud and held as a vagrant, until Mason came to his rescue and vouched for his good character and repute.

The most famous Callender pamphlet, *The Prospect Before Us,* is dated 1800. "The design of this book," the preface explains, "is to exhibit the multiplied corruptions of the Federal Government, and more especially the misconduct of the President, Mr. Adams." After digressing into a complicated indictment of Washington as "twice a traitor" for renouncing first the King and then the Articles of Confederation, and a sneering charge that he had composed his Farewell Address in the hope of being drafted for a third term, Callender gets down to his main subject by asserting that Adams's election was a stolen one. To support this contention he gives detailed accounts of ballot-box stuffing, and of the use of British campaign contributions to help the Federalist ticket: "That British gold, also, has descended in showers, is a fact now recorded in the supreme court of Pennsylvania. . . . If the *red book* of St. James's shall ever, like that of Versailles, meet the light of day, divers interesting discoveries will certainly transpire, as to the manufacture of British treaties, and of truly federal majorities. . . ."

The President's well-known hot temper also came in for comment: "The reign of Mr. Adams has, hitherto, been one continued tempest of *malignant* passions. As president, he has never opened his lips, or lifted his pen, without threatening and scolding. The grand object of his administration has been to exasperate the rage of contending parties, to calumniate and destroy every man who differs from his opinions. . . . Every person holding an office must either quit it, or think and vote exactly with Mr. Adams. A catalogue of these expulsions would fill a pamphlet."

Callender gleefully inserted a sarcastic story designed not only to ridicule the President but also to imply that his followers were low characters—in contrast with the gentleman who refused to bow the knee to his absurd pretensions of majesty:

"In summer, 1798, general Sumter of South Carolina, was grossly insulted at the new Circus in Market-street, Philadelphia, because he did not clap his hands, when the president entered the place . . . a rumor spread that Mr. Adams was coming in . . . one Fitzhugh called out, in a loud voice, asking why the general did not clap. . . . General Sumter represented . . . that he was a stranger to the gentleman and asked if the latter knew *who he was?* "Oh, damn you, we know you, and all your party," replied the royalist. "I hope, in six months time, to see you all banished from the country." . . . The second rumor of the approach of his majesty of Braintree proved, also, groundless. At last, Mr. Adams did appear. Fitzhugh then attempted to snatch off general Sumter's hat. . . . The general found out his name, and called for him, next morning, at his lodging, but Fitzhugh was gone."

Finally, lumping Washington and Adams together, Callender finished in a burst of indignation at the corruption of the Federal Government. He accused them both of appointing speculators, or "paper-jobbers," as Judges and Ambassadors, while raising an affected yelp against the French Directory—"as if any corruption could be more venal, more notorious, more execrated than their own . . . while the grand lama of Federal adoration, the immaculate divinity of Mount Vernon, approved of and subscribed to every·one of their blackest measures." He ended with a cry of reproach and exhortation: "Citizens of Virginia! *When will ye begin to think?*"

In June 1800, Callender was tried at Richmond under the Sedition Law. Countrywide interest was aroused by reports that Judge Chase had ordered the Marshal to keep all rascally democrats off the jury, or as we might say today, all "reds." Callender was fined $200 and sentenced to jail for nine months. While in jail he wrote a second and a third part of the *Prospect.* This trial set off a long controversy over the practice of allowing a Federalist marshal to pick the jury in sedition cases.

Much of Callender's material was embodied in a *History of the Administration of John Adams,* which was compiled by a hack writer named John Wood in 1801. When the book was printed in 1802 Vice President Aaron Burr got hold of an advance copy and decided it was too raw to be published. The whole edition was bought up and suppressed. But there was a violent disagreement over this suppression, and Wood finally published the book. Adams, however, was by that time well out of it and holed up in Braintree.

As the 1800 campaign opened, it was evident that Adams was in a weak position, between the repercussions of the Alien and Sedition laws on one hand, and the party split over foreign policy on the other. His enemies prepared to drive hard against him.

In Congress, the Republicans set out early in the year to abolish the standing army, which had been created to meet the fear of a French invasion. This motion led to a conflict between the irascible John Randolph of Roanoke and President Adams.

Randolph, who had been only a child at the time of the Revolution, made a speech in the House in which he denounced "mercenary armies" and asserted that free men must be defended only by militia. He went on to say that Americans dared not trust their liberties to "a handful of ragamuffins." Since the best of the Revolutionary armies had been Regulars and often ragged, these words caused some resentment among the older men as well as in the Armed Forces. Shortly afterward at the theater Randolph was insulted by a naval officer, and on the way out his cape was jerked. He wrote an angry letter to the President telling him that the independence of the legislature had been attacked and that "a provision commensurate with the evil" ought to be made "to deter others from any future attempt to introduce the reign of terror into our country."

Adams sent the letter to the House, saying it was a matter of privilege and "ought to be inquired into by the House itself, if anywhere." He would therefore submit Mr. Randolph's letter "without any further comments on its matter or style." The Republican papers leaped at the chance to accuse Adams of terrorizing the people. "How long," exclaimed the *Aurora,* "the servants of the people and the servants' servants shall trample on their masters, God only knows." According to the *New York Journal,* "Mr. Adams has done well to make no comment on the 'style.' Language so manly, so energetic, is new to him. The letter contained none of the shameful sycophancy of the obsequious addresses of the faction." The "faction," of course, refers to the Federalist Party.

The House, however, decided by a large majority that Randolph had acted improperly in carrying his complaint to the President, and that the affair at the play had best be forgotten, though the Republican newspapers still insisted that he was a martyr and one more man whom John Adams had tried to destroy.

Meanwhile on January 6 appeared the first number of *The Press,* a Republican paper dedicated "To the People of Virginia." This first number, essentially a prospectus, minced no words: "At a time when your firm and faithful adherence to the principles of your Fathers, has rendered you the objects of the coarsest abuse and most atrocious calumny to states that have apostasized from the venerable lessons of wisdom inculcated by the revolution . . . you must be short sighted *indeed,* not to discern the symptoms of an awful, and portentous *crisis,* which approaches. Have not the strongest tendencies of tyranny been seen among you? . . . Has not an alien and sedition law been enacted? Is not a war of *vandalism* waged against the PRESS? . . . Is not a standing army introduced among you; and have not the soldiers of this army in many instances exhibited the invariable character of such establishments by vexations and indignities on the people?"

Any impartial and intelligent jury, declared the editor of this fearless paper, would convict the Federalists of plotting from the beginning "the subversion of our present democratical form of government." In particular, Adams's *Defence of the American Constitutions,* published in 1787, was cited as proof of a predilection for orders of nobility and for a strong Executive. The paper quoted:

" 'I only contend (says he) that the English constitution is in theory, the most stupendous fabric of human invention . . . & that the Americans ought to be applauded instead of censured for imitating it *as far as they have done. . . .* The Americans have not indeed imitated it in giving a *negative* upon their legislature to the executive power: in this respect their balances are incomplete, very much *I confess to my mortification;* in other respects they have some of them *fallen short of perfection, by giving the choice of some militia officers to the people.' "*

In other words, Mr. Adams wanted the Presidential veto power made absolute, like that of the King. He also would prefer that Army officers, instead of being elected by their regiments, should have to look to the Executive as "in *all cases the fountain of honor,"* just like a king.

After a detailed account of the partiality of the Federalist Administration for the British, as manifested for instance in "the treaty of Mr. Jay, the root of incalculable evils to this country," the editors ask:

"To what can you ascribe these measures, unless to a disposition to trample upon the constitution of our country? Review the whole and say, is there, or is there not ground for distrust and suspicion?

"If we have shewn where the *monster* lurks, and have *rent* the *veil* that concealed him, it is for you, to *drag* him from his retreat. The interest these subjects involve, demand that they should not be slightly glanced at, and dismissed: If they be false, you are paid for your labor by the confidence of security: If they be true, and you take no measures for your safety, you are undone. . . . Every hour you are more and more entangled in the *wreaths of the serpent: One other convolution perhaps, and you are chained; while the reptile strikes his poison into your heart."

This prospectus has been ascribed to William Duane, of the *Aurora*, an interesting example of the eighteenth-century newspaper man. Duane was born in America of Irish parents, and was taken back to Ireland as a child. After he grew up he worked on newspapers in India and then in London, where he became editor of the *General Advertiser*, a paper which still exists under the name of the London *Times*. Duane returned to America in 1795 and worked on the *Aurora*, which he took over when Bache died in the yellow fever epidemic of 1798.

John Adams's feeling about the British Constitution is reported in Jefferson's diary where he says that in April, 1791, at an official dinner in Washington's absence, "after the cloth was removed, and our question agreed and dismissed, conversation began on other matters and, by some circumstance, was led to the British constitution, on which Mr. Adams observed 'purge that constitution of its corruption, and give to its popular branch equality of representation, and it would be the most perfect constitution ever devised by the wit of man.' Hamilton paused and said, 'purge it of its corruption, and give to its popular branch equality of representation, and it would become an *impracticable* government: as it stands at present, with all its supposed defects, it is the most perfect government which ever existed.' And this was assuredly the exact line which separated the political creeds of these two gentlemen."

John Adams was by no means so naive a royalist as Duane, by careful choice of quotations, made him seem. In 1787 he was honestly struggling to think out how a democratic society might achieve good government, a problem which we have not yet completely solved. Some of his speculations may be worth quoting here to illustrate how obscure certain questions were in the 18th century even to the Fathers of the Constitution.

Adams says in his *Defense of the American Constitutions*: "It is become a kind of fashion among writers, to admit, as a maxim, that if you could be always sure of a wise, active, and virtuous prince, monarchy would be the best of governments. But this is so far from being admissible, that it will forever remain true, that a free government has great advantage over a simple monarchy. The best and wisest prince, by means of a freer communication with his people, and the greater opportunities to collect the best advice from the best of his subjects, would have an immense advantage in a free state more than in a monarchy." Apparently he means more than in an absolute monarchy.

Adams goes on to praise a system having "A Senate consisting of all that is most noble, wealthy, and able in the nation, with a right to counsel the crown at all times, . . . another assembly, composed of representatives chosen by the people . . . gives a universal character, in every part of the state, which never can be obtained in a monarchy." Adams evidently regarded what he called a "monarchical republic" as the ideal, one bearing much more resemblance to the present British Government than to that of the eighteenth century.

As for the utility of a Senate, Adams wrote: "The rich, the well-born, and the able, acquire an influence among the people, that will soon be too much for simple honesty and plain sense, in a house of representatives. The most illustrious of them must therefore be separated from the mass, and placed by themselves in a senate: this is, to all honest and useful intents, an ostracism. A member of a senate, of immense wealth, the most respected birth, and transcendent abilities, has no influence in the nation, in comparison of what he would have in a single representative assembly. . . . The people have the power to remove him into the senate as soon as his influence becomes dangerous . . . you may still hope for the benefits of his exertions, without dreading his passions; for the executive power being in other hands, he has lost much of his influence with the people, and can govern very few votes more than his own among the senators." This was published in 1787, before Adams had had as much experience with senators as he was later to enjoy.

In June, 1800, the Government moved to Washington and the Adams family came into the White House. Meanwhile the Federalist Party showed marked signs of breaking up. The Republicans won a state election in New York, which cast serious doubts on Adams's chance of reelection. Adams accused Secretary Pickering of having conspired with Hamilton in a plot that resulted in this defeat. He demanded Pickering's resignation, and when Pickering refused to resign, he discharged him. The Federalists then were openly divided into what were called the Adamites and the Pickeronians.

The Pickeronians were extreme anti-French Federalists who resented Adams's willingness to make peace with France. Since he was popular in strongly Federalist areas such as Maryland, New Jersey, and parts of New England, they did not openly oppose him for reelection. But they plotted to run C. C. Pinckney for ostensibly the Vice Presidency, and then secretly switch enough electoral votes to make him President and degrade Adams to Vice President.

The Republicans sensed victory in the air and turned everything loose on the President. He was accused on the one hand of allowing British influences to infiltrate the Government, and on the other of being personally angry at the "British faction" in his own party. On his way home to Braintree for the summer, he had dropped some petulant comments that were picked up and expanded by the Republicans in order to help split the Federalist party. The *Aurora* quoted him as saying that since the mission to France the Federalists were the most factious men in the country, and that if Hamilton had been left in command of the army for two years longer the United States would have had to raise an army to deal with him. He was also reported to have complained that there was a strong British faction in the country, headed by the British Minister, and that Pickering and Hamilton belonged to it.

Hamilton, for his part, wrote a pamphlet attacking Adams. His friends, seeing at once that this would finally wreck the party, persuaded him to withhold it, but it came into the hands of Aaron Burr, who gave it to the public.

"Not denying to Mr. Adams patriotism and integrity," said Hamilton's pamphlet, "and even talents of a certain kind, I should be deficient in candor, were I to conceal the conviction, that he does not possess the talents adapted to the *Administration* of Government . . . he is a man of imagination sublimated and eccentric; propitious neither to the regular display of sound judgment, nor to steady perseverance in a systematic plan of conduct . . . to this defect are added the unfortunate foibles of a vanity without bounds, and a jealousy capable of discoloring every object."

Hamilton reports that in the election of 1796, he and his friends favored giving equal votes to Adams and Thomas Pinckney, the two Federal candidates, trusting to "casual accessions of votes in favor of one or the other, to turn the scale between them. . . . My position was, that if chance were to decide in favor of MR. PINCKNEY, it probably would not be a misfortune; since he, to every essential qualification for the office, added a temper far more discreet and conciliatory than that of MR. ADAMS." In other words, Hamilton believed Pinckney, as President, could be managed.

"It is a fact, which ought not to be forgotten, that MR. ADAMS, who had evinced discontent, because he had not been permitted to take an equal chance with General Washington [in the first election], was enraged with all those who had thought that MR. PINCKNEY ought to have had an equal chance with him. It is to this circumstance of the equal support of MR. PINCKNEY, that we are in a great measure to refer the serious scism which has grown up in the Federal Party."

Hamilton praises the firm stand Adams took when the Three were insulted in Paris, but goes on:

"Much is it to be deplored that we should have been precipitated from this proud eminence without necessity, without temptation.

"The latter conduct of the President forms a painful contrast to his commencement. It has sunk the tone of the public mind—it has impaired the confidence of the friends of the Government in the Executive Chief—it has distracted public opinion—it has unnerved the public councils—it has sown the seeds of discord at home, and lowered the reputation of the Government abroad."

When Adams was preparing his Message, on the French crisis, Hamilton recounts, it was suggested that he should say that if France were to show a desire for reconciliation by sending a Minister, he would be politely treated. "The suggestion was received in a manner both indignant and intemperate. MR. ADAMS declared as a sentiment which he had adopted on mature reflection:—*That if France should send a Minister to-morrow, he would order him back the day after.*"

In less than 48 hours, according to Hamilton, Mr. Adams decided that if France would engage to receive an American Minister politely he would send one. "In vain," says Hamilton, "was this extension of the sentiment opposed by all his Ministers, as being equally incompatible with good policy and with the dignity of the nation—

he obstinately persisted, and the pernicious declaration was introduced . . . it was the groundwork of the false steps that have succeeded."

After discussing Adams's recent policies at great length, Hamilton pronounces them evidences of "the desultoriness of his mind." He attributes the dismissal of Pickering and of Secretary of War M'Henry to "the ungovernable temper of MR. ADAMS. It is a fact that he is often liable to paroxysms of anger, which deprive him of self command, and produce very outrageous behaviour to those who approach him. Most, if not all his Ministers, and several distinguished Members of the two Houses of Congress, have been humiliated by the effects of these gusts of passion. . . . This violence, and the little consideration for them which was implied in declining to consult them, had occasioned great dryness between the President and his Ministers."

Hamilton went on to complain that, as he had heard on good authority, Mr. Adams had repeatedly indulged in virulent and indecent abuse of him and had stigmatized him as the leader of a British Faction. There was, of course, far too much truth in this charge for Hamilton to let it go unanswered. Accordingly, he climaxed his pamphlet by printing two letters that he had sent to the President, showing that he was so deeply disturbed as to forget his own dignity. The first was dated August 1, 1800, and said:

"Sir: It has been repeatedly mentioned to me, that you have, on different occasions, asserted the existence of a British Faction in this country . . . and that you have sometimes named me . . . as one of this description of persons. . . .

"I must, sir, take it for granted, that you cannot have made such assertions . . . without being willing to avow them, and to assign the reasons to a Party who may conceive himself injured by them. . . ."

The second letter he undoubtedly believed in his anger would speak for itself, and would bring all the wise and rich and good to stand with him and denounce the dastardly creature who had so cruelly denied him justice. This was dated October 1:

"Sir: The time which has elapsed since my letter of the 1st of August was delivered to you, precludes the further expectation of an answer.

"From this silence, I will draw no inference; nor will I presume to judge the fitness of silence on such an occasion on the part of the

Chief Magistrate of a Republic, towards a citizen who, without a stain, has discharged so many important public trusts.

"But this much I will affirm, that by whomsoever a charge of the kind mentioned in my former letter, may at any time, have been made or insinuated against me, it is a base, wicked and cruel calumny; destitute of even a plausible pretext, to excuse the folly, or mask the depravity, which must have dictated it."

The Washington *Federalist* answered Hamilton's pamphlet mildly but firmly, observing that with all its affectation of candor, it was clearly the production of a disappointed and embittered man, and that "few, we believe *very few*, will hesitate to pronounce Mr. Adams his equal in moral rectitude, and much his superior as a statesman." The editor went on to remark on Hamilton's complaints of the public service as a thankless job with little chance of reward and a sure harvest of obloquy, adding sarcastically that he seemed determined to prove his position by throwing mud at the highest officer in the public service. But though many Federalists were ashamed of Hamilton's peevish outburst, and perhaps the more inclined to come to the President's support, the whole incident was a net loss to their party in the election.

So John Adams, a strong-minded President, cursed by the strongest political leaders of his own party because he would not be controlled, and vilified by the Republicans for his aristocratic principles, went down to defeat in bitterness of spirit, carrying the Federalist Party with him; and Thomas Jefferson reigned in his stead.

CHAPTER III

CONTEMPTIBLE EGGHEAD

Thomas Jefferson was the first President to come into office with full knowledge of the unmerciful castigation that he must expect as part of the Presidency. He even tried to be philosophical about it, though he never pretended that the lying and slandering did not hurt him. After four years in the White House he wrote to a friend who as a judge had been subjected to a Federalist mudbath, that anyone who came into an eminent office was sure to be "anointed with this chrism." He noted that not too many men were to be found who were capable of filling the top places in government, and if they were to allow themselves to be driven out by merely being lied about, their enemies would be encouraged to make still more use of so cheap a weapon.

In Jefferson's opinion, if the treatment he himself had received, or anything close to it, had been applied to Washington, our first President "would have thrown up the helm in a burst of indignation."

Back in 1793, when Jefferson retired as Secretary of State, he went home in peace to Monticello, bearing the good-will of both parties. For despite the growing conflict between Republicans and Federalists, Jefferson's manifest disgust with Citizen Genet, and his firmness in upholding the dignity of the United States against the assaults of that mad character, had earned him the respect even of the Federalists—especially if it were true that he was out of politics. But in 1796 it became plain to everyone that Jefferson could not be out of politics, for the Republicans were looking to him to take the Presidency away from John Adams. Then there was no more peace.

The Federalists persistently attacked Jefferson for being a "philosopher," or, as we should now say, an egghead. He had "impaled butterflies," drawn up a report on weights and measures, and speculated on the causes of the differences between whites and blacks. One thing that particularly enraged the Federalist writers was his invention of the swivel chair. "Ability to contrive turnabout chairs," said a critic, "may entitle one to a college professorship, but it no more constitutes a claim to the Presidency than the genius of Cox, the great bridge builder." Another took up the same refrain: "Who has not heard from the secretary the praises of his wonderful *Whirligig Chair*, which had the miraculous quality of allowing the person seated in it to turn his head, without moving his tail? Who has not admired his fertile *genius* in the production of his *Epicurean side-board*, and other Gim Krackery?"

It may be permissible at this point to speculate on what the Federalists of 1796 would have said if someone could have told them that in the 20th century the Jefferson swivel chair would be universally adopted as the very seat of business executive power. It would not be fair, however, to laugh at these old worthies, since the contempt for eggheads has obviously not become obsolete. James Reston in the New York *Times* for February 23, 1958, quoted even the liberal Senator George D. Aiken as asking: "Who would want to see the Senate of the United States run by ninety-six Phi Beta Kappas?" As Reston commented, "If Senators scoff at Phi Beta Kappas and Presidents prefer the company of retired distillers, steel tycoons and mud-pack artists, who is to put an end to this silly and derisive joke about intellectuals?" Jefferson, and the nation, survived this ridicule a century and a half ago; the sputnik and similar developments raise the question about survival in our own day.

A lengthy pamphlet, lengthily entitled *The Pretensions of Thomas Jefferson to the Presidency Examined,* set forth the arguments against too much mental activity in the White House by enquiring how any President could hope to be respected by his cabinet officers and other staff members if they should catch him sticking a pin in a butterfly or experimenting with some new gadget—why, he would soon be the laughing-stock of the world. "The great *Washington* was, thank God, no philosopher; had *he* been one, we should never have seen his great military exploits; or should never have prospered under his wise administration."

Not only did the Federalists scoff at Jefferson as an intellectual, they also accused him of various shameful misdemeanors that would unfit any man for high office. One was that as Governor of Virginia he shamefully ran away when a British raiding party approached

Charlottesville. Actually Jefferson was one of the few state Governors who loyally supported the grand strategy of General Washington by denuding his own state of men and guns to reinforce the Continental armies. The Virginians, suffering helplessly under British raids, tended to be bitter at the Governor for failing to defy Washington and keep his troops at home.

When Tarleton's raiders chased the state government out of Charlottesville, the Governor fled with the Assembly across the mountain to safety. Since he had no armed men, escape was in order, expecially as Cornwallis would undoubtedly have hanged Jefferson and the Assembly all in a row, if Tarleton could have caught them.

But according to the Federalists "Mr. Jefferson discovered such *a want of firmness* as shewed he was *not fit to fill the first executive office,* for instead of using his talents in directing the necessary operations of defense, *he quitted his government by resigning his office,* at a time that tried men's souls. Is there any *security* he would not act *in like manner again, under like circumstances?*" The fact was that only at the end of his term did Jefferson resign in disgust, saying that the state needed a general as Governor, and General Nelson was appointed on his recommendation. But to the Federalists, the whole episode appeared to be shameful. They mercifully attributed the Governor's behavior not to any criminality but to "a constitutional weakness of nerves," and suggested that though the Virginia Assembly afterward gave him a vote of confidence it was merely trying to gloss over his conduct for the sake of the reputation of the state.

It was when the critics came to religion, however, that they really began to bite. They made much of Jefferson's unorthodox religious views, for, like a good many of our Presidents and other leaders, he was what is nowadays known as a Unitarian. As he explained to Dr. Joseph Priestley, the famous scientist who had been mobbed for similar views in England and had fled to America: "To the corruptions of Christianity I am, indeed, opposed; but not to the genuine precepts of Jesus himself. I am a Christian in the only sense in which he wished anyone to be; sincerely attached to his doctrines in preference to all others; ascribing to him every human excellence; and believing he never claimed any other."

To the orthodox this was outrageous. They suggested that his interest in freedom of religion might better be called a desire for

freedom from religion, and speculated that his mind had been corrupted by conversation with the French atheists while he was American envoy in Paris. It was also noted that Jefferson was a friend
of Tom Paine, who after the Revolution had taken to writing "impious
and blasphemous works reviling the *Christian religion*," which had
been much applauded in France and industriously circulated in the
United States by the very people who wanted Mr. Jefferson for
President. If he were to become President, "there is no doubt that
Tom would return to this country, to be a conspicuous figure at the
President's table where this enlightened pair of philosophers would
fraternize, and philosophize against the *Christian religion*."

Jefferson's encouragement of Freneau and the *Gazette* was of course
the subject of violent criticism. The idea that civil servants ought
not to be active in politics, now precariously embodied in the Hatch
Act, was far from being recognized by either party in 1796; but the
Federalists were naturally resentful at the success of Jefferson's
protégé in attacking Washington's Administration while Jefferson
himself was Secretary of State. It was noted that Freneau was on
the government payroll for several months before he inaugurated
his newspaper, the implication being that he was subsidized while
organizing the *Gazette* as well as after it got into operation. "There
perhaps never was a more *flimsy* covering for the *pensioning of a
printer*. Some ostensible ground for *giving him the public money* was
necessary to be contrived. The *clerkship of a foreign language* was
deemed a *plausible* pretext: but no man acquainted with human
nature, or with the ordinary *wiles* of political intrigue, can be deceived
by it."

The Federalists complained that the Republicans were spending
excessive amounts of money on the campaign. Why were so many
handbills in circulation vilifying Adams? They reported that in
Pennsylvania, hand-bills, post-bills, pocket-bills, and broadsides to
the value of one hundred thousand dollars had been sent off, and
trees along every road, the gate-posts, and the door-posts of every
farmhouse in the state were white with posters slandering Washington
and heaping abuse on the Government of the United States. For
this the Democratic Clubs were held to be responsible. Two years
ago they had hated the excise, and, to overthrow it, printed inflammatory addresses, nailed them on the trees, scattered them along the

A virulent attack on Jefferson, "The Providential Detection" (above) depicts him on bended knee before the "Altar to Gallic Despotism" upon which the works of Thomas Paine, Voltaire, and Rousseau are already burning. Jefferson is about to cast the Constitution into the flames but is stopped by an eagle ostensibly guided to the spot by a providential eye. Note that the eagle threatens Jefferson with one claw while the other protectively seizes the Constitution. This caricature was used against Jefferson during the election campaign of 1800. In denouncing the Sage of Monticello as "an atheist" in a fiery sermon, Rev. Timothy Dwight, president of Yale, warned that national catastrophe would be the inevitable result of Jefferson's election. In his eyes the future looked black indeed: the Bible would be burned publicly, the "Marseillaise" sung in the churches, and, worst of all, "We may see our wives and daughters the victims of legal prostitution; soberly dishonored; speciously polluted." Federalist newspapers were equally alarmed at the prospect of Jefferson in the White House. Declared the Columbian Centinel: "Tremble then in case of Jefferson's election . . . for your ruin is at hand."

This Federalist cartoon entitled "Mad Tom in a Rage" depicts Jefferson as a drunken anarchist tearing down the pillars of government.

roads and flung them into every tavern in the Western country.
Now they hate John Adams, and, to defeat him, have once more taken
up their old tricks. "Will the people of Pennsylvania be influenced
in their choice by the Democratic Clubs of the Capital, the founders
of the Western insurrection? If the Republican ticket is chosen, who
will govern the country? Mr. Jefferson? Alas, no! the Democratic
Clubs."

Some of the Federalist oratory was designed to appeal to the common man. Thomas Robinson Hazard, who was born in Narragansett
in 1797, recalled seventy years later in his *Jonny-Cake Papers* what
he was told by old Paris Gardiner, "who, in my boyhood, lived in a
house on the extreme north end of Hardscrabble." The old man gave
him an account of a speech made to the Hardscrabble voters by a
"veracious stump orator from Providence" during the 1796 campaign.
"He felt he could impart to such intelligent citizens as those before
him a profound secret which, when learned, could not fail to convince
every independent freeman present who had any regard for the
honour and well-being of his country, how immensely in all respects
John Adams, the profound and fearless patriot and full-blooded Yankee, exceeded in every respect his competitor, Tom Jefferson, for the
Presidency, who, to make the best of him, was nothing but a mean-
spirited, low-lived fellow, the son of a half-breed Indian squaw, sired
by a Virginia mulatto father, as was well-known in the neighborhood
where he was raised, wholly on hoe-cake made of coarse-ground
Southern corn, bacon and hominy, with an occasional change of
fricaseed bullfrog, for which abominable reptiles he had acquired a
taste during his residence among the French at Paris, to whom there
could be no question he would sell his country at the first offer made
to him cash down, should he be elected to fill the Presidential chair."
After the speech it was unanimously voted that in case any *individual* or *individuals* should dare to vote for that half Injun, half nigger,
half Frenchman, with a touch of the bullfrog, Tom Jefferson, he or
they should be rode on a green split chestnut rail, sharp side up.
This was all very well for Rhode Island in the effete East, but the
advancing frontier was gathering more and more political weight,
and the frontier was heavily Republican. In the nation as a whole,
undoubtedly the majority of the population wanted Jefferson; but

the property qualifications for voting, and the fact that in so many states the legislature chose the electors, gave John Adams a chance, which was further improved by Jefferson's refusal to go after the uncommitted electoral vote. So Adams squeaked through as President and Jefferson as runner-up became Vice President.

For the next three years, therefore, it was Adams who was anointed with "the unction of lying and slandering," and his Vice President was once more left relatively undisturbed.

Congressman Fisher Ames of Massachusetts, however, one of the leading orators of the Federalists, wrote to a friend in December, 1796, that Jefferson's hypocrisy might dupe very great fools, but it should alarm wise men. Underneath it a deep design lay hid. The Senate would give Jefferson no trouble. He would have no casting votes to give. He would bear no responsibility for any measure. He would be called upon to take part publicly in none. But he would go quietly on, affecting zeal for the people, combining the malcontents and the "antis," and, standing at their head, would balance the power of Adams with his own. During four years two Presidents would jostle and conflict. Then the Vice would become chief.

But there was no need for the Vice President to play politics in order to undermine the President. The Federalist Party was taking care of that, with the enthusiastic help of the Republican press. By 1800 the Republican tide was running strongly.

The party of John Adams, though badly split, still had plenty of ammunition to throw at Thomas Jefferson. The Federalists warned the public against the perversion of language which they had observed creeping into political discussions throughout the Republic. In the effort to convince the people of the need for a change, they complained, the Republicans were calling even the peace and prosperity of Washington's administration "the calm of despotism," and urging the people to embark on "the tempestuous sea of liberty." But. the people were sternly warned, "when tired of the voyage, vainly may we strive to regain our present peaceful haven. We must endure the unceasing storms, and deeply drink the bloody waves; and find no refuge at last, but in the calm of real despotism." The fear that Jefferson's followers were of a definitely bloody turn of mind

had deeply permeated the upper classes, much like some of the ideas
that prevailed in our own times under the New Deal.

One of the most persistent and voluminous of the Federalist attacks
during this campaign was a long series of articles by "Burleigh" in
the *New England Courant*, beginning on June 30. This paper, now
the *Hartford Courant*, had been founded in 1721 by Benjamin
Franklin's brother, supported by a group of "respectable characters"
calling themselves the Hell-Fire Club. In 1800, "Burleigh" still maintained the Hell-Fire tradition, and so did those other Connecticut
fire eaters, President Timothy Dwight of Yale and his equally sulfur-
ous brother Theodore.

"Burleigh" laid down as gospel that if Jefferson were to be elected
the Federal Constitution would be destroyed, since he was well known
to harbor a spirit of deadly hostility to that sacred institution.
"Jacobinism"—which in those days meant about the same thing as
"communism" in our day—would prevail, and the results would be
dreadful indeed. Just how dreadful, Burleigh took all the summer
of 1800 to spell out in dreary detail. Newspaper readers in those days
had only a few pages to look over once a week, and all the evidence
goes to show that if the writer were earnest and emphatic, the thought
that he might be dull never occured to them.

Burleigh warned that the radicals were infernally clever as well
as dreadfully depraved, and they had built up with the labour of
years their plots to overthrow the government. "Mixing with
Jacobinism," he pointed out, "is like scattering poison into the aliments
of life. The whole mass becomes impure, and if swallowed becomes
the certain cause of destruction and death."

Since Jefferson had been Secretary of State, it was obvious that
he had dabbled in treason, like so many of his successors in our own
day. As official keeper of the secrets of the government, he had the
power to do incalculable mischief, as he showed when with French
help he set off the Whiskey Rebellion, and when he offered to sell
out his country to the French for *"a few thousand dollars."* Apparently the smallness of the price was particularly shocking.

By September, Burleigh was painting in the present sunny background for a terrifying picture of the coming Jacobinical desolation:

"Look, my countrymen, over the face of our happy nation, and
see our towns flourishing, our ships multiplying, our territory popu-

lating, our markets thronged, schools filled with our children, our churches opened for the solemn worship of God! Where shall we look for a parallel? Where shall we search for happiness below the sun, if we find it not here? [i.e., "you never had it so good."] Are you prepared to part with this elysian scene; to exchange it for the delusive, the fatal phantom of 'liberty and equality?' Before this resolution is finally taken, let me call your attention to realities which will attend the *convulsion*.

"Accompany me in the survey, trace the bloody scene with a severe eye, mark its horrors, brood over its calamities, and then choose for yourselves—whether you will cleave fast to the government of your choice, the religion of your fathers; or will enter on board the crazy barque of Jacobinism, to be wrecked in the tempestuous sea of *French* liberty."

Pointing the finger at the Party of Treason, the prophet of doom predicted that if Jefferson should win there would surely be a civil war, with all the horrors so recently observed in the French Revolution. He took small comfort from the fact that in Connecticut the Federalists were in the majority, for there were Jacobins enough to subvert the state "with their arts, their plots, and their wickedness." He saw a fearful prospect when these desperate characters should come to power: "Murder, robbery, rape, adultery, and incest, will be openly taught and practiced, the air will be rent with the cries of distress, the soil soaked with blood, and the nation black with crimes. Where is the heart that can contemplate such a scene without shivering with horror!" In a burst of all-too-prophetic vision, he went on to predict that after a civil war we should have a nation exhausted with fighting but not cured of implaceable hatreds and a spirit of revenge that would embitter the national life for generations yet to come.

Easily shifting the spotlight to the widespread fear and distrust of foreigners, he called attention to the thousands of immigrants who had fled the pillory and the gallows in their home lands, of whom the most violent and dangerous were the Frenchmen and the United Irishmen. These characters were of course all devoted to the cause of Mr. Jefferson, and once let him get control of the government, they would burst all bounds, "This blood thirsty band will rush from their lurking places, whet their daggers, and plunge them to the hearts of all those who love order, peace, virtue, and religion." Had Burleigh known that a particularly wild Irishman, one Andrew Jackson, had already been in the Capital spying out the land as a Congressman, he would no doubt have said something of that portent—and if someone could have told him that in time Harvard College would give this Jackson an honorary degree, he would have been nonplussed indeed.

By the end of September, Burleigh was swinging into his stride. "Are you prepared," he demanded, "to see your dwellings in flames, hoary hairs bathed in blood, female chastity violated, our children writhing on the pike or the halbert? If not, prepare for the task of protecting your Government. Look at every leading Jacobin, as at a ravening wolf, preparing to enter your peaceful fold, and glut his deadly appetite on the vitals of your country. Already do their hearts leap at the prospect. Having long brooded over these scenes of death and despair, they now wake as from a trance, and in imagination, seizing the dagger, and the musket, prepare for the work of slaughter. GREAT GOD OF COMPASSION AND JUSTICE, SHIELD MY COUNTRY FROM DESTRUCTION!"

Finally in less strident though no less deadly tones, the Connecticut prophet called up in the hearts of his trembling readers the fear of the wrath of an outraged God. Pointing out that Jefferson was notoriously hostile to our holy religion, he demanded whether any Christian could be so reckless as to vote for such a man. It is a solemn thing, he declared, for a nation to repudiate God. Suppose once more we should be in national distress and in need of Almighty protection— there would be every reason to fear that God would turn his face away.

The Congregational ministers of New England were strongly entrenched in the political structure as well as fundamentalist in doctrine. They clung to the privileges of an "established"—i,e., tax-supported— church as desperately as their Episcopal brethren in Virginia. What the clergy hotly resented was that in 1776 Jefferson had drafted a bill to "establish religious freedom" in Virginia. After the war, in 1786, the legislature passed such an act in practically the form that Jefferson had suggested. It provided not only toleration but also "disestablishment," by which the Episcopal clergy lost their tax-supported incomes. It was the idea of disestablishment that doubled the rage of the Connecticut ministers.

In a Fourth of July sermon the Rev. President Timothy Dwight of Yale warned of the results that might be expected under President Jefferson: "For what end shall we be connected with men of whom this is the character and the conduct? Is it that we may change our holy worship into a dance of Jacobin frenzy, and that we may behold a strumpet personating a goddess on the altars of Jehovah? Is it that we may see the Bible cast into a bonfire, the vessels of the sacramental supper borne by an ass in public procession, and our children either wheedled or terrified, chanting mockeries against God, and hailing in the sounds of the *Ça Ira* the ruin of their religion and the loss of their souls? Is it that we may see our wives and daughters the cuncubines of the Illuminati?"

It is recorded that when, in spite of Dr. Dwight's warnings, Mr. Jefferson was elected in 1800, some women in New England buried their Bibles to save them from Government agents who would be sent to seize and burn them.

Dr. Dwight had a cross to bear in the fact that he inherited Jefferson as a Yale alumnus. In 1784 that man had traveled in New England, preparing himself for his mission to Europe as Minister Plenipotentiary. There he so impressed Ezra Stiles, then President of Yale, that a couple of years later Yale gave him the honorary degree of LLD. Harvard also give him a degree.

In further pursuit of the pious objective of saving America from Jefferson, a certain Dr. William Lynn published a long pamphlet entitled *Serious Considerations on the Election of a President*. Dr. Lynn was an early fighter in the war between science and religion that was later to rage so violently over Darwin's *Origin of Species*.

The pious Doctor pinpointed the charge that Jefferson was a dangerous egghead by pointing out how he had irreverently expressed the opinion that the shells found on the tops of high mountains could not have come there during the Flood. Jefferson had figured that if all the water in the atmosphere should rain down at once it would overflow the land to a height of only 52½ feet, not enough to cover the highest mountains. He admitted that he could not understand how the shells got there, but took the outrageous position that he would rather be puzzled than to know something that was not so. Jefferson, incidentally, was not the first thinker to run into this quandary. Leonardo da Vinci had been in trouble with the Church some 300 years earlier for timing a snail and doubting that the mountain seashells in Italy could have crawled up there during a forty-day flood. Dr. Lynn sternly called attention to Jefferson's neglect of the plain facts in the scriptural account which tells us that the fountains of the great deep were broken up, thus providing all the water needed to cover the mountains.

Jefferson was also accused of daring to speculate that the Indians, having developed so many radically different languages, must have been living in America much longer than the six thousand years that the churchmen gave as the age of the earth. This was obviously "an opinion repugnant to sacred history," and therefore deeply subversive of all that good folk held dear.

But even worse, the Sage of Monticello had boldly suggested that the schools should not put the Bible into the hands of children until they had grown old enough to handle religious questions. Rather, he said, their memories should be stored with the most useful facts of Greek, Roman, European and American history, which would not strain their immature minds but would be useful as background in mature life. This notion thoroughly outraged the good Doctor Lynn, who indignantly reminded his readers that "the Bible is the most ancient, and only authentic history in the world."

A story that served to stike horror into thousands of pious souls, and that haunted Jefferson's footsteps for the rest of his life, was started on its devastating rounds by this same pamphlet of the 1800 campaign. It was fathered on a Reverend Doctor John B. Smith, deceased and therefore beyond earthly cross-examination. It seemed that Dr. Smith had tried to argue religion with Jefferson's friend Philip Mazzei, and Mazzei in support of his own atheistic position, had exclaimed: "Why, your great philosopher and statesman, Mr. Jefferson, is rather farther gone in infidelity than I am." Mazzei then went on to tell that once when riding with Jefferson, and seeing a decayed church building, Mazzei had remarked, "I am astonished, that they permit it to be in so ruinous a condition." *"It is good enough,"* rejoined Mr. Jefferson, "for him that was born in a manger!" Dr. Lynn, in recounting this precious tale, commented that such a contemptuous fling at the blessed Jesus could issue from the lips of no other than a deadly foe to His name and cause.

Several of Jefferson's partisans, recognizing how badly this story was hurting his reputation, answered it at length, as well as they were able in the absence of the late Dr. John B. Smith. DeWitt Clinton pointed out that it had passed through several hands and many years of time without, apparently, ever before being reduced to writing, and it' had obviously been polished so as to throw a lurid light. Clinton remarked that the omission of a single word or a single circumstance might have reversed its whole meaning. Originally it might simply have meant that "the Lord dwelleth not in temples made with hands," and that a costly church is as often a monument to human pride as an evidence of piety. He also recalled that in 1791 Dr. Lynn in a Fourth of July sermon on *The Blessings of America* had quoted Jefferson's *Notes on Virginia* as a respectable authority on the progress of this country, failing entirely to observe the evidences of atheism that he discovered as soon as Jefferson threatened to defeat the Federalists in an election.

Another defender flatly accused Dr. Lynn of misstating the words of the Reverend Dr. Smith. "That venerable character told the truth of the story, as follows: Mazzei, on passing a church, which the episcopalians had suffered to go to decay, after being debarred the privilege of forcing other denominations to support them, addressed the philosopher Jefferson thus: 'Why do you leave your churches in so mean a condition! Our Italian priests would not consent to enter them!'—'Probably they would not,' replied the sage philosopher, 'and yet meaner places were deemed grand enough to dispense truth in, by him who was born in a manger.' Were Dr. Smith alive, he would bear testimony to the truth of this. The perverters of Jefferson's Notes, act confidently, in perverting his pious expressions, and wresting his virtuous essays for the vilest purposes."

In 1807 Jefferson wrote to Clinton to thank him for sending a pamphlet defending him on the Mazzei story. "The ground of defence might have been solidly aided by the assurance (which is the absolute fact) that the whole story fathered on Mazzei, was an unfounded falsehood. Dr. Lynn, as aware of that, takes care to quote from a dead man, who is made to quote from one residing in the remotest

While his highly disreputable cronies rant and rave, Thomas Jefferson (standing on table at right) spouts demagogy to the satisfaction of the Devil on left side. Entitled "A Peep Into the Anti-Federalist Club," this caricature was published in New York in 1793. Artist is unknown.

Reflecting the Federalist viewpoint, this contemporary print shows Jefferson, Secretary of the Treasury Gallatin, and French Ambassador Genet trying to block the wheels of responsible government while Duane, editor of the "Republican Aurora," lies prostrate as he is trampled upon by troops guarding the Federal chariot in which Washington is bearing down on the French cannibals. At left Terrorists are torturing Federalists.

Deliberately evoked to mislead the nation, the patroness of "The Order of Confusion" reportedly reigned supreme over the rabble who constituted Jefferson's supporters during differences with Federalists.

part of Europe. These are slander and slanderers, whom Th: Jefferson has thought best to leave to the scourge of public opinion."

Another charge in the 1800 campaign was that Jefferson would turn the nation over to French revolutionary agents supposed to be infiltrating the country. In the middle of September, Negro uprisings were reported in South Carolina and near Richmond, Virginia. According to the *Richmond Gazette* of September 16, the Virginia plot was engineered by two Frenchmen, and in the general massacre of the whites, all Frenchmen were to be spared. The attempt "was happily frustrated by the deluge of rain that fell and rendered the watercourses impassible on the evening fixed for the execution of their scheme." Ten Negroes had been hanged, the Gazette was pleased to report, and trials were still going on.

The charge of un-American activities in Jefferson's party was buttressed by calling attention to its ready adoption of foreign-sounding political terms. It was noted that the radicals in various European countries, being opposed to the monarchy, commonly called themselves Republicans, and "friends of the people," and so did the radicals in America. It was a sinister fact indeed, in view of the well-known history of the guillotine in France, that here as in France, the Jeffersonians had taken to openly giving their Federalist opponents the name of "Aristocrats." That was a name that might well make any respectable person's neck prickle with fear.

"Is it not evident," demanded one horrified commentator, "that the French begin to think that the plot is almost ripe for executiion? Is not insurrection already excited in the Southern States? Who was at the head? FRENCHMEN. Who were to be assassinated? The white inhabitants, men, women, and children. Were none to be spared? Yes, FRENCHMEN. Is not this the plain language of the business, that the FRENCHMEN view the opposition to the government as so extensive, as that it is time to let loose the southern slaves and the whole band of disaffected disorganizers to spread destruction among us! *'He that hath ears to hear let him hear.'*"

Finally, the Federalists tried to undermine Jefferson in the South by bringing out the fact that he disliked the slave system, and was even in favor of education and advancement for Negroes. It was true that many of the Southerners were Jeffersonians with qualms, as so many today are Democrats with qualms. They hated to swallow Jefferson's liberal democracy, but in the end they hated the Northern Federalists even more, so they gulped and swallowed.

According to a Federalist pamphlet published in South Carolina, Jefferson as a French-inspired theorist in politics was known to entertain opinions "unfriendly to the property, which forms the efficient labor of a great part of the southern states." For the record showed that during the Revolution he had proposed an amendment to the Virginia code of laws by which all slaves born thereafter would be educated at public expense, then sent to Africa, with arms and equipment, and declared a free and independent people under American protection and alliance.

The pamphlet also recorded for the edification of Southern readers, how when Jefferson was Secretary of State he had received a letter from Benjamin Banneker, a free Negro who had gotten out an almanac, to which he had replied with horrifying sentiments of cordiality. He had said that he rejoiced to find nature had given his black brethren talents equal to those of other colours, and that the appearance of stupidity was merely the result of their degraded conditions of life, both in Africa and America. In fact, he had gone on to say, "I can add, with truth, that nobody wishes more ardently to see a good system commenced for raising the condition of their body and mind."

"The meaning of these expressions," the reader was warned, "cannot be mistaken. *It is still a plain wish that they should be emancipated*— and this wish is so strong, that *nobody* (not even the Quakers, or the Abolition Society) wishes it more ardently."

But in the 1800 election, despite the most solemn Federalist warnings, the Republicans won handily. The Federalist Party was dying; it had failed to keep up with the march of history. The Republican victory, however, came out with an absurd dilemma, which soon led to a Constitutional amendment to prevent its happening again. Although Jefferson was universally regarded as the leader of the party, and Burr as its choice for Vice President, all the Republican electors voted for both of them without any scattering, so they were tied with 73 electoral votes each, to 65 for Adams and 64 for Pinckney, with one for John Jay. The election therefore was thrown into Congress, which practically meant inviting the Federalists to decide which Republican should be President.

Hamilton hated Burr personally for having outwitted him in New York politics. He threw his powerful influence in Congress on the side of Jefferson. "Upon every virtuous and prudent calculation," he said, "Jefferson is to be preferred. He is by far not so dangerous a man." After a long deadlock, Congress chose Jefferson as President, and Burr became Vice President. Hamilton's intervention was one of the reasons for the duel three years later in which he was killed by Burr.

When Jefferson arrived in Washington to take up the duties of the Presidency, he inherited a Civil Service which, having been built up under Washington and Adams, was naturally manned almost entirely by Federalists. Adams was bitter over the results of the election; and before leaving office he took particular pains to fill all vacancies with members of his own party. These were the so-called "midnight appointments," and they included the appointment and confirmation of Jefferson's enemy, John Marshall, as Chief Justice. Adams himself left Washington in disgust the day before the Inauguration.

Jefferson's Inaugural Address on March 4, 1801, was intended to be conciliatory. He told his audience and the nation that "Though the will of the Majority is in all cases to prevail, that will, to be rightful, must be reasonable . . . the Minority possess their equal rights, which equal laws must protect, and to violate which would be oppression. . . . We are all republicans—we are all federalists. . . If there be any among us who wish to dissolve this Union, or to change its republican form, let them stand undisturbed as monuments of the safety with which error of opinion may be tolerated where reason is left free to combat it."

The new President promised "A wise and frugal government, which shall restrain men from injuring one another, . . . and shall not take from the mouth of labor the bread it has earned." He called for "Peace, commerce, and honest friendship with all nations, entangling alliances with none."

Most people were favorably impressed, but the Reverend Manasseh Cutler, Federalist Member of Congress from Massachusetts, wrote home sourly: "Jefferson's speech, though a medley of Jacobinism, Republicanism, and Federalism, of religion and atheism, of sentiments consistent and inconsistent with the constitution of an energetic government, yet it is extremely smooth, and must be highly popular with the people at large."

Jefferson immediately began reducing the size of the Federal establishment, and succeeded in cutting it about in half. The reduction in force naturally enraged the Federalists, who accused him of a spoils system; but since he made almost no new places, it also enraged the Republican office seekers. It was Jefferson who contributed to American lore the saying that "Every appointment made gives me one ingrate and a hundred enemies."

The Dwights of New Haven were in no way reconciled to the new Administration. Theodore Dwight, the brother of Timothy and gifted with a remarkably similar vocabulary, delivered an oration on July 7, 1801, in which he complained that the government which had been established under the auspices of Washington was now the sport of popular commotion, adrift without helm or compass in a turbid and boisterous ocean. "The great object of Jacobinism," he declared, "both in its political and moral revolution, is to destroy every trace of civilization in the world, and to force mankind back into a savage state. . . . We have now reached the consummation of democratic blessedness. We have a country governed by blockheads and knaves; the ties of marriage with all its felicities are severed and destroyed; our wives and daughters are thrown into the stews; our children are cast into the world from the breast and forgotten; filial piety is extinguished, and our surnames, the only mark of distinction among families, are abolished. Can the imagination paint anything more dreadful this side hell?" His imagination failed to paint the even more dreadful situation so bitterly fought by conservatives in the 1930s, when under Social Security "human beings would be given numbers like dogs."

Jefferson was sufficiently aroused by the irreconcilables in Connecticut, to dismiss Elizur Goodrich, Collector in New Haven and a man inclined to agree with the Dwights. This led to remonstrances from Federalists who wanted to know if Jefferson had meant the conciliatory words of March 4th, and from Republicans who thought he should clean more of the rascals out.

The President's Message of December 7, 1801, drew a series of critical papers by Alexander Hamilton, writing under the pen name of *"Lucius Crassus."* Hamilton showed no such violent hatred here as in his attacks on Adams and Burr. He believed, according to a letter he wrote to James A. Bayard, that Jefferson's "politics are tinged with fanaticism—he is too much in earnest in his democracy . . . crafty and persevering in his objects . . . not scrupulous about the means of sucess, nor very mindful of truth . . . he is a contemptible hypocrite." That was mild compared with what Hamilton thought of Adams and Burr.

Hamilton called Jefferson's Message "a performance that ought to alarm all who are anxious for the safety of our Government." Jefferson had proposed that the excise taxes be abolished, on the ground that the remaining revenues would be enough to pay interest on the national debt and even to pay off the principal more quickly than planned. Hamilton asked why cut taxes till a surplus is certain? And why not keep the revenue and pay off the debt faster? "How is this reconcileable with the wanton and unjust clamors heretofore vented against those who projected and established our present system of public credit; charging them with a design to perpetuate the debt, under the pretext that *a public debt was a public blessing?*" Now, he complained, all of a sudden Mr. Jefferson wanted to postpone the payment of the debt, by throwing away part of the fund destined for its prompt redemption—"Wonderful union of consistency and wisdom!"

Hamilton himself had in fact argued in the past that a reasonable national debt would be a national blessing. It would create a necessity, he said, for keeping up taxation to a degree which, without being oppressive, would be a spur to industry—which was true since there were no income taxes and government bonds were in strong hands.

Hamilton suggested that if too much money were coming in, instead of cutting taxes it would be far better to invest the surplus in public works such as arsenals and dockyards, roads and bridges, aqueducts and canals. He accused the Jeffersonians of opposing public works and of being too much enamored of strictly private enterprise. This favorite dogma, he admitted, was true enough when taken as a general rule—enterprise ought, doubtless, to be left free in the main—but, he urged, in language that sounds strange coming from the original Hamiltonian, "practical politicians know that it may be beneficially stimulated by prudent aids and encouragements on the part of the government. This is proved by numerous examples which will be neglected only by indolent and temporizing rulers, who love to loll in the lap of epicurean ease, and seem to imagine that to govern well, is to amuse the wondering multitude with sagacious aphorisms and oracular sayings."

Hamilton offered as a further argument against tax reduction that the habits of our citizens made it so hard to get them used to taxes, that it would be "foolish to resign the boon" once a tax is established, perhaps in a short time to have to resort to it again, at the risk of another whiskey rebellion. Anyhow, if anything were to be reduced, he suggested, it should be the tariffs, to encourage trade.

When Jefferson came into office James Thompson Callender was still in jail under the Sedition Law. The new President regarded the law as unconstitutional, and therefore pardoned him forthwith. Callender then asked for the postmastership of Richmond, but Jefferson by this time had sized up his character and refused to appoint him. Callender, however, got control of the Richmond *Recorder*, and used it as an organ for attacking Jefferson. One of his contributions to misleading history asserted that the maid whom Jefferson's daughter Maria had taken with her to Paris in 1784 had borne a son, Tom, who showed "a striking tho' sable resemblance" to Jefferson himself. No one who knew Jefferson personally and was familiar with his family life believed this gossip, but it was eagerly spread by the Federalist papers. Callender's principal contribution, however, was the Walker story, which dated back thirty-five years.

Jefferson and John Walker were at school and college together, and Jefferson was "brideman" at Walker's wedding in June, 1764. He fell in love with Mrs. Walker, and in 1768 he took advantage of Walker's absence to make love to her. She rejected his advances and urged her husband, without saying why, not to go on having Jefferson as executor in his will.

Mrs. Walker's niece married Henry (Light Horse Harry) Lee— their son was Robert E. Lee—and Henry Lee in time became a Federalist and a bitter enemy of Jefferson's. After Jefferson entered the White House, Lee needled Walker into writing up the details of the ancient scandal, and the story came to public notice through an article by Callender in the *Recorder* of October 27, 1802. The Federalist papers kept it alive, and when the matter came up again in the New England *Palladium* in January, 1805, Jefferson told the facts to some of his intimate friends, saying that he wished "to stand with them on the ground of truth." Speaking of the attacks on him, he said to Robert Smith, Secretary of the Navy, "You will perceive that I plead guilty to one of their charges, that when young and single I offered love to a handsome lady. I acknolege its incorrectness [i.e., impropriety]. It is the only one founded in truth among all their allegations against me."

In March, 1805, Walker gave Lee a detailed list of the occasions when he said Jefferson had tried to make love to Mrs. Walker, including some after Jefferson was married. The ample evidence of Jefferson's devotion to his own wife had not served to convince Mr. Walker that Jefferson had given up his attempts after his marriage, but it is practically certain that Lee transmitted to Walker a statement from Jefferson assuring him that Mrs. Walker's conduct had throughout been irreproachable. For a letter from Henry Lee to Jefferson on September 8, 1806, says, "I repeated [to Walker] my conviction of yr. sincere desire to do every thing which truth and honor would warrant to give peace to his mind and oblivion to the cause of his disquietude."

Obviously the people who brought this episode to light nearly forty years after the event, especially Lee and Callender, were moved by personal spite; but it was Jefferson's political enemies who gave it countrywide circulation.

After these adventures in scandal Callender did not long survive. While drunk, he fell in the James River, where he met his end "in congenial mud."

During his first term Jefferson sent off the Lewis and Clark expedition to explore the Oregon trail, and bought the western half of the Mississippi Valley for $2\frac{1}{2}$ cents an acre, doubling the United States area. For this latter he received many reproaches, not merely because the Louisiana Purchase was plainly unconstitutional, but even more on the ground that the price paid was extravagant. It was hard then to foresee that within a hundred years the farm lands alone in this territory would be worth five hundred times the whole cost. Federalist objections to the westward expansion were based in part

on the fact that American business men still looked mainly to the
sea and the trade of Europe. They had already found, too, that the
opening of the West increased the number of westerners, who were
often difficult to deal with in politics.

As the election of 1804 came over the horizon Jefferson knew that
he would be showered with brickbats, but he refused to quit under
fire. He wrote to Mazzei in July: "The spirit of republicanism is
now in almost all its ancient vigor, five sixths of the people being with
us. . . . We have now got back to the ground on which you left
us. I should have retired at the end of the first four years, but the
immense load of tory calumnies which have been manufactured
respecting me, and have filled the European market, have obliged me
to appeal once more to my country for a justification."

In this campaign the Boston *Centinel* carried an elaborate series
of 27 articles by a commentator calling himself "Hume," who analyzed
Jefferson's administration in full detail, much to its disadvantage.
According to "Hume," the President had swindled the American
people, beginning with his first Inaugural Adress in 1801: "Though
a perusal of this designed piece of splendid deception must have caused
a belief, that the halcyon days of primeval simplicity were again to
be realized under his auspices, yet has his presidency almost termi-
nated, and must end in miserable disappointment to the expectations
of good men."

"Hume" in his final chapter on October 27 summarized the President's misdeeds in one mighty paragraph of 140 lines of fine print
that must have tired the eyes while raising the blood pressure of many
a Federalist old gentleman. The indictment included the following
highlights: "Persecution and intolerance have been prominent traits
in his conduct. . . . Falsehood and slander have been weapons to
assail and drive almost every revolutionary character [i.e. Federalist
veteran] from the government. Indeed the President has openly
declared, that honor, integrity, and a love of the Constitution are not
yet qualifications for office. . . . Foreigners have been lured to ill-
fated *America* in expectation of carrying on their nefarious projects
with impunity. The billows of the ocean have been whitened by the
canvas of vessels, conveying from *Europe* hordes of aliens, whose
backs were smarting under the crimsoned lash of justice. . . . A
committee of persecution, called a committee of investigation, has

Pointing up a satirical Federalist attack on Jefferson entitled "Remarks on the Jacobiniad," this illustration depicts his typical supporter as a strutting ignoramous. Attack's author was John Gardiner.

"Despotism, Anarchy, and Disunion" was the title of this cartoon against John C. Calhoun, prominent Presidential hopeful of the 1830's and 40's.

Accompanied by apes emerging from a "Tory Cave," a Federalist editor entreats sailors to throw in their lot with England rather (than) support the James Madison administration during the War of 1812.

been appointed, to make a report of pretended delinquencies. . . . Great indeed must be that depravity, which resorts to the highest national tribunal to sanction slander by an official act for the ruin of private reputation." "Hume" deplores "the purchase of a wilderness for fifteen millions of dollars, which might probably have been acquired much more cheaply. Over this territory has Mr. JEFFERSON been constituted absolute monarch, clothed with a patronage, which may ultimately be death to national liberty. . . . To complete this scene of ignominy, the President himself has hired an abandoned profligate to calumniate WASHINGTON, and those other great and good characters, who with him acquired national independence. He hastened the return of THOMAS PAINE to this country, who is not only an open reviler of our political Saviour, but a notorious blasphemer of him, by whose death alone there is hope of happiness beyond the grave. Such conduct must dwell in the memory of posterity, and be esteemed evidence of a want of principle, for a parallel to which history in vain may be searched."

"Hume" in his first paper on June 6 had gleefully recalled the self-righteous attitude of the Republicans when they first came into office: "The present administration in the commencement of their political career, with exultation at the victory they had obtained over their predecessors, often repeated, 'let our actions be displayed at the tribunal of public opinion, we are confident, they will be as honorable to us, as they are pleasing to the people. We never will defend ourselves with any other aid, than the brilliancy of our virtue.' Like a rash inexperienced, and boastful youth, sanguine in his own strength, they must by this time have learned, that there is no cunning, which may not be investigated; no secret wickedness and corruption which may not be discovered."

Just before Election Day The *Centinel* addressed the following "Short Sermon" to the MECHANICS OF BOSTON: "Your serious and candid attention for a few minutes is requested to what may be now offered, from the following words, which may be found in the 19th Chapter of the *Book*, called *Notes on the State of Virginia*, written by THOMAS JEFFERSON. . . .'while we have land to labor, let us never wish to see our citizens occupied at a work-bench. Carpenters, Masons, and Smiths, are wanting in husbandry; but for the GENERAL OPERATION of manufacture, let OUR WORKSHOPS REMAIN IN

EUROPE!—It is better to carry provisions and materials to workmen in Europe, than to bring them to the provisions and materials here.— The MOBS of great cities add just as much to the support of pure government as SORES do to the support of the human body.". . .

"MECHANICS! If with this knowledge, you can vote for *such a Man,* you are more deserving of his stigmas, than I am willing to allow. But no, my friends, you know better. . . . Your cry will be, 'No European Workshops;' and you will vote for the John Coffin Jones list of electors, and for the Honorable Josiah Quincy, as Representative."

This Sermon, though using the first person, was unsigned even with a pseudonym.

The same paper had this written down for the sailors:

"Sam Seaworthy to his Fellow Townsmen, once more.

"AHOI! MESSMATES! AHOI!

"Here I am tight as a *buoy* and as solid as a *pumpbolt*—returned from a four years voyage—. . . I find, howsomever, by axing my friend Joab, the Carfender, that things on board the good old ship Federal Constitution have altered for the worse since I sailed. . . . When I left *America,* old JACK ADAMS commanded the Federal Ship . . . as good a commander as ever kept a quarterdeck. . . . His officers, too, were all Americans—old salts, every inch of them— men who knew, and never feared to do their duty. Now, it seems, they have all been turned ashore; with the aid of the southern *blackskins;* and the old ship is now officered and manned with Cabin-Window gentry, and *Parley-vous;* . . . who are busy in making *comical* experiments. . . . My friend Joab tells me, that the new Commander is called Captain Thomas Doolittle. . . .

"Since I've got home, I have looked over some of the newspaper logbooks that my *Poll* had saved, and I find these Freshwater Companions, who have got the helm, make a palaver about *Economy,* and sich Dictionary words. . . . Old Hawser Trunnion, the Yellow Commodore, who was always considered a *sly jack,* receives more than SIXTEEN HUNDRED dollars a year out of the Economy money chest— and all for doing nothing at all; but superintending his Dry Dock House in *Charlestown,* which is building on the United States land. . . .

"All hands, ahoi, tumble up, and attend on Sunday Evening at the *Caucus* at Fanuiel Hall; and there vote, for the Old Federal List of Nineteen Electors; which has the name of John Coffin Jones at the head of it."

The Federalists were more and more outraged by Jefferson's pressure for "economy." They impatiently insisted that *"pounds are lost through a stingy unwillingness to spend pence,"* and quoted the Bible: "There is that withholdeth more than is meet, but it tendeth to poverty." They declared that the national independence was not gained by parsimony, and that it could not be protected by parsimony.

When the President, after handily winning the election, sent a Message to Congress reporting that "the state of our finances continues to fulfill our expectations," the *Connecticut Courant* burst into angry italics: "We arrive at this conclusion, that *Genuine economy, as it respects particularly the government of the United States, imperiously demands such liberal expenditures, as from time to time may be necessary for the defence of our national independence and dignity and for the protection of all classes of citizens."*

The President's Message was classed under "The Deceptive Arts of the Democrats"; *Democrat* was still a bad name for a Republican, meaning in modern language a radical. The radical yearning for economy was what the *Courant* found most deceptive:

"Why then is the last administration perpetually charged with profligate wastefulness . . Why is the economy of the present rulers of the nation trumpeted at the city of Washington and constantly rung, from New Hampshire to Georgia, through all the possible changes and on every note in the *Gamut?—Why* but to catch *Gulls?"*

The Federalist party was in its death throes, and Jefferson in the 1804 election had snared all but fourteen of the electoral votes. This sorry state of the opposition may account for one of the feeblest attacks ever made on a President, a criticism of his post-election Message as proof that he could not write correct English. The Washington *Federalist* contributed this gem of literary criticism. For instance, "It is your business to inquire whether laws are provided in all cases where they are wanting," is denounced elaborately as an Irish bull, since if they are provided they are not wanting. "But in the American seas, they have been greater from peculiar causes" is corrected to read "But in the American seas, from peculiar causes, they have been greater." When Jefferson spoke of "That tribe, desiring to extinguish in their people the spirit of hunting" the critic carps: "What is a tribe but the people composing it? *Dele* 'in their people.'" He objects to the word *one* in "expenditures for the last year, with estimates for the ensuing one."

All this is for the purpose of suggesting that Jefferson had a ghost: "Proofs, that Mr. Jefferson's literary celebrity is unmerited is (sic) important on more than one account. If it is discovered that all his boasted literary performances, such as are really correct, are the products of a *hired pen,* which he has artfully imposed upon the public as his own—his political character must stand in a new point of view. . . . When it is decided that he is ignorant of the definition of ordinary words, a miserable deficiency in common reading is proved." The critic particularly objected to the intrusion of business slang into official English. "And when Mr. Jefferson informs Congress that they 'may *count on* his hearty co-operation,' &c. the expression has a *nation deal* of vulgarity in it."

There is no reason to think that the *Federalist* had its tongue in its cheek. In 1776, although there had already been a number of local resolutions calling for independence, it was Jefferson who supplied most of the actual wording of the Declaration that the Congress adopted. This fame was a sore point with some of the Federalists; and the critic here wanted his readers to think that in the drafting committee the young Jefferson had secretly had some "hired pen" ghosting the Declaration for him, under the very noses of John Adams and the other committee members.

The discharge of some of the more obstreperous Federalist office-holders brought out some remarkable examples of high moral principle which the Federalists felt ought to be applied to the Civil Service. They could see that from the first the Republicans had been plotting to get those offices away from the incumbents, by sowing the seeds of discord in every town and village in the Union. There was of course a grain of truth in this charge, for Washington, like any revolutionary leader, had hoped for a one-party country, and it was the Republicans who brought in the two-party system and sowed the seeds of discord. Another source of resentment was that Jefferson's followers held the outrageous notion that execellent men should be driven from the government payroll for no crime but failure of zeal for the party in power.

"The man who would secure the countenance and patronage of this party . . . must relinquish the right of private judgment . . . must follow them in all their *crusades,* must approve all their plans of self-aggrandizement, must swallow all their potions and their pills, must lay his conscience upon the *iron bedstead* to be so stretched or contracted as to be brought to an exact conformity." It was going to be a long time before an incoming party would refrain from a reduction in force that would reduce mainly those who seemed unenthusiastic about its crusade.

In January, 1805, before Jefferson entered on his second term, the *New England Palladium* summed up in many words the case against him. It harped on the Democratic charge that the Federalists were monarchists, declaring that if Mr. Adams had committed all the crimes that Jefferson had in his record, no doubt he too would have been hailed as no monarchist but a good Republican.

Jefferson was accused of having paid a debt to a friend in depreciated paper dollars, though in actual fact he had sold property to pay that debt under conditions that caused him to pay it twice over.

He was accused of writing a book saying that it was no matter whether there were twenty gods or one, and of inviting Tom Paine, "the vilest blasphemer and infidel that ever disgraced the world," to come to America in a government vessel.

He was accused of attempting the honor of a friend's wife, and when repulsed, of "taking to his bosom a sable damsel," described in language that cannot be printed even in a book in our day.

He was accused of dismantling the Navy, of "inventing drydocks to rot our ships," and of providing puny gunboats to scare crows in our coastal waters.

He was accused of hiring Callender to concoct scandalous lies about Washington, and of flattering Napoleon, the vilest despot in Europe, and of appointing as Secretary of the Treasury Albert Gallatin, a man who had opposed the collection of the public revenue and had helped to stir up the Whiskey Rebellion, which cost the United States upward of a million dollars. He also had squandered *fifteen millions of dollars* in obtaining a doubtful title to an unprofitable wilderness.

"If, in fine," the accuser concluded, Mr. Adams "had been a coward, a calumniator, a plagiarist, a tame spiritless animal, a man who wrote pretty nonsense and thought it was fine writing, . . . if he had been a man without religion, a statesman without principle and a patriot regardless of his country's welfare, and entirely devoted to raise himself and his partizans upon the nation's ruin, then these Democrats would never have denounced him as a *monarchist,* but hailed him as *a genuine republican,* in whose mercenary smiles they sought for the reward of their baseness."

How did Jefferson feel about these accusations? There is ample evidence that he was painfully sensitive to the slanders that were so gleefully printed and reprinted about him all over the country. He knew that his enemies were glad to believe everything disgraceful that could be said about him. But, as James Truslow Adams has pointed out, Jefferson, unlike John Adams, was so strongly attached to the liberal principle of freedom of the press, that he would have no part in any attempt to hit back at the papers when they lied about him. His attitude toward the Federalist Sedition Law was simply that it was unconstitutional. He believed that in the long run history would do him justice, but in the short run he sat "writhing in the White House," trying as best he might to comfort himself with philosophy and his sense of public duty.

In Jefferson's second term he could see that war with England was coming, but he wanted to put it off as long as possible. He told Monroe, "If we can keep at peace eight years longer, our income, liberated from debt, will be adequate to any war, without new taxes or loans, and our position and increasing strength put us *hors d'insulte* from any nation." The most controversial of the measures that he adopted for keeping out of war was the Embargo Act of December, 1807, which prohibited the export of any produce from an American port.

Even New England at first was unable to smuggle more than about 25 percent of its normal trade, and the business men were roused to fury against the Administration. This controversy brought out two literary denuciations that have survived to this day in one way or another as parts of the American culture.

The first was a long poem, *The Embargo,* by a thirteen-year-old boy, in which Mr. Jefferson was told just who he was and what he could do. The poet addressed his suffering homeland in wingéd words:

> *Ill-fated clime! condemn'd to feel th' extremes,*
> *Of a weak ruler's philosophic dreams;*
> *Driven headlong on, to ruin's fateful brink,*
> *When will thy country feel, when will she think!*

Then, turning to the culprit himself, he cried:

> *And thou, the scorn of every patriot name,*
> *Thy country's ruin, and her council's shame!*
> *Poor servile thing! Derision of the brave!*
> *Who erst from Tarleton fled to Carter's cave;*
> *Thou, who, when menac'd by perfidious Gaul,*
> *Didst prostrate to her whiskered minion fall:*
> *And when our cash her empty bags supply'd,*
> *Didst meanly strive the foul disgrace to hide;*
> *Go, wretch, resign the presidential chair,*
> *Disclose thy secret measures, foul or fair.*
> *Go, search with curious eye, for hornéd frogs,*
> *Mid the wild wastes of Louisianian bogs;*
> *Or, where Ohio rolls his turbid stream,*
> *Dig for huge bones, thy glory and thy theme.*
> *Go, scan, Philosophist, thy ****** charms*
> *And sink supinely in her sable arms;*
> *But quit to abler hands the helm of state,*
> *Nor image ruin on thy country's fate!"*

Perhaps we may assume that where the venerable William Cullen Bryant walks now with his peers in the Elysian Fields, he has been permitted to forget this early effort. Here on earth, men have given a bit of immortality to the surge and thunder of the *Embargo*, by using it for a sort of plum to pop into a history text as a help in keeping the student awake. We may take it as showing a revealing glimpse of table talk in 1807 in a New England family corresponding to the Roosevelt-haters of the 1930s; and we can see the ardent youth glowing with the frustrated indignation of his elders and feeling the Epic Muse calling him to soar, an avenging eagle, on angry pinion into fame and glory as his country's savior. In launching his career as a poet, however, young William did better with *Thanatopsis*.

Washington Irving was so much more successful with his attack on Jefferson that after the immediate purpose and meaning of it had been forgotten, his *Knickerbocker History of New York* survived as a classic of American humor that few readers today recognize as having been partly designed to serve a political purpose. In this "veracious" history, Jefferson is represented by the worthy Wilhelmus Kieft, Governor of Manhattan when that budding colony was threatened with aggression by the Connecticut Yankees. Kieft is described as having studied at the Hague, where he "skirmished very smartly on the frontiers of several of the sciences," and ventured so rashly into metaphysics that "he came well nigh being smothered in a slough of unintelligible learning—a fearful peril from the effects of which he never perfectly recovered."

The brilliant Irving, no doubt influenced by his own political outlook on current affairs, had small patience with the policies adopted by Governor Kieft against the encroaching Yankees, or for any egghead whose learning could lead him to follow the Governor's example. For the Governor boldly defied the invaders, and assured his council "that he had been obliged to have recourse to a dreadful engine of warfare, lately invented, awful in its effects, but authorized by dire necessity. In a word, he was resolved to conquer the Yankees—by proclamation!" This deadly weapon had the great virtue of costing the treasury practically nothing, and all it needed to ensure complete success was that the Yankees should stand in awe of it. Provokingly enough, however, they treated the proclamation with contempt, whereupon, nothing daunted, the valiant Kieft resolutely determined to double the dose. He therefore fulminated against them a second proclamation, of heavier metal than the former; written in thundering long sentences, not one word of which was under five syllables. This, in fact, was a kind of non-intercourse bill, prohibiting "all commerce and connection, between any and every of said Yankee intruders, and the said fortified post of Fort Goed Hoop, and ordering, commanding and advising, all his trusty, loyal and well-beloved subjects, to furnish them with no supplies of gin, gingerbread or sour crout; to buy none of their pacing horses, meazly pork, apple brandy, Yankee rum, cyder water, apple sweetmeats, Weathersfield onions or wooden bowls, but to starve and exterminate them from the face of the land."

After recounting the sad failure of the embargo and the fall of Fort Goed Hoop, Irving turns to a discussion of what might have been wrong with the strategy of Governor Kieft: "The great defect of Wilhelmus Kieft's policy was, that though no man could be more ready to stand forth in an hour of emergency, yet whatever precaution for public safety he adopted, he was so intent upon rendering it cheap, that he invariably rendered it ineffectual." This defect resulted from an accident in his education, when in some obscure German text he had stumbled over "a grand political *cabalistic* word"—none other than the word *economy*.

"When pronounced in a national assembly," Irving observes, "it has an immediate effect in closing the hearts, beclouding the intellects, drawing the purse strings and buttoning the breeches pockets of all philosophic legislators. . . .By its magic influence seventy-fours shrink into frigates—frigates into sloops, and sloops into gunboats."

At this point it is of interest to recall that Irving's comments on governmental economy were aimed at a *Democratic* administration. Times and parties change, while arguments and even necromancy are more enduring. Jefferson had some arguments on his side which may have been somewhat more valid then than the same reasoning is today. As for preparedness, he was sure the country could "spring to arms" in time to meet any attack if one should start lumbering across the then broad Atlantic. Government credit, on the other hand, in the stress of the Revolution, had foundered in the inflationuary tide; Jefferson believed that financial strength was the best kind to lay up in advance of a possible emergency. As it turned out, history failed to give a clear judgment, for the outcome of the War of 1812 was confused by the serious lack of unity on the American side and the extraneous preoccupations of the British.

The New Englanders of course rapidly improved the art of circumventing the Embargo. One of Jefferson's last official actions was to persuade Congress to pass the so-called Force Act, authorizing federal agents to seize without warrant any goods that they suspected were intended to be smuggled abroad. New England responded with a wave of indignant town-meetings and threats of secession that Jefferson regarded as ominous. The Embargo, instead of being more effectively enforced, had to be repealed. But the war with England had been postponed, and Jefferson escaped from the Presidency with the feeling of having got off more easily than he had feared. He wrote to his friend Pierre S. Dupont de Nemours that no prisoner released from his chains ever felt more relief than he did at "shaking off the shackles of power."

After Jefferson's retirement the hopeless and frustrated Federalists continued from time to time to campaign against him, but they could no longer draw blood as they did when he was a public official. He wrote to a friend in 1810 that he appreciated the kindness of his friends in defending his reputation, and remarked that it was probably good for the country to have the Federalists diverted from disturbing the government, by wasting their time barking at the ex-President. All these years, as he put it, he had served the opposition faithfully "in the terrific station of Rawhead and Bloodybones," and if they wanted him to continue in that office he would do so—particularly if it could be "exercised at home, without interfering with the tranquil enjoyment of my farm, my family, my friends and books."

As time went on the Sage of Monticello, though busy managing his two estates and 200 slaves, still found occasion for long letters about his experiences and observations in public life. One such, written in 1813, renewed his defense of Washington against the charge of aristocratic leanings that had been so often made by the more rabid Republican writers twenty years earlier. He assured his correspondent that Washington "sincerely wished the people to have as much self-government as they were competent to exercise themselves. The only point on which he and I ever differed in opinion, was, that I had more confidence than he in the natural integrity and discretion of the people." Jefferson strongly criticized the "monarchists" for claiming the sanction of General Washington for their principles. But he was not looking for public argument. He ended his letter with a request that it be kept out of the papers, saying: "I am certain I risk no use of the communication which may draw me into contention before the public. Tranquillity is the *summum bonum* of a septegenaire."

One of the greatest pleasures of both Jefferson and Adams in their old age was the renewal of their friendship, which had been accidentally broken in 1801. When Jefferson came into office, John Adams's son John Quincy Adams held a government job which was abolished by a change in the law, and Jefferson, unaware of his situation, did not find him another job. His mother thought Jefferson had slighted him because of politics, and broke off the friendship between the two families, which was not resumed until a mutual friend succeeded in bringing them together again ·in 1812. From then on the two ex-Presidents corresponded steadily until they both died, within the same hour, on July 4, 1826, the fiftieth anniversary of the Declaration that they had helped to write.

Adams wrote to Jefferson in 1813 that he was mortified to find that the vilification he had suffered from 1797 to 1800 was being matched, now that the Republicans were in office, by the bad manners of his fellow-Federalists. "I know not which party," he protested, "has the most unblushing front, the most lying tongue, or the most impudent and insolent, not to say the most seditious and rebellious pen."

The two correspondents were not, however, entirely free from buzzing intrusion in their friendly philosophizing. The egregious Timothy Pickering, whom Adams had dismissed from his Cabinet for personal disloyalty, and who hated Jefferson as heartily as he hated Adams, heard that they had patched up their differences and were once more on friendly terms. He would soon put a stop to that. With this worthy purpose he prepared and published a long account of the history of Callender's attack on Adams, throwing the main responsibility for it on Jefferson.

"Who has not heard," enquired Pickering, "of the libels on President Adams (not omitting Washington) in the pamphlet called 'The Prospect Before Us,' written by Callender under the countenance, patronage, and pay of Mr. Jefferson? of which libels Callender was convicted by a jury at Richmond; for which he was fined and imprisoned; and for which he received (as he had a good right to expect) President Jefferson's pardon. The patronage and pay were evidenced by two letters from Jefferson to Callender, which, after they had quarrelled, Callender put into the hands of Augustine Davis, Esq. of Richmond. . . . I received them. Both were in Mr. Jefferson's own handwriting, to me perfectly well known."

The first letter quoted by Pickering mentions the payment of "50 dollars, on account of the book you are about to publish. When it shall be out be so good as to send me 2 or 3 copies. . . ." The other letter, dated Monticello Oct. 6, 1799, says: "I thank you for the proof sheets you inclosed me: such papers cannot fail to produce the best effect . . . you will know from whom this comes without signature: the omission of which has been rendered almost habitual with me by the curiosity of the post-offices. Indeed a period is now approaching during which I shall discontinue writing letters as much as possible, knowing that every snare will be used to get hold of what may be perverted in the eyes of the public."

Pickering went on to say that not only was Jefferson's encouragement of Callender, in order to beat Adams, "to the last degree dishonourable," but it was equally unjustified for Adams to forgive such an offense. It seemed obvious to Pickering that Adams was moved by unworthy care for the interests of John Quincy Adams, who had joined the Republicans in 1807, and that the father would basely take back all his former reproaches against Jefferson—"*lest they should have an inauspicious influence on the fortunes of his son.*"

Pickering failed in his attempt to poison the friendship between the two old statesmen. The famous Adams temper flared up, not against Jefferson but against Pickering; he avoided exhibiting his feelings in public, however. As he explained to Jefferson, his friends had persuaded him to keep his dignity, but internally he was still boiling: "My loving and beloved friend Pickering, has been pleased to inform the world that I have 'few friends.' I wanted to whip the rogue, and I had it in my power, if it had been my will to do it, till the blood came. But all my real friends, as I thought then, . . . insisted 'that I should not say a word; that nothing that such a person could write would do me the least injury; that it would betray the constitution and the government, if a President, out or in, should enter into a newspaper controversy with one of his ministers, whom he had removed from his office, in justification of himself for that removal, or anything else'; and they talked a great deal about the *Dignity* of the office of President, which I do not find that any other person, public or private, regards very much."

In 1814 Jefferson was shocked to learn that during the burning of Washington the British had destroyed the Library of Congress, a collection of some 3,000 books which he had personally organized and catalogued. His own private library of nearly 6,500 volumes had been collected with care and expert knowledge of many subjects, much of it while he was living in France. He had intended that on his death Congress should have the first refusal on this material, but, as he said, "The loss they have now incurred, makes the present the proper moment for their accommodation, without regard to the small remnant of time and the barren use of my enjoying it."

The Republicans controlled both branches of Congress, and of course they were prepared to accept the offer, though they thriftily moved to pay only $25,000—less than half the value. Even this was shaved down in the final appropriation. As for the pitiful minority of Federalist members—including alongside the old relics young Daniel Webster, just elected from New Hampshire—they were swept by a wave of hysterical fury. What, pay out the taxpayers' money to bring into the Nation's Capitol a mass of radical, immoral, atheistical pamphlets, many of them even in French? Not to speak of subsidizing the very High-Priest of Republicanism himself, sitting on his hill at Charlottesville and still corrupting the minds of young and old who came to sit at his feet! All the latent conservative hatred of the intellectual came out and war-danced for the edification of the reporters.

A Congressman pointed out that instead of squandering $25,000 on books, Congress could well use the money to buy rifles for 2,000 soldiers. Others urged that the books were not such as Congress wanted, and at least a fourth were in foreign languages, many even in the dead languages. What use, for instance, would Congress have for a pamphlet on architecture, or for the ten cook books, nine of them foreign? The debate in some ways resembled the conservative furor that arose in Congress during the 1930s when some joker spread a story that the Department of Agriculture had spent money printing a bulletin on the love life of the frog.

One statesman named Cyrus King, a graduate of Phillips Andover and Columbia College, moved that if the library were bought a committee should cull out the useless and the immoral items and sell them, investing the proceeds in useful books. On a suggestion being offered that they should rather be burned, Mr. King replied that he had at first so intended, but then thought the committee "might be unwilling to perform a task usually allotted to the common hangman."

But all protests were vain. Congress bought the books, as the conservative *Niles' Weekly Register* reported in disgust, "putting into the pocket of Thomas Jefferson 23,900 dollars for about six thousand volumes . . . many which cannot be read by a single member in either house of Congress, and more which never will nor ought to be read by a member—while the library is destitute of other books, absolutely necessary, in doing the public business. This is true Jeffersonian, Madisonian, democratic economy, which has bankrupt the treasury, beggared the people, and disgraced the nation."

The subject of Jefferson's library came to public notice once more, after his death in 1826. This time the reference was not to the books that had been bought by the government, but to those that he had collected since 1814. He had continued to live the life of a prosperous country gentleman, but his prosperity had gradually declined. The profits of his farms diminished, but even more serious was the growing cost of being the Sage of Monticello, to whose shrine flocked hosts of pilgrims, distinguished and undistinguished. His visitors literally ate him out of house and home. When he died, Monticello had to be sold; and two years later his final collection of about 2,000 books, which he had bequeathed to the University of Virginia and two grandsons-in-law, was reluctantly advertised for sale, since "the condition of his estate requires that this bequest be diverted to the payment of his debts."

But although the old patriarch died in debt he died contented. He had been well hated and well loved while he was engaged in the service of his country; he had been able to retire in peace and live happily as an elder statesman; and he knew that he would have an honorable place in history. He was the first of the Presidents to recover fully from the ordeal of the Presidency.

CHAPTER IV

DEFAMED PURITAN

John Quincy Adams wanted intensely to be President. But he had been brought up in the old school that required a candidate to stand in the attitude of a man who cared nothing about who would be chosen. He trembled before the breath of criticism, and he feared the risk of running openly and perhaps being defeated. Yet if only he could once reach the Presidency, he could relieve the ingrained feeling of failure that had haunted his whole highly distinguished career of public service.

Here it was 1822, and in two years it might be Adams's chance. Adams was Monroe's Secretary of State. Monroe was coming to the end of his second term, and the Secretary of State was the natural heir. But he could feel the beginnings of a tide of venomous opposition. As the pressure grew he wrote: "An undercurrent of calumny has been flowing in every direction adapting its movements to the feelings and prejudices of the different parts of the country. It has a story for Pittsburg and a story for Portland, a misrepresentation for Milledgeville and a lie for Lexington. . . I have no countermining at work. . . . I make no bargains. I listen to no overtures for coalition. I give no money. I push no appointments of canvassing partisans to office."

He little guessed what coalition he would be accused of making before the day when he would step up to take the oath as President in 1825. Nor did he sense that Andrew Jackson, the General whom he had boldly defended in the meetings of Monroe's Cabinet, would be the man to turn the taste of his Presidency to dust and ashes.

As the fateful year of 1824 gradually approached, the attacks grew in intensity and bitterness. Adams was accused of nearly everything from "aristocracy" to betrayal of his country's interests. Most of the attacks he wisely ignored as beneath the dignity of his office. One that called for remarkable self control was a vicious diatribe by his father's old enemy Timothy Pickering. Adams decided not to advertise the aged Pickering by a reply. But he did hit back at an attempt of Henry Clay, the Speaker of the House, to discredit him with the voters in the West. Under cover Clay had his friends bring to light a secret letter from Jonathan Russell to Ssecretary of State Monroe at the end of the War of 1812, when Adams was one of the peace negotiators at Ghent. As published, Russell's letter accused Adams of trying to trade off the West's navigation rights on the Mississippi in exchange for New England fishing privileges off Nova Scotia. However, as Adams was able to prove, the published copy was widely different from the original letter in Monroe's file. Russell was "completely destroyed," but Adams did not directly accuse Clay.

Another attack came from Congressman Alexander Smyth of Virginia in the form of a longwinded distortion of Adams's Senate career. Adams replied by publishing an "address" to the voters of Smyth's district and they responded by not reelecting Smyth.

It gradually became evident that Adams would have four chief rivals for the office: Secretary of the Treasury William H. Crawford, Henry Clay, Secretary of War John C. Calhoun, and Andrew Jackson.

John Quincy Adams and Andrew Jackson, who at the end came to be bitter enemies, began as warm friends, for each in his own way was an intrepid fighter. When General Jackson, stretching his orders to the limit, invaded the Spanish province of Florida in 1818, Adams, as Secretary of State, was in the midst of negotiations for the purchase of the territory from Spain. The Spanish Government, on receiving news of the invasion, broke off the negotiations and threatened war. Adams called the bluff; he wrote a strong note upholding Jackson and threatening more and worse unless Spain would do business. Spain backed down, and Adams developed a vast admiration for Jackson, which was cordially reciprocated.

In 1821 Jackson said in a letter to James Gadsden: "You are at liberty to say in my name to both my friends and enemies, that I will as far as my influence extends support Mr. Adams unless Mr. Calhoun should be brought forward. . . . As to Wm. H. Crawford you know my opinion. I would support the Devil first."

Jackson's feelings had strong personal reasons. In July, 1818, after his raid into Florida, the Cabinet had had a violent argument over whether to disavow him and knuckle under to Spain. Adams stood alone or almost alone for three prespiring days as Jackson's champion.

An 1828 cartoon used against John Quincy Adams. It appeared shortly
after the distribution of a letter which reportedly urged Adams supporters to assign "at least six strong and courageous men" to each polling
place. In this cartoon a neutral citizen is being "convinced" that he
should vote for Adams. Looking on from the second story of the building at left, Adams remarks: "Let us not be palsied by the wishes of our
constituents." Andrew Jackson, depicted at the extreme right, says:
"Let the people's unbiased will prevail." Name of cartoonist is unknown.

WANTED

Not until March 4th 1825, an honest, intelligent and faithful MAN SERVANT, to serve the People of the United States as their President, for the next term of four years. He must have the following character:

He must be at least thirty-five years old. A College education will not be insisted on as indispensable, provided he has by his own genius and industry acquired as much general knowledge as did Benjamin Franklin, the Printer, or Roger Sherman, the shoemaker, who signed the Declaration of Independence, and has the steel and the flint to strike out sparks of political truth to light this nation to their most direct way to prosperity and plenty. He must be true to his promise, and not a courtier who will say YES to every one.

It is expected he will do his best to restore the industrious, intelligent, honest Farmer to his pristine rank and consequence in society, and the Artizans and Manufacturers of equal merit may be placed by their side, and useful industry be made fashionable and honorable, and the idle speculator be no longer rated a gentleman, but a vagabond in society, a drone in the political hive —and make the industrious, intelligent boy, who is seen at work in the field, workshop or factory, to be more respected by society, and more sought after by the girls, than the young dandy who is selling grog in a store, or studying in an office with a gown on, how to cheat legally, steal according to law, and tell lies in the words of truth.

Whether this campaign handbill of 1824 was more of a criticism of President Monroe than an attack on his successor, John Quincy Adams, is not clear. Either of them might well have been the author's target.

Crawford had wanted Jackson repudiated and punished, and Jackson knew it. Whether Calhoun was also against Jackson is still a disputed point, but in any case the General did not hear the story until twelve years later, after he had accepted Calhoun as his Vice President. Clay in the House had openly led an unsuccessful attempt to put through a vote of censure against Jackson. So Jackson, who had little interest in the Presidency in 1821, naturally favored Adams and Calhoun.

Even after the campaign was well under way, in January, 1824, Secretary Adams gave a great ball in Jackson's honor, to celebrate the anniversary of the Battle of New Orleans. In his biography of Adams, Bennett Champ Clark describes this ball as the most impressive social function in the history of the Republic up to that time. Neither Adams nor Jackson could foresee that their friends, in the heat of political conflict, would manoeuver them into the position of implacable enemies.

The torture of John Quincy Adams really began after the election, when it became clear that the Presidency would be decided by the House. Jackson had won 99 electoral votes, Adams 84, Crawford 41, and Clay 37. Calhoun had been eliminated early and had taken the Vice Presidency. The House had to choose between the first three in the list, and the fourth man, Clay, as Speaker, might well be king-maker. The question was, would he make a deal?

Crawford had had a stroke, though his followers tried to conceal his condition; the actual choice was between Adams and Jackson. The people obviously preferred Jackson, but in Congress the states were so evenly balanced that the vote of one state could turn the election, as in the end it did.

Exactly what really happened has been much disputed, but it is certain that Jackson was more openly opposed to a deal with Clay than Adams appeared to be, and so it was Adams who got hurt in the scramble, although he won the Presidency.

The story as Jackson recalled it was published in 1827: "Early in January, 1825, a Member of Congress of high respectability visited me one morning and observed that he had a communication, he was desirous to make to me; that he was informed there was a great intrigue going on and he thought it was right I should be informed of it."

The Congressman told Jackson that he had been approached by friends of Mr. Clay with the information that the Adams people had offered a deal by which if Clay would throw his strength to Adams he could be Secretary of State. The question was whether Jackson would match that offer, as in that case, "the West did not wish to separate from the West." That is, since Clay was from Kentucky, his followers would rather help Jackson if they could get an equally good price for their votes. The Congressman advised that in his opinion, if the Adams forces were going to play it that way, "it was right to fight such intriguers with their own weapons."

To this proposition the General reported that he gave a plain answer: "Say to Mr. Clay and his friends that before I would reach the presidential chair by such means. . . I would see the earth open and swallow both Mr. Clay and his friends and myself with them. If they had not the confidence . . . that I would call to . . . the cabinet men of the first virtue, talent and integrity [tell them] not to vote for me."

It soon came out that the highly respectable member of Congress had been James Buchanan, the future President. He may have assumed the privilege of an interpreter to soften his report of Jackson's answer. According to an account that Clay made public many years later, Buchanan after his talk with Jackson had met Clay socially and sounded him out. He led the talk to the subject of cabinets, and predicted that Jackson would have the best Cabinet in the country's history. On someone asking where he would find such ministers, Clay reports that he replied, "he would not have to go outside this room for a Secretary of State." This sounds like a self-serving story of Clay's: for if he could make it appear that both candidates had offered him the same deal, he might be less blamed for taking up with Adams.

Meanwhile Adams was finding his position more and more complicated. For one thing, Thomas Jefferson was heard from, and what he said was not simple. First Daniel Webster came back from a visit to Monticello and reported Jefferson as saying: "I feel alarmed at the prospect of seeing General Jackson President. He is one of the most unfit men I know for such a place. . . . His passions are terrible." Senator Thomas Hart Benton had also been to Monticello, and his report balanced Webster's. He had told Jefferson of the report that Clay would support Adams and that Adams would "make up a mixed cabinet," and asked him how it would do. Jefferson answered, "Not at all—would never succeed—would ruin all engaged in it."

It seems clear that friends of Adams brought word that Clay might be disposed to support him, and that in return he told them he "harbored no hostility" for Clay's part in the Russell attack. On December 17, Adams confided to his diary that "Clay would willingly support me if he could thereby serve himself . . . if Clay's friends could know that he would have a prominent share in the Administration, that might induce them to vote for me."

By December 23 Adams had a feeling that in his relations with Clay he was on dangerous ground. He wrote in his diary, "Incedo super ignes [I walk over fires]." On January 1 he and Clay met at a state dinner for General Lafayette, and "He told me that he should be glad to have with me soon some confidential conversation upon public affairs. I said I should be happy to have it whenever it might suit his convenience. At the beginning of this year there is in my prospects and anticipations a solemnity and moment never before experienced, and to which unaided nature is inadequate."

On January 9th "Mr. Clay came at six, and spent the evening with me in a long conversation explanatory of the past and prospective of the future. . . . He said . . . that he had been applied to by a friend of Mr. Crawford's, in a manner so gross that it had disgusted him; that some of my friends also, disclaiming, indeed, to have any authority from me, had repeatdly applied to him . . . urging considerations personal to himself as motives to his cause. . . . He wished me . . . to satisfy him with regard to some principles of great public importance, but without any personal consideration for himself . . . he had no hesitation in saying that his preference would be for me." This entry is silent on what Adams said during the long evening, before Clay came to his concluding assurance of support.

From there on, the diary tells of a vast amount of normal politicking, consultation with friends about who was leaning toward whom, and who would get the Crawford votes. On February 3 Adams was assuring Webster that if elected he would not treat the old Federalists as a proscribed party, but would give them a fair chance at appointments. This was a straw in the wind that was blowing the Adams branch of the Democratic-Republican Party away from the

Jackson branch and toward the business men represented by Webster. The two-party system was beginning to reappear.

So step by step in the course of what seemed to be ordinary political manoeuvering, John Quincy Adams settled himself into the trap that Jefferson had seen waiting for him, and forgot about the fires underneath.

Long before the time for action by Congress, rumors of a deal were spreading over the country. Jackson wrote to a friend: "There are various rumors . . . but whether any of them is founded in fact I do not know, as I do not . . . join in any conversation on the subject of the presidential election. . . . Mrs J and myself goes to no parties." But with Adams it was different. Clay and his friends came and went in the Adams house. Webster called to lay the groundwork for a job as Minister to England, and then went to work lining up Federalist congressmen.

On January 24 it was announced that Kentucky and Ohio would vote for Adams—which seemed to offer plain evidence that Clay was delivering their votes—and the storm began to blow. One of Clay's lieutenants in Kentucky wrote to him: "For God's sake be on your guard. A thousand desperadoes would think it a most honorable service to shoot you." Senator John Henry Eaton, one of Jackson's closest friends, had a friend editing the Philadelphia *Columbian Observer*, and on January 28 the *Observer* said flatly that Clay's followers had "hinted that they, like the Swiss, would fight for those who pay best." The friends of Adams, the *Observer* reported, had offered a promise of the Secretaryship of State, while Jackson's men had refused to bid.

In the House it was finally so close a squeeze that a silent prayer of one distracted old man decided who should be President. New York was the pivotal state. Martin Van Buren of the Crawford faction had seventeen votes lined up for Jackson, and there were seventeen for Adams. Whatever would break the New York deadlock would win the election.

Van Buren kept bachelor hall with three other men including old General Stephen Van Rensselaer, a rich patroon from Albany, whose mind had become somewhat vague in his old age. Clay had taken the General to visit Adams, but Van Buren had brought him back into line, and he promised to support Jackson. Actually, his interests would naturally lie with the business party, but the lines were not yet clear, and he was moved by loyalty to his friends. On the fateful ninth of February Van Buren escorted the General to the Hill, but once there he was seized by Clay and Webster, who frightened him with stories of what might happen to his properties if the wild man from the West should get in. Then his friends retrieved the confused old gentleman and urged him to stand by his promise. Finally he braced up and declared, "I am resolved. Here is my hand on it."

At last, after various preliminaries, the states were told to poll their members. Poor old General Van Rensselaer put his head down for a moment of prayer. Then he opened his eyes and saw on the floor an Adams ballot that a member had thrown away. His prayer was answered by someone. He picked up the ballot and put it in the box when it came by. So John Quincy Adams became President of the United States. Incidentally Martin Van Buren, though he had failed to keep his hold on the old General, became an established Jackson man, and in due time Jackson's heir to the Presidency.

Jackson had not been desperately anxious for victory, and at the Inauguration Ball he took occasion to shake hands with Adams and wish him well. It was their last meeting. Before many days Clay was appointed Secretary of State, and the fat was in the fire.

Some months later Jackson wrote to a friend: "When rumor was stamping the sudden union of his friends and the friends of Mr. Clay with intrigue, barter and bargain I did not . . . believe that Mr. Adams participated in a management that deserved such epithets. Accordingly . . . I manifested publicly . . . my disbelief of his having had knowledge of the pledges which many men of high standing boldly asserted to be the price of his election. But when . . . Mr. Clay was *Secretary of State*, the inference was irresistible. From that moment I withdrew all intercourse with him."

So Adams came into the White House under a cloud that became particularly galling to his puritanical spirit, for he had at least partially persuaded himself that he had made no "deal," but had disinterestedly chosen Clay as the best man for the job. In addition he was temperamentally unable to fit into the requirements of the Presidency. He needed to be a good fellow and win friends in Congress and the country; instead he was shy and reserved, and often petulant like his father. With all his lofty ideals and vision of a noble future for his country, he could not attract an enthusiastic following or even gain widespread assent to his policies, for lack of the common arts of the politician. Only in his home town, among his taciturn fellow-puritans, was there a public that could understand and love him—and in the end bring comfort to his tired, bruised and battered spirit.

In his first Message to Congress Adams showed how far he was from understanding the majority feeling of his day. He soared off into unpopular Hamiltonian theories of the aristocratic welfare state: "The great object of . . . civil government," he told the legislators, "is the improvement of the condition of those who are parties to the social compact." To be specific, the Government should build roads and canals, maintain a national university, promote scientific research, and map the coasts, rivers and mountains. Adams ended with an ineffective clarion call: "While foreign nations, less blessed with that freedom which is power than ourselves, are advancing with gigantic strides . . . are we to slumber in indolence or fold up our arms and proclaim to the world that we are palsied by the will of our constituents? Would it not be to cast away the bounties of Providence and doom ourselves to perpetual inferiority?"

But this drastic federalism, so much like a foretaste of the New Deal, served only to infuriate the old Jeffersonians in 1825. They were more than half convinced that Federal public works were unconstitutional; and in any case, such extravagances were a threat to the Treasury and to their fond hope of paying off the national debt. The Democratic Party had a long road to travel before coming to F.D.R.

And more bitterness was to come, over Adams's Latin-American policies.

Back when Adams was Secretary of State, he had been the first to state the policy that in due course became the Monroe Doctrine, and when he became President he followed along the same line, as a friend to the newly liberated Spanish colonies. So when the great Liberator, Simón Bolívar, called a Congress of Republics in 1826, to be held at Panama, and invited the United States to take part, Adams accepted and appointed two ministers to attend the meeting.

Just why this action should have aroused such a storm is not at first apparent, until we note that the agenda included a discussion of the abolition of the slave trade. This served as an excuse for the Crawford and Jackson men in Congress, who were drawing together into an anti-Adams coalition, it rise in fury against the President.

R. Y. Hayne of South Carolina—the same who in 1830 engaged in the titanic debate with Daniel Webster described in the school books—led the attack on the Panama visit. He proclaimed that the South would not agree to any action that would contribute to the abolition of slavery in Haiti and Cuba; and he threatened secession if the Federal Government should make any "unhallowed attempt" to interfere with slavery in this country. He attacked the Monroe Doctrine as contrary to Washington's advice to avoid entangling alliances. Hayne was joined by Northeners who objected to the Monroe Doctrine as an entangling alliance, or who objected to Secretary Clay on general principles. Martin Van Buren asserted that if Clay's advice were followed, "the fair fame of our republic would be tarnished—shame would precede our approach—and disgrace follow in our path." In the House, the irascible John Randolph of Roanoke, harking back to the Adams-Clay deal, denounced "the coalition . . . of the Puritan and the blackleg," a saying that was repeated all over the country.

In the end the mission was approved, but its departure was so delayed that it arrived after the end of the conference. The importance of the slavery argument against Adams is shown by the fact that in the election of 1828 the "Solid South" appeared for the first time: Adams got no electoral votes in the slave states that year except six in the border state of Maryland.

As 1828 came on, it was plain that the tide was turning against the reelection of Adams. The electioneering was bitter on both sides. The Democratic-Republican Party was splitting up, into a conservative wing that favored public works, a protective tariff, and a strong central government; and a largely agrarian wing resting mainly on the West and South, and devoted to states' rights. The Adams party came to be called National Republicans and later Whigs; the Jacksonians came to be called simply Democrats. The reader will of course have noted here and elsewhere in this book that parts of the early conservative platform now belong to the modern Democratic Party; and parts of Jackson's—or Jefferson's—Democratic platform are now firmly nailed to the Republican structure. This does not indicate any lack of principle in our two-party system, but merely the importance of interest as well. When the shoe is on the other foot the principle is in the other platform, and party tradition adjusts itself to suit.

Jackson had the advantage because of the growth of the new frontier and the fact that the property qualifications for voting—similar to the modern poll-tax—in nearly all the older states were being gradually reduced. The small farmers and workers were getting more political power, and the conservatives, with Adams as their standard bearer, were on the losing side. In addition, the Jackson men mercilessly pressed the charge of a corrupt deal between Adams and Clay. On their side, the Adams men played undeniably dirty politics, attacking not merely Jackson's military career but also the reputation of Mrs. Jackson. Jackson blamed Clay for organizing these attacks on his wife, and believed Adams could have restrained them if he had wanted to do so. As a result, when Jackson was triumphantly elected he burned with contempt and hatred for his old friend Adams.

On January 1, 1829, Adams wrote in his diary: "The year begins in gloom. . . . The dawn was overcast, and as I began to write, my shaded lamp went out, self-extinguished. It was only for lack of oil; and the notice of so trivial an incident may serve but to mark the present temper of my mind. . . . I began the year with prayer, and then, turning to my Bible, read the first Psalm." The first Psalm starts with words that stung the defeated President like a whip: "Blessed is the man that walketh not in the counsel of the ungodly. . ."

A month later Adams wrote: "Mrs. Jackson having died in December, the General has signified his wish to avoid all displays of festivity or rejoicing, and all magnificent parade. He has not thought proper to hold any personal communication with me since his arrival. . . . His avoidance of me has been noticed in the newspapers. The *Telegraph* newspaper has assigned for the reason of this incivility that he knows I have been personally concerned in the publications against his wife in the *National Journal*. This is not true. I have not been privy to any publication in any newspaper against either him or his wife."

Adams found himself shunned in Washington. In the summer of

1830 he went home to Quincy feeling that he had ended his political career in defeat and shame. But in September he was invited to run for Congress. Overwhelmingly elected, he wrote in his diary on November 7: "No one knows, and few conceive, the agony of mind that I have suffered from the time I was made by circumstances, and not by my volition, a candidate for the Presidency till I was dismissed from that station by the failure of my re-election. . . . But this call upon me by the people of the district . . . has been spontaneous . . . No election or appointment conferred upon me ever gave me so much pleasure." So, at the age of sixty-three, John Quincy Adams at last began to come into his own.

There was one unpleasant interlude in June, 1833, when President Jackson was traveling in New England. Congressman Adams was called out of his garden in Quincy by a visit from his kinsman Josiah Quincy, the President of Harvard, who came to tell him that the University was giving Jackson an LLD degree, and to invite the ex-President to attend. "I said that . . . as myself an affectionate child of our Alma Mater, I would not be present to witness her disgrace in conferring her highest literary honors upon a barbarian who could not write a sentence of grammar and hardly could spell his own name. Mr. Quincy said he was sensible how utterly unworthy of literary honors Jackson was, but the Corporation thought it was necessary to follow the precedent, and treat him precisely as Mr. Monroe, his predecessor, had been treated. As the people of the United States had seen fit to make him their President, the Corporation thought the honors which they conferred upon him were compliments due to the station, by whomsoever it was occupied. . . . I adhered to my determination to stay at home."

In the House Adams became the champion of the right of petition against the famous "gag rule." Under this rule, which was adopted in 1836, all the numerous antislavery petitions coming to Congress were to be "laid upon the table, and that no further action whatever shall be had thereon." This fight over the right of petition became one of the chief elements in alienating Northern sympathies from the South. Although Adams was not an Abolitionist, his resistance to the Southern gag rule on the discussion of slavery kept the subject a sore one, and aided the growth of abolitionist sentiment. So he was soon well hated by the Southerners, and so, in 1842, he came to be engaged in the great debate that was probably the high point of his career.

On January 25, 1842, Adams rose and presented a petition from Haverhill, Massachusetts, urging Congress to take action "peaceably to dissolve the Union." This petition did not directly mention slavery, though of course it was aimed at the South. It did not technically come under the gag rule, and Adams moved that it be referred to a committee with instructions to prepare an answer showing why the request ought *not* to be granted.

The Southerners thought they saw a chance to destroy their enemy. Forty members held a caucus that night and drafted a resolution of censure. The resolution stated that to present a proposal for breaking up the Union was an insult to the House and involved the crime of high treason. It said that Adams might justly be expelled, but that the House in its mercy would "only inflict upon him their severest censure . . . for the rest, they turn it over to his own conscience and the indignation of all true American citizens." Such a resolution, if passed, would have necessitated his resignation.

The attack was led by Thomas F. Marshall of Kentucky, nephew of the late Chief Justice, and the greatest of the Southern orators. He was backed by Henry Wise and Thomas W. Gilmer of Virginia. These men were in the prime of life and well equipped to stand the physical strain of a long fight with no holds barred. Adams was seventy-four years old, with rheumy eyes, a feeble frame, and hands shaking with palsy, but he was spoiling for a fight.

An eyewitness account of that classic battle has been left to us by a member who had a seat close to Adams in the House—Congressman Richard W. Thompson, of Indiana. When Adams heard the resolution, Thompson reports, "In so far as he exhibited the least emotion it seemed to indicate satisfaction, because he could see at a glance that he would be afforded a fit opportunity . . . to leave such a history of his life as would thoroughly vindicate his loyalty to the Union."

Marshall opened for the resolution in "a speech of great ability— exhibiting occasional touches of magnificent eloquence." He accused Adams of inviting the members of the House to commit high treason. Adams replied in a speech defending the right of petition and defying his enemies. He went at Marshall without gloves: "It is not for the gentleman from Kentucky, or his puny mind, to define what high treason is, and confound it with what I have done." His voice, Thompson says, was "tremulous with emotion, yet sharp, fierce, and piercing."

Wise joined the attack with an impassioned speech. Among other things, he accused Adams of treachery in deserting his father's "English" party after 1800 and going over to the "French" party. "When Wise, alluding to the anti-slavery sentiment . . . said, in his emphatic tones—'the magazine is under the walls, and the torch of the incendiary may level the beautiful edifice in the dust,' the scene became such as no language at my command can describe."

The next day Wise spoke for two hours with unabated violence. But "he changed the issue to a personal one . . . and thus, unwittingly, threw himself into the lion's mouth." He closed with a sarcastic lament that the once illustrious Adams had fallen so low as to attempt "to excite a spirit of disunion throughout the land. . . The gentleman is politically dead; dead as Burr—dead as Arnold. The people will look upon him with wonder, will shudder, and retire."

Adams in reply recalled that a few years earlier Wise had been threatened with censure by the House on a charge of murder for his part in a fatal duel, at which time Adams had opposed legislative action, in the absence of a verdict from a regular court. "It is very possible," he said, "that *I* saved this bloodstained man from the censure of the House . . . although his hands were reeking with the blood of murder." Thompson reports that "Wise felt the wound keenly and winced under it." Adams sat down "perfectly composed and unconcerned," for he had the measure of his opponents.

Day after day the battle raged back and forth. Threats of assassination came to Adams in the mail, but as the fight went on petitions from the North poured in protesting against the attack on the old champion. The slaveholders began to see that they had made a mistake, and Adams had not yet unlimbered his heavy artillery. Gilmer spoke for two days, February 2 and 3, but Thompson reports that he "fell below the demands of the occasion." Finally Adams replied, in a speech that began on February 3, and lasted through Friday and Saturday, February 4 and 5.

"It soon became apparent," says Thompson, "that he had reached a point where he could not only fling his thunderbolts with deadly effect, but thoroughly and triumphantly vindicate his whole life.

And he did this so effectively, and with such a surprising exhibition of power, that his prosecutors . . . were dwarfed into pygmies before him. They appeared like children in the grasp of a strong man.

"So anxious were all to hear every word that the stillness was broken only by his peculiar and somewhat shrieking voice. Every eye was fixed upon the extraordinary old man as tremblingly he uttered his words of fiery eloquence and scathing sarcasm. The members gathered around him so closely that they could observe every expression of his face. Lord Morpath, of the British Parliament, had a seat upon the floor nearby, and gave marked exhibition of both wonder and admiration. . . . When he referred to his services at the Russian court, it was impossible to restrain the outburst of applause." For Adams told these men of 1842 how he alone had stood up for the return to their owners of neutral vessels seized by Russia at the demand of the victorious Napoleon, when no other minister at St. Petersburg dared to speak up, whereby he stimulated a Russian policy that led to Napoleon's invasion and catastrophic retreat.

Saturday night, when he went home, he wrote in his diary, "I saw my cause was gained, and Marshall was sprawling in his own compost. I came home scarcely able to crawl up to my chamber, but with the sound of 'Io triumphe' ringing in my ear."

On Sunday, he reports that he attended St. John's Church, and "My attention involuntarily wandered." And the entry for Monday records that he had prepared an outline of further speeches "which would have occupied at least a week. But I saw on Saturday that the House was tired of the whole subject." His enemies had had enough and his friends knew he was the victor.

On Monday morning, as Thompson tells the story, the old man stood up "and calmly surveyed the scene for a few moments, without uttering a word. . . . With a piercing glance, first at Marshall, then at Gilmer, and last at Wise,—he calmly and slowly said: 'I am ready to go on if necessary, but for myself I am satisfied.'" After a short silence, someone moved to table the resolution of censure, and it was tabled. "Adams, among them all, was the only one apparently unmoved. . . . He sat for a little while like a statue," and then rose and presented a batch of two hundred more petitions. "Not a word was spoken except by himself; and there he stood,—that wonderful man, weak from age and physical infirmity, but strong as a giant in the invincibility of his courage—as completely master of the battlefield as the iron-duke of England was at Waterloo."

It was in this same year of 1842 that Tennyson published *Ulysses*. Adams was undoubtedly familiar with the poem before the year was out; he could hardly have missed the comforting pertinence of the last two lines:

> *Made weak by time and fate but strong in will*
> *To strive, to seek, to find, and not to yield.*

Three years later, on December 3, 1845, the old fighter recorded another victory in his diary. After long years of struggle the House, on his motion, had rescinded the gag rule. He wrote: "Blessed, forever blessed, be the name of God!"

Less than three more years, Mr. Adams rose from his seat in the House and toppled in a stroke that was his death.

The room in the Capitol where the House sat in Adams's time is now Statuary Hall. In the southwest part of the floor, set into the marble, you may see a small bronze plate with no inscription on it. Here is the place where John Quincy Adams had his seat, and where after a life of disappointment, in his old age he fought his great battles and knew himself triumphant, and where at the last he fell at his post of duty.

CHAPTER V

KING ANDREW THE FIRST

One day in August, 1776, word went around Waxhaw district in upland South Carolina that the mail was in from Charleston with the Philadelphia newspapers. The people gathered from miles around to hear the news. Nine-year-old Andy Jackson, who had been to school and could read a paper without stumbling, was delegated to read aloud to the assembled company. What he read that day was the news of July 4, the *Unanimous Declaration of the Thirteen United States of America,* beginning: "When in the course of human events. . . ."

By the time Andrew was thirteen the war had come to the Carolinas and he was enlisted in the Revolutionary forces as a mounted orderly. In 1781 he and his brother were surprised and taken prisoners. Then it was that a British officer made a costly error in public relations. He ordered Andrew Jackson to clean his boots, and when the boy refused cut him on the head with his sword. From that cut the future victor of New Orleans got a white scar that he did not forget.

In 1795 we find Jackson in Tennessee, twenty-eight years old, and just back from a business trip to Philadelphia, telling his friends that Washington ought to be impeached for supporting the Jay Treaty, which in his opinion was a "Daring infringement of our Constitutional rights." Jackson favored war with England. The following year he was back in Philadelphia as a Congressman, and was noticed by Albert Gallatin as a tall, lanky backwoodsman with his queue tied in an eelskin. At the time when twelve irreconcilable Congressmen voted against giving a courteous reply to President Washington's final Message, Congressman Jackson was one of the twelve. In 1797 he appeared again briefly in the Capital, having been elected Senator from Tennessee. In the Senate his chief recorded accomplishment was to create an unfavorable impression on Vice President Jefferson, who remembered him as a firebrand with an uncontrollable temper. He resigned in 1798.

A glimpse of how Jackson's enemies in Tennessee regarded him at about this time is provided by a letter in the Washington *Federalist* in 1800:

"The mania of poor Jackson has so far increased of late that there has been a union of all parties to get rid of him by sending him back to Congress.

"With pistols always in his hand, or in his pockets, and a most ferocious phiz, he is either avoided or *sent to coventry* on all occasions. . . . What you will do with him I know not, unless somebody among you will resent one of his insults and challenges *which you will be sure to meet,* and thus rid the unfortunate man of an existence which has become as much a burthen to him as to his associates."

Actually, the unruly Andrew Jackson was prospering in the wild western state of Tennessee. He made money in land and became a cotton planter on his "Hermitage" estate. In 1798 he was elected a superior judge, and in 1802 he won the elective office of Major General of the Tennessee Militia. In 1812 he was called into active service against the marauding Creek Indians, and finally he was the victor over the British in the Battle of New Orleans. So he was already a national hero long before he became President.

The full-scale punishment customarily meted out to Presidents began to reach Jackson in the campaign of 1828. There were two main lines of attack—one against his military career, another against the reputation of Mrs. Jackson.

As early as July, 1827, the situation had become so unpleasant that a pro-Jackson journalist, pretending, tongue-in-cheek, to be an Adams partisan named "Tobias Holdfast," addressed his *Dear Uncle Toby* as follows:

"Why does not Binns came out with some new forgery? A certificate signed by somebody, no matter who, setting forth that Jackson is a coward, and skulked when the British attacked his lines at New Orleans, would be admirable. The opposition would not notice it, and just before the election comes on we can republish the certificate, and say that the charge of cowardice was publicly made against him sixteen months ago and has never been contradicted. The lies which have been invented and published concerning Mrs. Jackson were excellent, and have produced a wonderful effect in this part of the country. Mrs. Charles King, who is the highest authority on such subjects, has decalred that Mrs. Jackson should not be placed at the head of 'good society.' "

The Adams faction attacked Jackson's career in a voluminous pamphlet with the long-winded name *A Brief Inquiry into Some of the Objections Urged Against the Election of Andrew Jackson*:

"Many powerful and alarming objections have been raised against the propriety of intrusting a mere soldier with the control of the nation as its Chief Magistrate—an office requiring peculiar talents, and long experience, prudence, and wisdom. Some of these objections it is the object of these pages to unfold and support. . . . It has not been attempted to even refer to most or all that has been objected to the character of General Jackson, showing his utter incapacity to fill the office of President with honour and safety to the country. . . . Let us regard as unwise and perilous . . . to attempt to put at the head of government, a man who was never known to govern himself, and whose whole career, in private life, has been, until a few years, a scene of disgraceful riot and murderous outrage, and whose public ministrations have been at the sacrifice of law and the constitution, which he has never failed to trample under foot, when they opposed any barrier to the gratification of his vehement and arbitrary will."

The pamphlet gives details of a gunfight between Jackson and Thomas Hart Benton, in which no one was killed, though Jackson got a bullet in his arm that stayed with him for nearly twenty years. Later the two antagonists met as Senators and became fast friends. The pamphlet cited this reconciliation as a point against Jackson, who was also accused of being an implacable hater: "He has, to promote his own views, taken to his bosom a man long his deadliest enemy, and whose life he once murderously attempted."

An account is given of the death of Charles Dickinson in a duel with Jackson arising out of the maligning of Mrs. Jackson by Dickinson. Jackson is also accused of arbitrarily maintaining martial law in New Orleans after the news of peace had arrived, and imprisoning a judge who had issued a habeas corpus on behalf of a member of the legislature whom Jackson had locked up. (It was true that the news of peace had arrived, but it came from the defeated British forces, and Jackson, fearing treachery, kept a tight hand until he got confirmation from Washington.)

BORN TO COMMAND

OF VETO MEMORY

HAD I BEEN CONSULTED

VETO

CONSTITUTION
of the
UNITED STATES
of America

Internal Improvements Bank

KING ANDREW THE FIRST.

To those who stood to lose most by Andrew Jackson's policies, he was a despot who was neither pure nor simple—as is plainly suggested by this caricature.

Some Account of some of the Bloody Deeds
OF
GENERAL JACKSON.

Jacob Webb   David Morrow   John Harris   Henry Lewis   David Hunt   Edward Lindsay

THOMAS HART BENTON, Lieut. Col. 39th Infantry.

Widely distributed in the campaign against Jackson, this notorious Coffin Handbill was highly effective in creating the impression that he had ordered the execution of disobedient members of the Tennessee Militia without any regard to extenuating circumstances. "His crown of laurels had not yet withered," declared the handbill, "when blood, the life's blood of his countrymen, of his fellow soldiers, flowed plentifully at his orders."

Finally, the pamphlet described the execution of six militiamen for "desertion" at the end of their three-months term of duty in face of Jackson's orders to serve for a six-month stretch.

The charge of bloodthirstiness was emphasized by the issuance of the famous "Coffin Hand-Bill" and by a pamphlet called *Official Record from the War Department.* This last was a garbled version of the court-martial records, made up to look official, and labeled "Ordered to be Printed by the Congress." When distributed under the franks of pro-Adams Congressmen, it could well deceive the voters.

The Jackson Committee of Correspondence in Baltimore published a 15-page defense of Jackson on the score of the executions, the most telling charge against him. This pamphlet quoted the acting Adjutant at the time of the desertions, as saying that all the officers of the regulars and of the militia who were with Jackson at the time approved his stern discipline because the British were nearby and threatening to attack, and the news of peace had not arrived. The Adjutant asserted that "the example had the most salutary effect, as it prevented another mutiny."

Another defender of Jackson, writing in the *Maryland Gazette,* offered a long list of his services to the country, including his discovery of the treasonable designs of Aaron Burr, protection of the frontier settlements from Indian raids, and preserving New Orleans from pillage and destruction. The writer taunted Clay and Adams with having never risked their lives in any military service, and at the end burst out poetically with the rallying cry:

Freemen! cheer the HICKORY TREE
In Storms its boughs Protected YE!

The most inhuman aspect of the campaign was the attack of the Adams forces against the reputation of Mrs. Jackson.

The story of Rachel Jackson is one of romance, misfortune, and lifelong loyalty. In the autumn of 1788, when 21-year-old Andrew Jackson reached Tennessee, he found lodging with a wealthy widow, Mrs. John Donelson, whose daughter had married a bounder named Lewis Robards. When life with Robards became impossible for Rachel, Jackson helped her escape to friends in Natchez, while Robards went to Richmond (Tennessee was then part of Virginia)

to ask the Legislature for a divorce. Robards on his return let it
be understood that he had divorced Rachel, and she promptly married
Andrew Jackson. Two years later Robards disclosed that there had
been no divorce, and he obtained one against Mrs. Jackson on grounds
of adultery. The Jacksons were then remarried. At no time, until
Robards filed his case in court, had they or any of their friends ever
doubted that the divorce and the first marriage were real. Although
their friends gave them nothing but sympathy and understanding,
there were enemies, especially as Jackson could not keep out of public
life, and their early mischance colored both their lives from then on.
Jackson personally suppressed gossip in his own state by the fear of
death, and this sacred duty accounted for much of his violence as
long as Rachel lived.

Rachel Jackson's appearance in the last summer of her life was
described by the daughter of one of Jackson's officers, who visited
the Hermitage in 1828. Years later this lady wrote, "My personal
knowledge of the Gen. and Mrs. Jackson dates back to the time when
I was not yet nine years old, the summer preceding his first election. . . .
Picture to yourself a military-looking man, above the ordinary height,
dressed plainly, but with great neatness; dignified and grave. . . . Side
by side with him stands a coarse-looking stout, little old woman,
whom you might easily mistake for his washerwoman, were it not
for the marked attention he pays her, and the love and admiration
she manifests for him. Her eyes are bright, and express great kindness
of heart. . . . I have heard my mother say that she could imagine
that in her early youth, at the time the Gen. yielded to her fascinations,
she may have been a bright, sparkling brunette; perhaps may even
have passed for a beauty. . . . The Gen. always treated her as
if she were his pride and glory, and words can faintly describe her
devotion to him. I well recollect to what disadvantage Mrs. Jackson
appeared . . . and I recall very distinctly how the ladies of the
Jackson party hovered near her at all times apparently to save her
from saying or doing any thing which might do discredit to their
idol."

Two years before the election of 1828 Jackson had already detected
signs of an attack on Rachel as well as on himself personally. He
wrote to his friend Sam Houston in December, 1826: "I am determined

to unmask such part of the Executive Council, as has entered into the combination to slander and revile me; and I trust, in due time to effect it, and lay the perfidy, meaness, and wickedness of Clay, naked before the American people. I have lately got an intimation of some of his secret movements, which, if I can reach with possitive and responsible proof, I will wield to his political, and perhaps, to his actual destruction. he is certainly the bases, meanest, scoundrel, that ever disgraced the image of god—nothing too mean or low for him to condescend to, *secretely,* to carry his cowardly and base purpose of slander into effect; even the aged and virtuous female, is not safe from his secrete combination of base slander—but *enough, you know me* I will curb my feelings until *it becomes proper* to act, when retributive *Justice will visit him and his pander heads.*"

Jackson told another friend: "The whole object of the coalition is to calumniate me, cart loads of coffin hand-bills, forgeries, and pamphlets of the most base calumnies are circulated by the franking privilege of Members of Congress, and Mr. Clay, even. Mrs. Jackson is not spared, and my pious Mother, nearly fifty years in the tomb, and who, from her cradle to her death, had not a speck upon her character, has been dragged forth by Hammond and held to public scorn as a prostitute who intermarried with a Negro, and my eldest brother sold as a slave in Carolina. . . . I am branded with every crime, and Doctor McNary, Col. Erwin, Anderson and Williams are associated for this purpose. I have for some days known that they were the issuers of old slanders that appeared abroad, but it is only lately that they have been unearthed, and was not my hands tied, and my mouth closed, I would have soon put an end to their slanders. This they know, but suppose when the elections over all things will die away. —*Not So,* I look forward to the first of Decb. next with much anxiety. The day of retribution must come. I am charged with Burr's Conspiracy and every other crime. Was Anderson and McNary as clear of purjury as I was of the Burr Conspiracy, it would be a pleasant thing for their conscience."

Jackson was mistaken about his vengeance. His overwhelming victory in the election wiped out the importance of the gentlemen whom he had looked forward to shooting in person. This was part of the growing up that the hero had to do after he was elected President of the United States.

Meanwhile Rachel in her quiet life at the Hermitage was protected from the knowledge that her name was being bandied about all over the country. But as early as July, 1827, she was being defended in a New York paper by a "Member of the Presbyterian Church," who testified to her piety and asserted that as a possible First Lady she was fully "entitled to be placed at the head of the virtuous female society." Most of the direct attacks on Rachel were in the form of privately printed material, the writers of which might hope to escape legal or personal reprisals by the hard-hitting General.

As the 1828 campaign proceeded it grew steadily dirtier on both sides. The partisans of Mr. Adams had no such fastidious scruples as their leader. They proclaimed that Jackson was a crude brawler, gambler, cock-fighter, and murderer, as well as an adulterer—all with enough color of truth to make the accusations sting, for the frontier life was no pink tea, and Jackson's blameless marriage had been called adulterous in a successful suit in court.

Jackson's friends did not hesitate to hit back with such ammunition as they could lay hands on. Adams was accused of personal stinginess and public extravagance, as well as of dealing corruptly with the "shyster" Henry Clay. Like his father, he was called an aristocrat who despised the common people.

In the unbridled fury of the contest, not only was the sensitive Adams cruelly mauled; even the outwardly tough old General was mercilessly battered through the unceasing attacks on Rachel, which he had to endure without letting her suspect what was being said. And as it turned out, the campaign was only the beginning of his ordeal.

When November came Jackson was triumphantly elected, but the fates had prepared for him and his lady a final, crushing blow. As to just how Rachel met her death, there are different stories. It is certain that much against her will she started to prepare for Washington with all its peril of hostile tongues. She said she "would rather be a doorkeeper in the house of God than to live in that palace at Washington." But finally she went off to Nashville to shop for clothes. According to one story, she grew tired and stepped into the private office of one of her relatives, a newspaper editor, to rest until time for her carriage to come. There she happened upon a pamphlet that Jackson's friends had published in her defense, meeting and denying the charges against her from which she had been carefully shielded in the sanctuary of the Hermitage. An hour later she was found crouching in a corner weeping and hysterical. On the way home she stopped to bathe her eyes in a creek in the hope that the General would not notice anything wrong, but he did.

A few days later Rachel had a heart attack, and on December 23 she died. She was buried in the garden of the Hermitage. Her tombstone calls her "a being so gentle and so virtuous, slander might wound, but could not dishonor."

The New York *American* struck a parting blow at the dead in an editorial saying: "We are forcibly reminded of the concluding passage of Tacitus' life of Agricola. With a little change it seems no less applicable to the deceased wife of the President elect: Illa vero felix, non tam claritate vitae, quam opportunitate mortis." This supposed quotation the editor translated: "She was, indeed, a fortunate woman, but not so much so on account of the blessings or splendour of life she enjoyed, as for the lucky death she met with, all in good time."

To which a correspondent replied that having looked up his Tacitus, he found that the editor had gratuitously inserted the disparaging phrase denying the splendour of her life. He continued, "I am at a loss for adequate terms to express the detestation and abhorrence with which I shudder at such cold blooded and inveterate malignity."

Although Jackson himself was for a time prostrated with grief and horror, his followers were of course elated over his election. For example, a writer for the New York *Courier and Inquirer* who was destined to become better known in future years, James Gordon Bennett, reviewed the ineffective efforts of the Adams faction with merciless taunts:

"The impotency of the attacks which have been made upon General Jackson during the last three years, by the Adams party, reminds us of an anecdote: 'Mother,' bawled out a great two-fisted girl one day, 'my toe. itches.' 'Well, scratch it then.' 'I have, but it won't *stay* scratched!' . . .

" 'Mr. Clay, Mr. Clay,' bawls out Alderman Binns, 'the old farmer's a-coming, a-coming.' 'Well, then,' says Harry, 'Coffin-hand-bill him.' 'I have,' says Binns, 'but he won't stay coffin-hand-billed.' 'Mr.

Clay, Mr. Clay,' says Charles Hammond, 'Jackson is coming.' 'Well,' says Clay, 'prove him an adulterer and a negro-trader.' 'I have,' says Charles, 'but he won't stay an adulterer or a negro-trader.' 'Mr. Clay, Mr. Clay,' bawls out the full Adams slandering chorus, 'we have called Jackson a murderer, an adulterer, a traitor, an ignoramus, a fool, a crook-back, a pretender, and so forth; but he won't *stay* any of these names.' 'He won't,' says Clay, 'Why, then, I sha'n't *stay* at Washington, that's all!' "

For Jackson himself it was a bitter triumph. Heartbroken and unsure of what he intended to do, he came to Washington and set up headquarters, where he was besieged by office seekers. He naturally leaned on a small group of his close friends from home, including Senator John Henry Eaton.

Jackson's first Cabinet was formed chiefly under the influence of Van Buren and of Vice President Calhoun. Van Buren became Secretary of State, and Calhoun placed his friends in the Treasury, Navy, and Justice Departments. In order to have one close friend of his own in the Cabinet, Jackson appointed Eaton Secretary of War. Except for Van Buren, the people chosen were generally weak, and trouble was guaranteed by the rivalry of Van Buren and Calhoun for the succession.

Jackson was bitterly attacked then and since for introducing the "spoils system." Civil Service replacements were, to be sure, more numerous under his rule than under his predecessors, though less so than in later administrations. There were 612 presidential officers, of whom 252 were removed. Out of more than 8,000 postmasters and their assistants about 600 were removed. Many removals were for good cause: frauds amounting to $280,000, for example, were found in the Treasury Department. Many civil servants were chronic bankrupts, and Jackson ordered all such dismissed. Another reason for changes was that Adams had been mercifully loath to replace anyone who was incapable of finding another position. Since there was no pension system many superannuated employees had been kept on the payroll out of charity. Discharging them was a cruel job, but the Jackson wing of the party was committed to economy and it had to be done.

Some of the most prominent newspaper editors who had supported Jackson were appointed to public office or attached to the intimate group that came to be called the "Kitchen Cabinet." This action raised a storm, since editors were universally regarded as low characters. One of these was Isaac Hill, of New Hampshire, whose paper had been especially violent against Jackson's enemies. His nomination was rejected by the Senate; but Jackson persuaded one of the New Hampshire Senators to resign (later to become Secretary of the Navy), and Hill came back to Washington as Senator-elect.

President Jackson's first months in office were devoted mainly to the troubles of Senator Eaton and his wife the famous Peggy O'Neal.

Margaret O'Neal was born in 1799. Her father kept a hotel, where many members of Congress boarded; the Jacksons had stayed there when he was in the Senate, and so had Senator Eaton. Margaret was married to a U.S. Navy purser named Timberlake. Mrs. Jackson was fond of young Mrs. Timberlake, which in itself was enough to convince the General that the gossip about her was as unfounded and malicious as that about Rachel. In 1828 Timberlake died at sea, and on January 1, 1829, Margaret married Eaton. Tongues immediately started to wag, for Eaton had lived at the hotel for considerable periods while Timberlake was at sea.

Mrs. Margaret Bayard Smith, the talented writer on Washington social life in her day, wrote to her sister about the other Margaret's wedding, in no charitable spirit:

"Tonight Gen'l Eaton, the bosom friend and almost adopted son of Gen'l Jackson, is to be married to a lady whose reputation, her previous connection with him both before and after her husband's death, has totally destroyed. . . . She has never been admitted into good society, is very handsome and of not an inspiring character and violent temper. She is, it is said, irresistible and carries whatever point she sets her mind on. The General's personal and political friends are very much distressed about it: his enemies laugh and divert themselves with the idea of what a suitable lady in waiting Mrs. Eaton will make to Mrs. Jackson and repeat the old adage, 'birds of a feather will flock together.' " (Mrs. Smith had not yet learned of Mrs. Jackson's death.)

Jackson's friends were indeed disturbed; one of them, Congressman C. C. Cambreleng, wrote to Martin Van Buren: "Poor Eaton is to be married tonight to Mrs. T---! There is a vulgar saying of some vulgar man, I believe Swift, on such unions—about using a certain household - - - and then putting it on one's head."

When Eaton was appointed Secretary of War in the new Cabinet, and Margaret acquired the protocol rights of a Cabinet lady, the revolt broke out. The other Cabinet ladies refused to call on Mrs. Eaton, and even Mrs. Andrew Jackson Donelson, the President's niece, who was his White House hostess, was barely civil to her.

Jackson believed the storm was blown up by the machinations of Clay, and he soon came to suspect Calhoun of being also involved. Margaret in her autobiography, written after she was seventy years old, says that in her opinion "Calhoun and his friends were at the bottom of the whole business." One Cabinet member who had no wife or daughters to restrain him was Martin Van Buren. He accepted the President's strong attachment to the Eatons and his violent defence of their innocence, and called assidously upon them when no man with womenfolk dared to go. This courtesy did not hurt his standing with the President. As James Parton says in his *Life of Andrew Jackson*, Van Buren was bright enough to see that a card in Mrs. Eaton's card basket was not unlikely to be a winning card.

As for Jackson, he spent the first six months of his Presidency in hardly any other activity but the effort to disprove the stories about Margaret Eaton. His secret and confidential writings devoted to this effort, nearly all in his own handwriting, amount to some 45,000 words, enough to fill over 100 pages of this book. As his friends understood, what Jackson was really doing was in defense of Rachel's memory, for he thought of the two cases as similar. In championing Margaret he was working off his blazing wrath against those who had attacked and finally killed his wife, especially Clay and Calhoun. In fact, the evidence collected by the President, together with Mrs. Eaton's autobiography, may be said to make a not unimpressive case for her, and for her illustrious champion.

In the autumn of 1829 the battle for Mrs. Eaton struck home to the President through the loss of his niece and her husband from his household, where they had been his invaluable helpers. Mrs. Donelson stubbornly refused to call on Mrs. Eaton, and Jackson in his obsession at last demanded that she choose one side or the other. She chose to go home to Tennessee, and her husband went with her, leaving her uncle deeply hurt and lonely, feeling that even

"Jackson is to be President, and you will be hanged" was the original caption accompanying this campaign cartoon of 1828. Designed to convey the impression that Jackson was personally responsible for summary execution of Army deserters during the War of 1812, this cartoon left no doubt as to how he might treat his political enemies if he were elected.

Characteristic of other attacks on Andrew Jackson, this cartoon of the 1840's left little to the imagination. For openly—too openly for those who preferred traditional customs—rewarding his supporters with political posts, Jackson was pilloried repeatedly throughout his administration.

his family had deserted him, "falling," as he said, "into the trap of the great intriguer, Mr. Calhoun."

All during 1830 there was social war in Washington. Jackson believed the Cabinet ladies were conspiring to get Mrs. Eaton ostracized—as of course they were—and he believed that Calhoun and his friends were behind it, as they may well have been. Probably the most important effect of Margaret Eaton's impact on Andrew Jackson's life, aside from giving him an outlet for his emotions while he gradually recovered from the shock of Rachel's cruel death, was to alienate him from Calhoun. For the time was approaching when he would have to act as President of the United States in defense of the Union, and Calhoun was fated to be his chief antagonist.

In May, 1830, friends of Van Buren considered that Jackson was prepared to accept evidence, which they had long been saving, that would break the last ties between him and Calhoun. They produced a letter written by Crawford saying that in 1818 in the Cabinet arguments over Jackson's Florida raid it was not he but Calhoun who had wanted Jackson to be punished. Calhoun obtained letters from Monroe and all the other Cabinet members of that time denying the charge; and he prepared a defence and counterattack on Van Buren, which he published in the middle of February, 1831. But it was much too late for a reconciliation. For on April 13, 1830, there had been an unequivocal incident at a Jefferson dinner that forecast the struggle over nullification in which Calhoun would be involved against the President.

Before this dinner Jackson was warned that the Southerners had arranged a series of toasts by which those present would find themselves committed to the old Jeffersonian doctrine that a state could nullify a Federal law by declaring it unconstitutional. Jackson prepared to spike the Southerners' guns. When the time came for him to offer a toast he rose, and looking directly at Calhoun he gave: "Our Union: it must be preserved." As Isaac Hill reported, "A proclamation of martial law in South Carolina and an order to arrest Calhoun where he sat could not have come with more blinding, staggering force." The President had made his position clear, though the need to act would not come until later. For the time being, nullification was once more driven underground.

Van Buren could see that with Calhoun men in the Cabinet, and with the Eatons disturbing the social and political scene, the Administration was in a weak position, and that it was time to reorganize the Cabinet. Finally in 1831 he persuaded Jackson to let him resign, which he did in such a way that the others had to follow. The Adams partisans greeted the apparent collapse of the Government with ill-timed mirth. There was even a cartoon showing "The Rats leaving the Falling House." They were wrong. The house was not falling but being cleared of rats and redecorated.

The new Cabinet was free of Calhoun men as well as of Secretary Eaton and his controversial wife. Van Buren was named Minister to London in a recess appointment and had already made himself popular there when in a fit of political folly the Calhoun faction in the Senate managed to block his confirmation. He came home to a triumphant reception when he arrived in New York in June, 1832, and was easily nominated for the Vice Presidency with every prospect of becoming President in 1837 if not sooner.

With a new Cabinet, Jackson was in a position to take action on the nullification threat as soon as it should come to a head, and meanwhile to begin moving toward the principal task of his administration, the destruction of the mighty Bank of the United States. These two objectives had been growing plainer to him since he entered the White House. Like Franklin Roosevelt, Woodrow Wilson, and Abraham Lincoln, Andrew Jackson came into the Presidency with little to indicate a capacity for greatness; he had greatness thrust upon him by the challenge of his times. The underlying quality that more than anything else gave Jackson the power to meet the challenge was his instinctive affinity with the people. As Van Buren said of him, "They were his blood relations—the only blood relations he had." He was born to be a folk hero, who would rise to leadership when the people called him to lead them into battle.

The battle for the people took the form of a war against the Bank.

The detailed story of the struggle with the Bank is told in the great biographies and historical studies such as Schlesinger's *Age of Jackson.* Schlesinger recommends C. B. Swisher's biography of Roger B. Taney as giving the best account of this struggle. Here only the briefest outline will serve as background for the growth of the legend of King Andrew, the merciless tyrant.

The Bank of the United States had a charter from Congress that was due to lapse or be renewed in 1836. The Bank, located in Philadelphia and headed by Nicholas Biddle, could issue paper money and could control local banks by its power to allow or withhold credit. This feudal banking system ruled the business world, and Biddle was King of the Bank. The Government had five of the Bank's twenty-five directors, but Biddle did not allow them to direct. He was the Bank's absolute ruler.

In the same way, as the struggle soon demonstrated, Andrew Jackson had absolute power over the one hold that the Government had on the Bank. The Government's funds were required by law to be deposited in the Bank, except that the Secretary of the Treasury could place them elsewhere, provided he explained his action to Congress. After dismissing two reluctant Secretaries of the Treasury, Jackson got the fact clearly established that when he said to withdraw the funds they were to be withdrawn. In wielding the Government's financial power he and he alone was King.

The "people" who were restive under the rule of the Bank and looked to Jackson to lead them out of bondage believed in two opposite theories, known as "soft money" and "hard money."

In general the West, being a debtor area, favored soft money. The Westerners wanted their own local banks with the uncontrolled issue of paper money. They readily accepted the accompanying risks of inflation, since inflation would be more hurtful to creditors than to debtors. They resented Biddle's power to control their finances from Philadelphia by allowing or withdrawing credit at will, especially since Biddle had no sympathy for their easy-money sentiments.

Among wage earners in the East, on the other hand, there was a growing suspicion that the right of banks to create money out of paper and ink and lend it out at interest was an imposition on workers who had to earn their money. An important labor committee, advised by the leading liberal economist William M. Gouge and other intellectuals, came out strongly against banks, and said, "if the present system of banking and paper money be extended and perpetuated, the great body of the working people must give over all hopes of ever acquiring any property." This was the "hard money" theory.

Jackson, though a Westerner, was a hard-money man, and so was his former antagonist and now powerful ally in the Senate, Thomas Hart Benton of Missouri. Among Jackson's fervent admirers was Father Jeremiah O'Callaghan, the fanatic priest who embarassed his own Bishops by his vigorous writing and preaching against the ancient sin of usury and against all banks.

In the struggle over the Bank, the theoretically incompatible easy-money and hard-money advocates united under Jackson against the arbitrary power of Biddle, though for different reasons. Thus Jackson came to represent more fully than Jefferson had ever done, not only the country folk but also the growing body of city labor.

In his first two Messages Jackson had mentioned that he doubted if the Bank were Constitutional or wise, but this was at first regarded merely as his personal view, with no fire back of it. War on the Bank was declared by Senator Benton early in 1831, in a speech attacking that institution as a monopoly using its powers to make the rich richer and the poor poorer.

On the side of the Bank were such conservatives as Clay and Webster in the Senate, and John Quincy Adams in the House. When the National Republicans nominated Clay as their candidate for President in the 1832 election, they chose John Sergeant, one of Biddle's lawyers, as his running mate.

On January 2, 1832, petitions for rechartering the Bank were presented to Congress, and Biddle sent a team of high-powered lobbyists to Washington. The issues had not yet been firmly drawn; and after a hard winter's work the rechartering bills passed the Senate in June and the House in July. Biddle threw a riotous party at his lodgings, but the President was still to be heard from.

Jackson had been biding his time, but he had had long talks with Benton and other advisers, and when the bill arrived at the White House he was ready for war. He told Van Buren, "The bank, Mr. Van Buren, is trying to kill me, *but I will kill it!*" For a week the White House group worked night and day, with the powerful legal help of the Attorney General, Roger B. Taney, later to be Chief Justice. When the veto message came out on July 10 it electrified the country. Jackson had declared war on the Bank, on behalf of the people of the United States. He had taken on the feudal lord of the business system, and there would be no quarter.

The veto message avoided emphasis on hard money, but stressed the cause of "the humble members of society" against "the rich and powerful." The rich and powerful whom Jackson had defied were not slow in hitting back.

Nicholas Biddle told Clay, "It has all the fury of a chained panther, biting the bars of his cage. It is really a manifesto of anarchy." He could not have been more wrong. The panther was neither chained nor caged. Meanwhile Webster in the Senate charged with considerable justice that the message "seeks to influence the poor against the rich. It wantonly attacks whole classes of the people, for the purpose of turning against them the prejudices and resentments of other classes." As Webster was getting a regular retainer from Biddle, he was naturally concerned. The conservative Boston *Advertiser* moaned, "For the first time, perhaps, in the history of civilized communities, the Chief Magistrate of a great nation . . . is found . . . endeavoring to stir up the poor against the rich." Most of the newspapers felt obliged to support the Bank, and so of course did its liege vassals the business men, not merely because disloyalty was dangerous, but because most of them sincerely believed that Biddle was their leader and protector against the mob.

Young Alexis de Tocqueville, taking his opinions from the respectable lawyers and business men whom he met, wrote that "since landing in America I have practically acquired proof that all the enlightened classes are opposed to General Jackson." Fortunately the country-wide clamor did not seriously point toward civil war. Popular feeling was able to find a healthy outlet, for it was an election year and the people could express themselves peaceably. The result: Jackson 219 electoral votes, Clay 49, scattering 18. The conservatives felt as bitter as their descendants were going to feel in 1936.

The Boston *Courier* offered a bit of hope in the gloom, noting that the Electoral College had still to act: "Yet there is one comfort left: God has promised that the days of the wicked shall be short; the wicked is old and feeble, and he may die before he can be elected. It is the duty of every good Christian to pray to our Maker to have pity on us."

After Jackson's reelection there was an interlude in the Bank war while he put down the revolt of South Carolina and incidentally strengthened his strategic position in the nation.

South Carolina felt aggrieved by the tariff law. Calhoun had been elected to represent South Carolina in the Senate, and he had come to be the leader of the nullification movement. On November 24 the State Legislature declared the tariff laws of 1828 and 1832 void within the state after Febuary 1, 1833. To this action Jackson replied on December 10 with a *Proclamation on Nullification* which Marquis James calls "the greatest state paper of the spacious Jacksonian epoch and one of the greatest to bear the name of an American President."

Jackson argued: "I consider, then, the power to annul a law of the United States, assumed by one State, incompatible with the existence of the Union. . . . To say that any State may at pleasure secede from the Union is to say that the United States is not a nation. . . . I have no discretionary power on the subject. . . . Disunion by armed force is treason . . . [Your] first magistrate cannot, if he would, avoid the performance of his duty."

It is recorded that in Illinois a young lawyer named Abraham Lincoln, just back from service in the Black Hawk War, pored over this proclamation, and that years later he remembered to read it over again in preparation for his own inauguration as President.

Jackson's only concession was a bill in Congress reducing the tariff and thus allowing South Carolina a face-saving way out. As February 1 approached and the state went on drilling soldiers, Jackson asked Congress for authority to send troops if it should attempt to stop the collection of duties. At the last moment the state gave in, and for that time civil war was averted. The storm had blown over leaving Jackson a hero, except to the states' rights extremists. Northern conservatives, seeing Webster and John Quincy Adams suddenly on his side, became so confused that some of them were heard to say that perhaps it was all for the best that Jackson had been reelected.

Jackson, however, was not confused. In the spring of 1833 he quietly began to prepare for taking the Government's deposits out of the Bank and transferring them to other banks. Biddle responded by lobbying a report through the House saying that the deposits were perfectly safe where they were.

Jackson reinforced his position by making a triumphal tour of the

Eastern states. It was on this tour that he was honored by Harvard, when Adams, though obliged to support the President against South Carolina, felt that calling him a scholar as well as a patriot was going too far. Practically everyone else, high and low, fell captive to his dignity and charm. In New Hampshire he collapsed with hemorrhages from the lungs, and was brought back to Washington on a stretcher to take up the fight of his life.

Biddle seized the offensive, calling loans all over the country so as to create business distress that could be blamed on Jackson's meddling, and the business men quickly forgot their momentary love for the bold President who had stood up to South Carolina. In fact, Calhoun was fighting on the side of the Bank, taking the ground that his enemy Jackson was usurping powers that properly belonged to Congress. Clay joined in accusing the President of aiming at "the concentration of all power in the hands of one man." He declared that "If Congress do not apply an instantaneous and effective remedy, the fatal collapse will come on, and we shall die—ignobly die—base, mean, and abject slaves; the scorn and contempt of mankind; unpitied, unwept, unmourned!" Webster charged indignantly, "I hear it boasted . . . that the solid ground . . . on which the recent measures rest, [is] that the poor naturally hate the rich."

In the House James K. Polk on the other side fought valiantly for his friend Jackson, and kept closely to the main issue that the Bank had too much pwoer, if it could blackmail the Governorment by paralyzing business at the will of Nicholas Biddle. This service did not hurt his chance of someday being President.

As the depression worsened, delegations of business men descended on Washington to demand that Jackson restore the deposits to the Bank. Jackson stood pat. James Fenimore Cooper was moved to remark that possibly "hickory will prove stronger than gold."

Jackson met the delegations with seemingly uncontrollable outbursts of fury against the Bank. He had learned to make deliberate use of his reputation as a wild man. Those who were close to him when he was President agreed that he never lost his temper; but any hostile group would find itself baffled by a torrent of furious denunciations, through which Jackson saved himself from having to listen to a vast amount of useless argument. As soon as the door closed behind the visitors, he would light his pipe and remark, "They thought I was mad." In his apparent madness he was stalling for time and stoking the fires until the iron was hot.

Then, suddenly, in a tirade before a New York delegation, he struck in a shower of sparks. "Go to Nicholas Biddle," he shouted, "We have no money here, gentlemen. Biddle has all the money." After the delegation left the President chuckled and asked, "Didn't I manage them well?" He had given them something to think about that would work in their minds and undermine their loyalty to Nicholas Biddle.

By the spring of 1834, the nation seemed in the grip of a fatal paralysis. Biddle would not let business have money, and Jackson would not let Biddle have the Federal deposits that had always been a vital part of his mobile resources. Biddle's position was that the contest was a revolt of the masses and that all loyal business men must look to him to lead them back to security even though in the battle the casualties might run high. The fury against King Andrew waxed hot. There were many cartoons showing the King in ermine with crown and sceptre. There was the usual political poetry. For example:

> And here is
> ## THE TYRANT
> Who, born to command,
> Is the curse of the country—the King of the land
> Against whom the people have taken their stand—
> The dotard of sixty—the plaything of knaves
> Who would make us obey him, or render us slaves.

But Jackson's word, "Go to Nicholas Biddle" was having its effect. As early as February the Governor of Pennsylvania was criticizing the Bank, and by June many business men were disaffected and were muttering that the credit squeeze was not a necessary measure but an arbitrary attempt to put pressure on the Government by bankrupting private business.

More and more business men and political leaders deserted Biddle, and by July he was in full retreat. He had to yield to one demand after another for financial help. Money began to flow again; the system of private banks to which the government funds had been

"A race obscene,
Spawn'd in the muddy beds of Nile, came forth
Polluting Egypt: gardens, fields, and plains,
Were cover'd with the pest;
The croaking nuisance lurk'd in every nook;
No palaces, nor even chambers, scap'd;
And the land stank—so numerous was the fry."

THESE ARE

THE VERMIN

That plunder the Wealth
That lay in the House,
That Jonathan built.

"Portentous, unexampled, unexplain'd!
What man seeing this,
And having human feelings, does not blush,
And hang his head, to think himself a man?
—I cannot rest
A silent witness of the headlong rage,
Or heedless folly, by which thousands die—
Bleed paid for Ministers to sport away."

AND THESE ARE

THE PEOPLE,

All tatter'd and torn,
Who lament the sad day
When the "Hero" was born;
Who once gave him praise,

"Ruffians are abroad—
* * * *

THESE ARE

THE VICTIMS,

Of high-handed power,
Who groan in a prison
To this very hour—
Who despise the base Traitor,
To glory unknown,
Who would put down the Thing,
   That despite of attacks,
And attempts to restrain it
   By villanous acts,
Will poison the Vermin,
That plunder the Wealth,
That lay in the House
That Jonathan built.

THE GUILTY TRIO.
"Great skill have they in palmistry, and more,
To conjure clean away the gold they touch,
Conveying worthless dross into its place;
Loud when they beg, dumb only when they steal.
—— Dream after dream ensues!
And still they dream, that they shall still succeed,
And still are disappointed."

AND HERE ARE

THE TRIO

Of cabinet fame,
Amos Kendall and Lewis, and Blair of bad name,
The scullions who grovel and revel in shame:
Ay—these are the tyrants—the rulers of him,
Who, enfeebled by years, is in intellect dim,
The dotard of sixty—who, "born to command,"
Dishonours himself, and would ruin the land.
Ay—these are the minions the People oppose,
Apostates, and Tories, and Liberty's foes—
The friends of the Traitor, to glory unknown,
Who would barter his country, and fawn at a throne.

Extracts from an anti-Jackson campaign booklet published in 1832.

Purpose of "Political Hydrophobia" (above) was to suggest that Jackson fiddled away cynically while his supporters looted the public treasury.

transferred began to operate effectively, and business boomed. The war was over, and the Bank had not recovered the Government deposits. Also, its charter would not be renewed.

Biddle gibbered to a meeting of Princeton alumni: "It cannot be that our free nation can long endure the vulgar dominion of ignorance and profligacy. You will live to see the laws re-established—these banditti will be scourged back to their caverns—the penitentiary will reclaim its fugitives in office, and the only remembrance which history will preserve of them, is the energy with which you resisted and defeated them."

William Cullen Bryant, who had grown up considerably since his unfortunate foray against Thomas Jefferson, was by this time editor of the New York *Evening Post,* and a leader of the Jacksonian Democrats. He reported in 1841 that Nicholas Biddle had withdrawn to his country seat, to pass his last days "in elegant retirement, which, if justice had taken place, would have been spent in the penitentiary."

On January 8, 1835, there was a great celebration, for the anniversary of the Battle of New Orleans, and at the same time for the payment of the last of the national debt. Jackson had fulfilled this Jeffersonian dream, partly by vetoing public works projects, and was inordinately proud of it. He provided a toast for the banquet: "The Payment of the Public Debt. Let us commemorate it as an event which gives us increased power as a nation, and reflects luster on our federal Union, of whose justice, fidelity, and wisdom it is a glorious illustration." The friends of the dying Bank, on the other hand, scoffed at the idea as primitive and puerile.

At the same time Jackson's opponents in the Senate were in a nasty mood, partly because in addition to wiping out the national debt he had taken a firm line with France on a matter of unpaid damage claims, which had made him so popular that even Henry Clay had had to go along. Any excuse for an attack on the Administration would be welcome. On January 27, they took up a report on the Post Office, which showed a moderate deficit and also some signs of poor management, with one case of conflict of interest that had, however, been voluntarily corrected. The report set off a burst of horrified oratory.

Three days later, while the President was coming out of the Capitol after a funeral service, Richard Lawrence, an unemployed house painter, tried to shoot him, but his two pistols both misfired. Mr. Wilson, "the keeper of the Rotundo," told the reporters that Lawrence had been hanging around the Capitol for some time.

The *Globe*, the Jackson party organ, blamed the Senators, who had been comparing the President to Cromwell, Nero, and Julius Caesar, and suggesting that only a Brutus could save the nation from the Tyrant. The editor particularly accused Calhoun of inciting to violence a few days earlier when he hotly demanded "reform or revolution!" Another Senator "spoke of the state of affairs as exhibiting ENORMOUS, NOT TO SAY, OUTRAGEOUS EVILS.' He asked if '*the Senate should follow up this* EXTRAORDINARY, ENORMOUS, HUMILIATING EXPOSITION, *with no other measures than a prospective remedy?*' He said, it was not the first occasion when such 'extraordinary developements of the *corruptions* of the Department had been made.' He said, the President was, by his own acknowledgement, '*alone responsible for the conduct of his officers.*'

"*Mr. Calhoun said he earnestly hoped that some Senator would present a resolution expressing the sentiment and feelings of the Senate, on the* GROSS CORRUPTIONS *which had been exposed in the report. . . . His most powerful feelings were those of the deepest shame and mortification. . . . He never could have conceived that such* ROTTENNESS, SUCH CORRUPTION, SUCH ABOMINABLE VIOLATIONS OF TRUST, *could ever exist in any of its Departments . . .* IT EXCEEDED ANY THING IN THE HISTORY OF THE ROTTENEST AGES OF THE ROMAN EMPIRE.

"The next day Mr. Preston shouted there were 'MAGGOTS WORKING IN THE VERY VITALS OF THE GOVERNMENT.' "

Mr. Lawrence's abortive effort was not, of course, the first sign of personal danger to the President. A year earlier, for instance, Congressman George McDuffie, a fierce nullificationist from South Carolina, in a speech on the removal of the deposits, had pointedly suggested that something drastic ought to be done to Mr. Jackson. The Congressman asserted that if the King of England or of France had seized the public treasure as Jackson had done, he would be in danger of having his head cut off. But here in these United States, for lack of such salutary discipline, "A great institution has been assailed, and the rights and property of widows and orphans trampled in the dust by the foot of a Tyrant."

After the assassination attempt The *Globe* took occasion to print specimens of more than a hundred threatening letters received by the President during the Bank fight. One specimen, for instance, pronounced sentence in the following burning words: "When you came into office, you found the country in a state the most prosperous and happy. . . . But, sir, how is it now? Why, sir, had 'war, pestilence, and famine' have spread its horrors and devastation o'er the land, the dismay and distress could not have been greater than now exists, as the consequence of your tyrannic measures. But a few months past, and this country possessed a currency superior to that of any other. The hand of despotism has been violently laid upon the sacred charter of our liberties, the constitution has been trampled under foot, and now lies prostrate in the dust, bleeding at every pore. . . . Sir, there is an earthquake slumbering beneath you; it is ready to open its jaws, to swallow you in its vortex. The country calls for a sacrifice, and when this reaches you, the victim may be ready for the alter. Beware; there is an eye upon you of one who seeks for immortality—it is the immortality of Brutus."

Another, from Cincinnati, came straight to the point: "Sir:— Damn your old soul, remove them deposites back again, and recharter the Bank, or you will certainly be shot in less than two weeks, and that by myself! ! !"

The Baltimore *Chronicle* called openly for violence: "He Tramples Upon the Feelings and The Hearts Of The People. Let the People Speak to Him in a Voice of Thunder. Let The Timid Tone of Supplication be Laid Aside, For The More Appropriate One of Command— And If He Still Persists, Let Him Share The Fate Due To All Tyrants. It Is Right That The President and Congress Should Know, That Relief or Revolution Will Soon Become Rallying Words; And That Of One Or The Other They Must Make Their Selection."

But Andrew Jackson was the last man to worry about threats of bodily harm; he had been shot at by experts. For many years he had been dying of tuberculosis, and he had won some of his most successful battles while he was too weak to sit up. He knew he was triumphant, and the people knew it. He had problems to worry him, such as the inflation that followed the breaking of Biddle's artificial depression; the growing danger of the slavery question with its undertone of nullification and secession; and in private the financial mismanage-

ment of the Hermitage property by his adopted son. But he was
well aware of the overwhelming love and admiration of the people
whose champion he had become.

One last minor wave of criticism came when the President insisted
on the nomination of Van Buren as his successor. At this point in
the present account it becomes possible to introduce the colorful Anne
Royall, newspaperwoman and publisher of the weekly *Paul Pry,* who
once was convicted of being a common scold, and who was said to
have once obtained an interview from John Quincy Adams by following him when he went swimming in the Potomac and sitting on his
clothes. After long wielding her vitriolic pen on Jackson's side, she
balked at the choice of Van Buren. In *Paul Pry* for July 9, 1836,
she repudiated the charge of inconsistency: " 'Why, Mrs. R., you have
changed—you have deserted the democracy—you are against Jackson
—you are a nullifier—you go for Harrison,' &c. So say those impudent
imposters to us. We throw it back in their teeth. We are precisely
where we were at the first, opposed to frauds, to all falsehoods, to all
political hypocrites, by whatever name they may be called. . . . Gen.
Jackson has changed; he has changed from a brave, high-minded,
honest, independent man, to a low, pitiful, political panderer, to force
his successor upon the people. Contrary to the Constitution, a man
of no party, and of no political principles. . . . He has stooped from
the acting Chief Magistrate of a great nation, to a franker of electioneering newspapers. He has left his friends, they did not leave
him, and all for a man who ought to have been beneath his notice.

"Gen. Jackson has done much for his country—few men have done
more; and he would have closed his public services with honor to
himself, and to the pride of his well wishers, had he not fallen into the
snares spread for him by political hypocrites and selfish knaves. All
we pray for is that Gen. Jackson may live to discover the impositions
that have been practiced upon him."

Nevertheless Van Buren was elected. Meanwhile the Senate,
by various deaths, defeats, and resignations, had at last come under
the control of Jackson's friends. Then Thomas Hart Benton, as a
parting gift to the old warrior, undertook to get the censure resolution of 1834 wiped off the record. For in March, 1834, in the middle
of the Bank fight and after Biddle's forces in the Senate had already

begun to waver, Clay had salvaged what he could from the wreck by getting the Senate to pass by a vote of 26 to 20 a resolution censuring the President. Jackson protested that the Senate had no constitutional right to censure him, but the Senate refused to receive his protest.

Now, at the close of Jackson's Administration, Benton pressed the Senate to expunge the censure resolution. Webster argued that it was unconstitutional for the Senate to destroy any part of its journal, since the Constitution requires it to "keep" a record of its proceedings. But Benton fought it through, and at last the Senate yielded. The old ledger was brought out and the offending resolution was crossed off, with an inscription across its face saying "Expunged by order of the Senate, this 16th day of January, 1837." As Marquis James records: "This tinsel, twilight triumph pleased the old man as much as if it had contributed something material to his fame. His eyes would kindle as he displayed the pen the Clerk had used—a gift from Benton."

During his last months in the White House the President was so ill that on March 4 when he came downstairs it was only the fifth time he had been down since November. But the day was bright and balmy. As he rode with Martin Van Buren to the Capitol, the crowds fell silent and stood with bared heads while the hero and his chosen heir rode by. After the ceremony, however, there came a moment when the feeble ex-President slowly started down the broad steps. Then suddenly, Thomas Hart Benton records, a mighty shout burst from the throng such as "power never commanded, nor man in power received. It was affection, gratitude and admiration, . . . the acclaim of posterity breaking from the bosoms of contemporaries. . . . I felt an emotion which had never passed through me before."

There have been many varying opinions about why Jackson was so great a man. It seems clear that the main reason the people loved him was that they thought of him as their friend. In his greatest adventure, the destruction of the Bank, he was fighting for the people, and they knew it. His understanding of economic theory may have been as sketchy as that of Franklin Roosevelt, but like Roosevelt he could sense the direction of progress and lead the people in that direction. As in Roosevelt's time, the financial dominion over the business world had become intolerable, and the political power of the nation had to be used to cut it down to size. That much was plain to both men, and that much they took as their duty. Neither one solved all the economic problems of his day; but each one renewed the vitality of the United States. The people felt strength flowing to them from these men, and they loved them for it.

Jackson built up the Presidency; that in itself made him a great man. The American people instinctively call for a strong Executive. Whenever they make the mistake of choosing a weak one they are unhappy; and when they get a strong one the majority will love him and admire his courage in face of the fervent hate of his enemies.

Jackson had entered the White House in 1829 sick with grief and anger; he left it in 1837 sick with tuberculosis, to be sure, but well content with his success as President. He had come in a popular hero; he went out after spending eight years in office under venomous attack, even more deeply rooted in the affections of the American people. He had struggled for years with a Senate controlled by his bitter opponents, but in the end he outlasted them. Clay and Calhoun, his chief enemies, had both seen the glittering prize of the Presidency slip beyond their grasp. As Claude Bowers sums up Jackson's experience: "Few Presidents have ever departed from the scene of their power with more for which to be grateful and less to regret."

Long afterward, however, the old fighter admitted to an intimate friend that he had two regrets: he had never been able to shoot Henry Clay or to hang John C. Calhoun.

Caricatured as an inciter of war, Lewis Cass, Democratic Presidential candidate in 1848, found it disadvantageous to continue using the title of General he acquired 35 years earlier during the War of 1812. His attitude toward Mexico during the late 1840's inspired this contemporary cartoon.

Subtitled "The First Qualification for a Whig President," this cartoon was widely reprinted in the campaign against Zachary Taylor. The skulls were meant to suggest that Taylor was personally responsible for unnecessary deaths during the war with Mexico in 1846-48.

FOR
SALT RIVER!
DIRECT.!!

THE FAST SAILING STEAMER

BLACK REPUBLICAN!
Capt. J. C. FREMONT, "No. 1,"

Has her Freight on board, and will have quick dispatch on

NOVEMBER 4TH, 1856.

The following is a list of the Officers and Crew for the voyage:

ENGINEERS.	MATE.
"FREE LOVE" GREELY, "FOXY" RAYMOND.	"DU DAH" DAY
FIREMEN.	**STEWARDS.**
"HOLY RIFLE" BEECHER, FRED DOUGLASS.	"SAUNEY" BENNETT. "LET THE UNION SLIDE" BANKS.
PURSERS.	**CHAMBERMAID.**
KANSAS WAR COMMITTEE.	MRS. "BLEEDING KANSAS."

A great number of "Political Parsons," who have stolen the Livery of Heaven to serve the Devil in, will be on board.

A patent "Caliope" is engaged, and will give several "Shrieks for Kansas."

The "Shaking Quakers" from Pennsylvania, "who did not vote" on the 14th inst., will amuse the Company during the trip.

This Boat is of light draft, and will reach nearer the "Head Waters of SALT RIVER" than any other craft.

☞ NO NIGGERS ALLOWED ON BOARD. ◁

For Passage only, apply to the President of the Fremont Club, at the "HUT."

N B — Passengers are to be on board at 5 o'clock. After that hour they will be brought on board on Litters, Wheelbarrows and Coffins.

P S.—Ship Stores must be sent on board as early as possible, for a 4 years cruise.

Typical of propaganda used against John C. Fremont, first Presidential candidate of the Republican Party, this poster helped contribute to his defeat in 1856. Considering that the party was then only two years old, that it had ineffective organization in most states, and that its opposition to slavery ruled out support in the South, Fremont did surprisingly well. He received 114 electoral votes to 174 for James Buchanan, the successful Democratic candidate, nicknamed "Old Fogey" by his opponents.

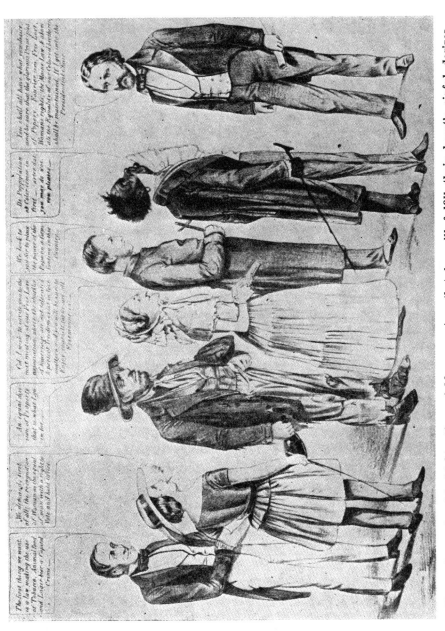

Fremont assuring his highly disreputable supporters that he will fulfill their heart's sinful desires.

Chapter VI

BABOON IN THE WHITE HOUSE

It was the night before Election Day in 1858. Abraham Lincoln had been campaigning for the United States Senate against Stephen A. Douglas, the "Little Giant," in a series of debates which had been eagerly followed by the whole nation. Now he was sitting with Henry Villard of the New York *Staats-Zeitung,* on the floor of a boxcar where the two had taken refuge from a black thunderstorm.

Lincoln was laughing about himself. "I am sure I am good enough for it," he said, "but in spite of all, I am saying to myself every day, 'It is too big a thing for you. You will never get it.' Mary insists, though, that I am going to be Senator, and President too." He paused to let that sink in. "Just think of such a sucker as me being President!" He roared with laughter, there in the dark. Outside, the storm thundered. The next day Douglas beat him for the Senate, but two years later he beat Douglas for the Presidency. With his election the storm came up across the whole nation. The hope of peace went glimmering as the Southern states began to secede. Lincoln's mail gave a foretaste of the hate that was to pour over his head until he died.

The incoming letters called him baboon, monster, idiot, mulatto. They told him in a hundred different ways that he would never live to sit in the White House. He was threatened with flogging, hanging, and burning at the stake. People sent him pictures of daggers dripping blood, and many of gallows with his body hanging. In January, Mrs. Lincoln received a large flat package sent by express from South Carolina. It contained an oil painting of Lincoln "with a rope around his neck, his feet chained, and his body adorned with tar and feathers."

Southern papers brought out a story that Hannibal Hamlin, of Maine, the Vice-President-elect, was part Negro. The secessionist leader R. Barnwell Rhett of Charleston declared that the Republicans had elected "a Southern renegade out of the bosom of Kentucky into Illinois, and a Northern whitewashed mulatto" to be President and

Vice President. How could honorable, high-spirited, proud Southern gentlemen submit to such an election? Three of these gentlemen, in fact, took the trouble to write a letter to Lincoln, saying that they understood he had a likely mulatto boy, "and if you will let us know what you will take for the boy Hanibal and you price is reasonable we will purchase him."

The New York *Herald,* adding its note of cheer, advised that here was Lincoln's great opportunity to avert national ruin and invest his name with immortality, by simply stepping aside in favor of "some national man" who would be acceptable to both sections. Such a noble sacrifice "would render him the peer of Washington in patriotism." Otherwise, the *Herald* could foresee he would probably be shot, leaving behind him "a memory more execrable than that of Arnold— more despised than that of the traitor Cataline."

On February 11 Lincoln set out, with a party including armed guards, on a roundabout journey to Washington, making speeches in an effort to calm the inflamed public mind. At Columbus, Ohio, he told his hearers that these were anxious times but that nothing was going wrong, "nobody is suffering anything." He meant only that so far there was no shooting war. "This is a most consoling circumstance," he went on, "and from it we may conclude that all we want is time, patience, and a reliance on that God who has never forsaken this people."

The newspapers had a field day. What sort of talk was this, with six states already out of the Union? The Baltimore *Sun* wondered what kind of a fool the nation had elected as President and remarked that if the state of the nation itself were not so grave his speechifications "would be ludicrous to the destruction of buttons." It went on to advise that "Mr. Lincoln is a man who ought never to be as funny as he can."

The arrival in Washington was not a happy one. At Philadelphia Lincoln was warned by the famous detective Alan Pinkerton of a plot to mob and assassinate him in Baltimore. He reluctantly consented to a secret night journey that brought him to the capital in the early morning, leaving a Baltimore mob to work off steam cheering for "Gallant Jeff Davis."

The New York *Times* was friendly to Lincoln, but unluckily for

Basest of all attacks on Lincoln, this cartoon gave currency to reports
that that man in the White House was of illegitimate Negro lineage.

THE REPUBLICAN PARTY GOING TO THE RIGHT HOUSE.

Horace Greeley leads the way while advocates of atheism, free love, and even women's rights bring up the rear.

him its Washington correspondent, Joseph Howard, was one of the most noted liars of his generation. This gentleman reported with glee that Lincoln had arrived in the capital disguised in a Scotch plaid cap and long military cloak, a costume that immediately appealed to the hostile press as a subject of caricature. "Lincoln ran from the first whispering of danger as fleetly as ever a naked-legged Highlander pursued the deer upon Scotia's hills," crowed one delighted journalist.

Down South the newspapers rejoiced in the undignified preliminaries of the new regime. A Mississippi paper commented on his silly speeches, his ill-timed jocularity, and his cowardly evasion of responsibility—presumably meaning his responsibility to the eager audience that had awaited him in Baltimore. "Had we any respect for Mr. Lincoln as a man or as President-elect," one paper sneered, "the final escapade by which he reached the capital would have utterly destroyed it." But worse was to be apprehended. "We have only too much cause to fear that such a man, and such advisers as he has, may prove capable of infinitely more mischief than folly when invested with power."

In face of the rising storm, the incoming President had to stand before the nation and make an Inaugural Address. He had begun work on it before he left Springfield. He remembered Andrew Jackson's Proclamation on Nullification, which he had read when he was a young man just back from service in the Black Hawk War. He got it out and read it over: "Disunion by armed force is treason. Are you really ready to incur its guilt?"

Lincoln took pains to assure the South that the rights of the states would be protected, but he declared the nation could not be dissolved by any one-sided action of the states. Finally, he pleaded for time and patience. "We are not enemies, but friends," he said. "We must not be enemies. Though passion may have strained, it must not break our bonds of affection. The mystic chords of memory, stretching from every battlefield, and patriot grave, to every living heart and hearthstone, all over this broad land, will yet swell the chorus of the Union, when again touched, as surely they will be, by the better angels of our nature."

But the time for reconciliation was long past, and both sides took the Inaugural address as meaning what they wanted it to mean.

The New York *Tribune* rejoiced to have a Man at least at the head of the government, but the Baltimore *Sun* considered it an assumption of despotic authority, "the knell and requiem of the Union, and the death of hope." In Charleston, Robert Barnwell Rhett's paper, the *Mercury,* advised "It is our wisest policy to accept it as a declaration of war."

So when at last the President refused to pull Federal troops out of Fort Sumter in Charleston harbor, and notified Governor Pickens of South Carolina that he was sending supplies to the fort, the Southern batteries opened fire. But meanwhile the secret plans for supplying Fort Sumter had taken a month to mature; during that first month of his term the President was under a drumfire of criticism from the North for inactivity and indecison.

The Northern papers demanded that he come to the point and accused him of unparalelled blindness and stolidity. The mail was equally unfriendly. Many of Mr. Lincoln's constituents were disappointed and disgusted. "I voted for you," one writer complained, "thinking that *in* you the country would find a defender of its rights and honor. I am totally disappointed. You are as destitute of policy, as weak, and as vassalating as was your predecessor. As the New York Times says this morning—'Your want of *policy* and *action* has demoralized the country more than all the 3 months of Buchanans did all together. Either *act,* immediately and decisively or resign and go home."

Among his friends, Lincoln made no apologies for his slowness of decision and action. As time went on his experience confirmed his habit of waiting for "the fulness of time." He received much advice, not only from ignorant letter writers but from "best minds," that would have led to disaster if he had followed it. He steered slowly through the fog, with many of the passengers and some of the crew screaming in his ears.

When the crisis came at Fort Sumter, the highly articulate abolitionist Wendell Phillips contributed his bit of confusion by deciding that the President had no right to hold a fort in the territory of South Carolina. If the Southern states wanted to secede, he declared, they had a right to do so: "Standing with the principles of '76 behind us who can deny that right?" Lincoln denied that right.

Sumter was attacked on April 12; it surrendered on April 14. As the news spread across the South the people went wild with joy. Cities fired salutes of a hundred guns. In one town the people gleefully hung Lincoln in effigy with a sign saying "May all abolitionists meet the same fate." A New Orleans paper informed its readers that the President had been seen in the White House "so drunk he could hardly maintain his seat in the chair." It was reported that Lincoln had been drunk for over thirty-six hours. "The man is nearly scared to death; and few people in that city [Washington] are in better condition." Though Lincoln's habit was to take lemonade when others were drinking whiskey allegations of his drunkenness continued in circulation for years.

When Virginia, after some hesitation, joined the South on April 17, the Richmond *Examiner* showed no semblance of restraint: "There is one wild shout of fierce resolve to capture Washington City at all and every human hazard. The filthy cage of unclean birds must and will be purified by fire. The just indignation of an outraged people will teach the Illinois Ape to retrace his journey across the borders of the Free negro States more rapidly than he came."

There were some signs that impatient volunters might try to take Washington before its defenses could be organized. The following letter may have been produced by someone not quite as illiterate as he tried to pretend. It was dated at Baltimore on April 11.

*"To Abe*ᵐ*. Lincoln Esqr*

"Dear Friend I take this method of informing you that you better prepair yourself for an assailing mob that is organizing in Baltimore as far as i can inform myself is about 12000m. strong they intend to seize the Capitol and yourself and as they say that they will tar and put cotton on your head and ride you and Gen. Scot on a rail this secret organization is about 70000m members in Maryland and Virginia and they can be all brought together in five days, the person that rits this was a member and is bound by a strong oath which if they now ho i was i wold not be suffer to live but justis to you and my country make me do this."

What sort of man was this who could draw such fierce hatred and yet be so loved by those who were close to him and by millions of simple folk who had never seen him?

Most people agreed with Lincoln himself that he was no beauty. He once said to a friend, "Thank God for not making me a woman— but if he had, I suppose He would have made me just as ugly as he did, and no one would ever have tempted me." In *The Education of Henry Adams,* the author tells of having seen Lincoln only once, at the Inaugural Ball of 1861, and describes him as having "a long awkward figure; a plain, ploughed face; a mind, absent in part, and in part evidently worried by white kid gloves." Adams thought at this time that no man living needed so much education or was so unlikely to get what he needed.

The New York *Times* carried an item from its Paris correspondent under the headline "Lincoln's Phiz in Europe." The correspondent urged that pictures of the President ought not to be sent out of the country. They looked so much like a criminal type that in France large numbers of them had been sold as pictures of a famous murderer of servant girls who had lately been executed near Lyons. "Such a face," he felt convinced, "is enough to ruin the best of causes; and people read the name inscribed under it with astonishment; the thing appears more like a hoax than a reality." The Southern papers copied this story with glee. Their usual name for Lincoln was The Baboon or The Gorilla.

But not everyone felt the same way. It was noticed that children liked to climb in Lincoln's lap. It is told that one little girl called across the room to her father, "Oh Pa, he isn't ugly at all; he's just beautiful!" It is perhaps easier today for people to understand how such feelings could arise in looking at so grotesque a figure, since so many millions of Americans, and of foreign visitors too, have had the experience of standing before the Lincoln Memorial in Washington.

When Francis Bicknell Carpenter, the portrait painter, was engaged to paint his group picture of the signing of the Emancipation Proclamation, his first sight of the President, as he described it afterward, was in a crowd at a White House reception, "Never shall I forget," the artist wrote, "the electric thrill which went through my whole being at this moment. I seemed to see lines radiating from every part of the globe, converging to a focus at the point where that plain, awkward-looking man stood, and to hear in spirit a million prayers, 'as the sound of many waters,' ascending in his behalf. Mingled with supplication I could discern a clear symphony of triumph

AN HEIR TO THE THRONE,
OR THE NEXT REPUBLICAN CANDIDATE

A Currier and Ives caricature suggesting that an illiterate Negro might be nominated for the Presidency with the support of Greeley and Lincoln.

"The Flight of Abraham." This Harper's Weekly cartoon added credulity to reports that Lincoln was fearful of being attacked by Southerners while enroute to Washington for his inauguration as President.

Under cover of darkness, Lincoln and his inaugural party changed trains at Baltimore with cowardly stealth, according to some newspapers, because of reports from Maryland that they would be jeered if seen in broad daylight.

and blessing, swelling with an ever-increasing volume. It was the voice of those who had been bondmen and bondwomen, and the grand diapason swept up from the coming ages."

Gideon Welles, who was afterward to be Lincoln's Secretary of the Navy, first met him at the end of the famous Cooper Union address in 1860. Welles admired Lincoln from the start, said he was no Apollo but no Caliban either: he was made where they had plenty of material for strong men. "His countenance shows intellect, generousity, great good nature and keen discrimination." Welles reported Lincoln as being effective "because he is earnest, strong, honest, simple in style, and clear as crystal in his logic."

On the other hand, Edwin M. Stanton, who was mentioned for Secretary of War in 1861 but was not appointed until the following year, had met Lincoln years before in a law case and had hated him at first sight. Stanton never tried to hide his contempt for the President and he pointedly failed even to leave cards at the White House. The Secretary of War always spoke of his chief as "the original gorilla;" once he told his friends that the famous explorer and naturalist Du Chaillu was a fool to go all the way to Africa for what he could have found so easily in Springfield, Illinois.

This book is not the place to describe the Civil War, but one Union General deserves a place because of his remarkable conceit and his contempt for the President. General George B. McClellan, intimate friend of the immortal Stanton, was in charge of the Army of the Potomac, but he kept his headquarters in Washington and showed little enthusiasm for fighting the enemy. Lincoln, who was not too well supplied with Generals of any calibre, tried hard to make the best of McClellan, and even went frequently to the General's home for consultation. One night the President went to see McClellan, taking along his two secretaries, John Nicolay and John Hay, and Secretary Seward. They found that McClellan was out but was expected home soon, so Lincoln decided that they would wait. An hour later, their host came in, brushed aside the servant who told him he had callers, and went straight upstairs. After another half hour the President sent word that he was still there, and the answer came back that the General had gone to bed.

McClellan has left for an admiring posterity a full account of his feeling for his chief, as recorded in his diary and his letters to his wife: "It is sickening in the extreme and makes me feel heavy at heart, when I see the weakness and unfitness of the poor beings who control the destiny of this great country. . . . I feel that the fate of the nation depends upon me and I feel that I have not one single friend at the seat of the government. . . . They have done all that cowardice and folly can do to ruin our poor country and the blind people seem not to see it. It makes my soul boil when I think of it. . . . The President is nothing more than a well meaning baboon. . . . I went to the White House directly after tea where I found 'the original Gorilla' about as intelligent as ever. What a specimen to be at the head of our affairs now! . . . I went to Seward's where I found the Gorilla again, and was of course edified by his anecdotes un-apropos and even unworthy of one holding his high position."

This was the man who felt it was his duty in 1864 to save the nation from Lincoln by running for President on the Democratic ticket. However, the "blind people" continued to prefer their favorite gorilla.

Not all the criticism of Lincoln came from unfriendly sources. One well-wisher who felt moved to do something for the President's own good was a Mr. Robert Colby of 47 Wall Street, New York. His letter of May 18, 1861, pointed out that people were worried about two things—the first being that the troops might not get good food, and "the second source of worriment is your personal manners . . . when you come to the receiving of military citizens (as all volunteers are) [it] becomes a serious question enough, whether you please them or not. . . .

"They say when you are on horseback, and platoons of men marching by you, that you lean about and turn your head to talk to people behind you, when they claim that you should sit erect and talk to nobody and look straight at the saluting soldiers. . . .

"You had better let some officer put you through a few dress parades . . . and get some military habit on you so you shall feel natural among military men—Don't let people call you a goose in these *very very* important relations to the Army— . . .

"My impression is that you will do well by paying more attention to your manners and make less effort at wit and storytelling—All well enough in private but publicly it is a nuisance—Your talent is conceded—be a gentleman and courtly in your manners when you ought to be . . . I voted for you and have a desire to be proud of your administration. . . . it won't do for you to be careless about any thing, not the least thing—

"P.S. There is one thing conceded—that you are a very warm-hearted, honest, and patriotic man . . ."

The postscript was a comfort anyway.

How did Lincoln feel about the attacks on him? One time when someone had sent him a batch of newspaper criticisms, he told a friend, half humorously, that after reading them he asked himself, "Abraham Lincoln, are you a man or a dog?" He smiled as he said it, but it was evident that he had read the clippings and that they had hurt. His sense of humor was some protection, but his skin was sensitive and many of the missiles reached him.

One time Lincoln told General Robert C. Schenck, "If to be head of Hell is as hard as what I have to undergo here, I could find it in my heart to pity Satan himself." To an old friend from Illinois he recalled the story about the man who had been tarred and feathered and was riding on a rail, when someone in the crowd asked him how he liked it. He said that if it wasn't for the honor of the thing he would much rather walk.

Lincoln was hurt by the gibes and curses of his enemies, but even more by attacks from extremists on his own side. He was pained and surprised at the bitter attacks of the impatient abolitionists when he seemed too slow in proclaiming the end of slavery. The criticism of such extremists as Horace Greeley and Wendell Phillips, he confided, was a source of "great grief" to him. He probably heard, among other things, of the meeting of the Massachusetts Anti-Slavery Society in January, 1862, at which Wendell Phillips remarked he believed Lincoln was honest, but "as a pint-pot may be full and yet not as full as a quart, so there is a vast difference between the honesty of a small man and the honesty of a statesman."

Early in the war the President wrote for himself a meditation which John Hay found on his desk and copied:

"The will of God prevails. In great contests each party claims to act in accordance with the will of God. Both may be, and one must be, wrong. God cannot be for and against the same thing at the same time. In the present civil war it is quite possible that

God's purpose is something different from the purpose of either party; and yet the human instrumentalities, working just as they do, are the best adaptation to effect his purpose. I am almost ready to say that this is probably true; that God wills this contest, and wills that it shall not end yet. By his great power on the minds of the new contestants, he could have either saved or destroyed the Union without a human contest. Yet the contest began. And having begun, he could give the final victory to either side any day. Yet the contest proceeds."

Late in 1861 Lincoln had some bitter medicine to take in connection with the *Trent* affair. On November 8th the USS *San Jacinto* stopped the British Royal Mail packet *Trent* in the Bahama Channel and took off James M. Mason and John Slidell, Confederate Commissioners to England and France. Immediately there was vast excitement in England and America and loud talk of war. But Lincoln, though he deeply resented the British government's flirting with the Confederacy, decided that one war at a time was enough. He released the envoys to a British vessel in Boston Harbor, and the war talk died out. He told a friend about a man in Illinois who felt himself dying and decided to make peace with his old enemy, Brown. So Brown was invited in and after a tearful scene he was softened up and shook hands. But as he was leaving the sick man rose on an elbow and called after him: "But look here, Brown, if I *should* happen to get well mind *that old grudge stands.*"

There was serious danger that England might recognize the independance of the Confederacy and give it all the rights of a belligerent nation. The British upper classes favored the South, but the workers, although the blockade cutting off the cotton supply caused heavy unemployment, stood heroically for the anti-slavery cause. The balance of public opinion abroad, especially in England, was precarious in the early part of the war until finally it was permanently tilted on the side of the North by Emancipation.

In his first year in the White House, Lincoln saw clearly that the war was bound to lead the North to demand the abolition of slavery, but he knew that most of the people were not yet ready to face this conclusion. He wrote to George Bancroft, the historian, that he had to move cautiously "and with all the best judgment I can bring to it." Some people were impatient, however. In December 1861 the

"The MacLincoln Harrisburg Highland Fling"—a Vanity Fair cartoon based on rumors that Lincoln disguised himself as a Scotsman when, upon arriving at Harrisburg while enroute to Washington, he heard that he was being pursued by Southerners.

Unfriendly cartoonists found the ungainly Lincoln an easy target.

generally friendly *Harper's Weekly* expressed keen disappointment with him: "He views his office as strictly an executive one, and wishes to cast responsibility, as much as possible, upon Congress." There have indeed been Presidents like that, but *Harper's Weekly* was wrong about Lincoln. This kind of criticism even about a strong President is to be expected when public opinion is moving ponderously and he has to pull with care or he will snap the tow-rope as Wilson did with the Treaty of Versailles.

Feeling about Lincoln among the Abolitionists improved early in 1862 when he refused to commute the sentence of a slave trader caught in New York, and the man was duly hanged. But there was a growing conflict between the "Radical" Republicans in Congress, who wanted no mercy on slaveholders, and the President, who steadily hoped that someday a peace with reconciliation might be achieved.

In the autumn of 1862 McClellan presented the country with half a victory at Antietam. His men had beaten Lee's army, but he had let Lee withdraw in good order under the noses of a reserve of 30,000 men who could have been thrown in to clinch the victory. At about this time Mrs. Mary Livermore of Chicago, in Washington for a meeting to organize relief for wounded soldiers, visited the White House and found the President sunk in depression. She asked how things were going and he answered, "I have no word of encouragement to give you. The fact is that the people have not yet made up their minds that we are at war with the South." Mrs. Livermore told her friends that Lincoln's face had ghastly lines, and his half-staggering gait was like that of a man walking in his sleep. "He seemed literally bending under the weight of his burdens," she reported, "A deeper gloom rested on his face than on that of any other person I had ever seen."

But the imperfect victory of Antietam at least could be used as an excuse for releasing the preliminary Emancipation Proclamation. Lincoln had held this document in his desk throughout the summer, for the war was going so badly he agreed with Seward that it might be considered a cry of despair. But now he felt he could take the initiative, and the Proclamation was issued. McClellan, of course, was horrified. He wrote to his wife that this and his other troubles "render it almost impossible for me to retain my commission and my self-respect at the same time."

The Southern papers in their rage laid special stress on a ticklish point that was worrying Lincoln a little—the danger of a slave rebellion that would horrify the world and turn public opinion against the Northern cause. The Southerners accused him of plotting to murder men, women, and children in their beds. "What shall we call him?" cried one angry editor, "Coward, assassin, savage, murderer of women and babies? Or shall we consider them all embodied in the word fiend, and call him Lincoln, the Fiend?" Actually the danger of a serious uprising was lessened by the fact that practically no slaves could read and write, and that they had no means of organizing over any large area. For the slaves themselves, in so far as they were aware of conditions at all, there were advantages in simply escaping through the lines.

Emancipation was to take effect on January 1, but only in areas under Southern control. Slavery would continue in the loyal border states, which Lincoln could not afford to drive into secession. He looked for abolition to come when the time was ripe, by Constitutional amendment, as he considered it to be beyond the powers of either President or Congress. The Emancipation Proclamation was a war measure that could be imposed only in enemy territory. The Radical Republicans, of course, violently disagreed with Lincoln's Constitutional theory.

Abroad the reactionary London *Times* had high hopes that emancipation would boomerang. "What will the South think of this?" sneered the editor. "The South will answer with a hiss of scorn. What will the North think of it?" In the editor's opinion, Northern businessmen would never agree to lose "the millions produced by the labour of the black man."

The *Times* may have overestimated the resentment of Northern businessmen, but it was right enough in being concerned. All over Europe, the conservatives who wanted to recognize the Confederate States were weakened by the Proclamation. More and more people believed the North was fighting for freedom.

By the end of 1862 the good impression created abroad by the preliminary Proclamation was reinforced by the lack of bitterness that Lincoln showed in his second Message to Congress. The

Edinburgh *Mercury* went so far as to rate the President's attitude toward the South as more civilized than that of many people in Britain at the time of the recent Indian Mutiny: "When we recollect the raucous hate in this country toward the Indian rebels, we feel humiliated that this 'rail splitter' from Illinois should show himself so superior to the mass of monarchical statesmen." While Lincoln was riding the storms of hatred blowing from the South, and from both Radicals and "Copperheads," or anti-war Democrats, in the North, his own inner fortitude and calm were winning the support abroad without which his cause would probably have been lost.

When the Emancipation Proclamation was issued in final form it was greeted with general rejoicing among loyalists in the North, but there were violent reactions among Northern Copperheads as well as in the South. The New York *Tribune,* for instance, spoke of the President as a tyrant and a usurper. Others criticized the action as illegal and unwise. Governor Parker of New Jersey, in a message to the legislature, denounced emancipation as based on an ill-founded notion of the "war powers" and as likely to prolong the war. Emancipation, he argued, should be left to the legislatures of the states. Southern papers found it hard to decide whether wickedness or folly were its most prominent features. To them Emancipation was at the same time a most startling political crime and the most stupid political blunder in American history. They hopefully proclaimed that it would attract sympathy to the Confederate cause in Europe; and one editor pooh-poohed it as "a Pope's Bull against the comet, not worth the paper it is written on."

But Henry Adams in London wrote that the Proclamation had done more for the Union cause than military victories or the efforts of diplomacy: "It is creating an almost convulsive reaction in our favor all over this country. The London Times furious and scolds like a drunken drab." Lincoln himself felt that "We are like whalers who have been on a long chase. We have at last got the harpoon into the monster, but we must now look how we steer, or with one flop of his tail he will send us all to eternity."

Lincoln believed thoroughly in his war powers and in his right to suppress treason and subversion. There was much argument in the newspapers and in Congress over whether the Constitutional power to suspend *habeas corpus* in time of rebellion lay with the President or with Congress. But in practice the Administration assumed the power, and Congress, though it passed a Habeas Corpus bill in March, 1863, requiring official reports of all arrests, clearly authorized the President to suspend *habeas corpus*. Whatever the legal powers may have been, there was an immense amount of open opposition to the war that was never successfully put down.

One of the most bitter of the Copperhead editors was Wilbur Fisk Storey, of the Chicago *Times*, who in March of 1863 was calling loudly for Lincoln's impeachment. At one point the *Times* and other like-minded papers united to give mass coverage to a one-sentence report that "The President's son 'Bob,' a lad of some twenty summers, has made half a million dollars in government contracts." No proof was offered and none was needed; it was obvious to all good Lincoln-haters he would be doing that. In June, General Burnside seized the plant of the *Times*, but that night a Copperhead mob of 20,000 gathered to shout defiance of the Government and threats of burning the plant of the Republican Chicago *Tribune*. The disorders went on several days while Republican leaders sent frantic calls to the President to get them off the hook. Finally he ordered the *Times* plant restored, and the paper happily resumed its poisonous attacks.

"Old Sam" Medary of the Columbus, Ohio, *Crisis* was a pacifist but no believer in pacific language toward Lincoln. His editorials were studded with such gems as: "If Abe Lincoln is the Government, with his army of official thieves, would it not be an act of patriotism to notify him to skedaddle?" One time a mob wrecked the *Crisis* print shop and Old Sam's office, but he was soon back on the job of cursing the President.

In Philadelphia the editor of the *Christian Observer*, a Virginian by birth, published a series of *Letters From a Virginian*, of which the following is a sample: "The gross, brutal, fiendish, demoniac outrages perpetrated by the chicken stealers sent here to ravage the country, pillage the houses and burn them, outrage the women, and shoot down for amusement peaceable citizens, and even children, on the streets, have greatly exasperated the people." His plant was seized by Federal officers, and he fled to Richmond where he reestablished his paper. But when another anti-Union journal, *The Jeffersonian*, of West Chester, Pennsylvania, was seized, the court ordered its return to the owner. The Post Office, however, barred it from the mails.

The New York *Daily News* published a list of 154 Northern newspapers opposed to what it called "the present unholy war," but the Government did little against them. The Post Office barred five New York papers from the mails, and some editors were locked up for a few months, charged with treason, and then released. The fact was that, as John Adams had found with the Sedition Law, suppression of the press is a poor weapon with a tendency to boomerang. In the main, Lincoln with all his war powers had to take the vituperation, like many another President before and since—even when its effect was not merely to hurt his feelings but to undermine the security of the nation.

In the winter of 1862-63 there was a secret movement to impeach Lincoln. Simon Cameron of Pennsylvania, Lincoln's first Secretary of War, long afterwards gave an account of this conspiracy in which he carefully named no names. He received an invitation from "a number of the most prominent gentlemen," to attend a meeting for discussion of national affairs. At the meeting he soon discovered that the real object was to find some way by which the President could be turned out of office because of his slowness in pushing the war: "These reasons, and the plan of attack, if I may use the expression, were all made known to me, and I was asked for my advice. I gave it, stating, with as much earnestness as I could command, that the movement proposed would be a disastrous one, and strongly urging that it would be little short of madness to interfere with the Administration."

Nothing came of this effort, but it indicated that early in the war the Radical Republicans were already feeling that Lincoln was expendable. The President had Copperheads to right of him and Radicals to left of him, and as he remarked to one of his friends, he felt fairly sure of being right so long as the thunder from both sides was about equal.

It was the Radical Republicans in Washington who avidly spread the story that Mrs. Lincoln was a Confederate spy, and that the repeated Northern disasters in the field were possibly the result of a betrayal of military secrets from the White House itself. This story had originated because Mary Todd Lincoln was from a border state and had several brothers in the Southern armies, though she also had many relatives on the Northern side, as was the case in numerous families. Finally the rumor grew to such a point that members of the Senate Committee on the Conduct of the War scheduled a secret session to consider Mrs. Lincoln's loyalty. One of the members afterward told what happened: "We had just been called to order by the Chairman, when the officer stationed at the committee room door came in with a half-frightened expression on his face. Before he had opportunity to make explanation, we understood the reason for his excitement, and were ourselves almost overwhelmed with astonishment. For at the foot of the Committee table, standing solitary, his hat in his hand, his form towering, Abraham Lincoln stood. Had he come by some incantation, thus of a sudden appearing before us unannounced, we could not have been more astounded. . . . No one spoke, for no one knew what to say. The President had not been asked to come before the Committee, nor was it suspected that he had information that we were to investigate reports, which, if true, fastened treason upon his family in the White House."

Finally Lincoln spoke: "I, Abraham Lincoln, President of the United States, appear of my own volition before this Committee of the Senate to say that I, of my own knowledge, know that it is untrue that any of my family hold treasonable communication with the enemy." Then he turned and went away.

"We sat for some moments speechless. Then by tacit agreement, no word being spoken, the Committee dropped all consideration of the rumors that the wife of the President was betraying the Union. We were so greatly affected that the Committee adjourned for the day."

In June, 1863, Lincoln wrote a letter which, as he told a friend later, he regarded as his best public document. He said that he had long kept a drawer where he put notes of the arguments that occurred to him about his wartime powers, and this letter was a summary of his matured judgment on the subject.

Erastus Corning of Albany, New York, had sent the President a set of resolutions passed by a Democratic state convention, denouncing him for suspending *habeas corpus,* and complaining because the Copperhead leader Clement L. Vallandigham had been arrested in Ohio for agitating against the raising of troops. In his reply Lincoln noted that the common constitutional rights had been established in England by civil war and in America by revolution, not during those conflicts but after they were won. The South had hoped to paralyze the North by persuading it to tangle itself in Constitutional limitations. "They hoped to keep on foot amongst us a most efficient corps of spies, informers, suppliers, and aiders and abettors of their cause." He pointed out that the Constitution itself makes the distinction between times of peace and times of rebellion or invasion, and that his own duty was to put down the rebellion. "Must I shoot a simple-minded soldier boy who deserts while I must not touch a hair of a wily agitator who induces him to desert?"

Instead of keeping Vallandigham in jail, however, Lincoln had him expelled across the Union lines in Tennessee, with the assurance that if he returned he would go back to jail. There was vast excitement in Ohio, where the banished leader was running for Governor on the Democratic ticket. Democratic orators blasted Lincoln before mass meetings of tens of thousands of applauding Copperheads. In the election that autumn Vallandigham got the votes of 185,000 civilians and 2,200 soldiers but the Union candidate, John Brough, got 247,000 civilian and 41,000 soldier votes. Lincoln regarded the Ohio situation as so serious that on Election Day evening he was in frequent touch with Brough's headquarters by telegraph. When Brough reported his majority had climbed over 100,000, Lincoln wired, "Glory to God in the highest. Ohio has saved the nation. A Lincoln."

Meanwhile, on July 4, ex-President Franklin Pierce had offered his feeble bit toward undermining Lincoln in an address before a great Democratic mass meeting at Concord, New Hampshire: "Here in these free states," he cried, "it is made criminal for that noble martyr of free speech, Mr. Vallandigham, to discuss public affairs in Ohio—ay, even here, in time of war the mere arbitrary will of the President takes the place of the Constitution, and the President himself announces to us that it is treasonable to speak or to write otherwise than as he may prescribe; nay, that it is treasonable even to be silent, though we may be struck dumb by the shock of the calamities with which evil counsels, incompetency and corruption, have overwhelmed our country." On the same day Governor Horatio Seymour of New York launched an even more dangerous attack, in which he accused the Government of "seizing our persons, infringing upon our rights, insulting our homes, depriving us of those cherished principles for which our fathers fought."

Considering that Seymour was in office and responsible for maintaining law and order in his state, his outburst was highly inflammatory. These official expressions of massive resistance were copied and embroidered upon by the Copperhead press, and on July 13 there began three days of draft rioting in New York. The mobs wrecked draft offices, lynched Negroes, and killed dozens of policemen. After troops had arrived and order had been restored, Lincoln's friends suggested that he appoint a well-known Judge to ferret out the organizers of the riots, but he refused to say either yes or no. Although Gettysburg had been fought and won in the first days of July, the loyalty of the North was still too precarious for any drastic move. He told a friend privately, "Well, you see if I had said no, I should have admitted that I dare not enforce the laws, and consequently have no business to be President of the United States. If I had said yes, and had appointed the Judge, I should—as he would have done his duty—have simply touched a match to a barrel of gunpowder. You have heard of sitting on a volcano. We are sitting upon two; one is blazing away already, and the other will blaze away the moment we scrape a little loose dirt from the top of the crater. Better let the dirt alone—at least for the present. One rebellion at a time is about as much as we can conveniently handle."

New York City, with its Copperhead Mayor, Fernando Wood, appropriated more than $5,000,000 to finance draft evasion, and out of 292,000 men drawn less than 10,000 were inducted.

In that summer of 1863 Lincoln was invited to address a meeting in Springfield, Illinois. Since he could not attend the meeting he decided to send a letter that would be a proclamation to the world. In this letter, after arguing that the only way to save the Union was to win the war, he launched into his main theme, the hope of victory:

"The signs look better. The Father of Waters again goes unvexed to the sea. . . . And while those who have cleared the great river may well be proud, even that is not all. It is hard to say that anything has been more bravely and well done than at Antietam, Murfreesboro', Gettysburg, and on many fields of less note. Nor must Uncle Sam's web-feet be forgotten. At all the watery margins they have been present. Not only on the deep sea, the broad bay, and the

Outcome of Lincoln's election as predicted by a Vanity Fair artist. Verging on hysterics, some magazines and newspapers warned not only that businessmen would shut their shops and cattle would graze in the streets, but also that the nation's currency would become worthless. The undismayed gentleman at the right is Horace Greeley.

A dissolute Lincoln drafts the Emancipation Proclamation. Note that his feet besmirch the Constitution while Satan (junior size) is providing him with counsel from a table decorated with Negro gargoyles and upheld by cloven feet.

"Oh, it's all well enough to say that I must support the dignity of my high office by force, but it's darned uncomfortable I can tall you." This cartoon appeared in a critical Northern newspaper when Southern resistance seemed to be more than equal to military resources of the Federal government.

rapid river, but also up the narrow muddy bayou, and wherever the ground was a little damp, they have made their tracks. . . . Peace does not appear so distant as it did. I hope it will come soon, and come to stay; and so come as to be worth the keeping in all future time. . . . And then there will be some black men who can remember that with silent tongue, and clenched teeth, and steady eye, and well-poised bayonet, they have helped mankind on to this great consummation, while I fear there will be some white ones unable to forget that with malignant heart and deceitful speech they strove to hinder it."

The New York *Times* led a chorus of praise for this letter from the Republican papers, saying "Even the Copperhead gnaws upon it as vainly as a viper upon a file," but the opposition papers did their best at gnawing. One of them charged Lincoln with managing the war not in the interest of the Union but in the interest of the Republican Party. Looking down its editorial nose, it credited the President with a certain homely untutored shrewdness and vulgar honesty, but deplored his lack of "that confident self-reliance and steady vigor of will which are the natural accompaniment of strong faculties. Indeed a hesitating infirmity of purpose which can with difficulty rescue itself from the suspense of conflicting motives and make a decision feeble when at last a decision is reached, is the key to Mr. Lincoln's character." Another critic sarcastically noted Lincoln's reference to "Uncle Sam's web-feet," and offered a poetic effusion to the effect that he had traded the American eagle for a goose.

After the Gettysburg memorial ceremonies on November 19 there were a few commentators who were pleased with the President's address, but they did not include the President himself. He told his friend Lamon "that speech won't *scour*. It is a flat failure and the people are disappointed." When Lincoln was a boy, if the plough gummed up with sticky mud and refused to clean itself, they said "it won't scour." He had felt the same trouble in ploughing through his speech. His numerous critics felt even worse about it.

It is hard for us in our day to understand just why so many people were, as Lincoln felt at the time, disappointed with his Gettysburg Address. It got a generally bad press. The fact that tastes have changed since 1863 can be easily recognized by trying to read, for example, either the famous orators or the famous humorists of the 1860s. Among the latter, Petroleum V. Nasby seemed much funnier to Lincoln than he does to the average reader who dips into his works today. Most of the mid-century stories and parables that still carry a sharp point have come to be attributed to Lincoln himself, some of them no doubt correctly.

In 1863 everyone naturally assumed that the proper ornament for a ceremony such as the Gettysburg dedication would be an oration of dignified length and solidity; and the famous orator Edward Everett was engaged to do the job. It was a good job and the audience liked it, though no one cares about reading his speech today. Everett himself was not puffed up by the applause. The next day he wrote to Lincoln, "I should be glad if I could flatter myself that I came as near the central idea of the occasion in two hours as you did in two minutes." Lincoln in reply praised Everett's performance.

The fact is that at Gettysburg the President had been given a secondary place. Although he could not make a long speech without competing against Everett, his critics regarded the shortness of his contribution as a defect, if not a palpable insult to an audience made up of people who had come long distances and were entitled to something more substantial. Some newspapers spoke of "the silly remarks" of the President, and his "exceeding bad taste." One felt that "Lincoln acted the clown," and another complained that "the ceremony was rendered ludicrous by some of the sallies of that poor President Lincoln. . . . Anything more dull and commonplace it would not be easy to produce."

But there were a few, in addition to Edward Everett, who thought the President had said something of value. The Chicago *Tribune,* for instance, ventured to predict that "The dedicatory remarks of President Lincoln will live among the annals of man."

In December, 1863, Lincoln sent to Congress a "Proclamation of Amnesty and Reconstruction." Resting on his Constitutional pardoning power, he offered amnesty to Southerners who would take an oath to support the Constitution and laws of the United States, and in particular to support the emancipation of the slaves.

This proclamation offended Senator Charles Sumner and other influential Radicals who wanted no mercy for rebels; and it drew violent reactions in the Confederate Congress, where it was recognized as a serious threat to the loyalty of Southern troops. Representative Henry S. Foote of Tennessee proposed resolutions denouncing "the truly characteristic proclamation of amnesty issued by the imbecile and unprincipled usurper who now sits enthroned upon the ruins of Constitutional liberty in Washington City." Another member, opposing Foote's resolutions on tactical grounds, thought that "The true and only treatment which that miserable and contemptible despot, Lincoln, should receive at the hands of this House is silent and unmitigated contempt. This resolution would appear to dignify a paper emanating from that wretched and detestable abortion, whose contemptible emptiness and folly will only receive the ridicule of the civilized world."

As 1864 approached the state legislatures began nominating Lincoln for a second term. It looked as though they had heard the People's voice, and to a great extent they had, but he still had widespread opposition in the North—Copperhead groups, Republican Radicals who thought Lincoln was too soft on the enemy, tired people who wanted peace even without victory, and rival candidates with powerful friends.

The Secretary of the Treasury, Salmon P. Chase, regarded himself as better fitted for the Presidency than the incumbent, and so did his clever and beautiful daughter Kate Chase Sprague, who had married the rich young Governor of Rhode Island. The firm of Jay Cooke & Company, in charge of selling war bonds, was also partial to Chase, and in the first months of 1864 a Chase-for-President organization with plenty of money for expenses was quietly active. Senator Samuel C. Pomeroy of Kansas was Chairman of the Chase committee, which secretly prepared an anti-Lincoln circular, signed only by Pomeroy, marked it "private and confidential," and sent it far and wide.

As Carl Sandburg says, "the Chase band wagon was trying at once to make a noise and be quiet," and naturally the noise prevailed. A Washington newspaper got hold of the circular and printed it, and it was copied all over the country. This precious document informed the world that a group of Republican leaders who called themselves Prominent Senators, Representatives and Citizens—but who were afraid to have their names known—had agreed that they must block the President's efforts to use his power for his own renomination. They asserted that he could not be elected anyway; if he were to be elected his second term would be worse than the first; and a second term would make him much too powerful. Chase, however, they were sure could be elected if all good men would rally round, and he would guarantee economy and purity in the Government. Nothing came of this movement, but it was clear that the President had plenty of enemies in Congress.

In April, 1864, he wrote a letter to a Kentuckian which was widely quoted and even drew from the hostile New York *World* the sour admission that the President "has an *affected* common-sense way of putting things." The *World* insisted, however, that the dishonesty revealed by this document would ruin the President's reputation with the people. The letter said: "I am naturally antislavery. If slavery is not wrong, nothing is wrong. I cannot remember when I did not so think and feel. . . . Whither it is tending seems plain. If God now wills the removal of a great wrong, and wills also that we of the North, as well as you of the South, shall pay fairly for our complicity in that wrong, impartial history will find therein new cause to attest and revere the justice and goodness of God."

Instead of ruining the President, this letter put into words what the people were beginning to recognize: that the abolition of slavery, which was demanded by only a small minority in 1860, had come to be a majority policy of the North, in time to become as essential a peace term as the restoration of the Union.

The Copperhead press in the North was pleased to contribute to the 1864 campaign a sarcastic piece copied from the *South Carolinian* picturing Lincoln as the typical Damned Yankee:

"If the Yankees had searched the length and breadth of their land for a fit representative, they could not have made an apter selection than the man, who, in the Presidential chair, is now playing fantastic tricks before high Heaven. . . .

"With a physiognomy which seems to have been purposely shaped in all its vulgar features to express sharpness of intelligence, blended with emotional insensibility, . . . we might suppose that warmed into life by some Pygmalion of a sketcher, he had just stepped out of the last numbers of *Punch* . . . he presents a more ludicrous appearance than that of Bottom crowned with flowers. . . .

Among cornerstones of the platform that made Lincoln's election possible were Negro Worship, Spirit Rapping, Free Love, Socialism, Atheism, and Rationalism.

Columbia: "Where are my 15,000 sons—murdered at Fredericksburg?" Lincoln: "This reminds me of a little joke." Columbia: "Go tell your joke at Springfield!" This cartoon appeared in Harper's Weekly, January 3, 1863.

"Comedy of Death"—a caricature depicting Lincoln as a macabre clown who treated his troops inhumanly and handled top Union officers like playthings.

"In the man's hopeless inability to apprehend the proprieties of time, place or person; . . . in the usual drawl with which he tells his absurd and inane stories; . . . in his smattering of an education, and in the utter impossibility of awing or abashing him by any exhibition of dignity or reserve, we recognize without difficulty the well-known characteristics of the Yankee, as they have been again and again depicted upon the stage.

"Better cringe under the sternest despotism of Europe—better the dominion of the fiend himself, . . . better, a thousand times better extermination from the very face of the earth, than to own as a master, . . . this mean, wily, illiterate, brutal, unprincipled, and utterly vulgar creature—in a word, this Yankee of the Yankees!"

In May the famous "ghoul editorial" was published in the New York *Herald* as a comment on a mass meeting of Lincoln followers:

"If Lincoln's re-election were not impossible . . . if the people had not long ago decided that General Grant is to be our next President, this ghoul-like meeting would alone destroy his chances and render his defeat a foregone conclusion. The trick of claiming credit for carnage, and trying to make capital out of wholesale slaughter was too transparent and too boldly played. In ancient times the ghouls stole slyly to their abominable festivals at midnight, by the pale glimmer of the sickly moon; but these modern ghouls parade themselves in open day, advertise their purposes in the daily paper, and gather publicly in a hall lit with the blaze of gaslight as if anxious to be universally abhorred and despised. The head ghoul at Washington had not sense enough to forbid the meeting. . . . Could the force of unblushing depravity much further go?"

Afterwards, for some mysterious reason, James Gordon Bennett, publisher of the *Herald*, changed his mind and by the time election came around was found supporting Lincoln. There is evidence that Lincoln bought him off with the offer of the post of Ambassador to France, which, however, he finally decided not to accept. Lincoln was not the first nor the last President to feel that the safety of the nation could justify a cynical use of patronage.

William Cullen Bryant's New York *Evening Post* was strongly pro-Union but not pro-Lincoln. Early in 1864 Bryant was hoping that the Republicans would not have to renominate Lincoln; and he went so far as to reprint the widely copied Brownson article. This was an attack on the President addressed particularly to the intellectual upper classes, among whom Bryant felt himself to be a natural leader. For Lincoln had been given a thorough analysis in *Brownson's Quarterly Review* by the learned and pontifical editor, Dr. Orestes Augustus Brownson.

"Mr. Lincoln," thundered the great Doctor in the tone of Dr. Johnson, "evidently knows nothing of the philosophy of history, or of the higher elements of human nature. He imagines that men act only from low and interested motives, and does not suspect, because he does not feel, the presence of a heroic element."

"His soul seems made of leather," the Doctor sadly observed, "and incapable of any grand or noble emotion. Compared with the mass of men, he is a line of flat prose in a beautiful and spirited lyric. He lowers, he never elevates you. . . . You ask not, can this man carry this nation through its terrible struggles? but can the nation carry this man through them, and not perish in the attempt? . . .

"He never adopts a clean policy. When he hits upon a policy, substantially good in itself, he contrives to belittle it, besmear it in some way to render it mean, contemptible and useless. Even wisdom from him seeems but folly. . . ."

"He is a good sort of man," Dr. Brownson admits, "with much natural shrewdness and respectable native ability; but he is misplaced in the Presidential chair. He lives and moves in an order of thought, in a world many degrees below that in which a great man lives and moves. We blame him not because he is mole-eyed and not eagle-eyed, and that he has no suspicion of that higher region of thought and action in which lie the great interests and questions he is called upon to deal with as President of the United States. . . . The fault that he is not fit for his position is the fault of us that put him there. His only fault is, the misfortune of being unconscious of his own unfitness for his place."

Thus Dr. Brownson managed to make one little thumbprint of his own on the page of history, and William Cullen Bryant succeeded for the moment in regaining the intellectual level he had attained a half-century earlier in *The Embargo*.

When the news came that Lincoln and Andrew Johnson had been nominated the Copperhead papers went into a snobbish fury at the insult offered to the people by putting forward a rail splitter for President and a tailor for Vice President. Evidently the age of statemen was gone, they scolded, and the age of ignorant boorish backwoodsmen and buffoons had taken its place. They spoke of the nominations as a triumph of thieves, plunderers, and shoddyites, referring to the undeniable fact that some future ornaments of high society were founding their fortunes on army contracts, including the supplying of uniforms containing reworked wool, for which by mis-labeling the contractor could obtain virgin-wood prices. The art of partially preventing army procurement frauds had not been devel-oped at that time, but the art of blaming them on the President was already in full flower. With all else that Lincoln had to contend with, therefore, he had to be charged with "the past three years' sway of fraud, corruption, and other Lincolnisms."

As for the Democrats, they had the much-frustrated General McClellan for a candidate, and plenty of excellent slogans denouncing "Old Abe" and affectionately upholding their own "Little Mac." On thousands of bobbing transparencies they proclaimed: "Old Abe removed McClellan. We'll now remove Old Abe" . . . "Time to Swap Horses, November 8th" . . . "The Constitution as it is, the Union as it was" . . . "We demand the habeas corpus" . . . "No more vulgar jokes" . . . "No emancipation; no miscegenation; no confiscation; no subjugation." It is recorded that never had there been so many marching clubs, such torchlight parades, such fireworks, such crowds at mass meetings, such enthusiasm. The story of that campaign raises a vision of what 1952 might have been, if the candi-dates had been Truman and General MacArthur.

In July, the Newark *Evening Journal* mixed politics and disloyalty in an editorial that got the editor in trouble: "It will be seen that Mr. Lincoln has called for another half million of men. Those who wish to be butchered will please step forward. All others will please stay at home and defy Old Abe and his minions to drag them from their families. We hope that the people of New Jersey will at once put their feet down and insist that not a man shall be forced out of the state to engage in the Abolition butchery, and swear to die at their own doors rather than march one step to fulfill the dictates of the mad, revolutionary fanaticism which has destroyed the best government the world ever saw, and now would butcher its remaining inhabitants to carry out a more fanatical sentiment. This has gone far enough and must be stopped. Let the people rise as one man and demand that this wholesale murder shall cease."

The editor was convicted and fined for interference with the draft. Back at his desk, he took up his pen to say: "We have no honeyed words for such a ruler as Abraham Lincoln, a perjured traitor, who has betrayed his country and caused the butchery of hundreds of thousands of the people of the United States in order to accomplish either his own selfish purpose, or to put in force a fanatical, impracticable idea." This much it was fairly safe to say about a Presidential candidate who by this time was inured to being merely called a perjured traitor.

The famous Antietam story had begun to circulate in the Copperhead papers sometime in December, 1862, and by the time the campaign of 1864 was well underway it was full grown with horns and forked tail. As the New York *World* reported it in June:

"Soon after one of the most desperate and sanguinary battles, Mr. Lincoln visited the commanding general and the army. While on his visit the commanding general, with his staff, took him over the field in a carriage and explained to him the plan of the battle, and the particular places where the fight was most fierce. At one point the commanding general said, 'Here on this side of the road, five hundred of our brave fellows were killed, and just on the other side of the road four hundred more were slain, and right on the other side of the wall five hundred rebels were destroyed. We have buried them where they fell.'

" 'I declare,' said the President, 'this is getting gloomy. Let us drive away.' After driving a few rods, the President said, 'This makes a fellow feel gloomy.' 'Jack' (speaking to a companion), 'can't you give us something to cheer us up? Give us a song, and give us a lively one.' Thereupon Jack struck up, as loud as he could bawl, a comic negro song, which he continued to sing while they were riding off from the battle-ground. . . ."

By September the story had gained some gory additional points in the same paper. "While the President was driving over the field in an ambulance, accompanied by Marshal Lamon, General McClellan, and another officer, heavy details of men were engaged in the task

"Trick versus Honors," a cartoon by Matt Morgan, shows a devious Lincoln dropping faked cards from his hands as he cringes before a Confederate soldier whose uniform proclaims victories at Bull Run, Frederick, Fort Hudson, and Charleston. Confidently the Reb remarks: "Oh, Don't give up Abe. Try another trick. I don't mind. I hold all the honors."

Lincoln depicted as a buffoon who joked callously as men lie wounded and dying all about him.

of burying the dead. The ambulance had just reached the neighborhood of the old stone bridge, where the dead were piled highest,
when Mr. Lincoln, suddenly slapping Marshal Lamon on the knee,
exclaimed, 'Come, Lamon, give us that song about Picayune Butler;
McClellan has never heard it.' 'Not now, if you please,' said General
McClellan, with a shudder, 'I would prefer to hear it some other
place and time.'" As McClellan was now running against Lincoln
for the Presidency, this last made a neat contrast.

The *World* also contributed some appropriate verses:

> *Abe may crack his jolly jokes*
> *O'er bloody fields of stricken battle,*
> *While yet the ebbing life-tide smokes*
> *From men that die like butchered cattle;*
> *He, ere yet the guns grow cold,*
> *To pimps and pets may crack his stories. . . ."*

By the time the song writer got at the incident, the men were not
even dead yet, and since the two officer witnesses could not be impeached, Lamon was both pimps and pets.

Lincoln' friends were worried about this story, which was being
constantly repeated and adorned with more gruesome details. Finally
Lamon wrote a description of what had happened, which he proposed
to publish, and Lincoln checked what he had written. Actually
Lincoln had visited the Army more than two weeks after the battle
of Antietam, and he and his party saw no dead bodies at any time
on the trip. The singing incident accurred while they were riding
from one camp to another, and neither General McClellan nor anyone
else made any objections. It was the kind of relaxation that easily
happens in any group of men engaged in a war, when traveling in
safe country and otherwise unoccupied.

Lincoln finally decided not to publish anything about the story.
He "disliked to appear as an apologist for an act of my own which I
know was right." At another time he told Lamon, "If I have not
established character enough to give the lie to this charge, I can only
say that I am mistaken in my own estimate of myself. In politics
every man must skin his own skunk. These fellows are welcome to
the hide of this one."

They were not, of course, welcome at all. It was at the time an effective piece of campaign literature, and to Lincoln it was particularly painful because it belied his real character and the agony that he suffered every day as his duty made him pour thousands of men into the furnace of the war.

The New York *Daily News* was owned by Congressman Benjamin Wood, the Copperhead Mayor's worthy brother. This journal contributed to the gloomy midsummer of 1864 a poem entitled *The Walpurgis Dance at Washington,* which included the following stanzas:

The night was heavy and murk, the moon shone dusky and red.
The air had an odor of sulphurous smoke and of corpses newly dead.
And I saw in fact or a dream, or both confused in one,
A dance and a revel and a maniac rout too hideous for the sun;
And out of it came a cry:
BLOOD! BLOOD! BLOOD! *Let the witches' caulron boil with a nations'*
tears for water!
BLOOD! BLOOD! BLOOD! *Slabby and thick as mud, to sprinkle the*
hungry soil for the carnival of slaughter!

One, tall, and bony and lank, stood forward from the rest,
And told a ribald story with a leer to give it zest,
And said: "Our fire burns feebly, we must pile it up anew;
Tell me the fuel to feed it with ye friends and comrades true!"
And they shouted with mad rejoicing:
BLOOD! BLOOD! BLOOD! . . .

Surely nothing could have been more comforting to the families of those Union soldiers who were reported dead or missing, or who lay in rows in the dirty hospital wards, where germs were still unrecognized and most of the wounded died of blood poisoning.

Lincoln's chances of reelection appeared to be threatened in July by a flareup of the conflict between the President and the Republican Radicals after Congress passed the Wade-Davis bill. This was a bill designed to override Lincoln's plans for reconstruction of the Southern states. Under this bill after all resistance had ceased the people of each state, not including former Confederate soldiers or civilian officers, could set up a new government, with the abolition of slavery and repudiation of Confederate debts. Lincoln received the bill a few minutes before Congress adjourned on July 4. Four days later he issued a statement in which he said that he could not approve abolishing the struggling new free states that the Union armies had helped to their feet in Louisiana and Arkansas. Morever, he told the country, he wanted to have slavery abolished by Constitutional amendment since Congress did not have the necessary power. This statement infuriated the Radicals.

Wade and Davis published a reply that was widely copied and became known as the "Wade-Davis Manifesto." The pocket veto, which had never been used before—"this method of preventing the bill from becoming law without the constitutional responsibility of a veto"—particularly enraged them as a dastardly trick. Like many Congressmen under other administrations, they felt it their duty "to check the encroachments of the Executive." They accused Lincoln of creating shadow governments in the South so as to have their electoral votes at his own disposal, and of not being sincerely in favor of emancipation. They stormed: "A more studied outrage on the legislative authority has never been perpetrated. . . . He must understand that our support is of a cause and not of a man; that the authority of Congress is paramount and must be respected; that the whole body of the Union men in Congress will not submit to be impeached by him of rash and unconstitutional legislation; and if he wishes our support he must confine himself to his executive duties—to obey and to execute, not to make the laws—"

In other words, the Manifesto restated the doctrine of the weak President, which Lincoln was so seriously violating that his party would forever after try to avoid nominating a strong-minded man to the Presidency.

Lincoln recognized that the fury of the extreme radicals was a sign of weakness, and he refused to come down and scuffle with them. As he told a friend, he was reminded of an acquaintance who bought his son a microscope. The boy went around experimenting with his glass on everything that came in his way. One day, at the dinner-table, when his father took up a piece of cheese, the boy cried out, "Don't eat that, father, it is full of *wrigglers*." But the old gentleman took a huge bite and replied: "Let 'em *wriggle;* I can stand it if they can."

Lincoln's judgment turned out to be correct. Wade and Davis were not only microscopic but harmless. As *Harper's Weekly* remarked, "It is simply impossible to make the American people believe that the President is a wily despot or a political gambler."

In August of 1864 all the war news was bad. Grant was making no progress before Richmond, and Sherman was stuck outside Atlanta. Discouraged by the stalemate, some of the more faint-hearted Republicans joined Lincoln's enemies in what was called the "Jonah movement," to dump him overboard and look for some more attractive candidate. How the President felt about it is indicated in an account left by his friend Carl Schurz of a visit with him one hot August evening. Lincoln told his visitor that he could carry his burden without complaining, but he was hurt that people in his own party should question his motives:

"They urge me with the most violent language to withdraw from the contest, although I have been unanimously nominated, in order to make room for a better man. I wish I could. . . . But I am here, and that better man is not here. And if I should step aside to make room for him, it is not at all sure—perhaps not even probable—that he would get here. . . . My withdrawal, therefore, might, and probably would, bring on a confusion worse counfounded. God knows, I have at least tried very hard to do my duty, to do right to everybody and wrong to nobody. And now to have it said by men who have been my friends and who ought to know me better, that I have been seduced by what they call the lust of power, and that I have been doing this and that unscrupulous thing hurtful to the common cause, only to keep myself in office! Have they thought of the common cause when trying to break me down? I hope they have."

When the lamps were lit, Schurz caught Lincoln for a moment with his eyes moist and his face showing strong emotion; and then he got control of himself and soon was joking with his guest. As he shook hands in parting, he said, "Well, things might look better, and they might look worse. Let us all do the best we can." In a few days things did look better. News came that Sherman had captured Atlanta.

Harper's Weekly remarked in September, 1864, perhaps not too accurately, that never since George Washington had a President been

A diabolical Lincoln consigning to the flames the nation's laws and, as the reader can clearly see, an effigy of the sacred Washington. Note that documents labelled Emancipation, Suspension, and the Draft are providing fuel for a fire that is burning States' Rights, Liberty, and, assumedly, every noble principle of democracy. In the original caption Lincoln is snorting at Washington's effigy: "I'll warn yer. Your old Constitution won't do U. S."

"Sinbad Lincoln and the Old Man of the Sea" shows the President as a harassed flunky for Secretary of the Navy Gideon Welles. Actually Lincoln had no more loyal supporter in his Cabinet throughout the war.

the target for so much mud. It offered in support of this opinion the following list of terms applied to the President by the friends of General McClellan: "Filthy Story-Teller, Despot, Liar, Thief, Braggart, Buffoon, Usurper, Monster, Ignoramus Abe, Old Scoundrel, Perjurer, Robber, Swindler, Tyrant, Fiend, Butcher, Land-Pirate;" and finally as a breathless and curiously anemic climax of fury: "A Long, Lean, Lank, Lantern-Jawed, High Cheek-Boned, Spavined, Rail-Splitting Stallion." The magazine observed, however, that the opposition was being baffled by the hard fact that most of the public knew the President's character and could not be moved by furious denunciations. "From the day when covert rebellion lay in wait to assassinate him in Baltimore, through all the mad hate of the rebel press to the last malignant sneer of Copperhead Conservatism and foreign jealousy, the popular confidence in the unswerving fidelity and purity of purpose of the President has smiled the storm to scorn."

It was noticeable by the middle of October that loyal Republicans were worrying more and more about the President's personal safety. Most of the President's visitors said something about hoping he would not be killed off by the cares of his office like Presidents Harrison and Taylor. Many letters also came in pleading with him to take care of himself. There seemed to be a foreboding sense of danger, not excluding the fear of foul play. It is not surprising that after months of accumulated suggestions Lincoln himself should have had a vivid dream, shortly before his death, in which he heard sounds of mourning and was informed that the President had been assassinated.

During the campaign crowds of Copperheads listened to oratory such as that provided by Congressman Samuel S. Cox on July 23 from the courthouse steps of Mt. Vernon, Ohio, which, according to the reports, was greeted with "immense applause."

"Mr. Cox: So far as Mr. Lincoln is concerned, he made peace impossible by his own conduct. . . . Will not history, nay, will not the living present, curse the execrable tool of fanaticism, who thus, even in the agony and article of our national demise, flings away the hopes and interests of this nation?

"A Voice: God damn him. [Laughter and cheers.]

"Mr. Cox: I cannot join in the earnest imprecation of my gentle friend. [Laughter.] While I do invoke that Providence may deal mercifully with the President, I pray that the people in November will damn him to an immortality of infamy. [Immense applause.] Think of it, in the very midst of the strife, . . . this retailer of smutty stories; this vulgar tyrant over men's thoughts, opinions, presses, persons and lives, rejects the blessed opportunity which the Angel of Peace tenders to our afflicted land. [Cheers.]

In November, however, not only was Lincoln elected—Cox was defeated.

When the election returns were in Lincoln had 212 electoral votes to 21 for McClellan. In the popular vote, however, he had only 55 percent of the total; there had been nearly two million votes against him. The Southern press tried to find comfort in the thought that Lincoln was an incompetent who had been unable to conquer them, whereas the defeated candidate was "an accomplished soldier," wishfully forgetting that Lincoln had dismissed McClellan for failing to accomplish victories. In New York, *The World* remarked sulkily that probably Lincoln would manage to lose the war, after which McClellan would come forward and save the Union after all.

Tough old Sam Medary of the *Crisis* found some comforting comments in the English Tory papers that he felt were worth reprinting. One of these pointed out that "Mr. Lincoln's predecessors were gentlemen; men of some experience either in military, diplomatic or political life, men at least of average intelligence, and of unquestioned personal integrity. . . . Mr. Lincoln is a vulgar, brutal boor, wholly ignorant of political science, of military affairs, of everything which a statesman should know. . . . We rejoice that the cause of oppression, robbery and injustice is entrusted to the hands of a vacillating, helpless imbecile rather than to those of an able, resolute and efficient soldier." Another, bravely hoping for the worst, was pleased to say that the South would never so dishonor all its noble traditions as to ask for peace terms from such a creature, and that there might even be a chance for a rebellion in the North to throw off the tyrant's reign of terror. It concluded that "Never were issues so momentous placed in so feeble a hand; never was so great a place in history filled by a figure so mean."

Not all the British press was Conservative, however. The *Spectator* showed a better understanding of the course of American history. It pointed out that this was a war of the people against the aristocracy that controlled the South, in which the people must win a clear-cut victory, or "the cause of liberty would have received a heavy, perhaps a deadly wound." It noted that under Lincoln's leadership the American people had gradually come around to the point of demanding an end to slavery, by a movement not of the "talking class," but of the common folk with whom Lincoln had the closest affinity. "Secure of their support, Mr. Lincoln can afford to disregard the clamor of city mobs and the apprehensions of the mercantile class."

Just before the 1864 election Governor Andrew of Massachusetts had written to the President about a widow in Boston, Mrs. Bixby, who, he said, had lost five sons in battle. He suggested that Lincoln send her an appropriate letter. Lincoln waited until the election was over, and then wrote to Mrs. Bixby:

"Dear Madam:

"I have been shown in the files of the War Department a statement of the Adjutant-General of Massachusetts that you are the mother of five sons who have died gloriously on the field of battle. I feel how weak and fruitless must be any words of mine which could attempt to beguile you from the grief of a loss so overwhelming. But I cannot refrain from tendering to you the consolation that may be found in the thanks of the Republic they died to save. I pray that our heavenly Father may assuage the anguish of your bereavement, and leave you only the cherished memory of the loved and lost, and the solemn pride that must be yours to have laid so costly a sacrifice upon the altar of freedom.

Yours very sincerely and respectfully,
Abraham Lincoln"

The millions of people who read and were deeply moved by the letter to Mrs. Bisby could not know with what a knife twisting in his own heart the President had written it. For the mother of his own twenty-one-year-old son was no such heroic character. Mary Lincoln was so close to madness that he had had to keep Robert out of the Army to avoid unspeakable horrors inside the White House.

The sudden death of Willie Lincoln, the second of the three sons, in February, 1862, had had much to do with Mrs. Lincoln's state of mind. Elizabeth Keckley, a former slave, who was Mrs. Lincoln's dressmaker and intimate companion, says in her reminiscences: "After

Willie's death, she could not bear the sight of anything he loved. Costly bouquets were presented to her, but she turned from them with a shudder, and either placed them in a room where she could not see them, or threw them out of the window. She gave all of Willie's toys—everything connected with him—away, as she said she .could not look upon them without thinking of her poor dead boy, and to think of him, in his white shroud and cold grave, was maddening. I never saw in my life a more peculiarly constituted woman."

The Copperheads seized upon the publication of the Bixby letter as an occasion for further twisting the knife in Lincoln's heart. Sam Medary led off:

"He speaks of the 'solemn pride that must be *hers,* at having laid so costly a sacrifice upon the altar of freedom,' " sneered the Copperhead editor. "This kind of sympathy is cheap, and easily manufactured; and when one reflects that the man who is ostentatiously shedding his tears over the remains of Mrs. Bixby's five sons has two sons who are old enough to be laid upon the 'altar,' but whom he keeps at home in luxury, we can easily understand the hypocrisy of all this sympathy for the poor bereaved widow. Why is it, we ask, that Mr. Lincoln's sons should be kept from the dangers of the field, while the sons of the laboring man are to be hurried into the harvest of death at the front? Are the sons of the rail-splitter, porcelain, and these others common clay? Or is it that Mr. Robert Lincoln, the young gentleman whose face is so familiar at watering places and billiard-rooms in the metropolis, has taken his younger brother into the speculation of cultivating cotton on Island Number Ten, through the agency of slave labor, and they can't be spared from their business?"

Since the facts about Mary Lincoln's condition had to be hidden in silence, it would have been futile for anyone to reply that the cotton story was made out of the whole cloth, and that Tad Lincoln was only eleven years old. In February of the following year, however, Robert Lincoln's insistent demands for military service were at last rewarded by a compromise. He was attached as a Captain to the staff of General Grant, where his mother thought he would not be in danger.

While Lincoln throughout his term of office lived in a storm of hate

"Daring American Acrobat." Prompted by sympathy for the South, this British cartoon shows Lincoln performing to the cheers of the Northern commonalty as the rulers of Britain, France, Italy, and Austria look on with distinct disapproval. Lincoln has one foot precariously hooked to a ring labelled Emancipation while his other foot moves toward Utter Ruin. Rings at right side are labelled Paper Money, Brag, and Buncombe.

This Vanity Fair cartoon didn't do General George McClellan any good
when he became the Presidential candidate of the Democratic Party in
1864. In depicting Little Mac as a huge whiskey bottle on the rampage
against drinking the artist suggested the General was a hypocrite.

and obloquy gradually diminishing after the black summer of 1864, his opposing President, Jefferson Davis, came to be more viciously hated by desperate Southerners as they felt themselves losing the war. The Charleston *Mercury,* in the very birthplace of the Confederacy, paid its respects to both Davis and Lincoln on January 10, 1865. The *Mercury* charged that the Confederate Government was "a pandemonium of imbecility, laxness, laxity, weakness, failure," made up of "tools and sycophants, men subservient to Mr. Davis' will and whims and dictations . . . whilst the country reels and staggers under the fearful burden of their helpless counsels, and their imbecile actions. On every side we see petty favorites lifted up to promotions and pushed into positions of importance, whilst men of magnificent gallantry and accomplished minds are suffered to fight on in the ranks, or to fall in some position of inferior command. . . . Never was a cause more enthusiastically loved by a soldiery—never was so much power, in numbers, in enthusiasm, in endurance, in courage, so frittered away, so broken down, so misapplied, so utterly disorganized, by an ineradicable vice of unscrupulous administration."

To Lincoln the *Mercury* gave reluctant praise: ". . . whether 'running his machine' in the pathway of his predecessors, or not, he has run it with a stern, inflexible purpose, a bold, steady hand, a vigilant, active eye, a sleepless energy, a fanatic spirit, and an eye single to his end—conquest—emancipation. . . . Blackguard and buffoon as he is, he has pursued his end with an energy as untiring as an Indian, and a singleness of purpose that might almost be called patriotic. If he were not an unscrupulous knave in his end, and a fanatic in his political views, he would undoubtedly command our respect as a ruler, so far as we are concerned."

As March 4th approached Lincoln viewed the coming inauguration with a quieter mind than he had had four years before; he was beginning to see the dawn of peace. Late in February, according to the painter Carpenter, he came into his office with a roll of manuscript which he put away in a drawer, saying cheerfully, "Lots of wisdom in that document, I suspect. It is what will be called my 'second inaugural.' "

On Inauguration Day it rained; the crowds stood in deep mud and with wet clothes, waiting. In the Senate Vice President Andrew

Johnson was being sworn in, and was contributing a long and embarrassing speech showing all too many signs of intoxication. Just recovering from typhoid fever, he had made the mistake of fortifying himself in Vice President Hamlin's office with two glasses of brandy. When at last the painful scene was over and the President was in the procession going to the East Front for his own inauguration, he told a marshal, "Don't let Johnson speak outside."

Outside, the rain had stopped. The tall, gaunt figure of the President advanced to the front of the platform, and a roar of applause thundered again and again across the vast crowd. As he began to speak, suddenly the noonday sun blazed down in splendor on him and on the people.

Lincoln told the people that four years ago neither side had wanted war, and the people cheered and applauded. Then he told them that both North and South had felt the just hand of God purging them of their guilt for the national sin of slavery, and there was less applause. (Later he wrote: "It is a truth which I thought needed to be told, and, as whatever of humiliation there is in it falls most directly on myself, I thought others might afford for me to tell it.")

And finally came the never-to-be-forgotten words, while people stood, unabashed, with sudden tears in their eyes: "With malice toward none; with charity for all; with firmness in the right, as God gives us to see the right, let us strive on to finish the work we are in; to bind up the nation's wounds; to care for him who shall have borne the battle and for his widow, and his orphan—to do all which may achieve and cherish a just and lasting peace among ourselves, and with all nations."

As the procession moved along Pennsylvania Avenue from the Capitol to the White House, it being then about two o'clock in the afternoon, people saw the evening star shining in the west. Lieutenant Ashmun of the cavalry escort reported it as "the first and only time that most of us ever saw that star at that hour of the day." Lincoln had been most impressed by the way the sun came out for his speech. He said to a friend, "Did you notice that sunburst? It made my heart jump."

Noah Brooks, a young newspaper man with whom Lincoln had developed an intimate friendship, has left some illuminating comments on how the President felt in the beginning of his second term. He was tired but sure of himself. Ten days after the inauguration he was so worn out that he had to lie in bed for a Cabinet meeting; and at the end of a hard day he spoke to Brooks of feeling flabby and of "the tired spot which can't be got at." But his courage was good, and he quoted the Old Testament passage, "His eye was not dim, nor his natural force abated." He blamed the newspapers for overplaying good news of the war, raising hopes that could not be soon fulfilled. But he was never weary of commenting on the longsuffering patience and courage of the people. Brooks reports: "I have been him shed tears when speaking of the cheerful sacrifices of the light and strength of so many happy homes throughout the land. His own patience was marvelous; and never crushed at defeat or unduly excited by success, his demeanor under both was an example for all men."

The Inaugural did not appease the Copperheads, for they were not ready to admit that the South was beaten and would need mercy. Insofar as they were concerned "the partially honest coward has been transformed into the unblushingly corrupt bully"; they "did not conceive it possible that even Mr. Lincoln could produce [anything] so slip-shod, so loose-jointed, so puerile, not alone in literary construction, but in ideas, its sentiments, its grasp."

But Lincoln could see the end, and he meant what he said about reconciliation. On March 28th, he had a long meeting with his two winning Generals, Grant and Sherman, on board the steamboat *River Queen*, lying in the James River. After his long years of working with a country that "didn't know it was at war," and with generals who refused to fight, at last the three strong men had found one another and had pushed the war close to a conclusion. Lincoln even hoped the Southern armies might collapse without a final bath of blood; but the three men trusted one-another's judgment to do whatever had to be done.

And all three agreed on the proper nature of the peace. All that they wanted, as Sherman recalled years later, "was to get the men composing the Confederate armies back to their homes, at work on their farms and in their shops." As to Jeff Davis, Lincoln told them he was hardly at liberty to speak his mind fully, but intimated that Davis ought to clear out, "escape the country," only it would not do for him to say so openly. It was not the "tyrant" Lincoln and his two implacable fighting generals who ever thought of taking vengeance on the defeated South. That was for the fuming politicians who called themselves "Radicals," and who would wreak their will only over Lincoln's dead body.

After the fall of Richmond, a young French diplomat, the Marquis de Chambrun, was riding through Petersburg in a carriage with Lincoln, when Lincoln stopped the carriage to look at a noble white oak with gnarled wide-reaching arms. Chambrun was deeply impressed by Lincoln's feeling for the tree and recorded that "he talked as if he might be some kind of a tree himself."

Lee surrendered on Palm Sunday, April 9. On the 11th Lincoln spoke to a crowd gathered on the White House lawn. It was a long, carefully prepared speech addressed to the country rather than to his immediate audience, calling for reconciliation and rebuilding. The Radicals muttered: " 'Magnanimity' is the great word with the disloyal who think to tickle the President's ear with it." "A universal amnesty must not be granted." "The President's speech and other things augur confusion and uncertainty." "Now we see the dregs of his backwardness." Even Vice President Andrew Johnson at that time was telling everyone he met, "Treason is a crime and must be made odious."

April 14th was the fourth anniversary of the fall of Fort Sumter, and it was Good Friday, the Day of the Crucifixion. "Everything is bright this morning," Lincoln said to a visitor. "The war is over. We are going to have good times now." He was gay and laughing as he worked through his appointments; and when he went for a carriage drive with Mrs. Lincoln late in the afternoon he told her, "I never felt so happy in my life." That evening supper was kept waiting while the President entertained two old friends from home, reading to them with shouts of laughter the latest sketch by Petroleum V. Nasby, in which he was called "the Goriller Linkin."

But finally he tore himself away from the happiest day of his life, and went to meet his fate. As he sat in his theater box, there came a sudden crash, and for him the day, and the life work, were over.

In the words of Truslow Adams: "The war was won; the Union was preserved; but peace and love and honesty and brotherly kindness had fled with Lincoln's soul."

CHAPTER VII

TARGET OF CALUMNY

On the night of April 14, 1865, Andrew Johnson, Vice President of the United States, went to bed early, in his room at the Kirkwood Hotel where the present Raleigh Hotel stands. A few blocks away, at Ford's Theatre, Johnson's friend L. I. Farwell was watching the show. When Farwell heard the shot and Mrs. Lincoln's scream from the box, his next thought was for the Vice President. Dashing out and down the street to the Kirkwood, he called to the clerk to guard the stair—that the President had been shot—and rushed up to pound on the door of Room 68. All was quiet inside, and his heart sank. He shouted and pounded, and at last there came a sleepy answer. Johnson was alive. The man in Room 126, who had been delegated to kill him, had got drunk instead and missed his chance.

So the Presidency came to the man whom Lincoln had picked in 1864 to be his running mate. Lincoln chose him because he not only agreed with Lincoln's policies, but also had been toughened by two years as Military Governor of the turbulent state of Tennessee, and before that by a long career as a Unionist Democrat in frequent danger of mob violence and assassination. He would need to be tough, for the political currents of the postwar period were going to be violent.

As the news Lincoln's death spread across the country, publicly all the world was in mourning. He had "exchanged the laurel wreath of time for the crown of immortality," and the Democratic press, both North and South, joined with the Republican papers in deploring the deed. The Southerners recognized at once that this was a disaster, that Lincoln had been the South's best hope of mercy and restoration.

Lincoln was not yet cold when the Radical Republicans in Washington were already organizing their forces to take advantage of his death. On the afternoon of April 15th leading Radicals held a caucus. The substance of their discussion has come down to us from a less enthusiastic fellow-traveler who attended. The prevailing mood was that Lincoln's removal was "a Godsend to our cause." Hostility to Lincoln's policy of conciliation, and contempt for his weakness, were plainly shown. Various accounts of those first Radical meetings emphasize their atmosphere of elation. "While the politicians were drinking, smoking, boasting, planning, indulging in profanity and obscenity in many conferences behind closed doors, the men and women of no importance were filing by the casket of the dead."

Johnson took his time about announcing his policies. All he would say was, "The only assurance that I can give of the future is reference to the past"; policies "must be left for development as the Administration progresses."

The new President already had a long and tumultuous past. He had come up in a hard school. By origin he was a Southern "poor white," born in North Carolina, the son of a hotel porter, with small chance of ever rising to a higher station. But when he migrated to East Tennessee at the age of seventeen and set up as a tailor, he found himself in a more Northern type of society, in which a successful tailor might go into politics. He prospered and in time came to have eight slaves of his own. But he hated the system of great plantations in the deep South, where, as he said, "the capitalist owned the labor," leaving no fair chance for the free worker, with nothing but his own labor to sell, to compete against the monopolized labor supply.

Johnson went into politics as a Unionist Democrat, taking Andrew Jackson as his hero and model. There is a legend that as the poverty-stricken Johnson family was trekking from North Carolina toward East Tennessee, with its pitiful household goods in a rickety cart, a troop of horsemen dashed by, spattering them with mud. The grim warrior at their head, however, came back and rebuked his men; then he dismounted to speak to the mud-spattered lad. According to the legend, he assured Andrew that Tennessee was a land of opportunity where he might well find success and fortune. Then, "I am General Jackson," he said and rode away. Whatever the truth of the legend, Andrew Johnson did find fame and fortune as an Andrew Jackson Unionist Democrat. Starting as alderman, he rose to State Senator, and by 1843 was already a Congressman.

Johnson's political position, however, guaranteed him an early initiation into some of the roughest aspects of Border-state life. He quickly came under the fire of "Parson" William G. Brownlow, for instance, whose Knoxville *Whig* announced in June, 1845, "Andrew Johnson is a VILE CALUMNIATOR, AN INFAMOUS DEMAGOGUE, A COMMON AND PUBLIC LIAR, AN IMPIOUS INFIDEL, AND AN UNMITIGATED VILLAIN." Brownlow also accused Johnson of trying to hire an assassin to murder him.

Another accusation that went the rounds in that year was that Johnson was an illegitimate son of a Judge in North Carolina. This charge got under his skin. When the campaign was over and he was safely reelected to Congress he took the trouble to go back to Raleigh and gather affidavits supporting the character of his mother, which he published in Tennessee.

As for Parson Brownlow, as fate would have it, nineteen years later, in 1864, he was a delegate to the National Unionist Convention in Baltimore, where were gathered old Whigs, new Republicans—including even some Radicals—and Unionist Democrats, to unite in renominating Abraham Lincoln. Parson Brownlow's part was to recommend for the Vice Presidential nomination none other than Andrew Johnson, "whom it has been my good luck and bad fortune to fight untiringly and perseveringly for the last twenty-five years." The delegates applauded, and in due course his man was chosen.

In Tennessee Johnson was hated not only by the Whigs as a Democrat, but also by most of the Democrats as a Unionist, outside of the Unionist area of East Tennessee. Nevertheless he did succeed not only in getting elected to the House by his own district, but later by the State Legislature to the United States Senate. Because of his dislike of the Southern plantation system, when he first went to Congress in 1843 he took as his special project the promotion of a Homestead Act, to provide opportunities for free workers like himself to settle in the West. He was a Senator by the time his Act was finally passed in 1862.

As a Senator during the desperate days of 1860-61, while the Southerners were defiantly resigning, Andrew Johnson distinguished himself by fiery orations in defense of the Union and the Constitution, rousing all the North to a fever of enthusiasm. He was hailed as a second Andrew Jackson and the reports of his speeches contributed greatly to the strength of Lincoln's position when he came into office on March 4, 1861. In the South the Tennesseean became equally well known and correspondingly hated. One letter, from Grand Junction, Mississippi, will illustrate how people felt about him:

"I have a mulatto slave remarkable for his impudence. . . . As a means of humiliating my slave it has been recommended to me to send him to Washington City with a *cowhide* and instruct him to give your back and shoulders some *marks of his attention.* . . . It is thought that Coming in Contact with *you,* will so effectually *disgrace* him, that the effect on him will be so humiliating, that he will make a good obedient slave." Johnson with his usual care filed this away with a notation on the envelope: "Threatened assault From Mississippi Attended to."

After such experiences it was natural for Johnson to be chosen by Lincoln in March, 1862, to serve as Military Governor of Tennessee and reestablish the Federal authority there. East Tennessee was overrun by Southern armies, and in the rest of the state Southern sympathizers were in the majority. Nashville, where he was surrounded and besieged for months, was itself "the very furnace of treason," and being Governor was a strenuous job. As one of his wool-hatted correspondents expressed a widely-held sentiment: "Go it Andy. This is your day. But while you are going so high you must not For get that every dog has his day And the day is not far advanse when you will have your Just day, and that day cannot come untill you are tared and fethered and burnt."

When 1864 came along Lincoln sent General Daniel E. Sickles to Tennessee to see how Johnson had been doing, with a view to considering him for the Vice Presidency. Sickles reported that his record was good and that with all his tendency to violent threats he had been no more severe than the desperate nature of his job required. On the basis of this report Lincoln decided to get Johnson as his running mate, being already convinced of his courage, and recognizing the advantage of having a Border-state Unionist Democrat on the ticket. Moreover, as a Southerner Johnson was free of the Radical thirst for vengeance, which Lincoln foresaw would be his most serious postwar problem.

When Johnson became President, he was soon in a relatively strong position with the public, both North and South. As the shock of Lincoln's death wore off there was a wave of appreciation for the

Caricatures of the dour countenance of Andrew Johnson in the course of a very typical day.

A cartoon that accompanied allegations that Johnson was inebriated when he took oath as President.

Johnson shown trafficking with the Devil, to Lincoln's disgust.

new man in the North, where people remembered how he had thrilled them four years ago by his eloquent defense of the Union in the Senate. The Southerners were slower to relax their hatred, but they were now a beaten people; they had suddenly recognized their loss in Lincoln's death; and as Johnson's policies unfolded they began to hope that he would follow the merciful policies of Lincoln himself. Here, however, was the material for violent trouble between the Democrat in the White House and the Radical Republicans in Congress.

Johnson believed that secession was the work of the plantation aristocracy, who had deceived and bullied the "wool hats" into fighting for their slave system. He therefore felt that the principal leaders ought to be punished for treason; and this well-known belief of his was at first taken by the Radicals as a sign that he would be easily persuaded to follow their lead. What they overlooked was that Johnson believed the common folk in the South had been helpless in the hands of the aristocrats, and that therefore they should not be punished, but should be encouraged to settle down and earn a living as good citizens.

The Radicals, on the other hand, wanted vengeance on the Southern whites as a people. From the Abolitionists among them they derived their ideal formula for vengeance and justice—to take the voting privilege away from the whites and give it to the Negroes. The fact that the illiterate Negroes would become helpless tools of corrupt Northern adventurers was no objection in their eyes. Their position was by no means based entirely on emotions built up during the war. The practical fact did not escape them that so long as they could exclude the Southern whites from voting and from Congress, the Republican Party would remain in secure control. Behind all the smudge, that was where the real fire lay.

The Radical leaders called assiduously at the White House and did their best to lead the new President in the way he should go. He was cordial but not always amenable. When General Ben Butler urged him to have Lee tried for treason, he went so far as to ask General Grant about it. But Grant said he had accepted Lee's parole, and that neither Lee nor any of his officers could honorably be tried unless they should violate their paroles. The President followed Grant's judgment. In the end the fact that none of the Southern leaders were hanged was mainly due to the influence of Grant and Sherman, the two stern warriors who had conferred with Lincoln on the *River Queen* just before the end of the war.

On May 29 Johnson issued two proclamations that ended his uneasy honeymoon with the Radicals.

The Proclamation of Amnesty granted pardon "to all persons who have directly or indirectly participated in the existing rebellion," subject to the taking of an oath of allegiance, and with fourteen classes of exceptions. The exceptions included chiefly men who had quit the United States military or civil services to join the Confederacy. Class 13 was notable, as it excluded from the general amnesty all persons who had voluntarily participated in secession and who had property valued at over $20,000. This proviso represented Johnson's firm belief that the war guilt rested on the rich plantation owners. At the end of the Proclamation was a paragraph saying that persons in the excepted classes could apply to the President for pardon and that it would be liberally extended. The President wanted no mass punishment, but he wanted to net all the big fish and then decide which ones to keep.

The second May 29 proclamation provided for setting up a loyal government in North Carolina. Other states quickly followed. Johnson made it clear that each state should start with the voting system as it existed before the war, subject to a loyalty test, and should make its own decisions as to admitting new classes of voters; for he believed that suffrage laws could be imposed on the states only by Constitutional amendment. Under his authority the states quickly organized themselves, and elected Senators and Congressmen to knock at the doors of Congress when it should meet in December.

These actions were correctly taken by the Radicals as a declaration of war against their plans. A look at Johnson's record, as he had already suggested, might have warned them, for on July 26, 1861, as Senator he had introduced a resolution on the meaning of the war. The resolution stated plainly that this was a war not for oppression or conquest, not to overthrow or to establish any institutions, but to maintain the Constitution and preserve the Union with the rights of the states unimpaired. When these objects had been accomplished, he maintained, the war ought to cease. That 1861 resolution passed the Senate by a vote of 35 to 5.

It was clear that the new President stood for clemency and reconciliation. He also stood for the Jacksonian doctrine of states' rights under the Constitution not including any right of secession. The Radicals insisted that the Southern states had committed suicide and their land was now conquered territory, from which new states could be formed and admitted to the Union only by consent of Congress. Johnson held that no state could cease to exist, and that it was the President's duty to see to it that each state reestablished "a republican form of government," as provided in the Constitution.

Legally there was much illogic in both sides of the argument, which can be found detailed in the histories. The point here is that Johnson stood for reconciliation and rebuilding; the Radicals, in their thirst for vengeance and political power, played fast and loose with Constitutional law. Johnson could not foresee the changes that within less than a century would make the New Deal Democrats under F.D.R. into federalists, and turn the reactionary Republicans into states' righters. This lack of prevision complicated his problems, but the verdict of history is that many evils came to both South and North in the next forty years that might not have happened if Johnson had succeeded in beating down the Radicals and winning reelection in 1868.

In August, 1865, the Johnson family moved into the White House. They included the President's son, Col. Robert Johnson, who had come to assist his father in routine work; D. T. Patterson, son-in-law, a Senator from Tennessee; two daughters, Mrs. Patterson and Mrs. Stover; and five lively grandchildren, in addition to Mrs. Johnson herself, who had been invalided by her hardships in the war but was still very much alive.

Life at the White House was now vastly different from that of the Lincolns. Instead of the shrewish Mary Lincoln, on her way to the madhouse, there was the remarkable Eliza Johnson, who, though she rarely left her upstairs room, yet was the center of the family. The simple and gracious personality of this shoemaker's daughter spread a spirit of affection through the household; and people noticed that the three broods of vigorous children never showed signs of quarreling. It was said of her that she was "an angel," and that "the nearest approach to ideal married life I've ever seen or known," as one of the staff put it, "was in the case of Andrew Johnson and his wife." To a newspaper reporter the First Lady said quietly, "We are plain people from Tennessee, temporarily in a high place, and you must not expect too much of us in a social way." This simple speech was widely quoted, and the plain people loved it.

Another difference was noted. Mrs. Lincoln had had a mania for extravagant clothes; in fact, her debts of over $25,000 would have shocked her husband if he had lived to know about them. But the humble tailor's wife, and the two daughters who relieved her as White House hostesses, were always dressed in perfect taste, and Johnson himself looked far more dignified than the neglected Old Abe. People liked this quiet dignity, and it was a solid base of emotional strength for a man around whose head such violent storms were to howl.

Four years later the ever-faithful Gideon Welles wrote in his diary about his farewell to the departing Johnson family: "No better persons have occupied the Executive mansion, and I part from them, socially and personally, with sincere regret."

In 1865 while the Radicals were simmering, the newspapers of other persuasions, Northern, Southern, and foreign, were praising the President for his wisdom and good heart. His Message to Congress in December, which was written under his direction by the historian George Bancroft, explained his position and asked for patience in working out the relation between the two races in the South. His popularity reached a high point; then Congress met and the Radicals had a place to work.

Congress came immediately under Radical control. They proceeded to entrench themselves by excluding all representation from the Southern states and by setting up a joint steering committee of fifteen to manage their program. The fifteen were headed by implacable Thaddeus Stevens, Congressman from the Gettysburg district of Pennsylvania.

The Radicals passed a bill to continue the Freedmen's Bureau, which had been set up in the War Department on March 3, 1865, to protect the rights of Negroes in the South. It had been manned by cheap political hacks, whom Grant reported to be "a useless and dangerous set." Johnson vetoed the bill on the ground that it in-

King Johnson turns away as his royal flunkies carry out the execution of Henry Ward Beecher, Wendell Phillips, and other opponents of slavery.

An unfeeling Caesar (Johnson) looks on as Negroes are massacred after the withdrawal of troops from South.

volved an unjustifiable continuance of martial law and suspension of many articles of the Bill of Rights, and the Radicals failed to override the veto.

Unfortunately this veto pleased not only the Republican moderates but also the Copperheads, whose support was the last thing Johnson wanted. He had not forgotten what the Copperhead press had said of him as recently as March, when he came in with Lincoln and the war was still on. They had called him a debauched demagogue without political principles but one who "could bellow his bastard 'loyalty' loudly." They shivered to think "that only one frail life stands between this insolent, clownish drunk and the presidency. . . . Should this Andrew Johnson become his successor, the decline and fall of the American republic would smell as rank in history as that of the Roman Empire under such atrocious monsters in human shape as Nero and Caligula." Johnson could rest easy as long as the unspeakable Copperheads talked this way about him; but their praise was poison. Even worse, the egregious Vallandigham insisted on snuggling up to the Administration and had to be pushed away.

On Washington's Birthday in 1866 the President greeted a serenading crowd with a speech accusing the Radicals of being as much enemies of the Union as the secessionists had been. The Radical press frothed with fury. The papers said he had made a drunken speech to a Copperhead mob, and that he had mistresses visiting him in the White House (somehow concealed from all his daughters and grandchildren). From then on it was open war on both sides. The Radicals prepared for overriding future vetoes by intimidating the Republican moderates and expelling Democrats on any half-plausible technicality. A series of reconstruction bills followed and one veto after another was overridden. Meanwhile Secretary of War Stanton, who had been false to President Buchanan and false to Lincoln, was betraying the Administration to the Radicals from his vantage point in the Cabinet, and Johnson was beginning to suspect his treachery.

In the summer of 1866, the President, irked by Radical control of Congress, decided to try a purge. He would "swing around the circle," as he had often done with good results in earlier years in Tennessee. He would take his case to the people, and ask them to choose a more conservative Congress in the Fall elections—a dangerous form of political intervention for any President to attempt.

In the North there were many moderate Republicans who enthusiastically supported the Lincoln-Johnson policies; but they were apt to be decent, scrupulous folk, no match for the Radicals, as it turned out. And there was the embarrassment of undeniable Copperhead support, soon labeled by the Radical press the "Copperjohnsons."

As Johnson set out on August 28, there were ovations in Washington, and through Maryland and Delaware, but by the time he reached Philadelphia he met organized opposition. The city officials were Radical, and they tried to prevent demonstrations by giving out false information on the time of Johnson's arrival. This trick failed, and the crowds were enthusiastic. The reception was good in New Jersey, and New York was a triumph. The hostile *Tribune* was forced to admit that "so far as popular demonstration and enthusiasm is concerned, the ovation . . . forms a striking contrast to all other displays of the kind that have preceded it in this city."

Johnson spoke that night at a banquet at Delmonico's. He said that his ambition was to pour the balm of Gilead into the nation's wounds, and to reunite the brothers who "have lived with us and been part of us from the establishment of the Government to the commencement of the rebellion. . . . That being done, my ambition is completed. I would rather live in history in the affections of my countrymen as having consummated that great end than to be President forty times." The diners rose and cheered. That was the high point of the trip.

By the time his train reached Schenectady, Johnson's voice was showing wear and tear, and he was visibly tired, but the crowds were still cordial. At Cleveland, however, the Radicals had organized a gang of rowdies to break up the meeting, and unfortunately the President cooperated by losing his temper. He told the hecklers some home truths that were good logic but poor politics, such as that they should not demand votes for Negroes in Louisiana until they let them vote in Ohio. The crowd went wild, and in no friendly way. They shouted, "You be damned!", "Shame!", "Traitor!", "Don't get mad, Andy!", "Hang Jeff Davis!" and "Three cheers for Congress!". They had the President's goat and they rode it; while he made the error of replying to the jeers with hot words of defiance.

The next morning there were signs that many people in the disorderly crowd had sympathized with the President, for great multitudes along the street cheered him as he was leaving town. But the Radicals had found his weak point. They organized heckling gangs at St. Louis and again at Indianapolis, where the howling was so successful that Johnson had to give up trying to speak. From there on back to Washington the Radicals had the mobs organized and the President received every possible insult.

The Radical press hounded him. He was called not only drunkard, but renegade, traitor, the great apostate, a faithless demagogue, the man made President by John Wilkes Booth, the Great Accidental, and the Great Pardoner. This also helped to exasperate his temper. At one point he even made the mistake of quoting "Come one, come all, this rock shall fly . . ." which may be good schoolboy poetry but is not what any fighting man should cry in the middle of a real fight. The unrighteous rejoiced.

In many cities the Mayor pointedly did not greet the President of the United States, and the Governors of half-a-dozen states showed him no courtesy. General Grant and General Custer, who were along on the trip, were outraged at the treatment the President received. At Newmarket, Ohio, when the mob called for Custer he came out and said, "I was born two miles from here, and I am ashamed of you." In Pittsburgh Grant responded and ordered the rowdies to go home.

After the trip the Radicals turned on a barrage of false reports. James Russell Lowell in the *North American Review* was one of the worst. He called the trip "an indecent orgy," which indeed it was though not in the way Lowell meant to imply. On the contrary, B. C. Truman wrote in 1913 in the *Century Magazine* that "As a member of the party I can say there was no drunkenness at all on the trip. Johnson, who had given up whiskey for sherry, indulged in but little of the latter, and Grant drank not at all." But the newspapers said that the country had watched "with a feeling of national shame the coarseness with which the President had turned a solemn journey to the tomb of a celebrated American into a stumping tour of an irritated demagogue." (The reference was to the fact that in Chicago Johnson visited the tomb of Stephen A. Douglas.) According to one paper his words would be read "with black brows and fiery eyes by an insulted people"; another called his speeches "vulgar, egotistical

and occasionally profane, full of coarse abuse of his enemies and
coarser glorification of himself." Friendly crowds were said to be
Copperjohnsons "sliming and crawling along" in the President's wake.

Johnson's appeal to the people failed. The election of 1866 went
strongly Republican and Radical. When Congress met, the President
sent a dignified Message asking Congress to admit representatives
of the Southern states, but the Radicals laughed at him. They
described his message as "a dreary, lifeless document and on a par
with one of Franklin Pierce's," and boasted "that Congress will deal
with him so as to make him realize his defeat and future insignificance."

Whipped on by the fierce Thad Stevens, Congress passed a series of
bills setting up provincial governments in the South, in calm disregard
of the Constitution and to the amazement of lawyers, courts, and later
historians. The President, knowing that argument was useless, was
bland. He used the help of the best minds in his Cabinet and among
his friends in preparing his vetoes, for the record, trusting that some
day the people would return to sanity and the Constitution.

Meanwhile Reconstruction was showing the deadly effects of
Johnson's loss of control over national policy. Many historians
believe that even Lincoln, if he had lived, could have made no headway
against the tide of savagery. In any case, the tide was running with
fearful strength. The flood of carpetbaggers poured into the South,
organizing the Negroes into Republican clubs, under the auspices of
those now most respectable of institutions, the Union League Clubs
of Philadelphia and New York. That, in detail, is another story;
it was simply the working out of the Radical policies that Johnson
had vainly tried to withstand.

If the tourist of today could get a glimpse of the Washington of
1867 he would readily conclude that the scene was a fitting one for
the unholy political orgy that was to take place the following year.

Through the center of the town from Capitol Hill to the Potomac,
in about the location of the present Constitution Avenue, ran the
B-Street Canal and Tiber Creek. These waterways had long been
open sewers without the slope or water supply to flush them out.
Back in Jackson's time Anne Royall described Tiber Creek in her
uninhibited vocabulary as being clogged with everything from plain

As is amply evident cartoonist Thomas Nast considered Johnson a traitor responsible for almost everything that went wrong during his administration.

Ticket to the impeachment trial of President Johnson.

success of Repu
...ating the measures that
...tended the principle of Mr.
... action to the entire service.

...ve
.dent upon
.w if his
form, he
in infla-
it then
he party,
onsistent
ild be the
f the party
dhesion to
have dis-
honey De-

the

DEATH OF ANDREW JOHNSON.

Ex-President Johnson died, July 31, at the residence of his daughter, Mrs. W. R. Brown, near Carter Station, Tennessee. On the 27th, when he left his home in Greenville, he was apparently in vigorous health; but soon after reaching his daughter's house, on the evening of the 28th, he was stricken with paralysis, which mainly affected his left side, and rendered him unconscious. He rallied occasionally, but finally passed away. Mr. Johnson was in his sixty-seventh year. We give his portrait on page 665.

PERSONAL.

The Rev. Dr. Alexander H. Vinton, forme
this city, but now of Boston, created sor
t in London on the evening of the Fou
en preaching in Westmin
the cer

When President Johnson died in 1875 this negligible obituary about him appeared in Harper's Weekly.

garbage to dead babies. In the 1860s it was still "hardly liquid enough for geese." Across from the old Willard Hotel was a swamp, and it is recorded in the history of the Willard that one of its guests, stepping out into a bright morning on Pennsylvania Avenue, was unfortunately killed by a stray shot from a hunter in the swamp. As late as the 1870s there was debate in Congress on how to control the numerous cattle, pigs, sheep, and goats that boldly shared the sidewalks of Pennsylvania Avenue with the Congressmen as they walked from their boarding houses to the Capitol.

Today there is far more pollution in the District waterways; but Tiber Creek has long since been put underground, and the vast deposit of sewage now lies several feet deep in the bottom of the Potomac off the shore from which in the old days John Quincy Adams and other citizens used to go swimming. In 1867, the sewage lay exposed between the White House and the Capitol; Washington was described as "one vast stench," and Congress in that year was not much less so.

In December, 1866, Representative James M. Ashley of Ohio had launched a long McCarthyite investigation of Johnson in the hope of finding evidence of disloyalty that might he used as a basis for impeachment. Ashley had been an unsuccessful Democratic editor who turned Republican and was elected to Congress, where he found himself amounting to very little. Then, as Ben: Perley Poore says, "he mounted the hobby of impeachment which enabled him to advertise himself extensively, and without expense." Being "a man of the lightest mental calibre and most insufficient capacity," he spent a year and a great deal of public money, and accumlated a stack of derogatory material that the Radical leaders reluctantly discarded as too flimsy even for their purpose. But they were still fascinated with the idea of throwing Johnson out and putting the President *pro tem* of the Senate, Ben Wade, in the White House.

When Congress met in December, 1867, Thad Stevens proclaimed with characteristic assurance: "Why, I'll take that man's record, his speeches, and his acts before any impartial jury you can get together and I'll make them pronounce him either a knave or a fool, without the least trouble." He went on sarcastically: "My own impression is that we had better put it on the ground of insanity or whiskey or something of that kind. I don't want to hurt the man's

feelings by telling him he is a rascal. I'd rather put it mildly, and
say he hasn't got off that inauguration drunk yet, and just let him
retire to get sobered." The pride that goeth before a fall was swelling in every Radical breast, as they exultantly counted their chances
of bringing Johnson down.

At last the great day came. On Saturday, Washington's Birthday
in 1868 the House was packed with Members and spectators and the
corridors crowded, when Thad Stevens, old and desperately feeble
but glowing with hate and triumph, rose and offered his impeachment
resolutions. Then, in speech after speech, the Radicals worked themselves into passionate fury. They called the President "this ungrateful, despicable, besotted, traitorous man," "a usurper of authority
and criminal violator of public trusts," and "the great criminal of
our age and country." His advisers were "the worst men that ever
crawled like filthy reptiles at the footstool of power," and he was
"the worst tyrant and usurper that history was ever called on to
record." "For a tithe of his usurpation, lawlessness and tyranny our
fathers dissolved their connection with the government of King
George, for less than this King James lost his throne and King Charles
lost his head."

They "waved the bloody shirt," accusing Johnson of encouraging
Southern whites to massacre the Negroes. Ahley bellowed and
thundered; he was in his madly boiling element. His mildest charge
was that Johnson was a more faithful representative and a more
formidable ally of the Southern traitors than any general of the rebel
armies, and that he was planning, if resisted, to start a new civil war.

Not all who roared their hatred for "King Andrew" were sincere
Radicals. At least two members of the Judiciary Committee are
known to have tried to resist the storm but to have finally decided
it was safer to go along and vilify the victim. The chief difference
between this scene and a modern purge-session of the Supreme Soviet
in Moscow was that there were still a few brave men in the meeting.
One was James Brooks, who told the House plainly what kind of
crime it was planning to perpetrate.

Brooks reminded his colleagues that it was, after all, Washington's
Birthday, saying that on this day of patriotic memories he could not
express with what deep solemnity he rose to resist "this untoward, this
unholy, this unconstitutional proceeding." He taunted the Radicals:

"Go on, go on, if you choose. You may strip him of his office, but you will canonize him among those historic defenders of constitutional law and liberty, in whose ranks it is the highest glory of human ambition to shine. . . . Suppose you succeed, suppose you make the President of the Senate President of the United States, you settle that hereafter a party, having a sufficient majority in the House and the Senate, can depose the President of the United States."

But with all the sound and fury of the Radical orators, the case rested entirely on what the Radical leaders hoped had been a fatal slip on the part of the President. Johnson had at last dismissed the treacherous Stanton in the face of a direct prohibition by Congress under the Tenure of Office Act, which forbade the President to discharge a Cabinet officer without the consent of the Senate. Johnson was sure the Act was unconstitutional, and proposed to test it in the courts. He had appointed Grant to be the new Secretary of War, with the understanding that Grant would refuse to yield to Stanton and would throw the case into court. But the General flinched; Stanton was barricaded in the War Department; and Grant had been welcomed with open arms by the Radicals. There was no way to get the case into the courts; it would instead be tried as an impeachment proceeding in the Senate, where not law but politics would decide. The Radicals were riding high.

On Monday, February 24, by a strictly party vote, the House impeached the President, and provided managers to take the case to the Senate for decision.

As for Johnson, he was used to danger, and he showed no sign of anxiety. One night Chief Justice Chase, who was to preside over the Senate at the impeachment trial, was giving a reception, and the guests were startled to hear the butler announce the President. Johnson came sailing in with his two daughters, looking entirely unruffled, and was cordially greeted by the host. The Radicals were scandalized. How could they trust the Chief Justice to preside at a trial "to enforce party discipline?"

It may be noted, that if this trial was not really for high crimes and misdemeanors but to enforce party discipline, as Brooks had plainly said, the effect, if it had succeeded, would have been to establish something like a parliamentary system, in which the President would be a sort of Prime Minister holding office at the pleasure of the legislature. In later years, Woodrow Wilson for technical reasons advocated a parliamentary system, but the idea never gained acceptance with the American people.

In the midst of the excitement, Congress received from the White House a stinging veto message on a bill intended to restrict the powers of the Supreme Court. Congress passed the bill over the veto, for it had long since grown defiant of the Constitution. But the veto made clear that Johnson was not begging anyone for mercy.

Charles Dickens was on a reading tour of the United States at the time, and passing through Washington in February called on the President. He commented: "He is a man with a remarkable face, indicating courage, watchfulness, and certainly strength of purpose. . . . I would have picked him out anywhere as a character of mark."

For his defense Johnson selected, among others, the distinguished lawyer Jeremiah S. Black, who had done good work for him before. When Black suddenly withdrew, the Radicals passed the word that he had found such shocking crimes that his conscience had revolted. The real story was different, but Johnson said nothing and let the storm blow. What had happened was that four leading Radicals had signed a petition which Black presented to the President, to have a warship sent to back up a claim of some of Black's clients on a Caribbean Island. Johnson had already refused to use the Navy for that purpose, but the conspirators hoped he might now be frightened enough to yield to blackmail. Instead the President stood up and told Black: "Rather than do your bidding I'll suffer my right arm torn from the socket. Yes, quit." Then, lapsing into East Tennessee language, he went on: "Just one word more: I regard you as a damn villain, and get out of my office, or damn you, I'll kick you out." The next day Black apologized, but the President said, "Tell General Black he is out of the case and will stay out." Johnson had other counsel who were more than capable of destroying the legal case of the impeachers, leaving the Radicals with no further resource but to put political pressure on the doubtful Senators.

The managers from the House took a week to present their case before the Senate, while the dying Thad Stevens sat and watched, hoping to live long enough to see his enemy destroyed.

Then came the President's chief counsel, former Supreme Court Justice Benjamin R. Curtis. His opening speech for the defense demolished the Radical case, showing that its only arguable point was the dismissal of Stanton, and that the Tenure of Office Act, even if Constitutional, by its own terms did not apply to an officer holding over from a previous administration.

There was other argument on both sides. For example, Thad Stevens came in with a speech which, as he was too weak to stand, had to be read for him. The fierce old Radical called Johnson "this offspring of assassination," and warned any Senator who would vote for acquittal: "dark would be the track of infamy which must mark his name and that of his posterity." It had become plain by that time that conviction could not be based on any evidence but must depend on unflinching hatred among the Radicals and successful intimidation of the moderate Republicans.

Meanwhile the President went on calmly with his duties, official and social. He continued his regular receptions at the White House, and his enemies who attended to see how he was taking it found him apparently undisturbed. In private, however, he was amusing himself somewhat luridly by reading of the subsequent lives of the famous "regicides," the men who had signed the death-warrant of Charles I.

Senator Wade, President *pro tem* of the Senate and heir-apparent to the Presidency, was busy selecting an all-Radical Cabinet.

During arguments in the Senate, the Radicals set about mustering votes. Their methods bore a striking resemblance to a modern communist operation. There was the same use of the Big Lie, such as accusing Johnson's friends of threatening murder, when it was the Radicals who were threatening every kind of punishment not excluding assassination. The home states of doubtful Senatore were invaded by detectives in search of material for blackmail. Well-meaning fellow travelers were brought into action. The Methodist Church General Conference was meeting in Chicago, and smugly voted for an hour of prayer "to save our Senators from error." Everyone present knew that these prayers were intended not so much to influence God as to put pressure on Senators to disregard the evidence and think prayerfully about the Methodist vote. The Radicals asserted that

Johnson's friends had a huge slush fund to buy Senators, hoping to cover the fact that they had one of their own. Ben Butler was quoted as saying of a Senator who threatened to vote for acquittal, "Tell the damn scoundrel that if he wants money there is a bushel of it to be had."

Altogether there were seven Republicans who refused to go with the tide. Of these the one in the weakest position at home was Edmund G. Ross of Kansas, who came to be the central figure in the fight, for if he should stick with the other six, combined with the Democrats, there would be one short of the two-thirds vote needed to carry the impeachment. The pressures therefore concentrated on Ross. In the process of searching Kansas for dirt with which to blackmail him the Radicals had a distressing accident, when evidence came out that one of their leaders, Senator Samuel C. Pomeroy, had offered to sell his vote and two others to the Johnson people for $40,000. But in the flood of lies this was glossed over at the time.

The story of how Ross stood up to every threat, and of how he took his punishment, has become one of the classic hero tales of America. His punishment lasted for most of his life, until Grover Cleveland came into office and appointed him Governor of the Territory of New Mexico; and a little before his death a repentent Congress voted him a Civil War pension.

Less widely known is the heroic story of Vinnie Ream. Senator Ross lived in Washington at the house of his old friend Robert L. Ream, whose daughter Vinnie was a talented sculptor. She had been awarded the contract for the full-length statue of Lincoln that now stands in the Rotunda of the Capitol, and she had been assigned a room in the Capitol crypt to use as a studio. Ross and other Conservative Senators sometimes met in Vinnie's studio for secret conferences. The Radical leaders suspected that she was urging Ross to follow his conscience, and George W. Julian was sent to make it clear to her that if Ross should vote for acquittal it would be the worse for her. But though badly frightened by platoons of growling Senators as the pressures built up, she refused to cave in. After the final vote some of the Radicals took a cheap revenge by ordering her to move her work out of the Capitol, but this was too raw for Thad Stevens himself, and he got the order rescinded.

A year later Vinnie Ream invited President Johnson to inspect her work in the crypt of the Capitol. "You are both good and great," she wrote, "and if you approve, the criticism of others would not so much dishearten me." She had a right to give him her approval too, having fought and suffered, with success, in his defense.

In the end all seven Conservative Republicans stood up to their sense of duty, and Thad Stevens lost his war. His final, vindictive, message was: "If tyranny becomes intolerable, the only resource will be found in the dagger of Brutus." After the impeachment was lost by one vote, Stevens was carried from the Chamber, his face black with rage, waving his feeble arms and crying, "The country is going to the devil." Which in fact it was, for many a long year to come, not because the impeachment had failed, but because in the main the Radical policies were succeeding in spite of President Johnson. Within two months, Stevens was dead.

Senator John B. Henderson of Missouri, one who voted against the impeachment, and who lived until 1913 when most of his colleagues were long dead, reported then that Senator Sumner himself had confessed to him in confidence two years after the event, "You were right in your vote and I was wrong."

In July, 1868, one of Johnson's friends sounded him cautiously about the Democratic nomination. "Before God," he replied, "I would rather this month pack up and leave this house and go to my old business than remain here subject to the insults and annoyances of the past."

In that same year John Quincy Adams 2d, grandson of President John Adams, wrote to President Johnson:

"I believe that those men who like yourself can dare to grasp great eventual gain to their country at the cost of temporary disfavor to themselves are doing as noble a work as men can do . . . today it seems to me high time for calm and patriotic men to be gathering around the organic law.

"When that day comes, and come I am convinced it will, when that great paper is is once more cherished as the most precious possession of the people . . . no name will be entitled to a higher place . . . than that of the President who dared alone to set his face against the momentary madness of the myriad, and at the risk of all that is dearest to a public man defend to the bitter end the Ark of the Covenant intrusted to his faithful keeping."

But the day that Adams hoped to see had not yet dawned. Grant was the Republican candidate, and he was elected.

On New Year's Day in 1869 President Johnson gave a grand reception at the White House. The place was jammed with great folks and common folks. Even Ben "The Beast" Butler had the effrontery to come, and the President calmly shook the hand of the man who had been as violent ten months ago as Thad Stevens himself. General Grant had pointedly gone out of town; he and Johnson were now bitter enemies. Later Grant told the Inaugural Committee that he would not ride with Johnson in the parade, and Johnson for his part refused to attend the Inauguration on any terms.

On March 4, the President finished his work at the White House at noon, said good-bye to his assembled Cabinet, and was driven to the home of his devoted friend John F. Coyle, one of the owners of the pro-Johnson paper the *Intelligencer*. There he remained for a few weeks occupying himself in the purchase of new furnishings for his Greeneville house, which had been looted by Confederate soldiers during the war. Before he left the White House, however, he issued a message to the American people, which was going out over the wires while Grant was taking the oath at the other end of Pennsylvania Avenue. Andrew Johnson, in his last few moments as President, called upon the people to protect the Constitution, the Union, and the interests of the common folk. He warned them of the evils of the Radical policies of Reconstruction, vengeance, and wholesale corruption. He concluded: "Forgetting the past, let us return to the first principles of the Government, and unfurling the banner of our country, inscribe upon it in ineffaceable characters: 'The Constitution and the Union, one and inseparable."

So Johnson returned to Tennessee, and the evils that he foretold, and more, came to pass and made the American people ashamed. One more thing he wanted to do: he wanted to go back to the Senate and say his say about the Radicals in their teeth. In 1872 he positively refused to let himself be nominated for the Presidency. He explained that he planned to run against Brownlow for the Senate in 1875, and added: "I would rather have the vindication of my

State by electing me to my old seat in the Senate of the United States than to be monarch of the grandest empire on earth. For this I live, and will never die content without. . . . Go to the convention tomorrow, and if my name is put in nomination, promptly withdraw it on my authority."

In 1874 he was on the stump again, running hard for the Senate, attacking Grant's administration with all the old fire, and being threatened in the old familiar way. It was a tough battle, but in the following January the Tennessee Legislature, on the 55th ballot, chose him once more as Senator.

Andrew Johnson came back to Washington a hero, his desk piled with congratulations from all over the country. The St. Louis *Republican* even called his election "the most significant personal triumph which the history of American politics can show," and the *Nation* recalled that his respect for the law and the Constitution had "made his Administration a remarkable contrast to that which succeeded it."

The Senate met in special session on March 5, and Johnson entered the Senate Chamber to be sworn in the presence of his enemies—those who still survived, only thirteen of the thirty-five who had voted to oust him from the White House seven years before. There was a moment of embarrassment while the old Radicals fidgeted and pretended not to notice him. Then as soon as he took the oath there was suddenly such a storm of applause that he himself was embarrassed and retreated to the cloakroom. In the press, even his ancient foe the New York *Tribune* had to swing with the tide, saying: "His bitterest enemies are compelled to admit his sterling honesty and unswerving rectitude. In these days of moral and official delinquency it is no ordinary gratification for the people at large to have their national councils honored by the presence of such a man."

On March 23 Johnson made his one speech, to a crowded Chamber. It was a vigorous attack on Grant and Reconstruction; and during the speech the galleries broke out again and again in wild applause. He was having his say, as he had longed to do one more time. He ended with his old battle cry, "God save the Constitution." Two days later the Senate adjourned and he went home to Greeneville.

Several weeks after he got back to Tennessee he was visiting his daughter, Mrs. Stover, when he suffered a stroke of paralysis. He had often said that when his time came he hoped to go like the one-horse shay, "all at once and nothing first," and here too he got his wish. The next day he lay in bed and talked of old days and battles; he had had a good life. Then he fell into a coma, and died quietly, on July 31, 1875.

Several years before he had told his friends: "When I die I desire no better winding sheet than the Stars and Stripes, and no softer pillow than the Constitution of my country." They also remembered that he had often ended a speech with the words: "I leave in your hands the Constitution and the Union, the glorious flag of your country not with twenty-five but with thirty-six stars." So they wrapped him in a fine new flag, now carrying thirty-seven stars, and under his head they placed his worn and much-thumbed copy of the Constitution of his country, and buried him on a hill that he had chosen in his own home town of Greeneville.

So Lincoln and Johnson, the rail splitter and the tailor, coming to power at the savage crisis of the mid-19th century, fought and won the struggle for Union; but were baffled in their hopes for peace, an ideal too high for the overwrought American people to accept in their time. But on Johnson's gravestone is the inscription, "His faith in the people never wavered." Future generations would see that his course had been right, and that even his faults were the consequences of his intrepid determination to do his duty.

In 1926 a case involving the long-since-repealed Tenure of Office Act happened to came before the Supreme Court. The Court made short work of the Act, saying:

"The executive power vested by the Constitution in the president of the United States extends to the removal, without the consent of the Senate, of executory officers appointed by him with such consent." So much for the one pretended legal basis for Johnson's impeachment.

Artist Nast felt strongly that Grant was made a scapegoat for others.

Grant doing a tipsy dance for Tammany Boss Tweed. Although Grant was Republican and Tweed Democratic the scandals attached to the latter were smeared on Grant by some of his critics.

Counselled by evil forces, Grant looks on as Louisiana's heart is torn out.

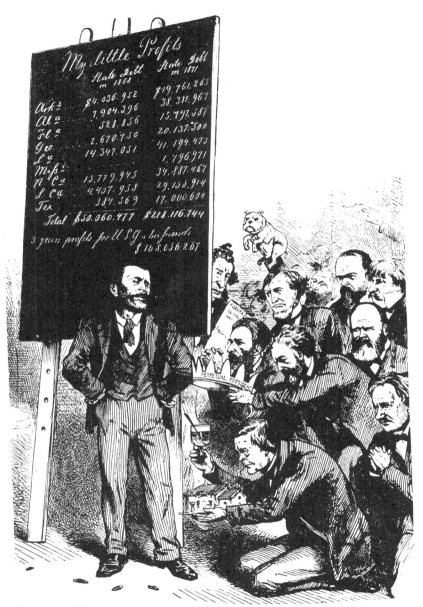

The only difference between Boss Tweed's "graft" and Grant's "profits," according to the cartoonist, was merely difference in arithmetic.

Like other drawings against Grant in Frank Leslie's Illustrated Newspaper, this cartoon by Morgan left no doubt as to the paper's attitude.

THE CHEAPEST PAPER IN THE UNION

New-York Tribune.

NEW SERIES   NEW-YORK, WEDNESDAY, NOVEMBER 6, 1872   DEAR AT ANY PRICE.

Of all the cartoons against Horace Greeley, Liberal Republican Party nominee in 1872, this was one of the cruelest. When it appeared, as historian Roger Butterfield pointed out, Greeley's wife had just died and Greeley himself was very ill. Several weeks later he died of a brain fever brought on by strain and mortification.

Diseased by Free Love, Fourierism, Political Corruption, Slovenliness, and Ambition, Greeley is shown drinking Pro-Slavery and Tammany slop while his misguided supporters feed on his corrupted body.

Reproduction of the front page of "Truth," a short-lived Democratic newspaper containing one of the most blatant falsehoods in American political history—a forged letter in which James A. Garfield purportedly expressed subservience to big business and advocated increased immigration of cheap Chinese labor. The letter achieved a sensation, causing considerable harm to Garfield's Presidential candidacy in 1880.

BLAINE

—THE—

PROSCRIPTIONIST.

RECORD

—OF—

JAMES G. BLAINE AS A KNOW NOTHING

AND

PERSECUTOR OF FOREIGN BORN CITIZENS

AND

ROMAN CATHOLICS.

The Know Nothing Oath—The Father Bapst Outrage—The Laws against Naturalization—Blaine's Attack on Catholic Church Property and Archbishop Hughes—No Foreign Born Militia— The Order of the American Union—Blaine's Know Nothingism in 1875—The Madigan Circular— Proofs that Blaine Wrote and Circulated it.

"Assserting the equality of all men before the law, we hold that it is the duty of the government, in its dealings with the people, to mete out equal and exact justice to all citizens, of whatever nativity, race or persuasion—religious or political.—[*Democratic Platform, 1884.*]

Inasmuch as Blaine's mother was a devout Catholic and there was little evidence he had participated in the Know-Nothing movement, this sort of attack during the 1884 Presidential election campaign was patently unfair. In arguing against his election an opposition editor declared that Blaine "had wallowed in spoils like a rhinoceros in an African pool."

"Stabbed in the Back," the title Judge magazine appended to this cartoon, referred to a blow that felled Blaine on the eve of the 1884 election. In the course of a routine reception for some New York clergymen, a Dr. Burchard made a speech in which he ineptly remarked: "We are Republicans and don't propose to leave our party and identify ourselves with the party whose antecedents have been rum, Romanism, and rebellion." Blaine took no notice of the anti-Catholic slur, possibly because he did not happen to hear it. However, Democratic newspapers took considerable note of it, giving the impression that he was personally responsible for what was said. Despite the consequent loss of New York's large Catholic population, Blaine came within a scant 1500 votes of winning the state's decisive electoral backing. Historians believe he would have been elected President if he had not been tagged with responsibility for Burchard's remark.

"Fee–Fi–Fo–Fum!" portrayed in no uncertain terms Benjamin Butler, Presidential nominee of both the Anti-Monopoly and Greenback parties in the 1880's. Strongly antipathetic toward Butler, Mark Twain described him in these words: "The forward part of his skull looks raised like a waterblister. He is short and pursy—fond of standing with his hands in pants pocket and looking around to each speaker with the air of a man who has half a mind to crush them and yet is rather too indifferent. Butler is dismally and drearily homely. When he smiles it is like the breaking up of a hard winter."

Even criminals are among those the artist lined up in support of the Presidential nominee of Greenbackers in 1884.

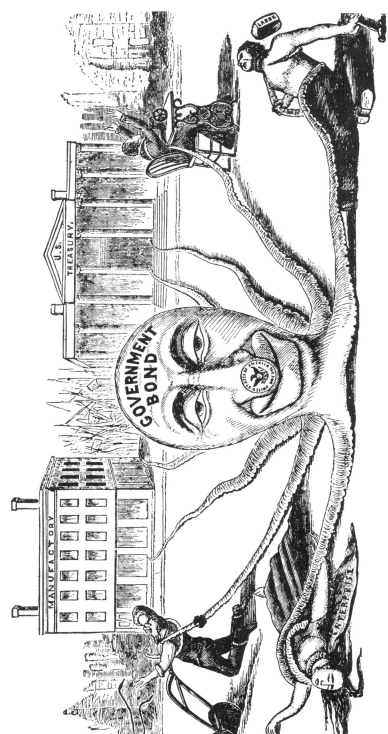

This grotesque cartoon expressed the attitude of Greenbackers toward the policies of President Benjamin Harrison.

Entitled "Another Voice For Cleveland," this cartoon was almost too much for the Democratic standard bearer to bear in the campaign of 1884. By way of retaliation for below-the-belt attacks on James G. Blaine, Republican newspapers sensationalized allegations to the effect that Grover Cleveland was the father of an illegitimate offspring of an illicit relationship with a widow named Maria Halpin. Although Cleveland admitted he had been intimate with Mrs. Halpin, he emphatically insisted he was not the father of her child. However, few believed him.

In deriding the personality and policies of Grover Cleveland the Los Angeles Times published this cartoon on March 6, 1885. Original title of drawing was "The Greatest Curiosity of the Nineteenth Century."

Invidious comparison of Grover Cleveland with Benjamin Harrison was exactly what the artist intended. In column at left Harrison is shown as a Civil War hero and friend of American labor. In column at right Cleveland is depicted as a saloon lounger, slacker during the war, and smasher of industry who had no regard for American workers or business.

"The Smallest Specimen Yet"—a cartoon deriding Benjamin Harrison as a President of such small stature that he could barely be seen through a microscope. Unfriendly artists frequently depicted him as a misfit for the hat worn by his grandfather, William H. Harrison.

The point artist Frederick Hopper sought to convey was that Theodore Roosevelt and William McKinley did pretty much what they were told by the trusts and G.O.P. boss Mark Hanna.

For not doing what he was told Roosevelt gets sat upon by Mark Hanna at the orders of the trusts while "Willie" McKinley expresses his delight.

CHAPTER VIII

WILD COWBOY

The Republican National Convention of 1900 opened in Philadelphia on June 19. As soon as the meeting was in order and prepared
to notice a late arrival, Theodore Roosevelt, the hero of San Juan
Hill, wearing his Rough Rider campaign hat, strode down the aisle.
He paid no visible attention to the wave of applause, but he knew
that everyone knew he was there.

Mark Hanna, the National Chairman, sat on the platform. When
Roosevelt made his entrance, Hanna's smile visibly faded. He knew
that his enemy, Matt Quay, was conspiring with Tom Platt, Boss of
New York, to get rid of Governor Roosevelt by shelving him in the
Vice Presidency. As Hanna said later, "Don't any of you realize
that there's only one life between this madman and the White House?"
For no one could be farther from the politician's ideal of a biddable
President than this all-too-active Governor of New York.

As for T. R., he was exhibiting himself not as a candidate for the
Vice Presidency, but as a coming man who might be nominated four
years later to head the ticket. For the time being he was contented
in Albany, where he could keep in practice and in the public eye at
the expense of the unhappy Mr. Platt.

Roosevelt's relation to Platt was a peculiar one. In 1898, when
Platt found that he could not avoid putting up the young hero for
the governorship, he had tried to tie a string to the office by extracting
a promise that T. R. would consult him about all appointments and
policies. To this T. R. readily agreed, adding, however, that he
reserved the right to use his own judgment afterward. This arrangement brought the Governor under fire from two sides. Platt was
frequently outraged, since the Governor frequently listened to his
advice, as agreed, and then did the opposite. At the same time, since
Platt was old and feeble, Roosevelt often journeyed to New York to
visit the Boss's house instead of summoning him to Albany. This
kindly habit outraged some of the reform zealots, who sputtered with

wrath at the thought of the pure-talking Roosevelt making pilgrimage
to sit at the horny feet of Boss Platt. T. R. cared little for either of
these criticisms, but he acquired an impatience with theoretical reform-
ers that lasted him the rest of his life, and toward the end may well
have helped to stoke the fires of his hatred for Woodrow Wilson.

Meanwhile, as the contented Governor of New York with an eye
on 1904, Roosevelt had no intention of being trapped at the 1900
convention in the innocuous office of Vice President.

McKinley was of course nominated for a second term. Then Platt
turned the pressure on the reluctant Roosevelt. When the crisis came,
a newpaper reporter was crouching on the fire-escape outside the
smoke-filled room and saw what happened. Roosevelt sat grasping
an empty chair, his fingers showing white with strain. Around him
sat a group of top Republicans, urging something on their victim.
Suddenly he rose, his face red with anger, and lifting the empty chair
smashed it down on the floor. Having expressed his feelings, he
threw up his hands. The reporter scrambled down and made for the
nearest telephone. Theodore Roosevelt had consented to take the
risk of being still on the shelf and unable to get off when the party
would be choosing a candidate in 1904.

So it came about that on September 14, 1901, Roosevelt was sworn
in as President, in Buffalo, where McKinley had just that morning died
from an assassin's bullet. Shortly after the ceremony Mark Hanna
arrived to pay his respects to the new President. Reporters noticed
that his face was gray with fear.

It was indeed a dangerous man whom the trembling Republican
Party had to accept as its new leader.

The conservative Washington *Post* was frightened but tried to be
hopeful. In an editorial it pointed out that so far it had seen very
little cause for encouragement in its observations of the Vice President
before or since he took office. "He has at all times been far too
theatrical for our taste. He pranced too much in war. He voci-
ferated too much in politics. We have not found him great in the
uniform of a soldier or impressive as the superstructure of a bucking
bronco. That he has amused us frequently and keenly we admit with
becoming gratitude. That he has ever suggested the perfect model
of a President we cannot truly say."

Theodore Roosevelt was not yet 43 years old when he became President. He was the son of a well-to-do New York businessman; his mother was from an aristocratic Southern family. Theodore was brought up to be a gentleman and graduated from Harvard, but quietness was not in him. Like so many Roosevelts, he differed from ordinary human beings much as uranium differs from ordinary metals: if he were to suffer some crippling injury he would give off power like an atomic pile. In his case the injuries were asthma, a puny body, and nearsight; in his later years he was blind in one eye. His reaction was vigorous; he taught himself to ride, shoot, and box, and when he was a rancher in the West he could rope a steer with the best of his men. He wrote to his sister in 1896: "I don't mind work; the only thing I am afraid of is that by and by I will have nothing to do; and I should hate to have the children grow up and see me having nothing to do."

Not long after this date he found something to do as McKinley's Assistant Secretary of the Navy, where he built up his reputation as a "combination of St. Paul and St. Vitus," driving Secretary Long close to distraction with his unauthorized preparations for the oncoming Spanish War. When the war came he resigned, organized the Rough Riders, and enjoyed himself hugely; so much so that Mr. Dooley, the famous Irish philosopher-columnist, said that T. R.'s book about his adventures should have been called "Alone in Cubia." It was a small war, but it led Roosevelt to the Governorship, and, as events turned out, to the Presidency.

This was the "madman" whose fate it was to usher in the Twentieth Century in American politics. Years later Julian Street in his book *The Most Interesting Man*, characterized him as a man who "just goes roaring on like a steam engine in pantaloons." Street described a meeting with Roosevelt: "As the Colonel advanced to greet me he showed his hard, white teeth, wrinkled his red, weatherbeaten face, and squinted his eyes half shut behind the heavy lenses of his spectacles, in suggestion, as it seemed to me, of a large, amiable lion which comes up purring gently as though to say: 'You needn't be afraid, I've just had luncheon.'"

When Roosevelt became President his first announcement was that he would carry on unchanged the policies of President McKinley; but that was merely an expression of his shock and bewilderment. He soon found his feet and began administering shocks to others. One of the first shocks was his invitation to Booker T. Washington to dine at the White House.

Roosevelt had consulted with Dr. Washington, the head of Tuskegee Institute, about appointments in the South, where the Republican office-holders were notoriously of low quality, and when Washington came north in October the President invited him to dinner. The reaction followed immediately. Angry Southerners called it "the most damnable outrage ever." A New Orleans paper cried: "White men of the South, how do you like it? When Mr. Roosevelt sits down with a Negro, he declares that the Negro is the social equal of the white man." Another suggested that the President was in favor of intermarriage between the races.

Afterward the President was attacked in the North, and in England as well, for failing to invite any more Negroes to the White House. He was accused of cowardly truckling to his Southern critics. The fact was that he had become convinced that the net effect of Dr. Washington's visit had unnecessarily stimulated racial hatreds and had done more harm than good.

In his December Message to Congress Roosevelt was still trying to calm the fears of business, but at the same time he indicated that he was not unaware of possible needs for reform. The message was full of balanced sentences. He said, for instance, that big business needed regulation, but it should be done carefully so as to avoid causing unrest. This drew a sarcastic comment from Mr. Dooley:

"Th' trusts," says he, "are heejous monsthers built up be th' inlightened intherprise iv th' men that have done so much to advance progress in our beloved counthry," he says. "On wan hand, I wud stamp thim undher fut; on th' other hand, not so fast."

But back in 1894 Roosevelt had told Brander Matthews, "I know the banker, merchant, and railroad king well, and *they* also need education and chastisement." Early in 1902 he felt that a bit of sound chastisement could well be applied, when J. P. Morgan incorporated the Northern Securities Company, to buy control of railroads in the Northwest for monopolistic purposes. The Supreme Court in 1895 had beaten down an attempt by President Cleveland to dissolve the Sugar Trust, after which the antitrust laws had come to be regarded as a dead letter. So when in February, 1902, T. R. demanded the dissolution of the Northern Securities Company, he was challenging the Court to reverse itself; and when two years later he won the case, he had brought the antitrust laws to life.

Morgan was surprised and distressed; he had felt that surely Mr. Roosevelt would do the gentlemanly thing—according to the Wall Street definition of a gentleman as one who stands loyally by the other gentlemen against the lower orders. He went to see the President and plaintively asked, if he had done anything wrong, why not send the Attorney General to confer with one of Morgan's lawyers, "and they can fix it up." But Roosevelt was not being a gentleman just then. This was a war to shift the balance of power in favor of the public interest.

Years later Roosevelt wrote that his attack on Northern Securities was necessary because when he came into office "the total absence of governmental control had led to a portentous growth of corporations. The Government was practically impotent. Of all forms of tyranny the least attractive and most vulgar is the tyranny of mere wealth."

After starting this legal battle, which was bound to move slowly, the President rested before going after the other trusts, whereby he opened himself to the charge of insincerity, which grew into violent accusations of a sellout in the campaign of 1904. Meanwhile, however, most of the business leaders felt themselves to be between the devil and the deep sea, facing a choice whether to stand by their wild Republican President or turn to the wild Democratic Party, possibly headed by William Jennings Bryan himself. The *Wall Street Journal*, however, was conscious of the dangers in arrogant business giantism. It recommended that the business men take their medicine and stop making faces, and advised that a strict enforcement of the law was in Wall Street's best interest and should be supported. "Meanwhile it is amusing to note that an easy way to notoriety and applause in quarters not usually open to the million is to be found in criticism of the President."

Though the President was going slow on the chastisement of the trusts, he managed to avoid a dull life by working on the Panama Canal. His highhanded action in November 1903, when he hastily recognized the new Republic of Panama, led to criticism that has continued in the histories to the present day. Pringle, for example, says that he "acted with haste that was indecent, not to say unwise." Colombia, which owned the Isthmus, had tried to drive a hard bargain, and T. R. was more than glad when the local people broke off and set up for themselves. It may be true that he had not personally promoted the revolution, but later he made unwise boasts that let him in for full responsibility. In 1911, after he was out of office, he said in a speech, "I am interested in the Panama Canal because I started it. . . . I took the canal zone and let Congress debate, and while the debate goes on the canal does also." This speech afterward cost the United States $25,000,000, which was paid under President Harding as an indemnity to Columbia—partly stimulated by the fact that Colombia had found oil and seemed to favor giving concessions to British companies rather than to Americans.

In 1908 another angle of the Panama story flared up. The New York *World* reported that William Nelson Cromwell was under threat of blackmail in connection with the mysterious disposal of the $40,000,000 that the United States had paid for the French company's rights in the canal. Cromwell had been the company's representative, and the paper hinted that a syndicate of Americans had secretly taken a generous cut of the money before it reached the French stockholders. Roosevelt was enraged and started a suit against the *World* under a wartime Act passed in 1898 "To Protect the Harbor Defenses" etc. This ill-conceived attack on the freedom of the press was thrown out of court, and the Judge remarked that personally "I have a curiosity to know what the truth was."

At the beginning of 1904 *Harper's Weekly,* which was sympathetic to Wall Street, reported a stern determination in the Street to beat Roosevelt, preferably with a Republican, or with a Democrat if necessary. "Anybody will do. It is a choice of evils."

In April William Randolph Hearst, for the Democrats, took a shot at Roosevelt on the ground that his antitrust sentiments were insincere. He recalled that George F. Baer of the Coal Trust had confessed on the witness stand that the Trust became part of the Republican machine in 1900. A great coal strike was on as the election was approaching, and the coal operators, to save the national Republican ticket from defeat, yielded to the miners and stopped the strike.

I am the will of the people. I am the leader. I chose myself to be leader it is MY right to do so. Down with the courts, the bosses and every confounded thing that opposes ME. I AM IT do you get me? I will have as many terms in office as I desire. Sate!

TR
REX

ABUSE

THE CONSTITUTION

THE SUPREME COURT

THE OFFICE OF THE PRESIDENT OF THE UNITED STATES

Artist E. W. Kemble minced neither words nor lines. Theodore Roosevelt invariably evoked strong feelings from both supporters and opponents.

"Mostly Smoke"—a cartoon by Bill Nye in the New York Daily News. To some it seemed that Theodore Roosevelt did little more than rave and rant about the trusts, but his supporters felt that his policies laid the basis for anti-monopoly regulation and other means of restricting big business.

Which was true enough, and a hard legacy for Mr. Roosevelt. When the next strike came, in 1902, the operators were determined not to yield again, lest they set a precedent, and he had to threaten the use of the Army before he got a settlement. Hearst went on to say: "Mr. Roosevelt's Attorney-General does not seek the indictment of Pres. Hill of the Northern Securities merger, . . . nor will he prosecute the criminals of the Coal Trust, because the Republican party does not dare to antagonize the Trust power at any time, and especially on the eve of a Presidential election.

"THE REPUBLICAN PARTY, THROUGH THE ROOSEVELT ADMINISTRA-TION, ACCORDS IMMUNITY FROM THE LAW TO THE TRUSTS, BECAUSE THE REPUBLICAN PARTY IS OWNED BY THE TRUSTS."

After Roosevelt's renomination the Democratic New York *World* described him as an all-round undesirable character, dangerous to Republicans, Democrats and neutrals: "One might as well expect the Kaiser to become St. Francis of Assisi as to expect Mr. Roosevelt to be sobered by authority and chastened by power. Eagles do not turn into doves when their wings grow stronger. An accidental President who in three years has trampled all Republican opposition under foot and made himself absolute master of his party can be relied on to extend his authority over our country by the same processes. . . .

"As for Mr. Roosevelt's fine moral courage . . . he has surrendered the ideal to political expediency. . . . The man who bearded the Northern Securities octopus has openly given hostages to Wall Street. . . . The man who made the better part of his political reputation as a civil-service reformer has taken all the spoilsmen and place-hunters of his party to his bosom."

The Democrats, hoping to attract disaffected Republicans, nominated the conservative Alton B. Parker, with the party line: "Judge Parker invites the support of every voter who conscientiously believes that President Roosevelt's policy of imperialism, militarism and imitation Europeanism is dangerous to the Republic." Parker was represented as standing for "conservative and constitutional democracy against radical and arbitrary Republicanism."

Carl Schurz, who had been a Republican under Lincoln, wrote a 15,000 word letter to the Parker Independent Club, explaining why he could not stomach this Republican candidate. He felt that the legendary Roosevelt had disappeared, and the present one was quite different. "The Government of this Republic must be a government of law, not a government of adventure," he said, failing to notice that the people that year were in love with adventure. Schurz somewhat belatedly found that the Republican Party was no longer the party of liberty and human rights for which he had fought forty years ago, but "is more and more becoming the party of rich men, who want to become through it still richer." He charged that the Republicans before every national election "fried the fat" out of the party's beneficiaries, with the understanding that the beneficiaries would be protected. "The upshot is a combination of bribery and blackmail, carried on with hardly any concealment."

On October 1st Joseph Pulitzer of the *World* unmasked the heavy artillery of the campaign. He accused Roosevelt of having purposely appointed George B. Cortelyou as Commissioner of Corporations in February, 1903, so that he might collect inside information on Wall Street firms. Then, without having made any of this information public, Cortelyou was allowed to resign and go to raising money for the Republican National Committee. Pulitzer could see no reason for this arrangement except that the new money-raiser had a portfolio of business secrets.

He quoted a sentence from one of Roosevelt's Messages: "Ours is not the creed of the weakling and the coward," and asked, "But may not peace also have her weaklings and cowards no less craven than those of war? . . . It is well enough to land marines in Hayti. Hayti does not contribute to the campaign fund. . . . But how about the great corporations that *do contribute* to the campaign fund? There is no Big Stick for them; no marines, no warship—nothing but secrecy, silence, solicitation, surrender."

All the Democrats joined in. George Foster Peabody, Treasurer of the Democratic Party, called attention to "the alarming dangers that lurk in the assumption that a man of character can properly do indelicate acts such as the putting of Mr. Cortelyou in his present unfortunate position." The Democratic press called it a public scandal, and an implied invitation to bribe the Executive. The "Cortelyou scandal" was hammered day after day.

Late in the campaign Judge Parker himself took up the charge of "Cortelyouism" and went so far as to use the word "blackmail," intimating that the big businessmen were buying Cortelyou's silence on secrets uncovered by the Bureau of Corporations. This gave T. R. an opening to turn loose his political vocabulary, against which Parker had no chance. He pointed out that the existence of contributions was not at issue. "Mr. Parker's accusations against Mr. Cortelyou and me are monstrous. . . . Inasmuch as they are false, heavy must be the condemnation of the man making them. . . . The assertion that Mr. Cortelyou had any knowledge, gained while in an official position, whereby he was enabled to secure and did secure any contributions from any corporation is a falsehood. . . . The assertion that there has been made any pledge or promise or that there has been any understanding as to future immunities or benefits, in recognition of any contribution from any source is a wicked falsehood."

If in fact any part of Wall Street was paying blackmail, there is every reason to believe that the President knew nothing of it. In those days campaign contributions did not have to be reported, and whatever Cortelyou collected, and whether he did have some business secrets that influenced the contributors, he told neither the public nor the President. The big men in Wall Street, after swearing never to accept T.R. and after luring the Democrats into offering a conservative candidate, decided after all that they would feel safer with the "madman" and a Republican administration than with Judge Parker and his accompanying Democrats. As the conservative New York *Sun* put it in a one-line editorial: "Theodore, with all thy faults." In Roosevelt's second term, however, he started several cases against the trusts, including one against the meat packers, who had openly supported him. Any deals that may have been made did not bind him.

Eight years later, when T.R. had bolted the party and the Republicans were after his scalp, a Senate committee brought out that J. P. Morgan had contributed $150,000 to the Republican campaign in 1904. Although Roosevelt had emphatically ordered Cortelyou not to take any Standard Oil money, John D. Archbold of that company testified that it had supplied $125,000 in currency to the National Committee. Even before he was out of the White House, however, Roosevelt had been embarrassed by the political facts of life in the Republican Party. Edward H. Harriman, the railroad magnate, wrote an indiscreet letter to a friend in which he remarked that his gratifying position as a political leader in New York was based on his help to Roosevelt in the campaign of 1904. When the results in New York State were looking doubtful about a week before election, the letter disclosed, "the President sent me a request to go to Washington to confer upon the political conditions . . . and asked me if I would help them in raising the necessary funds." Harriman went on to say that he raised $250,000, and that in return T.R. promised to name Chauncey Depew ambassador to France, which later he failed to do. A disgruntled employee sold this letter early in 1907 to the New York *World* for $150.

Mark Twain, who was writing his memoirs at the time, inserted a paragraph in which he noted that at last it was proved what he had thought all along: T.R. had bought the election of 1904 with Wall Street money. He agreed with Judge Parker's comment that at such a late hour in the campaign there could have been no conceivable use for a quarter of a million dollars except to buy the "floating vote" in the big cities.

When the Harriman letter came out Roosevelt blew up. He called it "a deliberate and willful untruth—by rights it should be characterized by an even shorter and more ugly word." Actually the correspondence on record shows that T.R. did ask Harriman to help in New York. There was nothing sinister about it but it was grist for the Democrats.

While Wall Street in 1904 was gulping and swallowing the distasteful Roosevelt, the ordinary voters were taking the hero with full-throated enthusiasm. The election was a landslide. The President voted at Oyster Bay early in the day and hastened to Washington to listen to the returns. When it was all over he said it was "the day of greatest triumph I ever had or ever could have." At last he was to be President in his own right.

On March 3, 1905, John Hay, who had started his political life as secretary to President Lincoln and was now Secretary of State, sent a ring to the President with a note:

"Dear Theodore,

"The hair in this ring is from the head of Abraham Lincoln. Dr. Taft cut it off the night of the assassination, and I got it from his son—a brief pedigree.

"Two Souls With But a Single Thought." Evoked by Theodore Roosevelt's friendliness toward Booker T. Washington, noted Negro educa-
tor, this highly offensive cartoon was drawn by L. C. Gregg, a Southerner. "On the Negro question," Theodore Roosevelt once declared,
"I hold myself the heir to the policies of Abraham Lincoln."

Some consolation for abuse T. R. was subjected to was provided by this McCutcheon cartoon in Chicago Tribune. The paper supported him briefly.

"Please wear it tomorrow; you are one of the men who most thoroughly understand and appreciate Lincoln. . . .

> Yours affectionately,
>
> John Hay"

The ring with Lincoln's hair in it added the final touch to the moment of triumph. Roosevelt wrote on March 9 to a friend in England: "Of course I greatly enjoyed inauguration day, and indeed I have thoroughly enjoyed being President. . . . As I suppose you know, Lincoln is my hero. . . . I am a college bred man, belonging to a well-to-do family so that I have not had to make my own livelihood. . . But the farmers, lumbermen, mechanics,˙ranchmen, miners, of the North, East, and West, have felt that I was just as much in sympathy with them, just as devoted to their interests, and as proud of them, as representative of them, as if I had sprung from among their own ranks. . . . How long this feeling toward me will last I cannot say . . . there will be a reaction. But meanwhile I shall have accomplished something worth accomplishing, I hope."

Once he was President in his own right, Roosevelt set out to bring Big Business under government control, by railroad regulation, workmen's compensation laws, elimination of child labor, supervision of insurance companies, and control of campaign contributions. He stole the useful planks from the Democratic platform, and calmly told Mr. Bryan at a Gridiron Club dinner that the Democrat had no use for them since after all he could not get elected. He was right in feeling that the people were behind him, and for four years he rode in glory, having what Gifford Pinchot called "a halcyon and vociferous time."

But in the depleted and sullen ranks of the diehard members of Congress and their business friends there was a bitter determination to outlast the madman and in the end destroy him. As early as March 7, 1905, a Standard Oil Congressman was writing to Mr. Archbold of the need to establish "a permanent and healthy control of the *Associated Press and other kindred avenues*. . . . No man values public opinion or fears it as much as Theodore Roosevelt. . . . Mild reproof or criticism of his policy would nearly paralyze him."

Congressman James W. Wadsworth, Sr., who had fought violently against Roosevelt's meat inspection legislation, and had then been retired by the voters of his usually Republican district, expressed the diehard feeling: "The whole thing stamps the President as unreliable, a faker, and a humbug. For years he has indulged in lofty sentiments, and violates them all for the sake of satisfying his petty spite. . . . Thank God, he can't fool all the people all the time, and the country is fast awakening to the real character of this bloody hero of Kettle Hill."

But though the heathen raged and the righteous cheered, not all was triumph. The Brownsville affair was one that troubled Roosevelt so much that he left all mention of it out of his autobiography.

Three companies of Negro troops had been sent to Brownsville, Texas, where they were at once made unwelcome by the townspeople. Two weeks after they arrived, at midnight suddenly firing broke out in the town and about a hundred shots were fired, though no one was killed. At the barracks, the troops were immediately ordered to fall in, and all were present except two who were on leave. But the civilians asserted that ten or fifteen soldiers had attacked the town, and as evidence offered army cartridge cases that they said had been found in the street. The fact that all the company rifles were inspected and found clean, and that marks on the cartridge cases showed they had been used in target practice at an earlier date, did not prevent a hysterical reaction from the officers. On the basis of official reports the President hastily ordered the whole contingent of 160 men dishonorably discharged.

Senator Foraker of Ohio, who had become T.R.'s bitter enemy in connection with railroad legislation, took up the cause of the Negroes in December 1906. He drew from the President a positive report based on an investigation by the Inspector General, which Foraker was able to demolish thoroughly. But Roosevelt hated to admit that he had made a mistake, and in December, 1908, when he was on the last lap of his Administration, he sent Congress a report of further investigations. This time he conceded that some of the soldiers might not have known about the alleged raid, but he still insisted that others undoubtedly were involved. This was meat to Foraker, who brought in evidence that one of the principal witnesses against the soldiers, whom the President had quoted in this latest report, had flatly denied having given any such information. The final result was a stinging defeat for Roosevelt. He had put too much trust in the War Department. Later some of the soldiers were reinstated.

In October, 1907, Mark Twain took the occasion of a Roosevelt hunting trip in Louisiana to go after him with no such gentle mockery as that of Mr. Dooley, who after all tickled T.R. more than he hurt. Mark Twain hated Roosevelt and he meant to draw blood. "Alas," he wrote, "the President has got that cow after all! . . . Some say it was a bear—but they were all White House domestics. . . . The fact that the President himself thinks it was a bear does not diminish the doubt but enlarges it. . . . His judgment has been out of focus so long now that he imagines that everything he does, little or big, is colossal. . . . But the circumstantial evidence that it was a cow is overwhelming. It acted just as a cow would act . . . thinking maybe he would spare her life on account of her sex, her helpless situation, and her notorious harmlessness. . . . When her strength was exhausted . . . she stopped in an open spot, fifty feet wide, and humbly faced the President of the United States with the tears running down her cheeks, and said to him with the mute eloquence of surrender: "Have pity, sir, and spare me. I am alone, you are many; I have no weapon but my helplessness, you are a walking arsenal; I am in awful peril, you are as safe as you would be in a Sunday school; have pity, sir—there is no heroism in killing an exhausted cow.'

"In the outcome the credit is all with the cow, none of it is with the President. . . .From a safe distance Hercules sent a bullet to the sources of its life; then, dying, it made a fight—so there *was* a hero present after all. Another bullet closed the tragedy, and Hercules was so carried away with admiration of himself that he hugged his domestics and bought a compliment from one of them. . . . Ennolds said: 'Mr. President, you are no tenderfoot.'

"Mr. Roosevelt responded by giving Ennolds a $20 note. . . .

"There were daily swims in the lake by members of the party, including the President. 'The water was fine,' he said, 'and I did not have the fear of alligators that some seem to have.'

"Mr. Ennolds lost a chance; if he had been judiciously on watch he could have done the alligator compliment himself, and got another twenty for it."

Roosevelt refused to take any blame for the panic of 1907. On the contrary, in January 1908, he sent a defiant message to Congress in which he declared that the Government would go on scourging sin in business, and would put behind the bars with impartial severity "the powerful financier, the powerful politician, the rich land thief, the rich contractor—all, no matter how high the station, against whom criminal misdeeds can be proved." He made it plain that he proposed the moral regeneration of the business world, and added that any business that would be hurt by moral reform was the kind that it would pay the country to hurt—the kind that had made the name of "high finance" a term of reproach. He refused to believe that the actions of his administration had brought on business distress; "it is due to the speculative folly and flagrant dishonesty of men of great wealth."

Wall Street was pained. Nicholas Murray Butler, an old friend of Roosevelt's, undertook the sad duty of reproaching the President: "Of all your real friends perhaps I, alone, am fond enough of you to tell you what a painful impression has been made on the public mind by your special message. . . . I am besought on every hand to know whether I, as a friend whom you trust and who has no ulterior motive to serve, cannot in some way bring you to see what damage has been done both to your own reputation and to the Presidency itself by the message. You may imagine that the task is anything but a welcome one."

Roosevelt replied coldly that if Butler's soul did not rise up against corruption in politics and in business, "why, then, naturally you are not in sympathy with me." And "thus," as Henry Pringle remarks, "passed Nicholas Miraculous from the Roosevelt years."

One incident of the panic turned out later to have been a time bomb. There came a moment when the brokerage house of Moore & Schley was in trouble, and if it fell it might throw the market into a dangerous tailspin. Now Moore & Schley held several million dollars' worth of Tennessee Coal and Iron Company stock, a valuable property desired by U.S. Steel. Judge Gary of the Steel Corporation went to Washington and explained to the President that as a patriotic service he was prepared to buy control of TC&I, and even pay more than its real value, if only he could be assured of freedom from anti-trust prosecution. T.R., who understood practically nothing of

Had this intemperate cartoon appeared in a Communist or Anarchist periodical it at least might have had some plausibility as an expression of the distorted mind of the artist. What made it shocking was the fact that it appeared in the Atlanta Constitution, one of the nation's most respected and respectable of newspapers. Possible excuse this paper had for such a vicious drawing was the fact that Theodore Roosevelt made no secret of his feeling regarding treatment of Southern Negroes.

"Here No One Dares Lay A Hand But Myself"—the Yankee peril as an Argentine journal saw it. More than previous Presidents, T.R. went out of his way to nurture good neighbor policies, but construction of the Panama Canal aroused strong animosity on the part of some Latin American governments, particularly those influenced by German interests.

high finance, had to decide what to tell Gary before the next day's opening of the market. Groping blindly for his duty, with the business world threatening to crash around his ears, he decided to save the markets from ruin first and think it over afterward. The wily steel tycoon got the assurance he wanted; Big Steel grabbed TC&I; and the looming catastrophe was staved off.

But a Congressional investigation in 1908 brought in evidence that to save the market it would have been enough for U.S. Steel to have lent Moore & Schley a few million dollars' worth of its bonds. Instead the Corporation had seized the opportunity to snap up the control of a property worth several hundred million at a total cost of less than fifty million, while hornswoggling the President into promising immunity.

T. R. indignantly denied that he had been hornswoggled, but it was an awkward moment. He had been badly scared at the time by economic forces that he had no skill to cope with; and for the moment he had had to forget about moral regeneration and follow what seemed to be expert advice on how to meet the crisis. It was this unpleasant memory that underlay the bitterness with which he greeted the news in 1911 that his successor had sued U.S. Steel for violating the anti-trust law in its acquisition of TC&I.

By 1908 it was clear that the progressive Roosevelt had not succeeded in imposing his brand of new Republicanism on the established leadership of his party. The unregenerate diehards still controlled much of the party machinery and many of the senior places in Congress.

The December session of Congress was not disposed to cater to the outgoing President, especially as president-elect Taft was openly consorting with the conservatives on Capitol Hill. Roosevelt, for his part, trod heavily on Congressional toes by criticizing an amendment that restricted the Secret Service to guarding the President and hunting counterfeiters. He said that the chief cause of this amendment was that Congressmen did not want to be investigated, and he rubbed it in by asserting that very little of such investigation had been done in the past. "But," he remarked, "I do not believe that it is in the public interest to protect criminals in any branch of the public service."

This tactful statement did little to calm the Congressional mind.

For during the previous spring there had been rumors that the President had agents watching the disorderly houses along Pennsylvania Avenue, to obtain information useful for influencing the votes of indiscreet Congressmen. The records show no evidence that any such system of applied blackmail was ever actually employed, but after being calmly assured that *not many* of the legislators had been under surveillance, the House indignantly passed a resolution calling on the President for proof of any wrongdoing by any of its members. He replied in a new message on January 4, which mentioned a case in the Senate of misuse of the frank, but denied any intention of systematically shadowing members of Congress. The House voted 212 to 35 to reject the President's message as lacking due respect. No President since Andrew Johnson had been so severely slapped.

On February 25 Congressman George Washington Cook of Colorado let off a parting blast in a speech which he called "Tyranny of Theodore Roosevelt." He deplored the President's lack of a legal mind and pictured him "riding through and around the arena of political action on his broncho of arrogant, egotistical impulses, pretending to throw his lariat of execution at the heels and broad horns of capital for the delectation of voting labor and ending the scene with the cunning catch of a prairie wolf or a gopher. . . . Mr. Roosevelt runs the Government on the same principles that the Beef Trust runs its sausage factory, from a personal standpoint, using legislative and judicial pork as the crude material of his fantastic administration."

But this was feeble stuff. Roosevelt was riding high on the way out. Though the politicians hated him, the people loved him, and he had got his chosen heir elected. On second thought, however, he was busily creating new forest reserves out of the public domain as fast as he could get the papers filled out, so that if any of Mr. Taft's friends wanted to get possession of these lands there would have to be an overt change of policy. And that might be dangerous for Mr. Taft; Roosevelt was confident that the people were with him.

So came March 4, and the halcyon days were over. James Bryce, British expert on American affairs, wrote from the British Embassy that in his judgment Roosevelt had "done more for the advancement of good causes, more to stir the soul of the nation and rouse it to a sense of its incomparable opportunities and high mission, for the whole world as well as for this Continent, than any one of your predecessors for a century save Abraham Lincoln himself. . . . The bringing about peace between Russia and Japan, the construction of the Canal, the setting on foot of the Conservation of Resources Movement, all fall into their places along with and cohere with this appeal to the Nation's heart and its larger thoughts for the future which you have made."

Some people were glad to see Roosevelt go. Owen Wister observed that the lawless elements in both Big Business and radical labor rejoiced to be rid of him; "both these groups hated Roosevelt as bitterly as the fanatics of Reconstruction had hated Lincoln." Nicholas Roosevelt, Theodore's cousin, testified that "It was the men who harbored crooked or dishonest schemes who most feared and hated T.R. while he was in the White House. . . . It was as an aggressive champion of right against wrong . . . of democracy against privilege that he contributed most to his age. . . . No wonder visitors to the United States regarded him as a phenomenon equalled only by Niagara Falls."

On March 23rd the ex-President sailed away to Africa on a hunting trip, and Taft was left in charge of the suddenly quiet White House.

Mr. Taft was not the man to wear the fast-moving shoes of Theodore Roosevelt. He tried loyally to carry on, and he enforced vigorously the antitrust laws which T.R. had succeeded in resurrecting. That job he could understand. But to his legal mind the duty of a President was to follow the law as laid down by Congress, not to sally forth against all sorts of evils at the expense of stretching the law. Taft was called "a pleasant person surrounded by men who know exactly what they want"—the party ideal for a quiet time. But he came at the wrong period in history. Though the world war was still unsuspected, it was not a quiet time. Those distant explosions and occasional earth tremors came from the mighty Theodore terrorizing the lions in Africa. If he lived, he would be back. And still hiding below the horizon was the strange portent of Woodrow Wilson. In such a world, Taft belonged in the haven of the Supreme Court—where, after much suffering, in the fullness of time a merciful Providence and President Harding at last brought him to rest.

In his very first year, Taft found himself in a violent and bewildering fight over conservation, in which he was cruelly hurt without ever understanding just what it was about.

The founding of the conservation movement in 1907 and 1908 was a triumphal progress for T.R. and his prophet Gifford Pinchot, which brought them little but praise. It therefore does not belong in this story except as background for the split between Roosevelt and Taft. The modern idea of conservation had been invented by Pinchot and joyfully adopted by Roosevelt, who in later years was inclined to regard it as his greatest achievement. When he departed he left Pinchot as in a special sense his deputy in charge of conservation, although officially only head of the Forest Service.

Roosevelt says in his autobigraphy that "Gifford Pinchot is the man to whom the nation owes most for what has been accomplished as regards the preservation of the natural resources of our country. . . . I believe it is but just to say," he adds not too modestly, "that among the many, many public officials who under my administration rendered literally invaluable service to the people of the United States, he, on the whole, stood first." Anyone, therefore, who would tangle seriously with Pinchot would be unpopular with T.R.

When Taft came in he appointed as Secretary of the Interior a conservative lawyer from Seattle, Richard A. Ballinger, who did not agree with the doctrines of Pinchot and the other conservationists.

The fight began when Pinchot learned that Ballinger planned to sell 5280 acres of coal land from the public domain in Alaska to a speculator for the Guggenheim Syndicate, which already controlled a large part of the territory. Pinchot regarded this as an undue encouragement to monopoly. Taft was in favor of conservation as he understood it, but could see no legal objection to putting the coal in strong hands that would develop the resource and build up the country. In the course of the fight Pinchot wrote a heated letter to a Senator which implied that Ballinger was making a fool of Taft; and Taft of course dismissed Pinchot forthwith from the Forest Service. Pinchot wrote to Roosevelt in Africa, and afterward met him in Italy on his way home. His report on the Ballinger affair undoubtely influenced the ex-President to feel disappointed in his sucessor.

From Italy Roosevelt proceeded to a tour of Europe, where he had a "bully" time visiting crowned heads and attending King Edward's

Predecessor of anti-semitic attacks familiar to Franklin D. Roosevelt, this cartoon was possibly evoked by TR's liberal stand on race questions.

Wall Street's image of the President as Collier's envisioned it.

funeral in London; and he returned on June 18, 1910, to be met by a great naval parade, a corral full of 2,500 governors, senators, and other dignitaries on the pier, and best of all, the cheering thousands whom he loved. It was a triumph that could not help being a cruel and unusual punishment for Mr. Taft. The whole situation was unavoidably loaded for trouble.

The explosion came on October 24, 1911, when the Attorney General filed an antitrust suit against U.S. Steel and specified that its control of Tennessee Coal and Iron was illegal. Roosevelt took this as a direct slap, since it implied that he had been fooled—as indeed he had. An added cause of estrangement was a careless reference in one of Taft's speeches to "political emotionalists and neurotics," which was not intended to apply to Roosevelt but which he took as personal. T.R. began to drift rapidly toward the feeling that it would be his duty to take the Presidency away from Mr. Taft. As late as November he was saying he was not a candidate, though pointedly not saying that he would not be one. Finally, on February 23 the New York *Times* reported his fateful words, "My hat is in the ring." Immediately the conservatives and the Democrats united in accusing Roosevelt of bad faith.

The New York *World* remarked that the Little Corporal was back from Elba but hopefully asserted that the populace had failed to respond. Not all of Mr. Taft's friends, it pointed out, were sordid office-seekers or Big Business champions of monopoly; many were just ordinary loyal Republicans who resented Roosevelt's effort to split the party. They resented his putting himself at the head of "noisy and vociferous and Populistic elements."

Above all, "the blackest page in the record is Mr. Roosevelt's treatment of Mr. Taft. Mr. Taft was not nominated by the Republican party. He was forced upon the convention by Mr. Roosevelt." As Taft's sponsor, Roosevelt should have stood by him and helped to make him a success; but instead he had stabbed him in the back, by supporting the anti-Taft junta (meaning largely the conservationists led by Pinchot). The editor went on to say that Grant had wanted a third term but never tried to climb back into power over the ruins of his party, and even Aaron Burr refused to wreck the Democratic party in order to prevent Jefferson's election.

"There was no dragging of Cincinnatus from the plough and there was no necessity that any Marc Anthony should thrice upon the Lupercal offer him the crown. He was willing to come with his own crown and frame a constitution of his own in accordance with the charming and alluring platform that he has promulgated."

The charge of violation of a pledge was repeated by the New York *Sun* over and over during the campaign in the following form:

THE DEADLIEST OF ALL PARALLELS

President Roosevelt's Decision on November 8, 1904: "Under no circumstances will I be a candidate for or accept another nomination."

Ex-President Roosevelt's Decision on February 25, 1912: "I will accept the nomination for President if it is tendered to me."

Logically, the weak spot in this charge was that a bargain is one thing, and a personal decision for which one has not been paid anything is another. A man has a right to change his own mind if he has not been paid to keep it unchanged, and Roosevelt's announcement in 1904 had come after he was safely reelected. But Roosevelt preferred to rest on the very real difference between consecutive and discontinuous terms, and the fact that once a President is out of office he has no further control of the machinery of renomination, "and is in the position absolutely of any private citizen."

The famous "cup of coffee" argument was supplied by the *Outlook*: "When a man says at breakfast in the morning 'No, thank you, I will not take any more coffee,' it does not mean that he will not take any more coffee to-morrow morning . . .'"

The press, of course, had fun. *Life* said: "The popular demand for Colonel Roosevelt is steadily increasing; but however great the demand may become, it can never be as great as the supply." The Brooklyn *Eagle* contributed the observation that "No place feels like home after you have once lived in the White House."

The campaign for the Republican nomination was a dirty one. At first Taft tried hard to avoid hitting back at the old friend who had chosen him to be President four years ago. But T.R. bore down without mercy, and at last Taft's patience wore out. On April 25 in Boston he launched an angry attack, taking up Roosevelt's charges in detail and accusing him of misquotation and misrepresentation. As the Boston *Post* reported: "His voice trembling with indignation the President declared Roosevelt has likened himself to Abraham Lincoln, and asked: 'I would like to ask the fair people of Massachusetts tonight if you think he is giving me a square deal; or if Abraham Lincoln would do what he is doing to me.' From all over the great auditorium came loud shouts of 'no' 'no' . . .So deeply was the President moved that he repeatedly abandoned the printed manuscript of his address to appeal to the multitude: "Do you think it is fair?' or 'Do you think that is giving me a square deal?' "

Taft remarked bitterly that "Theodore Roosevelt says all the bosses are supporting me. A man who supports me in politics is a boss. A man who supports him in politics is a leader." He also emphasized that to nominate Roosevelt would be a violation of the "useful and necessary" tradition against the third term.

The next day, at Worcester, Roosevelt answered. He called Taft a traitor to friendship, and accused him of being guilty of the grossest hypocrisy, of being disloyal to every canon of decency and fair play; of being responsible for assaults foul to the verge of indecency, of not being a gentleman, and of resembling Presidents Buchanan and Fillmore. As for not giving Taft a square deal, he said, "The trouble with President Taft is that he thinks that other people can tell you better what you need than you yourselves." As the *Post* reported it, " 'This is the crookedest kind of a deal,' he shouted in his high falsetto voice."

It was not a seemly exchange of views, and the country was embarrassed.

Many of Roosevelt's oldest friends, such as Elihu Root, Philander Knox, and Henry Stimson, fell away from him. The campaign became frantic on both sides. The New York *Times* printed a solemn article by Dr. Allen McLane Hamilton discussing whether T.R.'s mind had given way. Freudian psychology, which had just become the rage, was called upon to explain that subconscious longing for another term had undermined his judgment even while he was in the White House. Nicholas Roosevelt reports a conversation with "one of the leading socialites of Boston" to the effect that Theodore had a crazy brother in an asylum (which was not true), and that Theodore was even worse. Henry Adams wrote to his brother Brooks Adams that Roosevelt's mind had gone to pieces till it had become quite incoherent and spasmodic. "He is, as Taft justly said, a neurotic, and his neurosis may end . . . in nervous collapse, or a stroke, or acute mania." Taft's brother Charles commented on T.R.'s "utter failure in that poise, that breadth of human feeling and that lack of personal ambition that made Lincoln great, that is going to make Theodore Roosevelt when history throws its cold white light on him not a great but a pathetic figure."

History seems to indicate that a man may be great in one period and pathetic in another, especially if he lives past high tide.

The majority of Republican voters undoubtedly wanted Roosevelt, but the Taft men controlled the Convention in June, and Taft was nominated. Roosevelt bolted and was nominated as candidate of a third party that was quickly named the "Bull Moose."

It was a sad position for the man who had had such a glorious time in the Presidency. Many of the traditional Republicans whose memories ran back to Lincoln felt that the good old custom of renominating the incumbent had been rudely challenged; many objected to a third term; many felt that Roosevelt had been disloyal to the friend whom he had chosen and pushed into the White House. Those who did not believe he was crazy thought he was trying to make himself permanent President. It was suggested that if he should be elected "he will never quit the Presidency alive," and "Marse Henry" Watterson in the Louisville *Courier Journal* felt that if he did not land in a lunatic asylum there could be but one issue, life tenure in the Executive office.

Worst of all, when Roosevelt in the excitement of the Bull Moose Convention shouted that "we stand at Armageddon and we battle for the Lord," he was taking in too much territory. He had no monopoly on the Lord. Progressive Republicans who wanted to avoid voting for Taft could easily vote for Wilson, as in the end many of them evidently did. T.R. could still draw large and cheering crowds, but there was something wrong. Like Henry Wallace in 1948, he could see an unwelcome type of face appearing too often among his followers—members of the so-called "left lunatic fringe," whose support could mean nothing but failure.

One encouraging interlude, however, came on October 14, while

The New York Globe's attitude toward Roosevelt as the Presidential candidate of the Progressive Party in 1912 was quite unequivocal.

This cartoon helped contribute to T.R.'s defeat in 1912.

Roosevelt was in Milwaukee. As he stood in an automobile bowing to a cheering crowd, he was shot by a man who was opposed to a third term. The bullet, fortunately for him, went through a metal spectacle case and the manuscript of his speech before entering his chest. He was ordered to hospital but refused to go. He insisted on making his scheduled speech, saying, "It may be the last one I shall deliver, but I am going to deliver this one." When he pulled out the manuscript and saw the bullet hole in it he held it up and told the audience, "It takes more than that to kill a bull moose." He seized the chance to take a shot at the hostile press, saying that wild charges in the newspapers were influencing weak-minded fanatics to assassinate him.

This incident did something to salvage the badly battered Roosevelt morale. Lord Charnwood in his biography of Roosevelt says that in reply to a question from Lord Grey, he wrote: "I can answer with absolute certainty. You would have made the speech as a matter of course. . . . A good soldier or sailor or deep-sea fisherman . . . would normally act as I acted without thinking anything about it." The once-puny small boy took comfort, in his grown-up distress, that he could rank among the real men whom he so much admired. And like Andrew Jackson, he now had a bullet in his chest that he would carry for the rest of his life.

In the election Roosevelt lost all but his revenge. Taft carried only Vermont and Utah, with 8 electoral votes. Roosevelt got 88 votes, and Wilson 435.

Nearly three years after the election T.R. was restored to political vigor by the misguided efforts of one William Barnes, Jr., Republican boss of New York State. Roosevelt had issued a statement saying that Barnes and Murphy, the Democratic boss, commonly acted together to resist any reform of political corruption. This unpleasant truth roused Barnes, and he sued for $50,000 damages. Roosevelt's enemies were sure they had him in a trap, and Barnes's counsel boasted that he was going to nail T.R.'s hide to the fence. The first qualm of disappointment came when thorough investigation failed to turn up anything in the Roosevelt past that could be made into a scandal. Then on opening the case in court, Barnes's lawyers found they had a bear by the tail and were unable to let go. The defendant ran away with the case, and tied the plaintiff's lawyers in knots. He stretched out the proceedings, and seized the opportunity to preach the doctrine of clean politics at Barnes's expense, with a delighted public all over the country cheering him on.

One of T.R.'s bitterest enemies, observing how the trial was going, burst out at Barnes as a blithering idiot. "Here we had Roosevelt dead and buried politically. We were rid of him for all time. Now Barnes has not only opened the door for him to come back, but he has pushed him to the front of the stage and made him a greater popular idol than ever." T.R., meanwhile, was enjoying every minute of it, just as John Quincy Adams did the great treason trial of 1842.

At the end, too, there came a high moment. The case was closed on May 7, 1915, and on the next day the jury would retire to consider its verdict, after having breakfast and a chance to see the morning papers. On the afternoon of May 7 came the news of the sinking of the *Lusitania*.

Roosevelt had taken advantage of the opportunity of this public trial, as John Quincy Adams had done in his day, to lay his whole lifework and reputation on the issue, to win or lose it all. Now the *Lusitania* was sunk with fearful losses; he would be called on by the press to make a statement, and he must not flinch. But the jury, on whose verdict his place in history might well depend, included at least two German-Americans.

Roosevelt asked no advice from his lawyers nor from anyone else. That night when a New York paper called him to the telephone, he dictated a short and plain message condemning the sinking as murder and calling on the government to take action against Germany. In the morning he sadly told his lawyers that he had had to throw away the case, but "there is a principle here at stake which is far more vital to the American people than my personal welfare is to me." So they sat and waited for the verdict, but as it turned out the German-Americans followed the evidence and voted for acquittal. Barnes lost not only the case but his position as party boss. It was his hide that was nailed to the Roosevelt barn door at Oyster Bay.

A few months later one of Roosevelt's friends casually remarked that he couldn't recall how much damages the jury had awarded him. That put the frosting on the top of the cake. "But, my dear fellow," he screamed with glee, in his highest falsetto, "*I* was the *de-fen-dant!*"

Feeling his strength restored, T.R. began dreaming of military glory, for he was sure the United States would be drawn into the war. He wanted to raise a division of volunteers and go over to France. As word got around of what he had in mind he was overwhelmed with applications—nearly 250,000 of them had come in by May, 1917; so his dream was by no means his alone. But as America came into the war, and Roosevelt began hammering at the gates of the War Department, it soon became plain that he was not welcome. He was hopelessly at odds with Wilson. Actually both men were temperamentally unable to see the real possibilities of his proposal.

Roosevelt's own idea was unrealistically romantic. He longed to have a divisional brigade of cavalry, and possibly a couple of brigades of mounted infantry. He thought about Jeb Stuart, the Civil War cavalry raider, and pictured himself riding deep into German territory with his horsemen clattering behind him through the terror-stricken enemy villages in the night. He did not understand the muddy trench warfare, nor the difficulty of subordinating himself to General Pershing, nor that the real contribution he had to offer would be psychological.

Wilson, on his side, was blind to what was being offered. He was, to be sure, an artist in psychological warfare, who in the end would be the one to break the stalemate and shatter the German Empire with the power of his pen. But he would not see the propaganda value of the fabulous Roosevelt name, though Clemenceau wrote to him saying, "Our poilus ask, 'Where is Roosevelt?' Send them Roosevelt—it will gladden their hearts." And in Germany also, Roosevelt was a legend, the hero and mighty hunter, much admired by the Kaiser himself before the war. But Wilson could not bear to give Roosevelt the limelight, even to help win the war.

If the personalities had been vastly different, Wilson might have made expert use of the magic name; and Roosevelt might have adjusted himself to the role of inspiring devotion among the Allies and fear across the lines, even if he could have no crowded hour of glorious life with sword in hand and cheering men at his heels. But it could not be. On April 9, 1917, he called at the White House, and the two ill-assorted men talked affably together; but their minds did not meet. Finally on May 18 Wilson announced that he could not send any Roosevelt Expeditionary Force, adding cruelly and quite inaccurately, "The business in hand is undramatic, practical, and of scientific definiteness and precision." So Roosevelt angrily disbanded his paper division. His thousands of volunteers, his four sons among them, went unromantically to the trenches under less glamorous leaders, but the adventure was not for him.

He wrote to Georges Clemenceau in July, 1918: "It is a very sad thing to see the young die when the old, who are doing nothing, as I am doing nothing, are left alive. Therefore it is very bitter to me that I am not allowed to face the danger with my sons. But whatever may be their fate, I am glad and proud that my sons have done their part in this mighty war against despotism and barbarism. Of my four boys, Quentin, as you know, has been killed, and two of the other three wounded, and all three of these have been decorated for gallantry and efficiency in action."

He hated to grow old; and he was only sixty-one. But the vigorous body that he had built with such strenuous efforts out of unpromising materials was beginning to burn out; it had been a hard life. Early in 1918 he had a series of abcesses which left him deaf in one ear. On the day of the Armistice he went to the hospital with inflammatory rheumatism and did not get back to Oyster Bay till Christmas Eve. On January 5, he dictated an editorial opposing Wilson's policies; and suddenly in the night his heart failed and he was gone.

All across the country the flags were at half-mast. During his funeral, all the street-cars and subway trains of New York City stood still, the wheels of every factory stopped; policemen and school children stood to attention. In Washington the Senate and House adjourned, and even the Supreme Court adjourned without doing any business— the first time it had honored anyone in that way.

Lord Charnwood, in summing up Roosevelt's life, said: "Men have fought as stoutly as he, and more wisely—seldom so consistently for the right. That is the main thing. . . . He had those simple qualities which go to the hearts of common people, and of which the full possession is greatness, whether genius accompanies it or not. . . . He lived no restricted life of mere statecraft, any more than of mere scholarship, or mere sport, but he took life whole, as it offered itself . . . in like manner he respected worth when it met him and welcomed friends as God sent them, careless of differences between nations, or between classes, between gentle and simple, between the like and the unlike of himself."

Many different people, commenting on Roosevelt's death, compared him with Mr. Valiant-for-truth in the *Pilgrim's Progress*:

"After this it was noised abroad that Mr. Valiant-for-truth was taken with a summons . . . and had this for a token that the summons was true, 'That his pitcher was broken at the fountain.' When he understood it, he called for his friends and told them of it. Then he said, 'I am going to my Father's, and though with great difficulty I have got hither, yet now I do not repent me of all the trouble I have been at to arrive where I am. My sword I give to him that shall succeed me in my pilgrimage, and my courage and skill to him that can get it. . . . So he passed over, and all the trumpets sounded for him on the other side."

Examples of the vilification Charles Evans Hughes was subjected to when he ran for President in 1916 campaign.

In later years artist Rollin Kirby regretted that he had drawn these cartoons for the New York World.

Hughes was so badly smeared by rumors that he was pro-German
that his loyalty rather than his ability had to be played up prom-
inently during the bitter campaign of 1916. Wilson was elected.

CHAPTER IX

CRUCIFIED PEACEMAKER

In Wilmington, North Carolina, in the middle 1870s the Reverend Dr. Joseph Wilson was pastor of the First Presbyterian Church, and his son Thomas Woodrow Wilson was at home studying for entrance to Princeton College. On a fine summer morning young Tommy came to the breakfast table and addressed his father: "Eureka," says he, "Eureka, I have found it." "Found what?" says Dr. Wilson. "A mind, sir. I've found that I have an intellect and a first-class mind," says Tommy, vastly pleased with the discovery. He had spent most of the night with an abstruse treatise and found that he could understand the author's meaning, which, he was sure, only a first-class mind could grasp.

And so the jaws of the trap closed softly on him. For the other jaw was already in place: he had found the stern, Calvinistic God in the Church where he sat at his father's feet—"God, whose I am and whom I serve." Relying on his God-given intellect he could be sure that his will was God's will, and his duty was to proclaim it to men. A dangerous path for mortal man; for though in great part his gospel might be right, he might have to die for it like many another inflexible prophet.

To say that fate was preparing a sacrificial victim in anticipation of the crisis that would come forty years later is easy but of little use as a guide for future crises. Possibly a more practical interpretation of Wilson's preparation would be to appreciate the fact that the fertile soil of free America has developed innumerable specialized personalities, among whom from time to time the democracy has found one on whom to impose the fearful burden of leadership, in circumstances that forty years earlier were beyond human imagining. The apparently miraculous discovery of the needed great man has happened often enough to become a proverbial characteristic of American history; and Wilson was an example of a man trained for an unimaginable task. His intuitive sense of the meaning of peace on earth and of America's place and duty; his mastery of the language of prophecy; and his unswerving confidence in his own rightness, combined into a powerful if not always amiable character, capable of launching the vast enterprise that was first called the League of Nations and in its second incarnation the United Nations. For such an extraordinary feat the hero, being after all only a human being, might be expected to have the faults of his virtues—arrogance, extreme sensitivity to criticism or even friendly doubt, and lack of the political art of bargaining to win a less-than-perfect success. For these faults he was destined to be fervently hated by many honest and intelligent people, and at the last to suffer and die frustrated, though not without faith that in some distant future his cause would prevail.

With his Scotch and Scotch-Irish heritage, Wilson at times showed signs of the eerie Celtic tendency to see visions. One such is on record in his college oration on the Earl of Chatham:

"Under the deepening shadow of a gathering storm we obtain a last glimpse of Chatham, as he stands, himself a wreck, holding up before a blind Ministry a picture of the dark ruin which was awaiting them. With some of his old haughtiness the old man rises to answer one who had dared to reply to him, and falls, never to rise again."

Not long after he wrote this bit of unconscious prophecy, Tommy Wilson changed his name to the more dignified Woodrow Wilson, and set out on what seemed likely to be a dignified and unexciting academic career.

A quarter of a century later, while Theodore Roosevelt was leading the political uprising against Big Business, President Woodrow Wilson of Princeton, attacking the aristocratic club system in the University, had involved himself in a losing fight with the Big Business men among the alumni, whereby his somewhat conservative political opinions were rapidly being transformed into liberal ones. When he was offered a way of escape from the battlefield of Princeton into the Governorship of New Jersey in 1910, it was natural for him to leap onto the political scene as a liberal. It was a liberal era, for the country was tired of business domination. In the 1912 campaign, the auspices looked favorable for either Roosevelt or Wilson, whichever should win the Presidency, to have a successful and fairly peaceful line of progress ahead of him. The winner turned out to be Wilson, and on Inauguration Day in 1913 he was cordially welcomed to the

White House by President Taft, who though defeated had no resentment against a Democrat. After escorting Wilson to the Capitol, Taft accepted an invitation to lunch, and stayed to help introduce the new family to the mansion. Taft, as he said good-bye, remarked, "I'm glad to be going—this is the lonesomest place in the world." Wilson too was a man who would be lonely there.

But all was not as peaceful as it looked, for in the background was T.R., beaten down but still very much alive; and the two men, though both on the liberal side, were temperamentally bound to hate eachother. In fact, Wilson had criticized Roosevelt early in the campaign, to a group of newspaper men. With spectacular lack of his occasional prescience, he accused T.R. of too much promising the millennium. "You have no right to promise Heaven unless you can bring us to it," he told the newsmen, "for, in making promises, you create too much expectation and your failure brings with it only disappointment and sometimes despair. . . . The successful leader ought not to keep too far in advance of the mass he is seeking to lead, for he will soon lose contact with them." As early as 1907, Wilson had written to a friend, with equally spectacular blindness to his own weaknesses, that President Roosevelt was the most dangerous man of the age—all the more dangerous because he so sincerely believed in himself.

Roosevelt, for his part, despised Wilson as a sissy and phrasemonger. He told his friends that politically Wilson would be a joke if it were not for his power to make mischief. He called Wilson "a Byzantine logothete," a fairly innocuous dictionary word meaning a government bookkeeper in Byzantium; but it sounded so despicable that it became widely current.

The fundamental hostility between the two men was mainly derived from the difference in the way each had reacted to a feeble and nearsighted boyhood. Wilson could see well enough to be able to play some baseball, but he generally ended up managing the team. He did not go in for football or the more violent games, and he never became robust like Roosevelt; when he went to the White House he had a stomach pump with him. In Princeton he was more popular than Theodore was at Harvard, for he had wit and good spirits and an excellent tenor voice that gained him an honored place in the glee club. He missed the hard knocks that had driven Roosevelt to the grim determination to develop bodily strength and courage. It is impossible to imagine Wilson meeting T.R. for the first time as Pinchot did in 1899 at the Governor's mansion in Albany. Pinchot and Roosevelt, after a little conversation, decided to try some wrestling, which T.R. won; and then a bit of boxing, in which he got "knocked off his pins," as Pinchot delightedly reported the story years later. Now there was a man that Roosevelt could love as a brother. Wilson was something quite different. In view of all that T.R. had gone through to make a tough specimen out of himself, in sheer self-protection he had to despise the new President who had come up the easy way through social graces among his intimates and smooth oratory among the voters. To make these men bitter enemies no more was needed than the problem of what to do about a war.

Another source of future trouble in Wilson's career was his break with George Harvey. In the campaign for the Democratic nomination in 1912, Harvey, who was editor of *Harper's Weekly*, strongly supported Wilson. It was Harvey, in fact, who had brought Wilson forward two years earlier for Governor of New Jersey, and was widely regarded as having "made" him politically. But Harvey had Wall Street affiliations which, Wilson was informed, were hurting his chances among the Western liberals. So when Harvey asked him whether he felt embarrassed by the support of *Harper's Weekly*, Wilson tactlessly said that he did, forgetting to sugarcoat the dose with suitable hesitations and genuflections. Wilson's friends were aghast, and tried to pacify Colonel Harvey's hurt feelings by having Wilson write him an apologetic letter. It was in this letter that he made the famous excuse that "my mind is a one-track road," to account for his failure to give proper expression to his gratitude for all the Colonel had done for him. But Harvey was not appeased, and became Wilson's implacable enemy.

There was a wave of criticism against Wilson for going back on "the original Wilson man," and for a time it threatened his nomination. The situation was saved through a slick piece of advertising concocted by a young publicity man on the Wilson team. He invented and launched a story that the real cause of the break was that Wilson had refused to accept the help of Wall Street interests which Harvey

had pressed upon him. This tall tale succeeded in turning the tide
of public opinion, but did not endear Wilson to Harvey.

Wilson did not know about the advertising trick, but he did know
that his manners had been bad, and it worried him. After he was
President he was persuaded to offer Harvey the Ambassadorship to
France. But while tactful arrangements were under way for approaching the Colonel, that embittered gentleman gave an interview to the
New York *Times* in which he said such things about the President
that the matter had to be dropped.

Wilson felt keenly his failure to attract as many friends as he wanted.
This trouble grew out of his characteristic feeling of unlimited rightness with God. He said himself that he was prone to reject anyone
to whom he did not feel able to give his absolute confidence. Men
were too likely to disagree with something that he had decided to
hold sacred; he more than once broke with a loyal friend because
mere disagreement seemed to him to be disloyalty. And he was much
criticized, in whispers, because of his eagerness for friendships with
women who would offer him the unreserved and starry-eyed allegiance
that he wanted.

Ellen Louise Axson, whom Wilson married in 1885, gave him the
kind of home, with security of heart and peaceful shelter, that his
sensitive soul deeply needed; and she was never jealous of his numerous
and devoted woman friends. She and everyone else who knew him
intimately knew that his morals were beyond reproach; but, as Bess
Furman reports, "he was dependent on women in an extraordinary
degree. Their companionship, admiration, attentiveness, adoration,
brought out his original thought and scintillating conversation. Mrs.
Wilson was capable of serenely keeping a large party in after-dinner
conversation, while her husband was deep in tete-a-tete in the adjoining library with some newly discovered beauty."

To outsiders, Wilson's moral character was not so self-evident,
especially since his preaching of high ideals inevitably opened him to
personal attack by cynical political enemies. Roosevelt pointedly
refused to have any part in such tactics, but Wilson's less scrupulous
opponents reveled in whispered stories about the noble-talking President "chasing the chickens." Gossip centered most viciously on a

friend whom he met while on vacation in Bermuda, Mrs. Mary Hulbert Peck.

Mrs. Peck was no clandestine sweetheart. She visited the Wilsons, and the Wilson family, including daughters, visited her in Bermuda. The two hundred or so letters that he wrote to her during the course of some seven years were the kind that she would open on the porch, read, and hand over to a friend. When she was old and poor, she sold them to Wilson's friend and biographer Ray Stannard Baker. Since there was so much talk about them, and even a story that she was using them for blackmail, many scholars have read them with care, and found nothing to throw any shadow on the character of either Wilson or Mrs. Peck. According to Eleanor Wilson, her mother did wish Mrs. Peck would not smoke cigarettes, and the girls did not like her trying to make them wear more sophisticated clothes.

Wilson came under heavy pressure from the "suffragettes" demanding votes for women. During months on end the suffragettes picketed the White House. They burned Wilson in effigy, and whenever he said anything about freedom or democracy, they got copies and burned them in a bonfire in the park across from his front door.

As a Southern gentleman, Wilson was traditionally opposed to woman suffrage, but he was finally brought around by his daughters and their friends. The District Government asked his permission to break up the picketing, but he refused, saying that it did not bother him. After the United States was in the war, the District Commissioners asked the suffragette leaders to call it off as a patriotic gesture. When they refused to do so, there were riots, and finally on its own authority the Secret Service had the ladies arrested. They were given 60 days in jail, where they made publicity by going on a hunger strike. Then the President stepped in and pardoned them, but they went on accusing him of tyranny. It was a difficult situation.

Wilson started his administration as a promoter of liberal legislation along the general lines that had already been laid out by Theodore Roosevelt. To his credit are several notable institutions that were not wiped out by later events, such as the Federal Reserve, the Federal Trade Commission, and the Tariff Commission; and the settlement of a dispute with England over Panama Canal tolls. When the war broke out in the middle of 1914, at first it did not seem likely to bring the President under heavy criticism, for the people wanted to stay out of it—though many of them could not be neutral in thought as well as in deed, as he suggested in his neutrality proclamation.

Even the German invasion of Belgium did not seem to many Americans to warrant intervention. On September 23, 1914, Roosevelt himself, when he heard that a deputation of Belgians had arrived in Washington to ask American help, said that he did not know what action our Government would take, but that in his opinion it would be best to remain entirely neutral. He soon began to be irritated, however, by Wilson's neglect of preparedness, and in this he was joined by Taft and other conservatives.

Before T.R. came out publicly in opposition to the President, he had expressed his personal dislike in numerous private letters. He told Senator Lodge that Wilson was "the worst President by all odds since Buchanan, with the possible exception of Andrew Johnson; I am simply unable to understand how the American people can tolerate Wilson." To Mark Sullivan he spoke of "the common type of quality in Wilson, he has the regular professional cultivation and is a trained elocutionist, but at heart he is neither a gentleman nor a real man."

Wilson himself was never "neutral in thought," though he thought neutrality was a necessary policy for the United States. He told his secretary he would never "take action to embarrass England when she is fighting for her life and the life of the world." But he was determined that America must stay out of the war, not merely to avoid getting hurt, but so as to be in position to mediate a peace before both sides were hopelessly exhausted—or, as he called it, a "peace without victory." Roosevelt, who prided himself on having made peace between Russia and Japan, could not understand Wilson's peacemaking ambitions; this war had come too close.

The desire for intervention on the side of the Allies began to grow after the sinking of the *Lusitania* on May 7, 1915, and the mistake that Wilson made in his speech about it. The world looked to him to express the spirit of America in face of this horror; and to him it came as a challenge to maintain American neutrality with honor. He rested his case on the need for the United States to look forward to the duty of mediation when the war should have burned itself out. "The example of America must be a special example . . . of

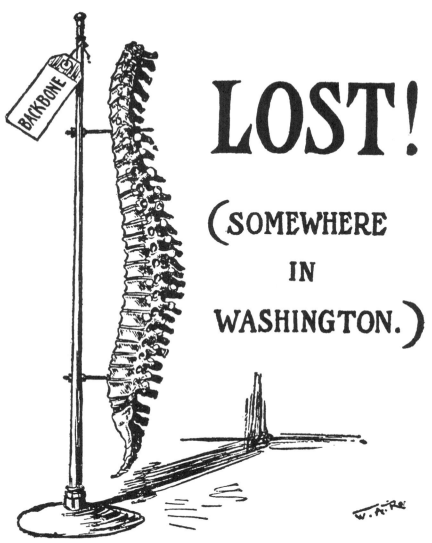

LOST!

(SOMEWHERE IN WASHINGTON.)

Aimed at Woodrow Wilson because of his reluctance to say or do anything that might plunge the nation into World War I, this blunt cartoon by W. A. Rogers in the New York Herald was probably the cruelest ever drawn about an American President. "No man can support Mr. Wilson," remarked the Kansas City Star in a caustic editorial about his policies, "without at the same time supporting a policy of criminal inefficiency as regards the United States Navy, of shortsighted inadequacy as regards the Army, and of failure to insist on our just rights when we are ourselves maltreated by powerful and unscrupulous nations. . . ." Similar criticisms were frequent.

Representing Uncle Sam, Woodrow Wilson turns his back on Lusitania victims. All but blamed for Lusitania tragedy, Wilson resisted clamor for a declaration of war against Germany after sinking of the vessel. A Cunard liner, the Lusitania was sunk without warning by a German submarine on May 7, 1915. Of 1,959 passengers and crew, 1,198 perished, including 128 Americans. Since the German Embassy in Washington had published in U.S. papers advertisements warning travelers against sailing in British or Allied ships, it was felt by some that no American lives need have been lost if Wilson had heeded the German warnings. On the other hand some considered the warnings as proof that sinking of the Lusitania was premeditated.

peace because peace is the healing and elevating influence of the world and strife is not." Later in his speech he said also that a nation may be so much in the right "that it does not need to convince others by force that it is right."

But between these carefully reasoned expressions of his ideal— an ideal shared at the time by most of his countrymen—he made the mistake of inserting an explanatory sentence that could be taken out of its context and used to convict him of rationalizing plain cowardice in the face of outrage. "There is such a thing," he said, "as a man being too proud to fight."

A man who in general is a magician with words, as Wilson undoubtedly proved himself toward the end of the war, must not make such mistakes. For a man like Wilson, a slip is far more disastrous than for a loud-roaring, often inaccurate fighter like T.R.; when Wilson said anything he was supposed to mean exactly that. He also suffered from his habit of thinking in high abstractions, the expression of which might be understood in lower terms than he had intended. As the implications of his unfortunate expression gradually sank into the public mind, the feeling spread that the President was a coward. Abroad it undoubtedly influenced the German attitude toward the United States; people in the Allied countries were discouraged and contemptuous; and Americans were ashamed before them. It was a poor preparation for the position of mediator.

Wilson's enemies publicly blamed him for the sinking of the *Lusitania*. Richard Harding Davis, for instance, in a long article pointed out that for three years in Mexico, bandits and cattle thieves had been murdering Americans and spitting on the American flag, and the only help Mr. Wilson offered was to advise Americans to stay out of Mexico. If Mr. Wilson had a son and the son told him the man next door had threatened to turn the hose on him if he came past the house again, "Mr. Wilson would not go to the neighbor and say, 'What do you mean you'll turn your hose on my boy?' Instead he would say, 'My son, tomorrow, on your way to school, you go out the back gate, and down the alley.' "

Davis asserted that the policy of "watchful waiting," as Wilson called it, had been approved by men who cared more for making money than for maintaining the nation's honor and prestige. He suggested that by a policy of drifting and shirking responsibility, the

President had been as much to blame for the sinking of the Lusitania as von Tirpitz himself.

"When the American ship *Frye* was sunk," he went on, "when bombs were dropped upon the American ship *Cushing,* when the American ship *Gulflight* was torpedoed and in consequence the lives of three Americans were lost, instead of indignant action, Mr. Wilson asked for time to think, and begged that while he thought, no one would rock the boat. . . . Mr. Wilson anchored our ships off Riverside Drive, and sent the crews to baseball parks and the movies. . . . Is it any wonder the highborn officers of the German Emperor deemed it safe, without warning or mercy, to massacre American women, men and babies?"

Finally, Davis accused Wilson of being a coldblooded schoolmaster without imagination, capacity for friendship, or understanding of human feelings—a man who while the entire nation was waiting with horror for the casualty lists, went out to the country club and played a round of golf. "This is no time," he exclaimed in disgust, "for the American people to sit still and say, 'Hush, our President is thinking!' "

Roosevelt was heard from immediately, but he spoke in urgency rather than blame against Wilson. In his message dictated while awaiting the verdict in the Barnes suit, he called attention "to the fact that the sinking of the Lusitania was not only an act of simple piracy, but that it represented piracy accompanied by murder on a vaster scale than any oldtime pirate had ever practiced before being hung for his misdeeds." What Wilson had called "strict accountability," in Roosevelt's opinion must mean immediate action in a case like this, "and our self respect demands that we forthwith abide by it."

Dr. Lyman Abbott of the *Outlook* also demanded action, complaining that the country had looked to the President in vain for leadership; Abbott, like so many others, compared Wilson with Buchanan. He recommended that something decisive should be done to "disown all fellowship with a power which perpetrates massacre of unarmed citizens on the high seas and calls it war."

There were, of course, quite different criticisms coming from German-Americans. At a mass meeting in New York a speaker attacked Wilson for "false neutrality" and said that the German boys lying dead in Flanders, killed with American-made instruments of murder, ought to haunt the President. He said America had become a hiss and a byword in the world, and urged his audience to "rise as Americans and end this murderous traffic." There was wild applause; and German sympathizers did in fact succeed in creating much confusion and sabotage.

When Wilson's note to the German government came out, demanding total abandonment of submarine warfare against merchant vessels, it attracted the approval of ex-President Taft and many other notables. The newspapers of all shades of opinion, except German, were generally favorable. The New York *Sun* commended the President. It recalled that his liberal domestic policies had alienated certain conservative groups, and he had reached the bottom of his popularity at mid-term in 1914. His cabinet had been regarded as feeble, especially Secretary of State Bryan; he himself was felt to be "remote, aloof, austere." But now "he is regarded with respect and trusted with sober confidence. . . . The minority President is become the majority President, the spokesman and protagonist of the American people." A survey of public opinion showed a strong feeling against Germany; but though the majority wanted "a firm stand," only a small minority of the telegrams coming into the White House called for war.

Roosevelt did not pursue the President at this time. On June 1 he told the press he had no further comments to make on the German situation. It seems clear that in the middle of 1915, although there were many cross currents, most Americans approved the Wilson combination of neutrality with expostulation.

But Franklin K. Lane, Wilson's Secretary of the Interior, wrote in disgust to a friend on July 18: "Of course those chaps think we are bluffing because we have been too polite. We have talked Princetonian English to a water-front bully." Lane, a Califorian of Canadian birth, was not given to pussyfooting, and could not quite understand Wilson.

By November, Wilson had decided that it was time to call for preparedness, and that by aiming it at the disorders in revolution-torn Mexico he could strengthen the United States without compromising his future position as peacemaker in Europe. In January, 1916, he went on a speaking trip to drum up sentiment for increased military appropriations, and got an increasingly favorable response. T.R. was angry at having his thunder stolen, and at Wilson's apparently inconsistent speeches, which were fitted closely to the slowly moving and complex currents of popular opinion. He commented: "From December 8, 1914 to February 10, 1916, there were fifteen messages, letters, and speeches of President Wilson's which I have read. . . . President Wilson took 41 different positions about preparedness and the measures necessary to secure it; and each of these positions contradicted from 1 to 6 of the others." He was particularly outraged by Wilson's use of "weasel words" which, as he explained, suck the meat from other words in the same sentence like a weasel sucking eggs. T.R. conveniently forgot that all Presidents have to use doubletalk, an art in which he himself was a practiced hand.

Roosevelt became increasingly hostile to the President, writing articles in the *Outlook,* the *Metropolitan Magazine,* and the Kansas City *Star,* and making numerous speeches. He had recovered from his political low point of 1912, and was leading a growing body of public opinion. "No man can support Mr. Wilson," he said, "without at the same time supporting a policy of criminal inefficiency as regards the United States Navy, of short-sighted inadequacy as regards the Army, and of failure to insist on our just rights when we are ourselves maltreated by powerful and unscrupulous nations." He called Wilson a pacifist hero, and said that he had the support of the professional pacifists, the flubdubs and the mollycoddles, who preached the utter flabbiness and feebleness, moral and physical, which inevitably breed cowardice.

Wilson's summer home on the Jersey coast, "Shadow Lawn," should be well peopled, Roosevelt said, "with the shadows of men, women, and children who have risen from the ooze of the ocean bottom and from graves in foreign lands; the shadows of the helpless whom Mr. Wilson did not dare protect lest he might have to face danger; the shadows of babies gasping pitifully as they sank beneath the waves. . . . Those are the shadows proper for Shadow Lawn; the shadows of deeds that were never done, the shadows of lofty words that were followed by no lofty action."

But what could one expect, he demanded, from an administration headed by a college professor with no first-hand knowledge of foreign affairs, and a crack-brained Secretary of State, the ineffable William J. Bryan?

"Bring Me A Copy of Our No. 1 Note to Germany— Humanity Series." Fiercely satirized by some American newspapers and even more by British periodicals, Wilson's reluctance to sever relations with Germany was frequently the subject of cartoons such as these.

"What's That? U-boats Blockading New York? Tut! Tut! Very Inopportune." A 1915 cartoon.

Lampooned because of his frequent diplomatic notes in his dealings with Germany, Wilson was shocked by misunderstanding of his motives. Rightly or wrongly, he felt that he had to exhaust every possibility that might lead to termination of the war. "There is such a thing as a man being too proud to fight," Wilson said in a speech on May 10, 1915. Until the United States entered the war two years later the phrase "too proud to fight" was hurled back at him almost daily by his political enemies.

In the growing tension after the *Lusitania,* Mr. Bryan, whom Wilson had appointed in the hope of keeping him "inside instead of outside," resigned. He told his friends that he could no longer go along with Wilson's increasingly severe notes; he thought they would lead to war. Once outside the Cabinet, he gave powerful leadership to the pacifists, who were active in much the same way as the "America First" groups during World War II before Pearl Harbor. Bryan, like the America Firsters, was careless about his associates; he addressed a meeting of the "Friends of Peace" in New York that was palpably pro-German. He hurt Wilson badly by encouraging the German government to develop an exaggerated notion of the pro-German influence in the United States, and by stirring up thousands of his followers to write to Congress, demanding an arms embargo against the Allies. After the United States got into the war, however, Bryan stopped talking about public affairs, and lectured only on morals and religion.

As the election year of 1916 dawned, the Republicans, who if not divided would probably be once more the majority party, began to see hopes of solving the Wilson problem by eliminating Wilson. Roosevelt still had too many enemies holding over from 1912 to be nominated, but he could see no future in the flimsy Progressive Party, and was ready to forget old scores and concentrate on helping to beat Wilson. He and his friends stepped up their attacks on the President.

Owen Wister, admiring friend of T.R., was roused to such a point that on Washington's Birthday in 1916 he gave out the following "poem:"

> Not even if I possessed your twist in speech
> Could I make any (fit for use) fit you;
> You've wormed yourself beyond description's reach:
> Truth if she touched you would become untrue.
> Satire has seared a host of evil fames,
> Has withered Emperors by her fierce lampoons;
> History has lashes that have flayed the names
> Of public cowards, hypocrites, poltroons.
> You go immune, cased in your self-esteem.
> The next world cannot scathe you, nor can this;

No fact can stab through your complacent dream;
Nor present laughter, nor the future's hiss.
But if its fathers did this land control
Dead Washington would wake and blast your soul.

Gifford Pinchot also followed his friend T.R. back into the Republican fold. The National Hughes Alliance had a two-page spread by Pinchot in *Collier's*.

Pinchot said that at first he had liked Wilson, but then was alienated by the discrepancies between his words and deeds: threatening Germany and not backing it up; declaring against intervention in Mexico and yet invading that country; pointedly neglecting the Navy, changing his mind, and then going back on that; running for office in 1912 on a platform calling for only one term and then trying for a second term; talking of pitiless publicity and conducting "the most secret administration of our time;" flouting the Roosevelt Progressives and now trying to conciliate them for the sake of their votes. "I have known official Washington from the inside for six Administrations. In that time Government business has never been so badly done and so extravagantly as it is now done under Wilson."

In particular, Pinchot could not forgive Wilson for giving lip-service to Conservation and then failing to help defeat the Shields water-power Bill, "the most dangerous attack on Conservation since Ballinger's effort to turn Alaska over to the Guggenheims." Finally Pinchot accused Wilson of forcing upon the country an ignoble standard of "profits over principle" in foreign relations that had left America without a friend among the great nations of the world; he said that all Wilson's fine talk was nothing but "molasses to catch flies."

A privately printed pamphlet by Hannis Taylor, who called himself "a lifelong Democrat," accused Wilson of being a Federalist at heart, and therefore a monarchist. He quoted Wilson's book, *Congressional Government*, in which he spoke with approval of the "King's Speech" by the President followed by a legislative response after the British manner, customs which had prevailed in the early days of the Republic. Wilson, with his well-known admiration for the parliamentary form of government, had of course always favored the theory of the strong President acting as nearly as possible like a Prime Minister; making the Presidency, as he put it, "a seat of the highest authority and consideration, the true center of the Federal structure, the real throne of administration, and the frequent source of politics." This sentiment Mr. Taylor found most obnoxious to good Jeffersonian doctrine, as of course it was. Wilson's resumption of the direct address to Congress, instead of sending a written Message, was held to be particularly offensive as a sign of monarchism.

There had, in fact, been a fundamental change in the positions of the parties since 1800. Economic policies for the benefit of the poorer people had come to depend mainly on federal action—as became even plainer in F.D.R.'s time. Meanwhile government regulation of business practices had become important, and business had found that it preferred to be regulated by the states, which could be more easily corrupted than the more visible government in Washington. Thus the modern Democratic Party was shifting toward Federalism and the opposition toward states' rights, to the vast confusion of simple, old-fashioned Jeffersonian Democrats like the good Mr. Taylor.

That gentleman also quite naturally found the same fault in Wilson that the old Jeffersonians had found in Washington—a shyness that seemed to betoken contempt for the common herd. He accused Wilson of an aversion to personal contact with the people, and in proof cited his "sudden and arbitrary abolition of the Inaugural Ball and of the New Year's reception, which, since the foundation of the Government, have been the sacramental ties binding the Presidency to the rank and file of the people." Those who did get to the White House entertainments, he complained, had to be invited "by a gilded and embossed card, delivered, not through the mails, but by Presidential messengers."

James M. Beck, on the contrary, was not afraid of King Woodrow. Writing on *The Passing of the New Freedom,* he regarded Wilson as an artist in generalizations of a literary and esthetic rather than a scientific kind, and entirely unable "to concrete his propositions and subject them to the test of reality . . . . since his own mind never compels him to be explicit and concrete, he quite naturally regards such demands on the part of others as captious."

Beck scoffed at the idea that Wilson was a dangerous man. "No man so weak in practical detail, so restive of opposition and delay, so incapable of using competent instruments, so lacking in elementary courtesy and tact, above all, no man *with such a genius for antagonism,* will ever jeopardize the liberties of the American people. . . . His amazing ineptitude is our salvation."

Robert E. Annin, one of Wilson's severest critics, also had no patience with his seeming impracticality: "He had a deftness in dallying with generalities which conveyed the thought that he alone was competent firmly to grasp and weigh the imponderables; but he was as impatient of an adverse fact as of a dissenting opinion. Like Gilbert's poet, he soared easily in the regions of the indefinable, but resented references to the multiplication table."

Wilson's problems of politics and neutrality had been rendered almost insupportable at the very beginning of the war by his loss of the steadying and comforting influence of his wife. Ellen Axson Wilson died on August 6, 1914, leaving to Dr. Cary Grayson the admonition to "take care of Woodrow." Finding after some months that the President was not recovering from the shock of his loss, Dr. Grayson saw to it that he was introduced to Mrs. Edith Bolling Galt, and he became engaged to her in September, 1915. Some of his friends feared that his remarriage might offend enough voters to affect his chances of reelection the following year, but he decided to take the risk, and the engagement was announced on October 7. The announcement was well received, and apparently did no political damage. The new Mrs. Wilson undoubtedly saved him from a breakdown until at last he was overborne by the strains of 1919, after which she did much to make his last illness tolerable.

Two weeks before the 1916 election, *Collier's* printed an enthusiastic article on President Wilson by Ida Tarbell, the famous "muckraker," together with a comment by the editor, Mark Sullivan, who was far from agreeing with Miss Tarbell.

Miss Tarbell had visited the Wilsons at the Summer White House, and had fallen under the spell of Mr. Wilson's charm. "A president, yes, every instant, but also a gentleman. . . . here at last we have a president whose real interest in life centers around the common man, and on whom we can count to serve that man so far as his ability goes . . ."

Asked how he happened to be democratic in spite of his academic experience, Wilson referred to his Scotch and Scotch-Irish heredity,

In the course of Wilson's illness toward the end of his administration rumors about his condition suggested that he had lost his sanity and was no longer capable of knowing what he was saying and doing.

"Teaching Him What To Say." Senator Henry Cabot Lodge blamed Wilson for practically all problems that arose at end of World War I.

and she quotes him as saying: "There is no real aristocracy in Scotland; there is no such thing as a Scotch peasant. . . . There is no difference between Scotchmen but the difference of education. There has never been a barrier between me and anybody, except the barrier of taste." This curiously obtuse reply came from the man who so deeply longed to be loved by the people and who yet succeeded in shutting himself off behind the high barriers of taste and assumption of superior knowledge.

Miss Tarbell, who had already written her biography of Lincoln, could not resist asking Wilson's opinion of him. Wilson replied that "He embodies what I take it we mean by Americanism more nearly than anyone," and went on to a comparison with his own experience that Mark Sullivan seized upon at once. To quote Sullivan: "Listen to this thoroughly fond description of a great man by himself. 'Do you not,' he says, 'get the impression in studying LINCOLN through the war of a man of great loneliness? He could make no associate in his great crisis. *I felt this profoundly in the acute stage of our difficulty with Germany.* The strongest men about me came with their opinions and suggestions. "I am offering this for what it is worth," they said, "but you must think it out." The awful and overwhelming thought was that the country trusted me. My determination from the start was to let nothing hasten me, nothing tempt me to override principles. I waited for clearer air. I made it a point not to read the details of what was happening in instances of personal suffering. I did not dare to do so lest I should see red. I feared to be overwhelmed by a storm of feeling.' "

Mr. Sullivan thought that a President who "could wait for a clearer air while the last smothered cries of the American women on the *Lusitania* were sounding in the ears of the world" could be in little danger of being overwhelmed by a storm of feeling in any circumstances. This is perhaps one of the best examples of that complete lack of communication between a President and his critics, which was so marked a feature of Woodrow Wilson's experience in the office.

According to what he said to Miss Tarbell, Wilson regarded himself as a practical man. "It bores me to have men waste my time in general terms. What I want to know is how it is to be done. . . . I suppose that in government I am a pragmatist; my first thought is, will it work?" This, it must be said, was in 1916, when he had piled up a gratifying record of liberal legislation, and had not yet tangled himself in the Fourteen Points and how to make *them* work.

Wilson regarded the 1916 campaign, he explained, as a contest between the people and Wall Street. "What the other side is trying to do is to bring Mark Hanna back. . . . I have lived with this group for fourteen years. They have no other ambition or desire but to control men's thoughts and lives. . . . Nobody can predict the profoundity of change in this country after the war; nobody can predict the hold on the country that privilege is going to take again if this class is put in power." He was sure the people would not want to make such a change if they understood the case. "I do not believe there is a man alive more saturated with American thinking than I am; I have lived it all my life. . . . I don't expect them to think with me at once, but I feel reasonably sure of how they will eventually think."

"If I understand myself," Wilson explained to Miss Tarbell, "I am sincere when I say that I have no personal desire for reelection." At this point Mark Sullivan started gleefully requoting: " 'It would be an unspeakable relief for me to be excused,' he says sadly, 'but I am caught in the midst of a process. Everything I believe in chains me here. Nothing is finished. Is it wise that the country should change now, leaving so much at loose ends?' "

"Is it wise?" Mr. Sullivan went on. "How modest the appeal. So like him. Let *us* who can with propriety say it, ask rather: Is it Decent? Is it Honorable? Is it Patriotic? Is it not Sinful? Does it not amount to Sacrilege? Yet such is the unstable quality of the American democracy that no one can depend on it for an instant. It has been known before to turn its back on 100 per cent goodness, advertised and guaranteed by the owner."

In fact the democracy came close to doing just that. On Election Day evening, Charles Evans Hughes was believed to have been elected. Only an upset in California saved Wilson for another term, and that was the last election the Democrats would win for many a long year.

The election returns made it clear that the South and West had reelected Wilson, and that the slogan "He kept us out of war" had been the main cause of the victory. So far as there was a mandate that was it. Roosevelt and others, mainly in the East, who had been impatient with the President's neutralism, were thus notified that 18 months after the *Lusitania* was sunk the country was not ready to declare war. A few days after election Wilson wrote to a friend: "Strange as it may seem, I went to bed that night feeling a great burden lifted. . . . Now the burden upon me is heavier than ever. If we can escape entering the war and bring about a rational peace, it is something worth dying for; and I believe the country feels that way or it would not have re-elected me."

To the Roosevelt faction Wilson's attitude was an exasperating and incomprehensible riddle. On November 4th, Owen Wister had had an article in *Collier's*, the gist of which was the Roosevelt objection to Wilson's neutralism and to his frequent shifting of policy. Wister's analysis of the relation between Wilson and the Kaiser was exactly the opposite of Wilson's own. Where the President felt that he was being repeatedly pushed toward war by German violations of neutrality, Wister says it was the Kaiser who kept us out of war by taking care not to go too far for Mr. Wilson's pacifism. There was, of course, some truth on both sides of that disagreement, for both Wilson and the Kaiser wanted the United States to stay neutral.

Wister could not see that the President had any limit to his cowardice and the ground he would yield under pressure. He said that Wilson has "filled the American eagle so full of white feathers that the bird cannot tell himself from a gander," and "by writing notes and eating his words brought the Stars and Stripes to dishonor in the eyes of the world."

The meaning of the neutrality policy had been defined more than a year earlier by Wilson in a letter to Colonel House, after the sinking of the *Arabic*. He said that the people were counting on him to keep the country out of war; and that it would be a calamity to the world at large if the United States should be drawn in and so lose "all disinterested influence over the settlement." Against Britain, he told the House, he would insist on the old American principle of freedom of the seas, but would not be too much excited by seizure of American property, since damages could be paid later; in dealing with Germany, he would not stand for destruction of American lives.

As the probability of being drawn into the war increased, Wilson's ideas became more definitely focused on that eventuality. He explained to his friend Frank Cobb, of the New York *World*, that he did not expect Germany to keep its promises, but he wanted them on the record. What concerned him was the attitude of the American people, who were divided into three main groups: pro-Ally, pro-German, and anti-war. Wilson did not want war, but Germany might go too far and make war unavoidable. If that should happen, he wanted the case to be so clear that the American people would be united. They must know that he had done everything possible to avoid war.

After the 1916 election Wilson began a new series of notes for the purpose of clarifying the position of Germany and the Allies, either to lay out a sound basis for mediating a peace, or to give the United States a justifiable set of war aims in case it should have to fight. To Roosevelt and his friends these notes were just more white feathers in the eagle's tail.

In December, 1916, Wilson sent identical notes to the belligerents, asking for their views on terms of peace, and also on how some kind of international arrangement might be set up to prevent all future wars. The Germans, confident that they held the winning cards, readily offered to accept an Allied surrender; but the Allies replied that the time was not ripe for a just peace.

On January 22, 1917, the President appeared before the Senate and outlined his own terms for a "peace without victory." He proposed that the nations should "adopt the doctrine of President Monroe as the doctrine of the World," in other words, no nation should trespass on any other nation's freedom, but every nation should be free "to determine its own polity, its own way of development, unhindered, unthreatened, unafraid, the little along with the great and powerful." He wanted a general concert of nations. Like Mr. Nehru in 1958, he wanted to see no special alliances that would draw the nations "into competitions of power." He urged freedom of the seas and "moderation of armament."

He could not of course promise that the United States would join the proposed "League of Peace," but he gave the world that impression by saying, "it is inconceivable that the United States should play no part in that great enterprise." This pronouncement was the real beginning of the League of Nations as a serious possibility. Both sides in the war were shocked by the suggestion of peace without victory, and so were many strongly partisan Americans. But the President believed his doctrine of peace on earth would sprout and grow—as in fact it did afterward.

For the moment, however, the Wilson peace proposals were blown away by the action of the German Government. Early in 1916 the Germans, hoping to keep America neutral, had agreed to Wilson's demands for restrictions on submarine warfare, but now they announced, on January 31, that beginning the next day they would use their submarines "to the full." Four days later the President went before Congress and announced that he was handing Count von Bernstorff, the German Ambassador, his passports.

Bernstorff reported to his Government that Wilson's main purpose had been to remain neutral so as to be the mediator who would dictate the peace; and so long as Germany let him believe in that possibility, he was neutral. But "after January 31, 1917, Wilson himself was a different man. Our rejection of his proposal to mediate, by our announcement of the unrestricted U-boat warfare, which was to him totally incomprehensible, turned him into the embittered enemy of the Imperial Government."

On the evening when Wilson was preparing his speech asking Congress for a declaration of war, he invited Frank Cobb to come and see him. Cobb arrived at the White House at one o'clock in the morning. The President had lost much sleep, and looked it. He told his visitor that he had tried every loophole to escape war, but that Germany had blocked every one with some new outrage. He hated to think what fighting would do to the spirit of the American people. "Once lead this people into war," he said, "and they'll forget there ever was such a thing as tolerance." That would be the end of his dream of a peace of reconciliation. Germany would be beaten so badly that there would be a dictated peace—a vengeful peace. "At the end of the war there will be no bystanders with sufficient power to influence the terms. There won't be any peace standards left to work with. There will be only war standards."

At that moment his eerie Celtic foresight came on him and he told Cobb that in victory he would be overwhelmed with adulation as a world savior, and then with the deflation of excessive hopes he would suffer attack and derision before all the world. But he had kept the peace as long as it could be kept. If he had it all to do over he would take the same course. So he faced his personal fate along with the fate of the nation, and that same day he went before Congress to ask for war.

Colonel Roosevelt at last saw the United States lined up on the side of the Allies where he thought it ought to have been long since, but he still despised Wilson for talking so much and in such lofty language. Mark Sullivan, who in later years came to admire Wilson, suggests that what irritated Roosevelt most was that Wilson was a "magician" who could do mysterious things with words that the downright T.R. could not understand.

Sometimes Wilson deliberately used words to conceal future questions that the people were not ready to face. In 1914, for instance, he told the people to be calm because the causes of the war could not concern us, knowing that most people would think he had said the war itself could not concern us, since they were not ready to think sensibly about the fact that it could and would if it lasted long enough. At the end of his war speech of April 2, 1917, as Sullivan points out, Wilson used a piece of black magic that escaped most Americans but was subtly calculated to be a time bomb in the German mind. Ending his description of the path America was obliged to follow, he said, "God helping her, she can do no other." To Germans in America or in Germany that sentence translated into German recalled the fateful words spoken by Martin Luther: "Ich kann nicht anders." Wilson's words, including this haunting phrase, sucked the morale out of the Germans, and in 1918 caused the home front to collapse before their armies were ready to surrender. But all Roosevelt could make of Wilson's messages, notes, and speeches was that the Professor was indulging in elocution "when the urgent need of the nation has been for action."

During the war the President was relatively free from direct attack, partly because war news was tightly controlled by the official "Committee on Public Information." This office of war information was headed by George Creel, who had a lively imagination which he used

for supplying optimistic items when the actual news was not encouraging. Progress in training and equipping the armed forces moved
with exasperating slowness while the Allies held on desperately and
waited for the Americans to come. On the other hand, the war
preparations were rather competently managed, and Herbert Hoover,
in *The Ordeal of Woodrow Wilson,* reports that there was practically
no corruption. He was familiar with the Washington scene, since
he was there as Food Administrator.

One notable offset to the enthusiasm dispensed by George Creel
was provided by the indomitable George Harvey, who was editing the
North American Review. In January, 1918, Harvey started a little
paper called the *War Weekly,* chiefly devoted to attacking Wilson
through Secretary of War Newton D. Baker, whom he called Newtie
Cootie, and accused of "sitting on top of a pyramid of confusion which
he has jumbled together and called a war machine."

Senator George E. Chamberlain, an Oregon Democrat who was
Chairman of a Committee on Military Affairs, was also highly critical
of Baker. On January 18, 1918, he told a luncheon in New York that
"the military establishment of America has broken down. . . . It
has almost ceased functioning." T.R., who was present, sprang to
his feet to lead the applause. Afterward he called a meeting of his
own and demanded a coalition Cabinet. Wilson reacted by calling
on Congress for dictatorial powers over industry, which he subsequent-
ly delegated to Bernard M. Baruch.

Throughout 1918 Harvey in his paper continued to harp on inefficiency in the Admininstration. On August 31, for instance, he cried:
"Out of the welter of incompetence emerges one luminous and overwhelming fact. It is up to the President to retrieve the shortcomings
and wrongdoings of his subordinates. The prospect is disheartening,
God knows, but it is not yet too late." It was shortly after these
discouraging words that the news began coming of the collapse, one
after another, of the German satellites in Central Europe.

As the end of the war and the off-year election of 1918 approached
together, Wilson was led into a political trap. His Fourteen Points,
which he had outlined as the American peace terms in January, had
at first aroused no dissent in Congress, but by August, Senator Henry
Cabot Lodge was expressing opposition, and the Republican floor

leader in the House was calling for a Republican Congress to control the President's rash activities.

In leading up to the armistice, Wilson, instead of flatly demanding unconditional surrender, was writing notes and arguing with the German Government about terms. Actually, he was playing for a German revolution that he hoped would drive out the Kaiser without letting in the Bolsheviks. Herbert Hoover characterizes the negotiations through which Wilson got his Fourteen Points accepted by both Germany and the Allies with the fall of the Kaiser thrown in, as "the greatest drama of intellectual leadership in all history." But Theodore Roosevelt and many other Republicans were disgusted, and accused the President of negotiating a soft peace.

On October 23, Roosevelt and Taft issued a joint appeal to the voters of Michigan in support of Truman H. Newberry for the Senate, and against Henry Ford, who was running for the Senate on the Democratic ticket. Roosevelt also sent telegrams to Lodge and other Senators, saying: "I earnestly hope that on behalf of the American people the Senate will declare against the adoption in their entirety of the fourteen points of President Wilson's address of last January as offering a basis for a peace satisfactory to the United States." He called the Fourteen Points thoroughly mischievous, and said that a peace based on them "would represent not the unconditional surrender of Germany but the conditional surrender of the United States."

Wilson felt that he had to defend his position against Republican attacks. He was already deeply engaged in negotiations with the Germans, who had asked for peace and had offered to accept the Fourteen Points as preliminary terms. Now he found that the two ex-Presidents, Taft and T.R., were joined with Chairman Will Hays of the Republican National Committee, to campaign for a Republican Congress as the only means of protecting the country from Wilson and disaster.

There was precedent for an appeal to the country for political support. T.R. himself, when he was running for Governor of New York in 1898, had called upon the voters to vote Republican as a gesture of support for President McKinley, who was still engaged in the peace negotiations following the Spanish War. Wilson needed even more the backing of a newly elected Congress to strengthen his hand in dealing with the victorious Powers on whom he hoped to impose a peace of reconciliation. President Johnson's unhappy experience in 1866 did not seem exactly analogous. So he fell into the trap, and on October 25 he issued an appeal to the nation to give him a Democratic Congress. Thereby he not only offended the American people but climbed out on a limb that was about to be sawed off.

George Harvey gleefully jumped upon this tactical error, crying that Wilson cared no more for the Democratic Party than for the Republican Party or the Prohibition Party, except as a vehicle for his own aggrandizement. "He is an autocrat by nature and by training," Harvey declared. "He is temperamentally incapable of meeting anybody upon a basis of equality. He aims, avowedly, through this election to achieve absolute mastery at home."

Wilson was cut to the quick when the voters elected a Republican Congress. The people had gone back on him: he had lost political touch. Stubbornly he determined to carry his policies through with a high hand. Against the advice of all his friends he decided to go to Europe as the head of the American delegation to the Peace Conference.

This too was a political error. Herbert Hoover, who was one of his most ardent admirers, has pointed out that so long as Wilson was in Washington no one could prevent his proclaiming to the world whatever he wanted to say, but when he became involved in personal negotiations inside a closed room with the other heads of state he could not talk freely of what went on. According to Col. House, "He was the *God on the Mountain,* and his decisions regarding international matters were practically final. When he came to Europe and sat in conference with Prime Ministers and representatives of other states, he gradually lost his place as first citizen of the world." But Wilson did not agee. He was convinced that he alone knew how to make a peace to end all wars, and he felt that the only way to keep the reluctant Allies on the true path would be for him to shepherd them personally.

Wilson's friends urged him to take at least a couple of Republican Senators with him, to help counteract the loss of bargaining strength resulting from his election defeat, and to reduce partisan opposition in the Senate itself. But he was sore and sensitive; he wanted only congenial people to go with him. The *George Washington,* on which he set out for Europe, was full of college professors, scientists, every kind of expert to advise him on the details of rebuilding the world. He was in high feather when he got out to sea with these people whom he understood and who understood him. "Show me the right," he told them, "and I will fight for it," and they applauded. It was not a good way for a hero to prepare for a bath of fire.

At home, Congress was appalled. Most members of Congress had no confidence in Wilson's experts. Especially in the Senate they were whetting their knives while Wilson, as William Allen White put it, "was spiritually pirouetting among his collegiate wood nymphs."

The New York *Evening Post,* which had loyally supported the Administration during the war, sadly enumerated the faults that had undermined Wilson's hold on the people. In his absorption in international problems, he had got himself out of contact with the true spirit of America on domestic matters. Instead of the democracy which the President had preached for years, he was taking advice from autocratic, bureaucratic, and provincially-minded advisers. The paper bitterly criticized his decision to take George Creel along to Europe, saying that Creel had "lost the confidence of the American press, and thereby of the people." It reported that the President's most loyal friends were shocked when the control of the Atlantic cables was taken over by Postmaster-General Burleson, with the evident intention of feeding the American people only such European news as Creel and the President might think best for them. "He is attempting to manage the Government in a personal and private way. . . . He has failed to take the people into his confidence with regard to what he means to do at the Peace Conference, or with his arrangements for the transaction of executive business during his absence from the country."

Meanwhile the *George Washington* made land, and Wilson went ashore as the man who had won the war and would bring peace on earth. He was "bronzed by a seven-day sea voyage, confident and courageous," as he set out to match his first-class mind with the hardened statesmen of Europe. But the former President of Princeton had gone up for his finals with an extraordinary lack of studious preparation. His good friend Ray Stannard Baker says, for instance, that he had apparently made no attempt to study the implications of the secret treaties that he knew had been negotiated among the Allies during the war. John Maynard Keynes observed that while it was commonly believed at first that the President had carefully framed a comprehensive scheme embodying the League of Nations and the Fourteen Points, he had in fact thought out nothing. "He had no plan, no scheme, no constructive ideas whatever, for clothing with the flesh of life the commandments he thundered from the White House."

While waiting for the Peace Conference to assemble, Wilson traveled around Europe. As he had foreseen, he was overwhelmed with adulation as the savior of the world and the prophet of peace. Herbert Hoover says of him that "never since his time has any man risen to the political and spiritual heights that came to him." The people lined the streets and threw flowers in his path. "No such man of moral and political power," says Hoover, "and no such evangel of peace had appeared since Christ preached the Sermon on the Mount. . . . It was the star of Bethlehem rising again." One American at least, who was in the mud of Eastern France at that Christmas season, wrote home that if the Lord were taking good care of the world the President would be assassinated before the new year, leaving his gospel of reconciliation shining in the sky along with Lincoln's. He still feels that perhaps it would have been better if Wilson could, as we now say, have been put permanently into orbit, instead of so quickly reentering the earthly atmosphere and burning up.

After the whole sad story was played out, Wilson's political opponents could dance with hob-nailed boots upon the memories of his day of glory, making it look like nothing but a successful campaign of bedazzlement organized by the Allied governments, to lure him into selling out his country. In the campaign of 1920 a canned speech prepared by the Republican National Committee was entitled "Mr. Wilson at Court: Royal Pageantry and Dazzling Splendor— A Suite of 1400." The President was quoted as saying when he came home from his first visit to Europe, "Was there ever so wonderful a thing seen before?" The National Committee concluded that he had been taken in by the King of England and other European royalty who had entertained him on his travels. "He dreamt he dwelt in marble halls." At Buckingham Palace he was greeted with "every royal formality which has attended epochal occasions . . . for two or three hundred years," (including, horrible thought, the times of George III). He and Queen Mary led the procession into the dining hall, followed by King George and members of the royal family. Many a gorgeous palace official "made obeisance," walking backward and shaking his wand, at imminent risk, says the script archly, "of tripping and falling on his—face!"

Most shocking of all, plate and ornaments valued at $15,000,000 were had up from the vaults for the occasion. Wilson and the King were seated at table with their backs to the empty throne, "a wise precaution."

There were gallant parades through the London streets—"up Haymarket way and past the statue of George III, where the King tactfully looked the other way." And at the end of a happy day, the canned speech continued, "they took the American President to Buckingham Palace to sleep, and tucked him in a bed of such royal splendor that even the trained American correspondents simply gulped and threw the whole dictionary at the telegraph operator."

Then the President went on to Paris and set up housekeeping in the palace of Prince Murat, where in anticipation of his coming, "telephones had been installed throughout and the electric lighting system had been improved." He dined at an inlaid mahogany table, and the Princess let her tenant have the use of her celebrated gold dinner service. A beautiful gondola-shaped bed was assigned to the President.

The cost to the American taxpayers was a pretty penny too. Wilson took with him to France 1400 of his favorites, a shocking list of high-brows—"statesmen, heliographers, geographers, astronomers, etymologists, biologists, economists, financiers," as well as common secretaries and clerks. "Money in a golden stream" poured into Paris, and at parties in the Hotel Crillon the motto was "Damn the expense," according to some newspaper reports.

The Republican National Committee found it not surprising that in this life of splendor the United States gradually came to seem to Wilson a mere speck on the map, and that in the end he surrendered the sovereignty of his country to a European super-government.

The first conference in Paris was devoted to the Covenant of the League of Nations. Here Wilson was able to get about what he wanted. The points of dispute were not there but in the coming Peace Treaty, through which the Allies intended to grab the spoils of war. With the Covenant in his pocket, he made a quick trip home, and then returned to take up with the Allies the drafting of the peace which they were to impose on the defeated Germans.

In the peace negotiations the President found himself isolated from home base and sitting in a game where his opponents were tough and unscrupulous. Like the Radicals after the Civil War, they wanted revenge and booty. Their people might like to cheer for Wilson and peace on earth, but they had no great desire to avoid "being beastly to the Hun."

Keynes afterward described Wilson as an innocent, lacking the intellectual equipment to cope with the dangerous Europeans "in the swift game of give and take, face to face in Council—a game in which he had no experience. . . .

"But more serious than this, . . . he was not sensitive to his environment at all. What chance could such a man have against Mr. Lloyd George's unerring, almost medium-like, sensibility to every one immediately round him. . . . The Old World's heart of stone might blunt the sharpest blade of the bravest knight-errant. But this blind and deaf Don Quixote was entering a cavern where the swift and glittering blade was in the hands of the adversary. . . . After all, it was harder to de-bamboozle this old Presbyterian than it had been to bamboozle him; for the former involved his belief in and respect for himself."

One of Wilson's handicaps was the knowledge among the Allies that he faced revolt at home. In the Senate a round-robin had been signed by more than a third of the Senators and had been published, saying that the signers would not accept the Covenant "in its present form." The European negotiators knew well enough that ratification would require a two-thirds vote; and that knowledge put the President in a weak position to insist on his Fourteen Points. So one by one the Fourteen Points were eroded as the President sacrificed one position after another in order to save at least the skeleton of the League, which he hoped might at some future time redress the wrongs that were done.

In April there was an incident that showed Wilson how far he was out of his depth. He felt that the Italian delegation was seriously

violating the armistice terms in its demand for possession of Fiume
on the coast of Jugoslavia. Using a technique that had sometimes
succeeded in putting pressure on the legislature at home, he issued
an appeal to the people of Italy to follow his lead instead of that of
their representatives. This was a worse mistake than his appeal to
the Americans to give him a Democratic Congress. His popularity in
Italy collapsed. Crowds in Rome shouted against his name. In
Brescia a Victory Statue that had been voted in his honor was cancel-
led. Streets that had been enthusiastically named Via Wilson were
changed to something else. His brief time of glory was already slip-
ping away into disillusion.

At last the wordy, impractical Treaty was completed and signed,
and a weary but determined President came back to the White House
in July to lay the document before the Senate for ratification. He
had insisted on having the Treaty and the League Covenant combined
in the same package, and he could not save one without the other.

A majority of the American people wanted to join the League, but
there were powerful elements of dissent. One consisted of returning
soldiers who had been kept waiting for their passage home, and who
had quarreled freely with the French people and regarded all Europe
with cynical disgust. Another discordant element was made up of
anti-British groups, chiefly German and Irish Americans, who thought
too much had been conceded to England. Anti-Germans thought
the Treaty was too soft toward Germany, liberals that it was too
harsh, particularly in demanding impossible reparations. Isolationists,
led by Senators William E. Borah of Idaho and Hiram Johnson of
California, wanted no league of any kind "to hoist its flag above the
Stars and Stripes." Finally there were those Republicans in the
Senate who hated Wilson on general principles. The lines were drawn
for a hard fight.

In his time in the Presidency, Wilson had not earned the affection
of the newspaper men, whose help or hindrance would now be so
important to him. During the war and at Paris they had resented
George Creel, and they had never felt congenial with the President
himself.

In 1921 Edward G. Lowry recalled attending Wilson's first Washington press conference, a "chill and correct performance." When the

newsmen filed in, they were greeted by an awkward silence. "Present-ly someone ventured a tentative question. It was answered crisply, politely, and in the fewest possible words. A pleasant time was not had by all."

George Harvey, looking back on Wilson's relations with the press, criticized his refusal to hold press conferences after May, 1916. He accused Wilson of thinking that public affairs were no business of the people—"that the people ought to be satisfied with the Creelings which are officially emitted from the Committee of Public Informa-tion." These impressions were deepened by the sending of Creel to Paris and the seizure of the cables. Harvey spoke sarcastically of the reports to be expected from Creel, " 'elaborated' in his well-known and justly esteemed style. . . . For such service the representatives of what he calls 'nasty newspapers' would doubtless be most grateful. Even the Congress would rejoice to get its news of the peace-making deliberations by the grace of the courteous gentleman who publicly likened its heart and mind to slums." These developments, "colored throughout by the attitude of the President himself," make one wonder "whether the Socialistic and paternal policy of the Administration . . . comprises also government control of the newspaper press. . . . The American people demur to any proposal for a 'reptile press.' "

In the Senate, Henry Cabot Lodge was Chairman of the Com-mittee on Foreign Relations. He recognized that there was strong public support for the Treaty, though there were many objections to specific points. Lodge was not absolutely opposed to the Treaty, but he hoped to add reservations that would cover the objections of all but the irreconcilable isolationists. Wilson hated Lodge and would have none of his reservations. There was a sufficiently large middle group of Republicans and Democrats who wanted some less drastic reservations; and if Wilson could have brought himself to cooperate with them they could have defeated Lodge and ratified the Treaty. But Wilson's health was already breaking down, and his physical weakness made him touchy and stubborn. He would listen to no counsels of moderation; he must have the Treaty as it stood or nothing.

William D. Hassett, who was a young newspaperman in Washington at that time, recalls that when Senator Martin of Virginia was con-

ferring with the President on the ratification problem, Wilson told
him bitterly that the main trouble was that too many Senators had
no head on their shoulders but only a knot to keep their bodies from
unraveling. Martin told this to his colleagues; they were not much
amused.

The summer was hot and while the Senate remained in a deadlock
the President sat and fumed. Finally he decided again to appeal to
the people. Like Andrew Johnson, he would swing around the circle;
and like Andrew Johnson, he quickly hurt himself by losing his temper.
At Indianapolis on September 4, he called on the opposition to "put
up or shut up," which missed the bullseye since they had put up a
definite set of reservations for discussion. At St. Louis he called the
opposing Senators "contemptible quitters." By the time he reached
Salt Lake City on September 23, his nerves were close to the breaking
point. The audience enraged him by applauding in the wrong places.
He declared that no reservations at all could be allowed. The following day he threatened to scrap the Versailles Treaty and negotiate a
separate peace with Germany.

The opposition tore the President to pieces. As one commentator
in the Chicago *Tribune* remarked, "When Mr. Wilson drops into slang
he reminds us of a nice girl trying to swear," and added that "shirt
sleeves and a silk hat make a queer combination, that arouses even
in the plainsman's simple breast an acute pain. . . . Manners maketh
man." It was pointed out that Col. Roosevelt could bust a broncho
and therefore he could wear chaps; Mr. Wilson did not look right in
oratorical chaps. And to call his opponents pro-German or Bolshevist
only served to throw an unfavorable light on his own lofty claims.

Senator Reed of Missouri accused the President of mistaking the
visions of ambition for the inspiration of idealism. "The President
marshals his syllogisms as a general marshals the battalions of his
army . . . but his soldiers are epithets, his battalions aggregations
of evil names, and his army an assemblage of denunciatory epigrams."
Senator Borah accused Wilson of usurping authority by sending
American troops into Siberia to attack the Bolsheviks, and quoted
him as saying that heretofore the United States was compelled to mind
its own business but that now it is in a position to mind other people's
business. "That is precisely what we are doing," he said, "in sending
troops to Russia to restore the old government."

Behind the President on his tour came a team of opposition Senators, speaking to great crowds, taking advantage of his mistakes, and winning thunderous applause. Hiram Johnson, for instance, speaking in Chicago on September 10, went through the Fourteen Points and told how each one had been ignored in the Treaty. "Who was the quitter?" he shouted, and the people howled, "Wilson." Borah denounced the League as a sacrifice of Washington's policy of no entanglements, and charged that England was getting the use of American soldiers for her adventures in Russia without the authority of Congress. The audience, heavily packed with England-hating Irishmen, went wild. "Impeach him! Don't let 'em go!" yelled the crowd, "Take the power away from him! Don't let him send them!" Borah accused J. P. Morgan of promoting the Treaty to protect his investments, and the crowd cheered when someone shouted, "Morgan belongs to England!"

On the same day in the Senate, returned soldiers in the galleries were loudly applauding Senator Kenyon of Iowa as he called for drastic reservations or rejection of the Treaty. And Senator George Norris, Progressive and friend of T.R., attacked Wilson for spending money in Paris like a drunken sailor and "cavorting with royalty all over Europe." He accused Wilson of paying Bernard Baruch $150,000 as special adviser, and of taking with him to Paris "1500 people as advisers whose advice he did not take."

Editorially, the Chicago *Tribune* said on September 11 that Wilson should be at the Capitol, to deal with the ominous police strike in Boston and other threatened disorders. "Our own house is not in order. Mr. Wilson is filled with a sense of his duty to humanity. We wish he would consider that his duty, and our duty, begins at home. . . . In storm and danger the post of the captain is on the bridge."

On September 27 at a Republican meeting on Long Island Senator Miles Poindexter of Washington called Wilson a world menace, the greatest pro-German in the country, and the leader of the Reds of the world, and accused him of stirring up civil war in Italy and encouraging revolts in Egypt and Korea by his doctrine of self-determination.

On the day before the President had had a physical breakdown at Wichita, Kansas, and his train was hurrying him back to Washington. The press reported on the 29th that "he walked from the train to his motor with a weak step, lifting his hat with trembling hand and smiling wanly at the greeting throng." So ended his appeal to the people. Years later Senator Albert Beveridge told Claude Bowers that in his opinion, if Wilson had only had the good fortune to drop dead on the platform, his martyrdom "would have lifted him overnight to a position higher than Lincoln's."

But he had no such luck. The blows continued to rain on him. George Harvey, for one, tore into him with an editorial entitled "The President at his Worst." On general principles, Harvey sneered, Wilson was at his worst in defending a policy of betraying the sovereignty of the United States and violating all its traditional principles. Then in swinging around the circle, it was bad enough to renew his gross neglect of his duties in Washington. But worse, at a time when above all things the country needed harmony and confidence, he set forth upon a mission of dissension, intent upon coercion of the Legislative Branch and subversion of the most essential principles of the Constitution. "Never before was so shameless and so mischievous an errand undertaken by a President of the United States."

The President was also at his worst, Harvey went on, in his "unworthy diatribes," which had no title to be considered the addresses of a scholarly statesman. They were rather "the shrill railings of a common scold, substituting personal vituperation for the arguments which he could not convincingly command. For the President of the United States to go about the country shouting at the majority of the Senate . . . 'Put up or shut up, you contemptible quitters, before you are hanged upon a gibbet!' is the most humiliating spectacle our political history records. Not even poor, passionate, uncultured President Johnson . . . ever descended to such depths of coarse abuse."

Harvey charged Wilson with thinking himself the sole representative of the nation and sole originator of national policies, not executing the laws enacted by Congress but directing Congress what laws to enact. Even if that theory were correct, he added, no one could have shown himself more unfit for such a position than President Wilson had done in this amazing exhibition of himself at his worst.

A week after reaching Washington Wilson had a stroke that paralyzed his left side. For some weeks he could not see any visitors except occasionally his secretary, Joseph Tumulty. During this time

Mrs. Wilson and his physician, Dr. Cary Grayson, did not dare tell the public how ill he was, lest there be an overwhelming demand for the Vice President to take over. They hoped he would get better— as in fact he did—and could not bear to think of the effect on him if he were to recover and find himself superseded. There were, of course, wild rumors. People suddenly noticed the bars on some of the White House windows, put there in T.R.'s day because his children playing ball had broken the glass; the bars led to rumors that a madman was locked up inside. The Senate sent a "smelling committee" nominally to discuss Mexican policy, really to get a look at the patient. It was headed by Albert B. Fall, the same who later went to jail in the Teapot Dome affair. When the President learned that the Senators insisted on seeing him, at first he was angry. Then the humor of it overcame him, for he knew his mind had not failed. He had them in and put on a gay half-hour of jokes and stories, including personal gibes at his guests, such as accusing Fall of wanting a Mexican war to protect his interests in New Mexico. Fall assured the President that he was praying for him, but what gave the President even more comfort was the knowledge that he had foiled Fall's efforts to prove him crazy.

After about seven months he began holding short Cabinet meetings. "He looked old, worn and haggard; it was enough to make one weep. One of his arms was useless." He could tell jokes, but found it hard to concentrate long on business.

During the winter of 1919-20 there was evidence of organized support for joining the League with mild reservations of a type that would not call for renegotiation. A poll of 17,000 clergymen, Catholic, Protestant, and Jewish, gave a vote of 16,200 to 800 for the Treaty, and a poll of the colleges supported it by two to one. Similar support came from Chambers of Commerce, Granges, women voters, and organized labor.

Evidently the active majority of the people still wanted the Treaty. If Wilson had been willing to negotiate he could have had a ratification with reservations that would have only added to its realism, bringing it a little closer to what was later adopted as the Charter of the United Nations. But he could not bear to listen to reason, and the diehards in the Senate, aided by the confusion among those favoring some form of Treaty, were able to prevent its approval.

On March 19, 1920, a majority of the Senate voted for the Treaty, but not the necessary two-thirds. It did not come up again.

Wilson stubbornly called for a "solemn referendum" in the election of 1920. He hoped the people would elect a Democratic President and Congress, and that they would at last ratify his Treaty. The issues of the election were, however, confused in several ways. Republican voters were assured in a statement by 31 leading citizens, including Elihu Root, Charles Evans Hughes, and Herbert Hoover, that a vote for Warren G. Harding was a vote for the League with suitable reservations. There was no clear separation of pro-League and anti-League political parties.

The "Speakers' Series" prepared by the Republican National Committee, in addition to the one on Wilson among the kings, contained prefabricated speeches under such titles as: "The High Cost of Living;" "Burning Up Billions" (in Government operation of the railways); "$30,000,000 in Spruce" (for construction of airplanes); "The Budget System: Enacted by Republicans to Stop the Deluge of Waste and Promptly Vetoed by President Wilson;" "Wilson's Fatal Policy in Mexico: Murder, Ruin, Robbery and Desolation Left in Wake of His Deadly Decisions;" and "British or American? Bond or Free?"

The election was really a referendum on Wilson himself, although he was not a candidate. Now that he was down and could not fight back, all the people whom he had offended had a field day, while the local Democratic leaders went their local ways, knowing that their national ticket had no chance to win. Aside from the Germans and Irish, there were business men who resented the income tax, and the spending of their money for a dam at Muscle Shoals (out of which later grew the TVA). There were Negroes, still strongly Republican in memory of Lincoln, who criticized Wilson for allowing segregation in Washington. There were, of course, the standard outcries against his dictatorial methods, emphasized by the limitations of access to him because of his illness.

But what mainly determined the outcome was that the people were tired of being grown-up and responsible. They had had seven active years of T.R., and enjoyed them. After Taft, they had been ready for some more progress, and had welcomed the bold leadership of Wilson. But after that had come the sacrifices of the war, and the long emotional strain of Wilson's struggle for his Fourteen Points and the League. The normal dislike of highbrows welled up. The people had had enough; they wanted as near as possible to no President at all for a while. The Republican nominee had a new, fascinating name for what the people wanted: "Normalcy."

So Warren Gamaliel Harding won the election; he immediately declared his opposition to the League in any form; and that was that.

The result was a hard blow for Wilson, but it did not shake his faith that in the course of time his vision would be vindicated. Looking at the situation from the perspective of nearly forty years later, it can be easily argued that the outcome in 1920 was fortunate. For the short run, the people were in a moral recession; and for the longer run, isolationism was still so powerful that any fruitful cooperation with the League would have been doubtful. As one historian has put it: "the American people were one war short of accepting leadership in a world organization for peace."

On March 4, 1921, the crowd saw "a tragic figure, broken physically, his face drawn in pain and misery, shuffling slowly across the White House veranda and being lifted into a waiting car, . . . as Woodrow Wilson laid down to President-elect Harding the burdens which had all but crushed out his own life. The silk hat, the long black coat and the cane comprised all that could be reminiscent of the Wilson that was."

Two days earlier Jan Smuts of South Africa, who had done much to help Wilson in Paris, had commented in the New York *Evening Post*, "On those whom the Gods love, they lavish infinite joys and infinite sorrows. For a few brief moments he was not only the leader of the greatest state in the world; he was raised to far giddier heights and became the center of the world's hopes. And then he fell, misunderstood and rejected by his own people. It was not Wilson that failed, it was the human spirit that failed at Paris. The Covenant is Wilson's souvenir to the future of the world."

But in the *North American Review* William Roscoe Thayer, who had been a close friend of Theodore Roosevelt, drew together into eighteen pages of bitter denunciation all the hatred and the exultation of Wilson's enemies in his defeat. Thayer rejoiced that such an egotist, happening to gain the Presidency, had been foiled in his attempt "to assemble in his own hands extraordinary powers which made him a despot of unlimited reach. . . . There can be no doubt that Mr. Wilson came to regard himself as a man of Destiny, preserved and guided by the Almighty to save civilization."

Thayer called attention to the autocratic power of college professors and college presidents, "which seems to make them autocrats and doctrinaires, unable to mix, as man with man, with the masses who constitute the statesman's material." Wilson "took counsel with hardly anyone; he wished to direct and control everything himself."

"Fate assigned to Wilson, the most incompetent President in foreign affairs for half a century, a six years' task which was almost wholly occupied with foreign affairs. . . . President Wilson chose for the head of his Cabinet Mr. W. J. Bryan, which was like choosing a blind man for jockey in a horse race."

Thayer accused Wilson of being pro-German. The efforts that Wilson made, as he himself said, "to find loopholes" through which he could escape war, seemed to T.R.'s friends to be signs of pro-Germanism or plain cowardice, or both. And his desire to avoid disunity at home, by holding back and letting the American attitude ripen, was described by Thayer as an even mixture of effrontery and cowardice. "The President, who admitted he was afraid to act for fear of enraging a part of the American people, had nothing in common with Abraham Lincoln, or U.S. Grant, or Grover Cleveland, or Theodore Roosevelt. He had nothing in common with any average American, for cowardice is not an American trait."

In Mr. Wilson's conduct of the war, Thayer pointed out various "baneful effects" of his temper and character. One was his habit of surrounding himself with only second- or third-rate men in order to get all the glory for himself, and rejecting first-rate men such as General Leonard Wood and T.R. Another was his plagiarizing of the League to Enforce Peace, originated by several Republicans including President A. Lawrence Lowell of Harvard and William Howard Taft, which Wilson stole and made his own, hoping to be chosen President of the World.

Thayer accused Wilson of wasting at least four billion dollars, mainly by the incompetence of Newton Baker in the War Department, though significantly he did not charge corruption. As for making the world safe for democracy, "Woodrow Wilson has done more to denature and destroy democracy in the United States than all our enemies have been able to do since our Government was founded in 1789. As I write these lines, he exercises an Autocracy which the Hohenzollerns and the Hapsburgs would have envied." President Wilson went to Paris, Thayer insisted, not like the other delegates, as a representative of the home Government; "he made it perfectly clear that he regarded himself as the American Government."

When people at home had doubts about some aspects of the League, "Mr. Wilson did everything possible to make them distrust his project. Not being in any sense a statesman, he did not try to propitiate. . . . He strove to inflame the country against the Senate, which was duly appointed by the Constitution to pass on the treaties negotiated by the President. . . . He had taken the precaution, several months before, to spread the insinuation that the Senate was a wicked body, which, for political reasons solely, was bent on thwarting him." Blinded by egomania, he imagined that the people were with him although they had defeated him in 1918 by over a million majority.

Finally, Thayer exultantly pointed to the evidence that Wilson had looked to the election as a referendum in which the American people should ratify his "vision" and place him among the world's few supreme men. "But the Great and Solemn Referendum turned out to be the Greatest Repudiation in American history." In his closing paragraph, Thayer piously gives praise to the sovereign people who had given the Republicans a thumping majority. The people "were sound and sane. They saw that the capital issue was Wilson and Wilsonism, and, having at last an opportunity to record their opinion, they repudiated both."

After leaving the White House the Wilsons lived on S Street in Washington, and he was well enough to receive many visitors, ranging from old Princeton faculty friends to Lloyd George and Clemenceau. He once remarked to Mrs. Wilson that he was having the unique experience of attending his own obsequies. His mind was still clear; he wrote an article for the *Atlantic* deploring President Harding's "normalcy," and observed to Lloyd George that President Coolidge was "no one in particular." On his last Armistice Day, in 1923, he made a speech in which he said many bitter things, but he prophesied that some day America would "assume once more the role of courage," and play an honorable part in world affairs.

One day he told one of his daughters that it was probably best after all that the United States had not entered the League, because it might have been only a personal victory for him. When finally they do join, he said, his Celtic foresight coming strong upon him, it will be because they are convinced that it is the right thing to do, "and then will be the *only right* time for them to do it."

When "the lame lion of S Street" died on February 3, 1924, most of the world spoke well of him, though German papers were bitter. The *Deutsche Rundschau* called on the German people to shout their curses after him into the grave, but except for the left-wing London *Daily Herald,* the British and most of the French papers spoke gratefully of his services to the world. His old friend Professor Bliss Perry declared what Wilson's loyal followers have felt down to the present day: "If his career ended with his burial, as in some stormy Elizabethan play, it would be fitting to call Woodrow Wilson's life a tragedy. . . . Upon idealists such as he the curtain does not fall: the play evolves into the eternal drama that makes up the life of humanity. The illogical, impertinent bullet that pierced Lincoln's brain has now become a portion of his glory. . . . Those who hated Wilson in his lifetime and those who loved him can agree at least in this: that his ultimate fame will depend upon the triumph of the political ideals which he clothed with fitting words."

"The Canned Candidate in Action," a New York World cartoon. Supporters of Warren G. Harding felt that he never had a fair chance as President because of persistent prejudice.

To the Men and Women of America

AN OPEN LETTER

When one citizen knows beyond the peradventure of doubt what concerns all other citizens but is not generally known, duty compels publication.

The father of Warren Gamaliel Harding is George Tryon Harding, second, now resident of Marion, Ohio, said to be seventy-six years of age, who practices medicine as a one-time student of the art in the office of Doctor McCuen, then resident in Blooming Grove, Morrow County, Ohio, and who has never been accepted by the people of Crawford, Morrow and Marion Counties as a white man.

Extract from an anonymously issued handbill alleging that Harding had Negro blood. The New York Herald claimed it a "foul, eleventh hour attack." Democrats repudiated circular and denied responsibility for it.

A vote for Coolidge is a vote for the Klan.
A vote for Davis is a vote for the Klan.
A vote for La Follette is a vote against the Klan, against invisible government, against mob rule;

Another example of anti-Coolidge, anti-Davis propaganda sponsored by zealous Progressives.

Evidently alliteration was considered the better part of calumny in the absence of substantiation of the item at side.

Kool Klammy Kal Koolidge Kant Kondemn the Ku Klux Klan. You Kan Kill the Kruel Ku Klux by Kanning Kunning Kwiet Kal.

Why the People Cannot Support Davis or Coolidge for the Presidency

> "As between Mr. Davis and President Coolidge, it is hard to discern much difference. Essentially the Democratic and Republican nominees for the presidency stand for the same thing."—Chicago Journal of Commerce Editorial, July 10, 1924.

"The Wall Street Twins"

J. M. Baer in "Labor"

Big Business Made J. W. Davis

"I have a fine list of clients—what lawyer would not want them? I have J. P. Morgan & Co., the Erie Railroad, the Guaranty Trust Co., the Standard Oil Co., and other foremost concerns on my list. I am proud of them. They are big institutions and so long as they ask for honest work I am pleased to work for them. Big business has made this country what it is. We want big business."—From an interview by J. W. Davis to the Brooklyn Eagle before his nomination.

Coolidge Depends on Capital and Profits

"Modern civilization depends to a large extent on accumulated and invested capital, and for its advance will depend more and more on accumulation and investment of capital. Civilization and profits go hand in hand."—Candidate John Calvin Coolidge.

"We justify the greater and greater accumulations of capital because we believe that therefrom flows the support of all science, art, learning, and the charities which minister to the humanities of life, all carrying their beneficent effects to the people as a whole. Unless this is measurably true our system of civilization ought to stand condemned."—From President Coolidge's new book, "The Price of Freedom," p. 9.

"Human action can be modified to some extent, but human nature cannot be changed."—ABRAHAM LINCOLN.

LA FOLLETTE-WHEELER PROGRESSIVE HEADQUARTERS
HOTEL MORRISON, CHICAGO, ILL.

"A plague on both their houses" was in effect the main theme of propaganda distributed by LaFollette Progressives in 1924.

"The Whirlwind Campaign," a 1924 cartoon by
Rollin Kirby, reflected the image of Calvin
Coolidge nurtured by some newspapers.

"The Fourth Estate," a 1930 cartoon by Kirby,
did not put Coolidge in a better light when
he expressed views after leaving White House.

"Gulliver and the Lilliputians" was drawn by Jay N. Darling at the height of attacks on Hoover. A close friend of the President, Darling (known professionally as "Ding") was distinctly sympathetic to Hoover.

From Hoover's viewpoint publication of this photograph of a relief line in front of an ironic billboard was patently unfair and inconsiderate.

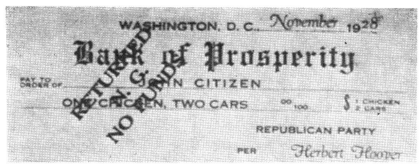

Copies of this bad check kept turning up during the early 1930's.

Who concocted the term "Hooverville" isn't known but widespread, sometimes unwarranted use of the term did the President great harm during the depression.

"It seems there wasn't any depression at all"— Fitzpatrick in the St. Louis Post-Dispatch.

What happened to many farmers during Hoover's administration was not soon forgotten. Nor did Democratic propaganda often pass up an opportunity to blame him for farmers' troubles.

Drawn for a veteran's newspaper, this cartoon appeared shortly after U. S. troops evicted ex-servicemen from an encampment near the nation's Capitol in July, 1932.

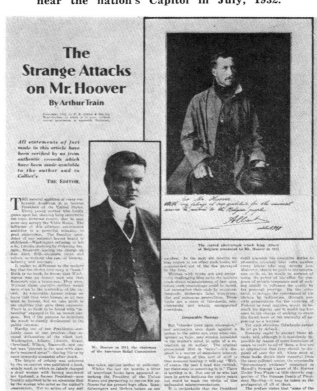

Collier's came to Hoover's defense in this article.

CHAPTER X

THEY HATED F. D. R.

The story of the defamation of Franklin Roosevelt differs from other accounts in this book, partly because he was in the White House longer, partly because a greater variety of crises and problems arose during his twelve years in office and partly because he was what he was.

More than half of those now living in the United States have some memory of F.D.R. as President and of how they loved or hated him. No one who lived through that period can write about him with complete detachment. Certainly no President in modern times was the object of such extremes of strong feeling.

Roosevelt was both idolized and detested, blindly followed or bitterly fought—sometimes by the same people. Many earlier supporters, like Senator Burton K. Wheeler of Montana, became his implacable enemies. Some one-time antagonists later joined his administration; Frank Knox, who was Republican Vice-Presidential candidate in 1936 and referred to F.D.R. as an S.O.B., entered the Roosevelt Cabinet four years later as Secretary of the Navy. F.D.R. was booed in Cambridge, Massachusetts, by Harvard undergraduates, and on the White House lawn by Communist-sympathizing students of the American Youth Congress. No one group held a monopoly of malice toward him, but most of the rabid Roosevelt-haters during the New Deal period came from among the rich and well-born.

Behind the intense hatred of the wealthy was the memory of their deadly fear in early 1933, when every god in their Olympus had failed them, and they saw ruin, perhaps bloody revolution, staring them in the face. In those despairing weeks before Inauguration Day bars of gold were lugged on board at least one yacht in Newport Harbor in the hope that, come the Revolution, the family might escape and find, somewhere in the South Seas, a haven where gold would still buy food and safety. Then came March 4 and the magnificent Roosevelt radio voice assured the nation that it had nothing to fear but fear;

and many of the shaken souls looked up in admiration and gratitude to their brave rescuer—a man of their own class, too.

Once the terrified ones were rescued, however, and found that their savior had scant respect for their old gods, and even thought they should pay increased taxes on their reviving incomes, the memory of their tearful relief and adoration on Inauguration Day turned to gall. They had been fooled—worse still, had fooled themselves. That they could not forgive. To be stripped of self-confidence was a shattering blow, and the natural reaction was anger. Roosevelt was in the line of fire—the more so because, with all his mistakes, he was not so comprehensively wrong as they had been.

Franklin D. Roosevelt's attitude toward problems of the depression was, from the beginning, frankly experimental. He spoke of himself as a quarterback having to make quick decisions on the football field. In view of the quality of the technical advice available to him this was a reasonable approach. Orthodox and respected experts had been woefully wrong about many of the events leading up to the 1929 crash; the unorthodox were still indistinguishable from the crackpots who hovered around in a buzzing swarm. The President was a layman, but it was he who had to call the signals and run the team. At times he terrified those supporters who understood, or thought they did, the dangers of some of the plays he called.

Not all criticism of Roosevelt came from reactionaries. Among the New Dealers there were many conflicting theories and plans which led to frequent disappointments with what the President chose to do. One high official, standing on the sidewalk after a dinner party, was heard to cry, while slapping his leg, "God, if we could only sell Roosevelt the New Deal!" In August, 1935, the *Nation* said editorially that the President had lost the confidence of many liberals because of unworthy political appointments, disorganization and inefficiency in his administration, and his refusal to state his real objectives and chart his course so that people could know what to expect.

This complaint, by both friends and enemies, of unwillingness to chart his course in advance, has been a common one whenever a strong President has steered the country through rough seas. Some of Roosevelt's worst political errors came when he charted his course too far ahead, promising what he would do in future circumstances he did not yet understand, as in the campaign of 1932, and in 1940 when he said that American soldiers would not be sent overseas. It is not the Captain's duty to satisfy the apprehensions of the passengers, or even of the crew; part of his job is to take criticism for not doing so.

In the early years of the New Deal it was not uncommon for supporters of Roosevelt who were sure they knew how to cure the depression to feel that if the President would only take the right course and stick to it, he would soon and triumphantly restore prosperity. That, however, was impossible, for his mind was not adapted to the study or understanding of economic relations. Moreover, public opinion was so confused that a rugged attack on the depression would probably have been unacceptable. It may well be that Roosevelt's chief contribution was his carefree energy and vitality—the very qualities that so enraged the conservatives. Inevitably some of his activities were less successful than others, and his enemies were quick to take advantage of this fact.

During the campaign of 1932, before he had encountered the facts of life in Washington, F.D.R. was led into saying things that as President he found could not be made good. One of the most embarrassing was the famous Pittsburgh speech in which he excoriated President Hoover for failing to balance the budget and cried in shocked amazement: "If the present rate on the budget continues, the true deficit as of June 30 next year will be over a billion six hundred million dollars—a deficit so great that it makes you catch your breath."

In the 1936 campaign, four years later, when President Roosevelt had to discuss his own budget situation, he asked one of his advisers what to say if the opposition brought up the Pittsburgh speech. "The only thing you could do, Mr. President," was the reply, "is to deny you were ever in Pittsburgh." F.D.R. was neither the first nor the last President to change his mind under the pressure of hard reality, but in doing so he provided his enemies with field-day opportunities.

There was a certain unreality about the argument between the conservatives and the spenders over the budget because neither side quite grasped the potential size of the United States. After World War II, when national income and the budget had grown more nearly to full size, relatively small variations in a $70 billion budget, if properly managed, might be effective for steering between deflation and inflation; but when the budget was only $7 billion, the rudder was too small to steer the ship, no matter who was at the wheel.

In 1932, Candidate Roosevelt denounced the Republicans for fostering regimentation, and for their doctrine of legislation by "master minds." He denied that human beings could be so unselfish, "almost God-like in their ability to hold the scales of justice with an even hand," as to rank as master minds. He took the traditional Democratic anti-federalist position against "the tendency to concentrate power at the top of a government structure alien to our system," and laid special emphasis on states' rights. He did not foresee then that under his administration the Democratic Party would become the modern Federalists, and the Republican Party the States' Righters.

Others changed, too. One of the radio phenomena in the 1930s was Rev. Charles E. Coughlin of Royal Oak, Michigan, a parish priest who had built up an enormous country-wide audience for hour-long Sunday afternoon broadcasts. Gradually his subject matter changed from theology, on which he was eloquent, to banking and currency, on which he was equally emphatic though ignorant. With the slogan "Roosevelt or Ruin," he was one of F.D.R.'s most stentorian supporters in 1932. But he was reputed to have a considerable investment in silver bullion for his Shrine of the Little Flower, on which the profit would be gratifying if the government would raise the price of silver. When the new administration failed to abolish private banks' right to create credit and thus compel them to use more silver in their transactions, the Coughlin text became "Roosevelt *and* Ruin." He charged the President with supporting godless communism and pagan plutocracy. "Franklin Double-Crosser Roosevelt" and a "scab President leading a scab army" had not "driven the money changers from the temple;" instead he had sold out to them.

The climax came when, over the air, Father Coughlin called the President "a liar" and made a sarcastic "apology" a week later. Couglin's attacks were not easily laughed off, for his following was largely among the poorer people to whom F.D.R. had to look for the bulk of his political support. Eventually, however, the Coughlin tempest blew itself out.

Dame Rumor was plenty busy during the Presidential campaign of 1932. She probably did Hoover more harm than Franklin D. Roosevelt, but it cannot be said that she worked only one side of the street.

Women of America, Wake Up!

No good housewife uses a recipe that always turns out badly.

The NEW DEAL RECIPE guaranteed every American family a happier and more abundant life.

Where is this happier and more abundant life?

Read the directions for the New Deal recipe. Any housewife can tell why it failed.

NEW DEAL RECIPE FOR THE MORE ABUNDANT LIFE

1/4 of every worker's pay envelope in taxes.
$150 debt for every man, woman and child in the U. S.

99/100 of business big and little
2/3 of all U. S. farmers
1/5 of all Americans dependent on Govt. aid.

Take the entire carcass of private business and clean thoroughly by unnecessary strikes, excessive taxes and New Deal laws. Cook in boiling water, salted with Government competition. Cool with a 59c dollar. Remove skin, and any overlooked profits.

Cover bottom of baking dish with what is left, add layers of U. S. farmers soaked in AAA sauce. Just before election throw in the birthright to a free vote of every American. First cut it into fine pieces by the shameful use of relief funds.

Cover with New Deal deficit prosperity sauce, a twenty billion dollar debt, season with the hard earned dollars of every worker. Sprinkle lightly with liberal promises and dishonest politicians. Clamp on the lid of government dictation.

Bake mixture in New Deal oven for five years, basting frequently with Un-American ideas.

This sorry New Deal dish has poisoned our national health. It has brought scarcity to a land of plenty, the threat of inflation and bankruptcy to every home and a fear of government to a proud people.

Are the housewives of America going to keep the New Deal cooks in Washington who follow this foreign recipe, until every safeguard of a free America is destroyed?

Or, are we going to DISCHARGE the New Deal cooks and again eat the plain American food of free enterprise, thrift and hard work.

Plain American food made the United States of America the most prosperous nation in the world.

If your Senators and Representatives are trained chefs who know their business — if they believe in the old American recipe which uses the ingredients of thrift and hard work, whether they are Republicans or Democrats, keep them on the job.

But if your cooks preparing your food in Congress belong to the New Deal Union — DISCHARGE THEM THIS FALL. They have made a sorry mess of our National Kitchen.

We will gladly send you a list of the New Deal Cooks if you write to

WOMEN'S REBELLION

SARAH OLIVER HULSWIT, Housewife,
Chairman.

Suffern, N. Y., July 1938

What Mrs. Hulswit lacked in polished English she more than made up for in her richness of metaphors. It's possible that she could have cooked up something more delectable if she had had the help of GOP literary chefs.

"THE GOOD NEIGHBOR"

"One of the great curses of American life has been speculation," said President Roosevelt in December, 1935

United European Investors, Ltd., was formed, with Franklin D. Roosevelt as president, to speculate in German marks. This is a reproduction of one of its advertisements.

"Camco's" barrage of high-pressure stock selling included the reproduction above. The stock unit price of Director Roosevelt's company in 1928 was $55. Today it is $0.00.

Extract from circular that was widely distributed during 1936 campaign.

A portion of the jacket of a book by Elizabeth Dilling entitled "The Roosevelt Red Record and Its Background." A highly articulate woman, Mrs. Dilling shouted in bold type and unequivocal words that the New Deal was just a front for Moscow-directed and supervised Communists and Socialists.

A cartoon by Art Young entitled "A Greek Fable Up To Date."

INDEPENDENT
EDUCATIONAL
UNMUZZLED

ENLIGHTENING
PROGRESSIVE
NEWSY

GENERAL OFFICES, PITTSBURGH, PA.

Vol. XLIII—No. 7   New York, N. Y.   Topeka, Kan.   Philadelphia, Pa. HARRISBURG, PA., OCT. 8, 1936 Los Angeles, Calif.   San Francisco, Calif.   5 Cents the Copy

A ROOSEVELT SENSATION

The Story of Roosevelt and Non-Union Soft Coal

By LOUIS McGREW, Editor of Labor World, Pittsburgh, Pa.

Some eighty years ago, James Roosevelt, the father of Franklin Delano Roosevelt, and Warren Delano, his mother's brother and possibly others of the kin, went to the anthracite region to make their fortune in the hard coal country. They established the town of Delano, Pennsylvania, now a railroad center, and possibly had other hard coal mines. It is well known both by the coal miners, in the anthracite region and by others, that they advocated the "Divine Right" to crush unions. That is they believed in their hatred toward unions, that God gave them the right to break up unions, and pay wages said to be from fifty cents per day for outside labor, up to as high as $3.00 per day for skilled miners. This story is written not for the purpose of merely smearing the President, but to prove conclusively, that he is not the great humanitarian, the modern Santa Claus, as it were, but rather a cold blooded, cruel coal baron. In this the fifth of our stories, which deal almost exclusively with the Roosevelt-Delano soft coal mines, we tie up the President definitely to the notorious Vinton Collieries Co., the Graceton Coal and Coke Co., at Graceton, Pa., and the Rochester and Pittsburgh Coal Company, at Indiana, Pa.

It is said the Roosevelts and Delanos left the anthracite region about 1887, to run non-union mines in Central Pennsylvania, as they willed. They bought thousands of acres of coal land, and built thereon their own towns. In 1879-80, James Roosevelt and Adrian Iselin, started to build the Pittsburgh, Rochester and Buffalo Railroad. We find they paid from fifty cents per day up to a dollar a day, and employed Italians just off shipboard. They had much labor trouble. It is said they took out injunctions, had strikes and used the club at that early date. In 1887 the Rochester and Pittsburgh Coal Company was established to feed the railroad. James Roosevelt was for many years the treasurer of both. Then came Warren Delano into the soft coal picture. He established Vintondale, Pa., a 20,000-acre operation, then Graceton, Pa.. a 15,000-acre operation. We have

Its legitimate existence is difficult to trace today, but if its 1936 masthead is to be believed, "Labor World" once had offices in New York, Topeka, Philadelphia, Harrisburg, Pittsburgh, Los Angeles, and San Francisco. Absence of other place names could be explained by the paper's crowded makeup.

In addition to the epithets that a priest could safely shout over the radio, there were numerous less printable slanders and ribald stories which circulated among Roosevelt-haters and were repeated with relish by New Dealers as examples of the feebleness of their opponents. The President's close friend Harry Hopkins had in his White House bedroom a framed *Esquire* cartoon showing a child who had written "Roosevelt" on the pavement reproved for having used "a dirty word."

Recalling "Franklin" as a smug, self-righteous snob, some Groton and Harvard classmates charged that he had been a failure in both the law and business, and that the resulting inferiority complex caused him to turn against his own class and seek applause from disgruntled radicals. "Roosevelt failed in Wall Street seven times," ran one explanation. "When he became President, he closed all the banks in revenge." A frequently circulated rumor was that he was insane: White House callers were greeted with "manic laughter" and interrupted by silly giggles. And, of course, the original family name was not "Roosevelt" but "Rosenfeld."

The more rabid Roosevelt-haters did not mention him by name; they referred to him as "That *man.*" Others bluntly called him "That cripple in the White House." Some suggested that a mistress habitually visited him; others that he was completely paralyzed below the waist.

One of the more printable stories was of a great surgeon so skillful that he spliced a new arm on an injured baseball player who then became a star pitcher; after several other surgical marvels in a climax of virtuosity the surgeon grafted a smile on a jackass who then became President of the United States. Another story that Roosevelt-haters told with relish was about a boy who dragged a drowning man from the river and feared his father would give him a whipping when he discovered that his son had rescued F.D.R.

Men and women whose only means of support came from inheriting or marrying inherited wealth joined in scorning Roosevelt for "never having met a payroll" and for "living off his mother's income." One industriously circulated myth was that the President had taken public money to pay rent to his mother for use of her Hyde Park estate as a Summer White House. Quoted rentals varied from $17,000 to $100,000 a year.

After the name "Krum Elbow" had been given to the Roosevelt Hyde Park property, Howland Spencer, who lived across the Hudson, charged that his estate was the original "Krum Elbow" and that F.D.R. had stolen the name. Thus aroused, Spencer turned author and produced a number of derogatory leaflets. One, after charitably attributing Roosevelt's lack of intelligence to a prenatal injury, went on to say that "the flattery that fertilized for its purpose such a mind as our neighbor's can be traced to the cabal of the Morgenthaus, Lehmans, Frankfurters and Cohens. . . . Men like Frankfurter and Baruch are more dangerous to the American tradition and ideals than all the Communists that could find their way into Union Square."

One of the virulent anti-Roosevelt periodicals was *The Awakener,* edited by a group of super-patriots including Lawrence Dennis, Col. Eugene N. Sanctuary, Director of the American Christian Defenders, and Joseph P. Kamp, the same whose eager assistance embarrassed the Republicans in the campaign of 1958. *The Awakener* specialized in alarms over the imminent death of free enterprise and in linking the New Deal to communism and socialism. Typical headlines were: "Marxian Parallel to the New Deal," "A Christian Indicts the New Deal," "RFC Gives Millions to Russia While Americans Starve," "Air Channels Practically Closed to All Except Administration Yes-Men."

In one of *The Awakener's* stories an "avowed radical" named Shoemaker, with other members of the Socialist Workers Alliance, organized a subversive front which they called "Modern Democrats." For this action they were "unfortunately" mobbed by a "group of patriotic citizens," and Shoemaker was killed. In his effects was found a "telltale letter, dated April 28, 1932, and signed by Franklin D. Roosevelt." What was in the letter was not clear but the reader was left with the impression that F.D.R. was in close communication with the Socialist Workers Alliance.

Among Roosevelt's economic experiments, it is noticeable that those which have been most successful were in general the most bitterly criticized when they were established.. His greatest mistake, on the other hand, the National Recovery Administration, drew relatively little fire from the Roosevelt-haters. For though on one side the NRA was an imitation of Russian planning, its chief source was in the business world, where there were many conservatives who wanted to imitate Mussolini's fascist system of government-sponsored monopoly. Mussolini, they pointed out admiringly, made the trains run on time— and there was no foolishness about anti-trust. That experiment, in Italy and here, did not turn out a success.

But the TVA, probably Roosevelt's most outstanding economic achievement, was anathema from the start. This project was a direct descendant of Theodore Roosevelt's conservation program, and was promoted by the maverick Republican Senator George Norris, all of which helped to emphasize the taint of class-treason that clung so powerfully to F.D.R. himself. A sample of the feelings about the TVA is a pontifical analysis by George Winston, in the *Awakener*. Winston pointed out that emotional attitudes toward technical problems were sure to lead to fatal blunders. Then, neatly illustrating his point, he waxed emotional about the insensate vanity of Senator Norris and his dream of erecting a vast monument to himself and at the same time bringing in the social revolution. While Coolidge and Hoover were in office, they had saved the country from Norris; but with the advent of Roosevelt with his reckless willingness to try anything once (with the taxpayers' money) the Norris dream was at last taken seriously.

"The scheme was wildly impractical from the start," cried the horrified Winston, "It was an indefensible imposition upon the taxpayers. . . . The average cash income of many of the farm families in the region does not exceed $50 per year. Obviously there could be no possible market for increased electric production. . . ."

Oh well, that was long ago. Somehow there is a market, and official observers from all over the world come to the Tennessee Valley to admire and to learn.

While Father Coughlin was preaching to the lowly quite different inspiration was being offered on higher social and economic levels. The American Liberty League was organized in 1934 by conservative "Jeffersonian Democrats" and Republicans who had been horrified by Roosevelt's policies. They were entitled to call themselves Jeffersonian by their yearning for "economy" and their dislike of federalism, at least if the question were not raised about what century they were being Jeffersonian in. The Liberty League President, Jouett Shouse, had been a Democratic Congressman from Kansas, and in the 1928 campaign was assistant to John J. Raskob, Al Smith's choice as Chairman of the Democratic National Committee. Shouse was therefore as authentic a Democrat as Al Smith, Raskob, and John W. Davis, who all helped to found the Liberty League.

Shouse was the main sparkplug and orator of the League. He sadly pointed out how he and his Democratic friends had been shocked at Roosevelt's new and outrageous policies. Who would ever have thought that Roosevelt would adopt "the amazing theory that a nation can spend its way back to prosperity?" Where had he ever given any warning of the death-sentence for holding companies, or the TVA and other socialistic experiments? "The program choked down the throat of the Congress fulfills to the letter the promises . . . of the Socialist Party." So he called upon all good men to rally in defense of the hard-pressed Constitution before it should be too late.

Every important business group was represented in the League, including the Morgans and Rockefellers as well as numerous DuPonts. There were 70 presidents or directors of corporations, and 70 eminent lawyers. Charles Michelson, the famous publicity expert of the Democrats, took pleasure in working over the list of eminent lawyers who were lining up to save the Constitution and pointing out how many of them had lost cases in the Supreme Court through the refusal of that august—and at that time conservative—body to accept their Constitutional interpretations. The New Dealers scoffed that the Liberty the League wanted was "Freedom for Freebooters." It was reported to have some 100,000 members, but since these were men who would vote against Roosevelt in any case, it had little effect on the 1936 result except perhaps through exhibiting who was opposing Roosevelt.

The Roosevelt family was a favorite topic for defamers. The marriages, divorces and business affairs of the children received imaginative, gloating attention. Many a Roosevelt-hater was sure that Eleanor Roosevelt planned to take over after her husband's death and hold the White House until one of her sons should be ready to succeed to the throne. Wendell Willkie, who was himself the target of calumny in the rough-and-tumble 1940 presidential campaign, expressed wonder how Mrs. Roosevelt ever stood the abuse that was heaped upon her.

In the cartoonist's opinion the Capitol became a madcap playground for "crackpot" schemes of FDR. For some critics of the administration NRA was an esoteric abbreviation for "New Revolutionary Administration."

Roosevelt Behind the Bars!

WHERE HE BELONGS
ACCORDING TO HIS OWN ADMISSION AND .. VISION

"Franklin D. Roosevelt was Secretary Daniels' assistant in the Navy Department throughout the war, and on a recent occasion declared that he furthered plans for the entry of the American Navy into the war on the side of the Allies from the first day of hostilities in Europe."

"Mr. Roosevelt boasted of his aid to Mr. Wilson's policy of 'following his designs far-sightedly'."

"Speaking last February in Brooklyn he declared that as acting head of the Navy he had committed enough illegal acts to send him to jail for 999 years, and his admission was applauded."

(The above quotations are from The American Monthly of August 1920.)

THIRD TERM? HELL !! ·· I'm in for Life !!!

If the man Roosevelt considered himself a criminal while Assistant Secretary of the Navy, and betrayed this country during the last war—will it then be wise for you, and patriotic, to trust this very same man as President, and, to believe him when he says: "I will keep us out of war"? —

Remember — President Wilson also "kept us out of war" and Franklin D. Roosevelt boasted—he was "following Mr. Wilson's designs far-sightedly".

—Ernst Goerner.

Reprint from "Is President Franklin D. Roosevelt Betraying Us Again?"

(Published October 1940)

Senator Holt of W. Virginia stated that Roosevelt boasted in 1920 "that he had violated enough laws to be sent to the penitentiary for 999 years."

(Milwaukee Sentinel, Sept. 20, 1940)

A VOTE FOR ROOSEVELT IS A VOTE FOR WAR

Additional copies 100 for $1.00—Address Ernst Goerner, P. O. Box 1824, Milwaukee, Wis.
Special Prices for Larger Quantities.

Let no one minimize this circular. Its justification can be found in the small type citing Senator Holt as authority for statement that FDR had boasted he had "violated enough laws to be sent to the penitentiary for 999 years."

ROOSEVELT—OR THE CONSTITUTION?

In his mad march toward war, Roosevelt each week flouts the Constitution in some new way—with or without the acquiescence of a servile majority in Congress. Will you defend Roosevelt and Tyranny? or will you take your stand to restore the Constitution and the Republic? The hour when you must make your choice is at hand.

It Has Happened Here

American fascism has become a reality. By his own admission, Roosevelt has left us only four freedoms—freedoms such as slaves had a century ago. But freedom of person, freedom to own property, freedom from foreign domination—these he has taken away. He has seized special presidential powers in the name of an emergency: *yet when the American Revolution was fought and won, we had no President at all.*

War to Conceal Failure

To obscure the complete collapse of his recovery program in 1938 Roosevelt resolved upon war. Since we had not an enemy in the world, he set out to make as many as he could. Now, America must indeed arm.

Unity Now

The cry for unity echoes from one end of the country to another. But unity can never be achieved in the interests of any foreign power; and that is why Roosevelt, in order to serve the British Empire, must draft reluctant soldiers, seize industries, and coerce labor. The crisis he has created calls for new leadership which will serve America first and America only.

Roosevelt Must Go!

Demand a new Secretary of State worthy of the highest office, and then the resignation or impeachment of Wallace and Roosevelt, thus making the new Secretary of State the lawful President. Once that is done, you will see the British and German and Russian agents melt away like snow in spring—and with them, all un-American sympathies.

RESTORE THE REPUBLIC

On Memorial Day, the movement to bring back constitutional government was no more than "a little cloud like a man's hand." Today it is a gathering storm. An angry America is beginning to agitate for Roosevelt's removal. *Let your voice be heard.* Neither Roosevelt nor Congress can successfully defy the will of the people.

NORMAN H. WILSON
32 Rockland Avenue
Yonkers, New York
MARGARET NORTON
15 Caryl Avenue
Yonkers, New York

SECOND BULLETIN.
INDEPENDENCE DAY, 1941.

NOTE: *Pass this along. Send us the names of other interested Americans—but no Tories, Nazis, or Communists.*

Somewhat more reasonable than most anti-FDR fanatics, signatories Wilson and Norton urged the "resignation or impeachment" of Wallace and Roosevelt, thus giving them the opportunity to step aside gracefully while "the British and German and Russian agents melt away like snow in spring—and with them, all un-American sympathies." Moreover, the patriotism of the authors should not be hastily impugned. Note that they request readers to send along "the names of other interested Americans—but no Tories, Nazis, or Communists." Unlike other vilifiers of Roosevelt, they were at least verbally discriminating in their choice of supporters.

AMERICA! A NEW CHALLENGE.

E. N. S.

E. N. SANCTUARY.

1. Said Frank-lin D. on 'lec - tion night, I'll find a crew to cure our plight,
2. "Fac-ing-Both-Ways",(b) but most-ly Left, Our free - dom rights he has be - reft,
3. This "Bug - gy" man who's at our head, with bu - reau-crats he has us fed;
4. From Lex - ing - ton to York-town's field, our fa - thers fought nor did they yield,
5. In God of Hosts we must re - ly and al - ien plans and schemes de-fy;

And head - ed by his Tug-well boy to Mos - cow did they then de - ploy,
As su - pine men in Con-gress Hall, o - beyed his ev - 'ry beck and call;
He part - y plat-form prompt-ly shed and de - vious ways be - fore us spread;(c)
On bat - tle-field their blood was shed, for lib - er - ty they fought and bled;
Sup - port a cause that's near our heart and nev - er cease til foe de - part;

Re - turn - ing with a plot so bold, ex - act - ly fit - ted Mos-cow's mould,(1)
Co'hn and Corc-'ran and "Hot-Dog" boys have writ - ten bills which much an -noys,
Our Con - sti - tu - tion served us well un - til there came a plan from hell,
Shall we be pol-troons in this hour? Shall en-trenched foe cause us to cow'r?
A - mer - i - ca—we sing of thee, where man once found true lib - er - ty,

On men once free, in ways un-kind, be - gan on us slave chains to bind.(a)
And steal - ing rights we once en-joyed, for this by Frank-lin were em-ployed.
Let's turn it back from whence it came and spon - sors brand with last - ing shame.
Or shall we rouse this sleep-ing land and for our he - roes firm - ly stand?
Turn back thy foes that now as - sail and cher-ished rights once more pre-vail.

Considering that copies of this song could be bought for 5c ($1 per hundred), it was a mighty good buy as sheet music goes. If its words and tune left much to be desired only an unreasonable Democrat could complain with clear conscience. Whether E. N. Sanctuary was both the lyricist and the composer isn't ascertainable, but it's a matter of record that he was in the forefront of the "Hate Roosevelt" parade that marched down the dark alleys of U. S. history.

29th EDITION (800.000 Total Circulation)   MARCH 15th. 1939

PUBLIC WARNING

ROOSEVELT & KIDNAPED CHILDREN

The below named committee believe it their duty in the interest of innocent youngsters, unsuspecting citizens and American high school girls to warn the American people that assassins, fiends, cutthroats, kidnapers and bomb throwers are at large with the connivance and protection of Franklin Delano Roosevelt's democratic administration.

The Department of Justice, the nation's highest law enforcing agency shields and protects them from exposure and imprisonment the most vicious heartless brutal band of criminals in history.

It is another angle to the long list of brazen scandals now confronting the American people, committed by their paid servants in office high and low.

Franklin Delano Roosevelt's Department of Justice has willfully failed to enforce existing laws honestly and honoral` with a view of shielding prominent, innuential, wealthy persons.

The DUTCH-GERMAN-ROTHSCHILD international banking crowd, with the aid of English-hating Irish sympathizers, long enemies of the Anglo-American-Morgan interests are responsible for all of this nation's unsolved horror murders, kidnapings, girl assassinations, and bomb outrages of the past years. They have been politically shielded through their wealth, power and influence. Relatives of the President are linked with this murder machine. All were trapped fully and completely in the Lindbergh baby kidnaping by citizens. Registered documents sent by the High Command in Germany to this country directing the Lindbergh baby kidnaping were seized by these citizens. But the Department of Justice promptly suppressed and concealed them. Had they been made public and our witnesses permitted to testify the names revealed and testimony offered would have cleared up a raft of the nation's murders and kidnapings.

Franklin Delano Roosevelt's administration with all the power at its command is successfully keeping these facts from becoming public while the murderers are going right along kidnaping, raping and murdering.

In addition to murdering our children and citizens these bankers held secret communication with foreign governments, which we believe is some kind of treason — for less influential citizens.

Following are some of the crimes this international banking crowd through convicts recruited from German and civil prisons have committed.

DOROTHY ARNOLD; STAR FAITHFUL; JIMMY GLASS; WILLIE McCONNELL; AMBROSE SMALL; JOSEPH BROWNE ELWELL; JUDGE CRATER; EDWARD RIDLEY, HIS CASHIER AND HIS BOOKKEEPER; THE 3X KILLINGS; THE SAN FRANCISCO PREPAREDNESS DAY BOMBING MURDERS; CHARLES MATTSON; CHARLES LINDBERGH, Jr.; THE WALL STREET BOMBING OUTRAGE; MARY BROWN; MARY COYLE; MARY MARTIN; FLORENCE KANE; BENJAMIN COLLINGS; MRS. FROHM & DAUGHTER; THE LIP STICK VICTIMS; PETER LEVINE and 500 or more other victims which lack of space prevents us from printing.

Jimmy Glass, (4); Willie McConnell, (9); Charles Lindbergh Jr., (20 months); Peter Levine, (12); and Jimmy Cash, (4); were all youngsters that had been kidnaped with the accompanying ransom demand and later frightfully murdered. THERE NEVER WAS ANY INTENTION TO RETURN ANY OF THE CHILDREN.

All of the females when found were nude. Most of them had been raped. With one exception, all had their exposed bodies ripped open with stilettoes. Mary Brown was burned alive with flaming gasoline. Mrs. Frohm and daughter had their hands burned off. The bombs were planted to explode in crowded streets among unsuspecting men, women and children. BALLISTIC EXAMINATION OF THE BULLETS TAKEN FROM SOME OF THE VICTIMS SHOWED THAT ALTHOUGH MURDERED YEARS APART THE SAME REVOLVER WAS USED.

Alien killers, haters of Americans, were the paid killers. The ones that gave them the signal were the DUTCH-GERMAN-ROTHSCHILD banking crowd. The ones that promised them police protection and made good on their promise by providing it, was the DUTCH-GERMAN-ROTHSCHILD international bankers and lawyers. Every time they got a shellacing in Wall Street by the Morgan crowd, or did not have their

way in certain things, or a servant, employee, or girl friend knew too much, or one of their undercover agents betrayed them, or transfered their affections to the hated Morgan interests, (Lindbergh and Levine come under this heading) it meant assassination or kidnaping of a youngster of their enemies, with the resultant false clues, and arrest of bums and tramps on suspicion.

WE ARE PREPARED TO PRESENT DOCUMENTARY EVIDENCE CLEARING UP EVERY ONE OF THE ABOVE NAMED CRIMES AND OTHERS THAT ARE FRIGHTFUL AND SENSATIONAL.

SAD BUT TRUE

When the true administration of justice falls down, as it has now; and laws are not honestly enforced, and officials are in league with criminals, as they are now; and evidence is available that said criminals are known and shielded by the very authorities themselves, then the door is left open to suspicion, as far as this committee is concerned, that the reason the criminals are permitted their freedom from exposure and punishment is because of the link of relationship of some of them to the President, Franklin Delano Roosevelt.

Since we began years ago, in publishing these circulars, in which we charge that the Federal Bureau of Investigation of the Department of Justice "G" men, arrest bums and tramps and friendless criminals while permitting the man of wealth and political connections to escape punishment, over 100 members of the Department of Justice have resigned from that Department.

Prior editions of these circulars containing many interesting features are on file at the New York Public Library, 5th Ave. and 42nd Street, N. Y. C. Note: The Library has no circulars for distribution.

HAL WALTON

Chairman for the Committee of Witnesses
Volunteer in the World War - Served in France with the 29th Engineers - General Headquarters Intelligence Division. G 2 C - Topographical Section
32 West 32nd Street   New York City

If the information in the upper left hand corner can be believed, 800,-000 copies of this circular were distributed by the "Committee of Witnesses" without the benefit of correct spelling or much concern about plausability. Note how deftly Roosevelt is blamed for the kidnapping of Charles Lindbergh, Jr., the Wall Street bombing in 1920, the disappearance of Judge Crater, and an assortment of other events dating back to the beginning of the century. Note too that it is irrefutably contended that Roosevelt had some sort of nefarious association with the "Dutch—German—Rothschild." Although "criminal" relatives and friends of the President, were, according to Mr. Walton's "Committee," part of "this murder machine," they were understandably "permitted their freedom from exposure and punishment because of the link of relationship of some of them to President Franklin Delano Roosevelt." Need any more be proven in this connection?

Robert Moses, New York's versatile and controversial public servant, contributed to the chorus the curious observation that a President of the United States has "certain immunities," particularly against aspersions that other political figures must endure with equanimity. He observed that the same immunity extends also to members of the President's family even when they don't behave well. Then, boldly daring to asperse the inaspersible, he went on: "It protects his wife when she romps up and down the country discovering economic ills and prescribing quack remedies. . . . It protects her when she uses the immense prestige of the White House to market scribblings which a college freshman would hesitate to hand to the professor."

The offspring of Theodore Roosevelt, comprising most of the Oyster Bay branch of the family, refrained from open, personal attack upon their Hyde Park relatives, but what they said and thought in private did manage to get substantial publicity. Alice Roosevelt Longworth had plenty to say; her remark that "Franklin was one-third Eleanor and two-thirds mush" was repeated with glee across the country. Nicholas Roosevelt, a distant cousin of the Theodore Roosevelts and an office-holder under Coolidge and Hoover, was author of a magazine article "Wanted: An Honest President." He was revolted by "the voice with a smile" and he deplored the presence of "an opportunist and melodious promiser" in the White House.

The virulence of the extreme Roosevelt-haters seems to have had a boomerang effect by arousing many people to vote for him who otherwise would not have bothered to vote. Roosevelt himself was inclined to regard his defamers as political assets. He told Frances Perkins that it was good politics never to mention an opponent's name. He had the advantage that everyone had heard of Roosevelt, including some back-country people who still thought he was Theodore. And some of his bitterest enemies were the most persistent in reminding everyone of his name. In the end, he said, a surprising number of voters go into the booth with no definite idea of whom to vote for, and they are apt to vote for someone whose name looks familiar. "I know it sounds feeble-minded," he admitted, "but it's true."

As the election of 1936 approached with Roosevelt certain to be renominated, *Fortune Magazine* discussed the question why people

ORDEAL OF THE PRESIDENCY

should hate anyone of such undeniable charm as the President. No doubt Roosevelt's connection with the repeal of Prohibition had earned the hostility of the drys, and his failure to go regularly to church had hurt him in the Bible Belt. But in *Fortune's* opinion the chief case against him was dislike of his personality. "For one criticism of New Deal measures you will hear ten criticisms of the presidential voice, the cocksure manner, the gladsome face, the cheerful elusiveness, the happy heart. There is nothing about the man that may not be made the cause of dislike." *Fortune* also noted a strong tinge of anti-semitism in the opposition, though only about thirty of the top thousand officials in the Federal establishment were Jews. In the main the deepest Roosevelt hatred, *Fortune* found, was among business men. It was clearly not due to red ink, it pointed out, for though taxes had gone up so had incomes; the net effect for most business men was a gain. The main criticism seemed to be based on lack of confidence in the future, caused by the experimental attitude of the President. No one could plan on what he would do next.

But accusing a President of breaking his promises is a feeble gesture, *Fortune* observed, since no one in the memory of man, or in either party, had been shocked at the disregard of platforms. "The important point is not whether the people were promised something they didn't get but whether they approve of what they did get." Some of our most popular Presidents, including Theodore Roosevelt, had been among those most often accused of lying. *Fortune* regarded the charge of extravagence as also a dud. Voters whose children are hungry are not going to be shocked by what they see of the receiving end—and, after all, business men will get the money when the beneficiaries spend it. To be effective, the extravagance charge would have to be connected with a visible danger of national collapse, and the voters could see no such danger.

Though there was a deep desire among the Republicans to defeat Roosevelt for reelection in 1936, there were not so many signs of a desire among possible candidates to run against him. Herbert Hoover, to be sure, after licking his wounds for three years, went before the Republican Convention with a fighting speech comparing the New Deal with the programs of hate and wild promises of the Nazi and

Fascist dictatorships. "Republicans and fellow-Americans!" he cried, "This is your call. Stop the retreat, and turning the eyes of your fellow-Americans to the sunlight of freedom, lead the attack and retake, recapture and reman the citadels of liberty!"

The convention hall shook to thunderous applause, but the shouting died down, and so did the Republican Party. Alf M. Landon, the budget-balancing Governor of Kansas, was nominated for President. He sallied forth "roaring like a fighting rabbit" against the dastardly record of the Roosevelt administration: its departure from the gold standard and devaluation of the dollar, NRA and its labor code, agricultural crop limitation and "plowing under the little pigs," Social Security, increased taxes on upper-bracket incomes, stock market regulation, the Tennessee Valley Authority. Actually, the issue was: are you for or against that man in the White House?

Roosevelt, in his acceptance speech, gaily stirred up the conservative propensity for advertising the enemy, and spoke severely of Big Business leaders who wielded monopoly powers as "economic royalists." This phrase was hotly resented by thousands of harmless rich people, most of whom operated no monopolies and exercised no king-like powers unless over a few household servants. Crowding to put on the ill-fitting shoe they loudly cursed Roosevelt for betraying his class and plotting to soak the rich. Since many millions of the unemployed and other poor people thought the rich ought to be soaked, the effect of this trick was to lure the Roosevelt-haters into giving him a large amount of free political advertising.

Two of the most relentless Roosevelt baiters and foes of the New Deal were Westbrook Pegler and Fulton Lewis, Jr. Pegler, who began as a sports writer and thus became well-exercised in the art of high-flown language, worked himself into fury in his syndicated column—and still does—on the subject of Eleanor Roosevelt. He was must reading for consistent Roosevelt-haters. Then, at 7 p.m., Eastern Standard Time, the anti-Roosevelt faithful tuned their radio dials to the snarls and sarcasms of Fulton Lewis.

Although Pegler and Lewis stimulated the adrenal glands and shot many a blood pressure perilously high, they could not match the cheerfully outrageous calumnies of Henry L. Mencken in the *American Mercury*. The sage of Baltimore was no respector of Presidents, although he did once have a good word for Grover Cleveland's admission of having fathered an illegitimate child. Mencken's roasting of Calvin Coolidge and Herbert Hoover during their terms in office was mere indoor practice for the wide-ranging synthetic conniption fits he performed while Franklin Roosevelt was in the White House.

"Quacks," he observed, "are always friendly and ingratiating fellows, and not infrequently their antics are very amusing. The Hon. Franklin D. Roosevelt, LL.D., is typical of the species." Like all quacks, Mencken explained, Roosevelt took in the patient by diagnosing an imaginary disease, then gave something to warm the patient's insides, and hoped that nature would produce a sensation of well-being for which he would get a testimonial. The New Deal "began as a din of alarming blather about the collapse of capitalism . . . and is ending with claims that the failure of these catastrophes to come off has been due to the medicaments of Dr. Roosevelt and his Brain Trust. In neither half of this imposture is there any truth whatever."

In 1932 Roosevelt had some "leaning toward what may be called ethical practice," since Senator Glass vouched for him, and the Senator was far too foxy a man to be fooled. Moreover, Roosevelt appointed as Attorney-General Thomas J. Walsh, an honest and intelligent defender of the Constitution. But Walsh died, and there was no one to restrain the New Dealers who forgot all about the homely remedies such as balancing the budget, getting rid of surplus officeholders and protecting the dollar. "Recourse was had to unadulterated quackery . . . Wizards of the highest amperage were at hand. . . . They would give us a Planned Economy, scientific in every detail, and out of it would flow the More Abundant Life, with everyone rich and happy, and the very birds in the trees singing hallelujah."

These wizards "turned out to be the sorriest mob of mountebanks ever gathered together at one time, even in Washington." Their secret remedies were stale mixtures of old quackeries, "from Free Silver to the Single Tax, and their methods were those of wart-removers at county fairs." But all agreed in hating the thrifty man and plotting his ruin.

"There is not a man in the whole outfit, who is worth the powder it would take to blow him up. They are, one and all, flagrant and incurable asses, and the higher their rank in the hierarchy of buncome,

Venomous anti-FDR outpourings of Father Charles Edward Coughlin, pastor of Detroit's Shrine of the Little Flower, alarmed both Catholics and Protestants. A blistering critic of the New Deal, he gained powerful support through his nationwide radio addresses on non-religious subjects.

AMERICA – NOT ENGLAND – WON
ENGLAND'S LAST BATTLE

IT is England's boast that she always wins the last battle. That was true in the day of Cromwell, when the Irish peasants could not compete with British artillery.

That was true during the Sepoy mutiny in India when the British generals tied the Indian chieftains to the mouths of cannon and blew them to kingdom come.

That was true at Waterloo when the forces of Blucher and Schwarzenburg saved Wellington.

That was true in Ireland, Easter week of 1916, when the King's soldiers, violating all rules of warfare, slaughtered Irish patriots.

That was true in South Africa when Kitchener and Lord Roberts brought the "might" of Britain to bear on a handful of Boers who were fighting for their national liberty against the cupidity of Cecil Rhodes and his minions for the diamond mines of Kimberley and the gold of the Rand.

But in the World War, England did not win the last battle. When the Allied line was sinking under the German thrust, it was American boys at Belleau-Wood, Chateau-Thierry and in the Argonne, who broke the back of the German army.

It was American money— $4½-billions of it, that has never been repaid—"that helped to win in this last British battle."

It was 300,000 American wounded, many of whom still lie in our Veterans hospitals, who won the last British battle.

That is how England wins her last battles!

Father Coughlin has been energetic in the cause of American neutrality. The saving of America from a becatomb of Europe is one of Father Coughlin's main purposes in his weekly broadcasts. If you have not contributed to Father Coughlin's broadcast, do so with from $1 to $20—please.

Skillfully attacking FDR's foreign policy, Father Coughlin's weekly "Social Justice" created the impression that it was merely averse to the shedding of American blood in behalf of the nefarious British.

WILL ONE OF THESE
Bundles FROM Britain
BE YOUR SON?

WILL YOUR BOY BE THE NEXT UNKNOWN SOLDIER?

NO UNDECLARED OVERSEAS WAR — PEACE PLEDGES MUST BE KEPT

THE PRESIDENT HAS COMMITTED US TO A SHOOTING WAR WITHOUT THE CONSENT OF CONGRESS. IT'S A DECLARATION OF SHOOT FIRST ANYWHERE ON THE SEVEN SEAS. HE HAS VIOLATED HIS OATH OF OFFICE TO UPHOLD AND DEFEND THE CONSTITUTION OF THESE UNITED STATES. — HELP US RETAIN OUR CONSTITUTIONAL GOVERNMENT AND THESE CONTINENTAL UNITED STATES.

The heads of nations who have betrayed other peoples are many, but only ROOSEVELT has betrayed his own The hour has come to press for the impeachment of
WALLACE and FRANKLIN D. ROOSEVELT
START ACTION NOW - - WRITE YOUR
CONGRESSMAN TODAY

CRUSADING MOTHERS OF PENNSYLVANIA
PRESIDENT, MRS. CATHARINE BROWN, 106 Main Street, Colwyn, Pa.

UNITE FOR AN HONEST MONEY SYSTEM

Note outright demand for impeachment of FDR and Henry Wallace in this leaflet available from Mrs. Catharine Brown at "One Dollar Per Hundred." Note too that Mrs. Brown doesn't give the President the benefit of any possible doubts in her mind. Considering that her main objective was (or appeared to be) the prevention of aid to the British, it's somewhat puzzling why her leaflet is climaxed by "Unite For An Honest Money System."

Dr. Francis Townsend and his emaciated calf gave Roosevelt some trying days for about ten years. Distinctly dissatisfied with the New Deal's modest pay-as-you-go social security program, Dr. Townsend offered $200 per month to everyone over 60 not engaged in gainful employment and not known to be "an habitual criminal." Since FDR didn't go along with the good Doctor even part of the way, Townsendites berated the President at every opportunity.

the more patent their asininity. . . . Their pretensions are as utterly
bogus as those of Lydia Pinkham or Dr. Munyon. They possess no
useful talent of any kind, and seem to be quite incapable of anything
colorably describable as sober judgment."

"The blame for this dreadful burlesque of civilized government
is to be laid at the door of the Hon. Mr. Roosevelt, and at his door
alone. . . . He has thrown away billions to no useful end or purpose . . . He has saddled the country with a camorra of quarreling
crackpots. . . The greatest President since Hoover has carried on
his job with an ingratiating grin upon his face, like that of a snake-oil
vendor at a village carnival, and he has exhibited precisely the same
sense of responsibility in morals and honor; no more."

Bolstering up his feelings with his incomparable vocabulary,
Mencken observed that, openly or covertly, F.D.R. had been repudiated by practically every literate American not actually employed
by the Government: "From the solid gold offices of the Liberty
League to the dismal cells of the Communist Party a roar of disapproval has been launched at the grinning Dr. Roosevelt until it
swells to the proportions of a national raspberry; while in the privacy
of select salons and Virginia mansions, self-respecting Democratic
senators, and even members of the President's official family, denounce
him with cold dislike." Indeed, all classes hate him. The plutocrats
hate the Happy Borrower—speak his name and the response "approaches, in its sincerity, the apoplectic." Mencken notes, in a flash
of insight, that much of the venom among the captains of industry
stems from the recollection of having swallowed the New Deal in
1933—bottle, label, and cork—an intolerable thought. The professional men hate him. The doctors see the horrid vision of socialized
medicine. The lawyers are solidly lined up against a man who flouts
the law. The professors who are not on the payroll look on Roosevelt
with the scorn of the expert for the amateur. All newspaper men
above the contemptible level of the Newspaper Guild, except for a
few old dodos in the New York *Times*, look on the Squire of Hyde
Park as no better than a lady reporter. Throughout the professions
nowhere except among the mentally feeble is anything to be seen
but repudiation for F.D.R.

The opposition was powerless to pry F.D.R. out of the White
House, Mencken wryly admitted, because of the greater numerical

strength of a long-standing Mencken hate, the American "booboisie."
Dr. Roosevelt, he pointed out, represents the final refinement of a
type of demagogue that has been developing "ever since Andrew
Jackson first found the range of a White House cuspidor. . . . He is
a tri-motored Mark Hanna with air-conditioning and free-wheeling"
but he would "probably be elected by the mass of voters commonly
called 'the backbone of America,' because they can be counted on to
do whatever is stupid. A fascinating phenomenon, that the most
widely-repudiated leader in our history will probably be given four
more years of repudiation."

The usually jocular Irvin S. Cobb was cheerless on the political
situation. He likened the New Deal to a rotten egg, "yellow and it
stinks. It's got a smooth, slick shell outside and it's all foulness
within. . . . I'd rather risk despotism from without than from within."

Many felt that way about "dictator" Roosevelt. They hated him
more than they hated Hitler. Many wrote him letters addressed to
"Franklin D. Russianvelt," or to "Franklin Deficit Roosevelt."

The 1936 election brought not only the reelection of the "widely-
repudiated" Roosevelt, who carried every State in the Union except
Maine and Vermont, but as a mighty anticlimax, it brought on the
demise of the *Literary Digest*. In earlier presidential elections, the
Digest's poll had given an extraordinarily accurate prediction. The
periodical sent out postage-prepaid "ballots," together with six-months
trial subscription blanks, to more than 20 million persons—those
whose names were in city and telephone directories, and holders of
automobile licenses and postoffice boxes—and asked them to indicate
their choice in the present election and for whom they had voted
in the previous election. This poll reached a fairly close cross-section of the registered voters of the country, and the enterprise worked
out to the advantage of the *Literary Digest* in two respects; nationwide publicity for the magazine and between 200,000 and 300,000 trial
subscriptions.

When the time came for its 1936 poll, the magazine was low in
funds, and the management thriftily cut down its mailing to some
6 million, chiefly automobile owners. Both parties took heart at
the results: Republicans were happy because a big majority of the
ballots were for Landon; the Democrats noted with glee that the

majority of those included in the poll had voted in 1932 not for Roosevelt but for Hoover. What had happened was that, seeking the highest percentage of trial subcription returns, the magazine had concentrated on the more prosperous people. These, as it turned out, were overwhelmingly but ineffectually for Landon. The *Literary Digest* curled up and died.

On Election Night the Republican Party was at low ebb. At the St. Regis Hotel in New York there was one New Deal table, standing as an oasis in a dismal desert of disappointed Republicans. Dorothy Thompson, wearing a Landon campaign sunflower, was one of two non-New Dealers at the table. After a bulletin was read in which Landon conceded the election, Miss Thompson rapped on a tumbler with a spoon for silence. "I propose a toast to Franklin D. Roosevelt, President of the United States," she said. Not a soul at other tables followed her lead. The toast was drunk only by her table-mates, and the dance band immediately struck up a tune. Perhaps no sadder sight was ever seen again until Election Night in 1948.

Six months after Roosevelt's sensational victory, he received his most humiliating defeat—and from a Congress hitherto reviled as "a mere rubber stamp." Smarting under the Supreme Court's unanimous condemnation of the NRA, a decision which he said put the country back in "horse and buggy days," and its rejection of other New Deal measures, the President proposed to "pack" the court. Most of the justices were old, and some had grown more conservative than when they were appointed; if he could enlarge the court with young Roosevelt appointees, he could change its complexion.

But the Court turned out to be a more sacred institution than the President had supposed. Many firm New Deal supporters who had been irritated by the Court's backwardness were shocked at the idea of swamping it by an act of Congress. When the Roosevelt message reached Capitol Hill and was being read in the Senate, Vice President Garner went outside the chamber and was surrounded by a knot of questioning Senators. His reply was a gesture of unmistakable meaning: one hand holding his nose, he pointed "thumbs down" with the other.

Walter Lippmann described the President's plan as "audacity without parallel in American history. For while other Presidents have quarreled with the Court, no President has ever dreamed of asking the power to remake the Court to suit himself. . . . This is a bloodless *coup d' état* which strikes a deadly blow at the vital center of constitutional democracy."

The Court message and bill were presented February 5, 1937. One hundred and sixty-eight days later, the Senate voted to send it back to committee, which meant its legislative death. The debate that led up to this action, for earnestness, passionate conviction and temporary superiority to the backbiting of petty politics, was probably the greatest political drama of the Roosevelt administration.

Elsewhere, the backbiting, scandal mongering and whispering campaigns continued.

In May, 1937, while Roosevelt was on a fishing trip in the Gulf of Mexico, accompanied by the usual White House correspondents, the McClure Newspaper Syndicate sent to its 250 subscribers a "confidential background report":

"Unchecked. A New York specialist high in the medical field is authority for the following, which is given in strictest confidence to editors:

"Towards the end of last month Mr. Roosevelt was found in a coma at his desk. Medical examination disclosed the neck rash which is typical of certain disturbing symptoms. Immediate treatment of the most skilled kind was indicated, with complete privacy and detachment from official duties. Hence the trip to southern waters, with no newspaper men on board and an inpenetrable naval convoy."

Another "confidential background report" stated:

"At a recent private dinner in New York an official of the American Cyanamid expressed in extreme form the bitterness towards the administration which is typical of the personal reactions of many right-wing leaders in business and finance.

"The gentleman in question asserted in so many words that 'the paranoiac in the White House' is destroying the nation, that a couple of well-placed bullets would be the best thing for the country, and that he for one would buy a bottle of champagne as quick as he could get it to celebrate such news."

The head of the syndicate, who is now dead, refused to disclose

Traitors Three

Brutus, Arnold and Franklin D.,
Sat in the shade of a sour apple tree.
Their conversation took a turn
As to which one was the most traitorous worm.

"It's I," cried Brutus, "I betrayed my friend,
I double-crossed Caesar until his end.
I won his trust and history books say,
His final words were 'Et tu, Brute'."

"Not bad," said Arnold, "but listen awhile,
Your small record just makes me smile.
You fooled one man, but look at me,
I sold out a whole army."

Up jumped Franklin, haughty and sure,
"You boys are a couple of amateurs.
When I took charge in '33
A nation put her trust in me.

I promised this and I promised that,
I calmed their fears with fireside chats.
I spent millions right and left
And that, my friends, is no small theft.

I told them just to feel at ease,
I had them chanting their A. B. C.'s
I promised that I would soak the rich,
Ain't I the lying ——————————?

I promised a land of milk and honey
Where everyone would be rolling in money;
I promised this and what did they get?
I gave them beer and 'Haufen Mist'.

They called me the great humanitarian,
(I should have been in a sanitarium).
Blue buzzards were on every window pane,
New born babies bore my name.

Beware of Wall Street, I dinned in their ears,
Trust in me and have no fears.
I will keep you safe from harm,
To hell with work, plow under your farm.

And believe in me, both husbands and wives,
But the little pigs can run for their lives;
They alone can see thru me,
I killed them off with the greatest glee.

I fooled those yokels both old and young,
I was the greatest scoundrel to remain unhung;
I ruined their country, my friends, and then
I placed the blame on nine old men."

Brutus stood there filled
    with awe,

Arnold sat with fallen jaw.

Then Brutus said, "We've
    had our fling,

Get up, Arnold, and salute
    your king."

With good reason author remains anonymous.

Covers of a few of several thousand anti-Roosevelt books, pamphlets, and circulars distributed during the 1930's and 1940's. Many were fugitive publications that did not include names of publishers.

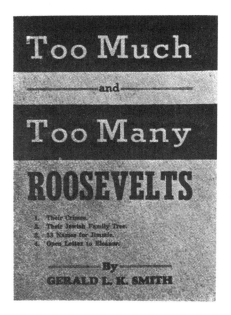

Countless copies of this derisive leaflet were distributed by Republicans.

PROPOSED OATH OF ALLEGIANCE
TO THE DEMOCRATIC PARTY

I pledge allegiance to the Democratic Party, and to the Roosevelt Family for which it stands, One Family Indespensable — with divorces and Captaincies for all.

Four thousand years ago Moses said to his people: "Pick up your shovels, mount your asses, load your camels, and ride to the Promised Land".

Four thousand years later Mr. Roosevelt said to HIS people, "Throw down your shovels, sit on your asses, light a Camel: THIS IS the Promised Land.

SIGN HERE_____

At least this item has a little more sophistication of thought, phrasing, and art work than other anti-Roosevelt literature printed in 1930's and 1940's.

Businessmen who supported FDR were not disturbed by stickers of this sort.

ROOSEVELT JEWISH ANCESTRY

THIS IS THE ROOSEVELT FAMILY TREE

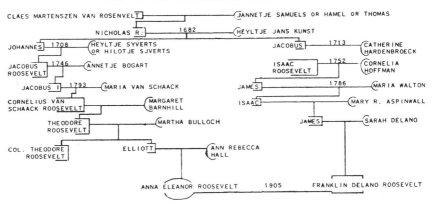

Above is the exact family tree of the Roosevelts, establishing their Jewish ancestry.

Note: Millions of dollars are being spent by powerful Jewish financiers to put another Roosevelt in the White House. Every sensible Christian and loyal American will fight the campaign of Leftists, Communists, Jews and Internationalists to return the Roosevelt dynasty to power.

Extra copies of this family tree may be had in tract form by addressing all orders to the CHRISTIAN NATIONALIST CRUSADE, P. O. Box D-4, St. Louis 1, Missouri. 50 copies, $1.00. 300 copies, $5.00. 1000 copies, $10.00.

NOTE: THIS FAMILY TREE CHART WAS PREPARED BY THE CARNEGIE INSTITUTION OF WASHINGTON, D.C.

An anti-Semite's delight, this family tree probably would have angered Theodore Roosevelt even more than his latter day cousin in the White House. Primary credit for this genealogical masterpiece belongs to the Christian Nationalist Crusade, a highly versatile group.

the source for both stories but he was one of the few who have ever
been dropped from the National Press Club for unprofessional conduct.
The president of American Cynamid denounced the "couple of well-
placed bullets" story as an outrage, but the hope was echoed in many
an exclusive club, and numbers of Park Avenue physicians expressed—
for free—their professional opinion that F.D.R. showed symptoms
of paranoia.

By 1938 fear of a third term haunted Republicans and not a few
Democrats. In discussing the question, Frank R. Kent, the nationally-
known Baltimore political writer, expressed the belief that the force of
tradition would prevent a third term, but he reminded his readers
that all Presidents have hated to give up the White House, and F.D.R.
hated the idea more than any others. Even the 1937 business collapse
had not been enough to dull the keen edge of his delight in the vast
powers of the Presidency. This unusually avid enjoyment of the
job Kent attributed partly to Roosevelt's overweening conviction
of his own goodness and wisdom, partly to sheer pleasure in power,
glamor, and perquisites, and partly to his skill in disregarding unpleasant realities.

Moreover, Kent pointed out, there was the family, unanimously
determined to cling to the fat incomes that had come to Mrs.
Roosevelt, and the children too, as a result of their illustrious connection. As a rule, he said, it is not considered good taste to mention the
President's relatives in a political article, but their own lack of taste
obviated that question here. Who wanted to hire any of them before
they got into the White House? And who doubts that once the
head of the family leaves the White House the market for magazine
articles, radio talks, and baking powder advertisements will dis-
appear completely?

This article was one of many on the same anxious theme that were
written early in Roosevelt's second term. The subject bothered the
Republicans like a sore tooth; they could not keep their tongues out
of it. A distinguished psychologist remarked at the time that they
were unwise in trying so persistently to disgust and frighten the people
with thoughts of a Rooseveltian monarchist plot. By crying every
day that a third term was "unthinkable," they might well make it
not only thinkable, but familiar, and in the end acceptable.

Marquis Childs reported in late 1938 that talk against Roosevelt had taken on a more menacing and violent tone. The mildest expression of wishful thinking among the Roosevelt-haters, he found, was in such words as "Oh, if Garner were only President!" and often the word assassination was openly used in conversation. Foreigners, recognizing that from the European standpoint Roosevelt's policies were mild indeed, were shocked and puzzled by the violent language of American tourists abroad.

Childs attributed this growing hatred to a fear that Roosevelt was undermining traditional middle-class privileges and was pampering the poor and shiftless. A *Fortune* poll had shown only 55 percent approving in general of the President; his policies and advisers drew far less than 50 percent approval. The unwillingness of the Roosevelt-haters to admit any good in the New Deal, however, had helped to limit the President's loss of popularity. It had led a majority of the ordinary people to feel that it was Roosevelt or nothing, and so to cling to him, regardless of his mistakes. In fact, Childs believed, one of Roosevelt's best political assets had been the evidence of upper-class hatred. One shrewd anti-New-Deal Democrat told him that the famous Liberty League dinner in February, 1936, when Al Smith sat at table with a row of furbearing DuPonts, was enough in itself to give the election to the Democrats.

With the approach of war in Europe the traditional isolationism of the American people was aroused, and much of it took the form of suspecting that the President would be meddling in foreign disputes. American isolationism came from many different sources and took many forms. In general, the American people or their ancestors had come across the Atlantic to get away from Europe, and did not want to be dragged back. Americans, as it has been well said, are born with their noses pointing west; and in general their isolationism has meant a determination to keep out of Europe—but no objection to being involved in China.

Special groups were suspicious of Roosevelt and his obviously pro-British bias. Many Irishmen still cherished their ancestral hatred for England. Even second-generation Germans were attached to Germany, and though not many approved of Hitler they remembered the ill-treatment of German-Americans in World War I and wanted no repetition. Midwesterners in general suspected the people of the East Coast of taking too much interest in European affairs. Pacifists after World War I had developed a strong belief that the United States had been sucked into that war to protect the profits of international banks and "merchants of death." Overlapping the pacifist group came many of the innocent souls who were susceptible to communist propaganda; and that in turn was directed sometimes by simple opposition to Wall Street—supposed by communists to be in league with Roosevelt in taking the country into war—and at other times by Russia's alliance with Hitler. Finally there were those who had not sensed the growing interdependence of the nations, and who felt that the United States had troubles enough at home without trying to settle those of the world.

The total effect, when the forces of isolation became closely organized after 1939, was the sight of some strange companions sitting cheek by jowl on the platforms at their meetings and joining to denounce the President of the United States.

The Democratic Convention of 1940 created much ill-feeling against the President among the party leaders, largely because he delayed announcing that he would run, and several hopeful candidates and their followers had worked hard for the nomination up to the point in the Convention itself when they discovered that they had no chance. Another source of bitterness was that Harry Hopkins was in charge of Roosevelt headquarters in Chicago, with a private wire to Washington. The professionals hated to have to look to him for orders from on high. They also hated to have Wallace imposed on them as Vice President, and almost refused to nominate him. Roosevelt's friends were seriously worried by the bad feeling, and tried to persuade him to come out to Chicago and turn on his charm. But he was afraid of being cornered and forced to face questions if he were there in person.

An extraordinary feature of the 1940 campaign was the wave of hooliganism against the Republican candidate, Wendell Willkie. All across the country from Massachusetts to California, people in the crowds threw things at him. *Life Magazine* showed pictures of 19 separate missiles, ranging from eggs and rocks to a wastebasket and a chair. Willkie took it with a grin, and the effect was to attract sympathy and probably votes; the Democratic high command was worried. Al Smith, who by this time was quite at home among the upper classes of the Liberty League, blamed it on the New Deal for "setting class against class."

The third-term campaign roused the Roosevelt-haters to new desperation. They warned the physicians in wordy telegrams that a third term meant socialized medicine. Insurance companies mailed notices to their policyholders that another Roosevelt administration would render their policies worthless. A big Chicago bank advertised that "In a last stand for democracy, every director and officer of this bank will vote for Wendell Willkie," and depositors were advised to do the same if they wished to protect their money. When F.D.R. was campaigning in Boston and paid a short visit to his son John in Cambridge, members of an undergraduate club at the Massachusetts Institute of Technology intoned in unison "Poppa, I wanna be a captain," in ridicule of a recent commission given to Elliott, the second Roosevelt son. A Philadelphia judge declared "The President's only supporters are paupers, those who earn less than $1,200 a year and aren't worth that, and the Roosevelt family." "Mothers of America!" cried one radio speaker on the night before Election: "When your boy is lying across the barbed wire on some foreign battlefield with his lifeblood dripping away, and he's crying out 'Mother! Mother!' don't blame Franklin D. Roosevelt because he sent your boy to war. Blame yourself, because YOU sent Franklin D. Roosevelt back to the White House!"

Anne O'Hare McCormick reported that foreign refugees told her the campaign sounded like the last free elections in European countries before the dictatorships came.

As *Life* said on November 11, the campaign, which began on a high level of honesty and fair play, degenerated at the end into a free-for-all of vituperation. The fact that the pro-Germans were working for the defeat of Roosevelt because of pro-allied sympathies was mentioned by Wallace, and even that was assailed as a foul blow. "Willkie is Hitler's Man, Says Wallace," the headlines screamed.

Roosevelt himself, in an address on October 23, gave a list of what he considered the "more fantastic" misstatements of the campaign. It is wrong, he said, "to state, for example, that the President of the United States telephoned to Mussolini and Hitler to sell Czechoslova-

Roosevelt's Impeachment Demanded by Klein

●

WHY DOESN'T CONGRESS ACT ?   WHY DO NEWSPAPERS, COLUMNISTS and RADIO COMMENTATORS SUPPRESS THE TRUTH ?

READ THE CHARGES — THE PROOF IS OVERWHELMING

ONLY AN IMPEACHMENT TRIAL CAN SAVE THE REPUBLIC

April 26th, 1943

To the Members of
The U. S. Senate
and
House of Representatives

Gentlemen:

The first count in the first of my fifteen charges against Franklin D. Roosevelt, asserts that he is disqualified by statute from serving the U. S. Government. You cannot ignore that charge; it is based on the law that you made. (Sect. 129 U. S. Criminal Code; 235 Federal Code annotated.)

If the charge is true, Mr. Roosevelt has never held legal title to the office of President, since his disqualification dates back to the time when he was Assistant Secretary of the Navy. You did not know of this disqualification; nor did those who voted for him three times. The statute of limitation does not protect him in a trial for impeachment.

A logical wind-up for such an impostor is summary removal from office. If Thomas Jefferson were alive, not only would he condemn a President who broke the two term tradition, but he would no doubt recommend penal servitude for one who committed that offense while under legal or moral disqualification from serving the government in any official capacity.

If the five million families that lost the bulk of their savings through the mortgage bond racket, knew the part that Mr. Roosevelt played in that racket, he could not have been elected President even if not disqualified.

Henry H. Klein meant every word of this open letter to Congress. The rest of his statement is equally strong in its phrasing, but somewhat more fuzzy in its thinking. If the above has whetted your appetite for more of same be sure to read his pamphlet entitled "Frankfurter Over the White House—Baruch Over Congress—Rockefeller Over the World."

These are the subjects King Noodle commands,
    Hauling in boodle His Highness demands.
These are the vassals, the serfs and the slaves
    Who bow their necks down to the insteps of knaves
Once wholly unfettered, now bonded they be.
    Oh where is the Lincoln to battle them free?

From "Mother Goose in Washington," a collector's item well worth preserving for the kiddies of tomorrow, this selection is only mildly indicative of its delightfully uninhibited contents.

"The President Solves Their Problem" is Communist-oriented cartoon designed to keep the faithful from being deluded into thinking that Roosevelt had the slightest humane concern about the welfare of veterans, young people, or, needless to say, anybody else. This cartoon was inspired by establishment of the Civilian Conservation Corps.

As a lackey of J. P. Morgan, Roosevelt served
Communist purposes well in this cartoon by
Jacob Burck. "Morgan goes to the White
House" was the accompanying title.

Despite the fact that trade unionists considered Section
7A of the National Recovery Act a greater boon to labor
than any other single federal measure, cartoonist Burck
didn't let his pen deviate from the Communist party line.

kia down the river; or to state that the unfortunate unemployed of the nation are going to be driven into concentration camps; or that the Social Security funds of the United States will not be in existence when the workers of today become old enough to apply for them; or that the election of the present government means the end of democracy within four years." He accused the Republicans of adopting Hitler's technique of the Big Lie—repeatedly hammering on falsehoods to impress them on the public mind.

Thirteen months after the 1940 election, the United States was at war. During those months, the country was sharply divided over two Roosevelt policies: first lend-lease to the Allied belligerents, then the protection of lend-lease shipments against Axis U-boats.

The lend-lease proposal naturally roused the fury of the isolationists. Senator Burton K. Wheeler took to the air to oppose the proposal and throw doubt on the sincerity of F.D.R.'s promise that there would be no American Expeditionary Force. He scoffed at the notion of a German attack on the United States, and said that the only threat to our independence would be to join in some "union of free nations" in which we would be outnumbered and out-generaled by our good neighbors across the sea. He urged his hearers to tell their Congressmen that "you have not surrendered the independence of America to warmongers and interventionists."

President Robert M. Hutchins of the University of Chicago, who had supported Roosevelt since he came into office, parted with him on lend-lease, saying he could not avoid the conclusion "that the President now requires us to underwrite a British victory . . . by supplying our friends with the materials of war. But what if this is not enough? . . . We must guarantee the victory." He called this policy the path to war, and said "we are drifting into suicide."

Two opposing organizations spearheaded the controversy over Lend-Lease: the Committee to Defend America by Aiding the Allies, and the America First Committee. The Committee to Defend America by Aiding the Allies was formed in May, 1940, to resist the isolationists and pro-Germans who were fighting Roosevelt's policies. William Allen White was Chairman. This committee, which included many Republicans, later came to be a tie between the Roosevelt and Willkie groups. The redoubtable Father Coughlin expressed his

Irish feelings about the committee in his paper *Social Justice*: "Like thieves who operate under cover of night, there are in our midst those who operate beneath the cloak of protected auspices to steal our liberty, our peace and our autonomy . . . 'The Committee to Defend America by Aiding the Allies' is a high-sounding name composed of high-handed gentlemen who are leaving no stone unturned to throw everything precious to an American to the dogs of war. . . . Sneakingly, subversively and un-Americanly hiding behind a sanctimonious stuffed shirt named William Allen White, these men form the most dangerous fifth column ever to set foot upon neutral soil. They are the Quislings of America. They are the Judas Iscariot within the Apostolic College of our nation.

"They are gold-protected, Government-protected, foreign-protected snakes in the grass who dare not stand upright and speak like men face to face."

The America First Committee held numerous mass meetings and, like the William Allen White Committee, collected funds to pay for radio time. Among prominent America First leaders were Senators Gerald P. Nye of North Dakota and Wheeler of Montana, John L. Lewis, Charles A. Lindbergh, General Robert E. Wood, John T. Flynn, Robert Young and Col. Robert R. McCormick of the Chicago *Tribune*. Snuggling up in the meetings were Coughlinites, the Rev. Gerald L. K. Smith with his lily-white Protestants, and the German-American Bund.

Irish and German opposition to Roosevelt's pro-British policies could be counted on to remain unchanged so long as the United States was not actually at war; but the Communist Party line varied with the shifting Soviet position. The war began with Russia and Germany allied; the communists and their fellow-travelers were isolationist and strongly pro-German, strange bedfellows in America First for such conservative patriots as General Wood, Lindbergh, and Flynn.

The charge that there was a Jewish plot to get America into the war was often hinted, though there were some rich Jews who subscribed to the America First Committee. Col. Charles Lindbergh said openly in a speech that the only people urging the United States toward war consisted of the Roosevelt family, the Roosevelt administration, the British, and the Jews.

Senator Wheeler contributed the highly effective slogan: that lend-lease would mean plowing under every fourth American boy. This roused F.D.R. to say that it was "the most untruthful, the most dastardly, unpatriotic thing that has been said in public life in my generation."

After Congress passed lend-lease in March, 1941, the question naturally arose of guarding our shipments against the U-boats. Senator Nye called on his radio audience to flood Washington with telegrams opposing the use of American naval vessels for convoying ships to England. He charged that Roosevelt was insincere when he promised in 1940 to keep out of war unless attacked—and accused Willkie of being no better. "Let me remind you," he said, "that however much assurance may have been given to the people by the President—Mrs. Roosevelt so very recently gave notice that the President had never given any such assurance, or made any such promise."

Nye attacked the notion "spread by British propaganda," that Hitler was a bad character with whom no peace could be made. He quoted Lord Beaverbrook as saying in 1938, "We certainly credit Hitler with honesty and sincerity," and Lord Rothermere: "There is no man living whose promise given in regard to something of real moment I would sooner take. He is simple, unaffected and obviously sincere."

One of the most memorable America First meetings took place in Pittsburgh on the afternoon of December 7, 1941. As Senator Nye, the principal speaker, was about to go on the platform, he was handed a news bulletin of a White House announcement that Japanese planes were then bombing Pearl Harbor. "It sounds fishy to me," he said. "I'm amazed that the President should announce an attack without giving details."

Then, cool as a cucumber, Nye went on the platform where another speaker was denouncing the President as "the chief warmonger in the United States." An interruption came from a reserve officer in the audience. "Can this meeting be called after what has happened in the last few hours?" he cried. "Do you know that Japan has attacked Manila, that Japan has attacked Hawaii?"

"Warmonger!" yelled the crowd. "Throw him out!"

"Don't be too hard on this poor bombastic man," the speaker urged as the heckler was escorted from the hall, "he's only a mouthpiece for F.D.R."

Having hired the hall, the America Firsters were bent on getting their money's worth, for the meeting continued with the usual demands for impeachment of the President for treason.

The coming of war failed to silence the Roosevelt-haters, many of whom though isolationists were also superpatriots. As Elmer Davis observed, "There are some people who hope that America will win the war but that Roosevelt will lose it."

One juicy source of "calumny as usual," was the secrecy of F.D.R.'s rest periods—so beautifully described in the diary of his secretary, William Hassett, published in 1958.

In 1942, F.D.R. began going to a camp in the Catoctin Mountains, which he called Shangri-La, afterward renamed "Camp David" by President Eisenhower. Since the place was of course top-secret and heavily guarded, rumor soon had it a sybaritic luxury camp, to be compared with Hitler's Berchtesgaden, where the tax-payers' money was wasted in wild orgies. One correspondent described the luxurious trout pond in front of the Lodge, kept stocked with big trout by the Fish and Wildlife Service, where the President could go boating at his pleasure, much like Cleopatra on the Nile. Actually, the "Big House" at Shangri-La was a rough seven-room cottage made by moving three log cabins together, with one bath for the President and another for the three other bedrooms. The great "trout" pond, about fifteen feet across, was put there to pump out of in case of fire.

War on the home front in September, 1943, was marked by F.D.R.'s famous attack on Drew Pearson, a clear indication that the strain of war abroad was telling on his nerves. Pearson had accused Secretary Hull of being anti-Russian, which was more true than comfortable in the ticklish relations between Roosevelt and his far-from-loyal war-partner Stalin. Roosevelt blew up. At his news conference he "simmered with fury," called the report a lie and an act of bad faith, and added that its unnamed author was "a chronic liar."

Drew Pearson was not entirely popular among his colleagues, but they were shocked by the Presidential tantrum. Raymond Clapper, one of the more respected commentators, reported: "President Roosevelt cut Pearson's throat from ear to ear in the most savage outburst of temper that I can recall at White House press conferences. It is barely possible that they are using Pearson to put the fear of God into all of us, and so far as I am concerned they have practically succeeded." To "practically" succeed in scaring Raymond Clapper meant not quite half—not enough to keep him from talking back to the President.

Many reporters thought this outburst was an indication that Roosevelt was "turning to the right," since Pearson had been consistently pro-New-Deal. The President got a "bad press." The Washington *Post* pointedly refused to drop Pearson's column. The St. Louis *Post Dispatch* said, "The Presidential anger becomes a captious and carping thing when it descends to an outburst like this." The New York *Herald-Tribune* observed that Russian-American relations called for a great deal more than angry castigation of an irreverent columnist. *Newsweek* headlined: "Roosevelt Blast Climaxes Longtime Feud With Press." The *Nation* reported that "the Hearst-Patterson-McCormick press was pleased, but most others were shocked, by the President's unprecedented, ill-tempered, and unfair attack on Drew Pearson," and went on to testify that when it came to chronically misrepresenting the facts concerning foreign relations, the State Department had a long record and so did the White House.

The idea of a fourth term was easier to imagine than that of a third term had been, though no easier for Roosevelt's enemies to swallow. In opposition to the Roosevelt-Truman ticket, the Republicans put up Governor Thomas Dewey of New York and Senator John Bricker of Ohio. Roosevelt opened the campaign with a speech to the Teamsters Union, which at that time had not yet become so well known as it is today. "The Republican leaders," he said, "have not been content to make personal attack upon me—or my wife— or my sons—they now include my little dog, Fala. Unlike members of my family, Fala resents this. When he learned that the Republican fiction writers had concocted a story that I had left him behind on an Aleutian island and had sent a destroyer back to find him— at a cost to the taxpayers of two or three or twenty million dollars— his Scotch soul was furious. He has not been the same dog since. I am accustomed to hearing malicious falsehoods about myself but I think I have a right to object to libelous statements about my dog." The audience ate it up, but this was only an appetizer. Roosevelt in this speech deliberately played rough, in the hope of getting Dewey's goat. He called the Republicans cheats, liars and swindlers, and the Teamsters cheered him on. Dewey lost his temper. In angry tones the Republican candidate accused F.D.R. of planning to hold men in the armed forces after the war because he could not find jobs for them in civil life. He pointed out that in March, 1940, after Roosevelt had been in office seven years, there were still ten million unemployed. The President had succeeded in keeping his depression going eleven years, twice as long as any previous depression in our history. That is why the New Deal is afraid of peace, he charged, that's why it is time for a change.

"We need," he proclaimed, "a new high standard of honesty in our Government. We need humility and courage. With the help of Almighty God we shall achieve the spiritual and physical strength to preserve our freedom in the pursuit of happiness for all. "

Hearst's New York *Journal-American* contributed the thought that "Roosevelt is embittered and frustrated because he knows it is true, as the Republicans are accurately and commendably emphasizing, that it is not the AMERICAN Democratic Party to which he is obligated for his fourth-term nomination and upon which he depends for the conduct of his fourth-term campaign. Mr. Roosevelt's candidacy is the responsibility and vehicle of the COMMUNISTIC Political Action Committee, a most ambitious and ruthless organization, not above having prison gates opened and immigration bars lowered for its benefit, as he himself has learned."

But the people decided that Roosevelt was a great man and they had better keep him.

They did not keep him long, however. As the world knows, Franklin Roosevelt died suddenly at Warm Springs, Georgia, April 12, 1945. The day before, he had written words that recalled his first Inaugural: "The only limit to our realization of tomorrow will be our doubts of today. Let us move forward with strong and active faith."

His death shook the world. Paranoiac Roosevelt-haters greeted the news with joyful telephone calls and hastily-gathered champagne parties. Whatever might be in store with the unknown Truman, they were rid of that That Man for good and all. In public, however, the comments from Roosevelt's enemies were generally decorous admissions that F.D.R. was a great man who had been of some service to the nation and the world.

But after Roosevelt's death and the decent formalities, there came bitter accusations from the Republicans that the real state of his health had been concealed during the 1944 campaign, since it was plain that if the Democrats had not been able to run him they might well have been defeated. Even Walter Lippmann wrote that the 1944 convention nominated Truman fully aware that it was choosing a future President. It was true that those who saw the President frequently had noticed occasional signs of age and weariness. His voice was not as strong as of old. Obviously, he was not the man he had been.

His appearance when he spoke before Congress March 1, 1945, upon his return from Yalta, shocked many of those who saw and heard him. He looked older, and his reading was listless and faint. But in Collier's for March 3, George Creel was denying whispers about Roosevelt's health that had been prevalent during the campaign —that he was suffering from coronary thrombosis, a brain hemorrhage, a nervous breakdown, and a cancerous prostate. His single ailment, Creel declared, was a bad case of flu that left him with a persistent cough which disturbed his sleep, cost him about ten pounds in weight, and made him look old. Creel did not pretend to quote Admiral Ross McIntire, the President's medical adviser, "for he has a close mouth, but it is significant that he has lost his worried look, and smiles clear back to his molars when asked about the President's health."

After F.D.R. died it was easy for persons who had seen him in the months before to project their memories back and believe that they knew all along he could not last. The result of these confused recollections, and the natural difference of judgment between partisans and opponents, was to prolong the futile argument that necessarily arises about the reelection of a President whose health has been questioned.

Roosevelt's death brought a curious reversal of the "warmonger" epithet; the accusation that instead of urging preparedness, Roosevelt had blocked it. Senator Owen Brewster of Maine charged him with responsibility for the loss of "thousands of lives and millions of dollars because he delayed putting into effect the industrial mobilization plans [that had been] drafted prior to the outbreak of war." A few isolationists, hoping that the country would forget how back in 1940 they had vociferously opposed rearmament and selective service, now declared that the late President's preparedness plans were neither prompt nor adequate.

Along with these post-mortems, the old, familiar drumfire continued: Franklin Roosevelt had been hell-bent for getting this country into war so as to perpetuate himself in power. He provoked attacks by Nazi submarines on American naval vessels. He made warlike gestures against Japan. And when these provocations failed, he bottled up the Pacific Fleet in Pearl Harbor where it would be helpless, in order to entice the Japanese into an attack.

As late as 1948, Charles A. Beard, who had taken a strongly isolationist stand before Pearl Harbor, brought out a book in which his enmity toward F.D.R. overshadowed his objectivity as an eminent historian. He charged Roosevelt with having plotted to get this country into the war. He accused him of acting "under the theory that the President of the United States possesses limitless authority publicly to misrepresent and secretly to control foreign policy, foreign affairs, and the war power." Beard said that F.D.R. planned to manoeuver the United States into the fighting through lend-lease and convoys, and that he forced Japan to fire the first shot. Behind the scenes, according to Beard, the deadly influence was that of Henry L. Stimson, Secretary of War, who had been Secretary of State under Hoover. Stimson, according to Beard, had tried to push Hoover into demanding that Japan keep hands off China, but Hoover refused to play. He succeeded with F.D.R., who was persuaded at a luncheon on January 9, 1933, before he was even in the White House; and from then on Roosevelt was craftily working toward Pearl Harbor.

Although the more rabid Roosevelt-haters had long and profanely wished for his death, now that it had occurred they suspected its reported circumstances. One rumor was that F.D.R. wasn't dead; always more or less unbalanced, he had succumbed to hopeless insanity and was a raving maniac behind the bars of a private asylum. Stories that Roosevelt had been a dying man for a year or more were accompanied by lurid tales of murder or suicide. The Roosevelt family custom of not allowing people to "view the remains" attracted no public notice when F.D.R.'s mother died, but the same custom prevailing at her son's funeral resulted in an orgy of ghoulish surmises.

A fascinating treasury of these weird theories was *The Roosevelt Death, A Super Mystery,* published in 1947 by the rabble-rousing Rev. Gerald L. K. Smith and purporting to be a "Manuscript Prepared by Mr. X." The "White House palace guard," according to Mr. X, refused to allow the Roosevelt casket to be opened for inspection even by the family because the body showed signs of either murder or suicide. When Stalin refused to believe that F.D.R. was dead and sent Ambassador Andrei Gromyko to investigate, Samuel Rosenman, who significantly had written most of the Roosevelt speeches against the Nazis, would not permit him to view the body. "From reliable sources," Mr. X heard that the President's face turned black less than four hours after death, a sure sign of arsenic poisoning. Roosevelt, he surmised, had been the tool of a cabal of international bankers— Rothschilds, Warburgs, Sassoons, Schiffs, Kuhns, Loebs, Morgans, Normans. This precious crew feared that in his senile raving he would expose their deadly secrets, so they either had him killed or forced him into suicide. The anti-semitic flavor of this last surmise is a common feature of this type of patriotic literature.

Another possible cause for suicide was remorse—remorse for having plotted to get us into war, or for having sold millions of German prisoners to Stalin for slaves, or for adopting Felix Frankfurter's sinister plan for lend-lease and betrayal of the American people. So, Mr. X concludes, no wonder the White House palace guard allowed no one to see the body.

Another book on this lurid subject was *The Strange Death of Franklin D. Roosevelt* by one Emanuel M. Josephson. At the Teheran Conference, this authority tells us, Roosevelt had a Russian waiter who was a physician, and who gave him a secret poison similar to curare, which made him extremely ill. At Yalta he had another physician-waiter, and General "Pa" Watson, his military aide, died suddenly on the way home. Photographs taken in 1944 were of one or more stand-ins when the real Roosevelt was unable to appear. And, the author asks, was it really Franklin Roosevelt who campaigned and was elected in 1944? He reports that Roosevelt had numerous slight strokes from 1937 on, which occasionally impaired his speech. But the "massive cerebral hemorrhage" from which he was said to have died, might have been caused by a bullet or a club, or by some form of poison. Several Russians were said to have been about when he died, and to have been mysteriously whisked away.

But the American people had no time to listen for the squeak of flying night creatures. They knew that the man who had been their friend had worked himself to death in their service.

*   *   *

Behind a high, century-old hemlock hedge between the Roosevelt home at Hyde Park and the Library is a rose garden. Here Franklin Roosevelt is buried beneath a simple ground cover of myrtle, directly in front of a block of plain white marble, eight feet long, four feet wide, three feet high. Here come thousands of visitors each year, most of whom never uttered any of the calumnies spread about him during his lifetime, and some others perhaps repenting of them.

In April, 1945, just eighty years after the long journey across the country of Abraham Lincoln's funeral train, Franklin D. Roosevelt's funeral train had ended its journey from Warm Springs, between the long lines of people mourning. When the procession came to this garden in Hyde Park, the neighbors had gathered, and they listened to the words of the old hymn:

> *Now the laborer's day is o'er,*
> *Now the battle day is past . . .*

There would be many a long day of labor and of battle for others to carry on, in the hope of working faithfully toward Franklin Roosevelt's ideal of prosperity and peace.

"Low Blows? Of Course!", a cartoon by Reg Manning distributed by the McNaught Syndicate, was evidently inspired by the feeling that Truman was less than fair in his remarks about Eisenhower in Oct. 1952.

CHAPTER XI

EPILOGUE

When John Adams was leaving the White House in 1801 with bitterness in his heart, a Boston paper offered this word of cheer: "Mr. Adams affects to believe that posterity will acquit him. It must be the posterity of a very distant age, so distant as to be wholly unacquainted with his conduct, that shall pass a favorable judgment upon him." A century and a half later, in fact, John Adams has come out rather well in the judgment of posterity.

In 1948, *Life* Magazine reported a survey of opinion on the greatness of Presidents made by Prof. Arthur M. Schlesinger of Harvard. Dr. Schlesinger asked the opinions of 55 leading authorities on American history, as to the relative greatness of all the Presidents, except William Henry Harrison and Garfield, who died shortly after being inaugurated, and Harry Truman, who was still in office.

The experts all agreed in grading Lincoln as the greatest President, in face of the contemporary judgment of the illustrious Dr. Orestes Augustus Brownson. Also listed as "great" were Washington, Franklin Roosevelt, Wilson, Jefferson, and Jackson. Classed as "near great" were John Adams, Theodore Roosevelt, Cleveland, and Polk. John Quincy Adams and Andrew Johnson, along with nine others, were graded "average;" six Presidents were counted as below average and two as failures.

The fact that the ten Presidents whose stories are told in this present book all come in the top three grades, as chosen by the historians, is not entirely an accident. It is to be expected that the greatest Presidents should be among those who were most bitterly hated, for as a rule they were the men who served in the most stirring times. Under their leadership wars were fought, periods of transition were safely passed, and important social and economic changes occurred. In part these great men no doubt caused these changes, and probably even more they were themselves formed by the pressure of great events; for it appears that more often than being definitely

From Republican viewpoint this cartoon by Frank Williams in Washington News was warranted by attacks on Nixon prior to 1960 campaign.

"Now You Kids Beat It"

From the Democratic viewpoint this cartoon by Herblock in the Washington Post was warranted even more than the item by Frank Williams on the previous page. Original title was "Now You Kids Beat It."

born great they were men whom the American people first chose as President and afterward thrust greatness upon them. In stirring times when a President is being hammered into the figure of a great man, it is natural that fierce passions should be aroused both for and against him.

It is also natural that the Presidents who will be counted by historians as most successful are likely to be not only statesmen but also expert politicians, whose art, like that of the expert physician, must include skill in avoiding the telling of untimely truth. John Fiske in his *Reminiscences of Huxley* remarks that "'The statesman's business is to accomplish sundry concrete political purposes, and he measures statements primarily not by their truth, but by their availableness as a means toward a practical end." Woodrow Wilson in his *History of the American People* said that Jefferson "deliberately practiced the arts of the politician and exhibited oft-times the sort of insincerity which subtle natures yield to without loss of essential integrity." And Wilson, of course, was describing his own deliberate moral standard for Presidential behavior.

Both these statements put the case mildly. More bluntly, the President's duty is to bring the ship safely through storm and battle, and if telling the truth would endanger the ship he must not tell it. He will therefore be hotly called a liar, and the more storms and battles he has to meet, the more hotly he is likely to be attacked.

Since it is not allowable for a President to deal in raw truth, it is also not allowable for him to demand justice in his own lifetime against his detractors. Theodore Roosevelt once went to court over a charge of drunkeness and won a verdict, with nominal damages, but that was a simple matter not involving affairs of state. In general it is not regarded as sporting for so powerful a man as a President to strike a common citizen in a personal quarrel—as was shown before 1800 by the disastrous repercussions of the Sedition Act, which was blamed on President Adams. Properly, the President's only immediate appeal is to the electorate when he runs for reelection, and in the end he appeals to the historians. As a rule, therefore, he keeps a diary, or its equivalent. The modern Presidential diary is a vast institution—the Roosevelt Library or the Hoover and Truman Libraries, where future historians may search for the truth that the

President could not disclose in time of crisis, and, he may hope, will do him justice.

The stories in this book necessarily illustrate only one aspect of the hardships of the American Presidency. George Washington, and the most vigorous of his successors, whose names are sure of honored places in history if the free world survives, cannot be depreciated now by any account of what the maddest of their opponents said about them in their time. But possibly in future times, if the United States is blessed with a great man in the White House, those who have made themselves familiar with what happened to other Presidents may be able to help discount and laugh away the most outrageous of the sticks and stones that will be thrown.

INDEX